25 CBSE

Class 12

BIOLOGY

Chapter-wise, Topic-wise & Skill-wise

Previous Year Solved Papers (2013 - 2023) Powered with Concept Notes

DISHA™
Publication Inc

DISHA Publication Inc.

A - 23, FIEE Comples,
Okhla Industrial Area Phase-II, New Delhi-110020
Tel: 49842349/ 49842350

By:
Rashi Chauhan
Shikha Kanojia

Typeset By
DISHA DTP Team
Jasmeet Singh
Shivam Kumar

Buying books from DISHA

Just Got A Lot More Rewarding!!!

We at DISHA Publication, value your feedback immensely and to show our apperciation of our reviewers, we have launched a review contest.

To participate in this reward scheme, just follow these quick and simple steps:
• Write a review of the product you purchase on Amazon/Flipkart.
• Take a screenshot/photo of your review.
• Mail it to *disha-rewards@aiets.co.in*, along with all your details.

Each month, selected reviewers will win exciting gifts from DISHA Publication. Note that the rewards for each month will be declared in the first week of next month on our website.

https://bit.ly/review-reward-disha.

Write To Us At
feedback_disha@aiets.co.in

CONTENTS

Trend Analysis (Year 2023-2019)
CBSE All India & Delhi

S. No.	Serial Number	Year of Examination								
		2023		2022		2021	2020		2019	
		All India	Delhi	Term-I	Term-II		All India	Delhi	All India	Delhi
1.	Sexual Reproduction in Flowering plants	3	3	11	—		3	3	3	4
2.	Human Reproduction	4	1	12	—		3	2	1	2
3.	Reproductive Health	1	3	4			1	1	1	1
4.	Principles of Inheritance and Variation	2	4	16	—		1	2	3	3
5.	Molecular Basis of Inheritance	6	2	17	—		3	4	3	3
6.	Evolution	3	2	–	—		2	2	2	1
7.	Human Health and Disease	4	5	—	1		3	3	1	2
8.	Microbes in Human welfare	2	—	—	4	Exam not held in 2021 due to Covid-19 pandemic	3	3	3	2
9.	Biotechnology: Principles and Processes	1	5	—	1		2	2	2	3
10.	Biotechnology and its Application	3	2	—	2		2	3	2	1
11.	Organisms and Populations	2	3	—	2		2	3	2	2
12.	Ecosystem	1	1	—	—		1	2	2	2
13.	Biodiversity and Conservation	3	3	—	3		1	1	2	1
	Total no. of Questions	35	34	60	13		27	31	27	27

Note: In this book all 25 papers (Years 2023-2013) including CBSE sample papers 2021-22, 2022-23 & 2023-24 are divided as per latest CBSE chapter-wise, topicwise & skill-wise – K (= Knowledge based), U (= Understanding), Ap (= Application based) & A (= Analysis) marked below the question.

Sexual Reproduction in Flowering Plants

Topic-1: *Pre-fertilisation: Structure and Events*

---

1 — Multiple Choice Questions (1 Mark)

1. The wall layer of microsporangium which nourishes the pollen grain is: **[CBSE Sample Paper 2023-24, K]**

   (a) epidermis   (b) endothecium

   (c) middle layers   (d) tapetum

2. The aquatic plant having long and ribbon like pollen grains is : **[All India 2022, Term-I, K]**

   (a) *Vallisneria*   (b) *Hydrilla*

   (c) *Eicchornia*   (d) *Zostera*

3. To overcome incompatible pollinations so as to get desired hybrids, a plant breeder must have the knowledge of ________. **[All India 2022, Term-I, U]**

   (a) pollen – nucellar interaction

   (b) pollen – egg cell interaction

   (c) pollen – pistil interaction

   (d) pollen – embryo sac interaction

4. Pollen grains retain viability for months in plants belonging to different families given below :

   [All India 2022, Term-I, K]

   (i) Solanaceae   (ii) Leguminosae

   (iii) Gramineae   (iv) Rosaceae

   (v) Liliaceae

   The correct option is :

   (a) (i), (ii) and (v)   (b) (i), (ii) and (iv)

   (c) (ii), (iv) and (v)   (d) (i), (iii) and (v)

5. In the tranverse section of a young anther shown below, identify the correct sequence of wall layers from outside to inside : **[All India 2022, Term-I, U]**

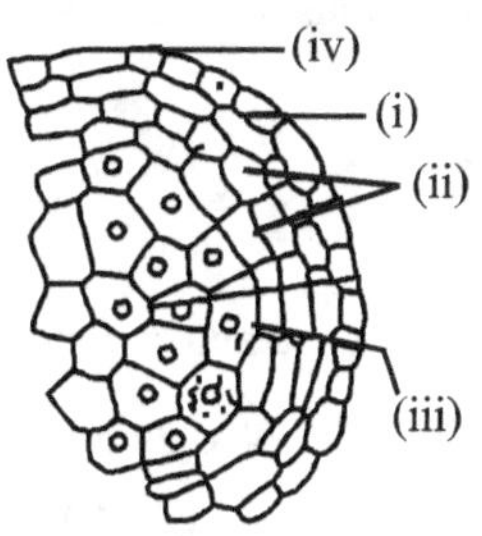

	(i)	(ii)	(iii)	(iv)
(a)	Middle layers	Endothecium	Epidermis	Tapetum
(b)	Tapetum	Middle layers	Endothecium	Epidermis
(c)	Epidermis	Endothecium	Middle layers	Tapetum
(d)	Endothecium	Middle layers	Tapetum	Epidermis

6. Floral reward/s provided by insect pollinated flowers to sustain animal visit is/are : **[All India 2022, Term-I, K]**

   (a) nectar and fragrance

   (b) nectar and pollen grains

   (c) pollen grains and fragrance

   (d) fragrance and bright colour

7. Which condition of gynoecium (pistil) is shown the figures (i) and (ii) ? **[All India 2022, Term-I, U]**

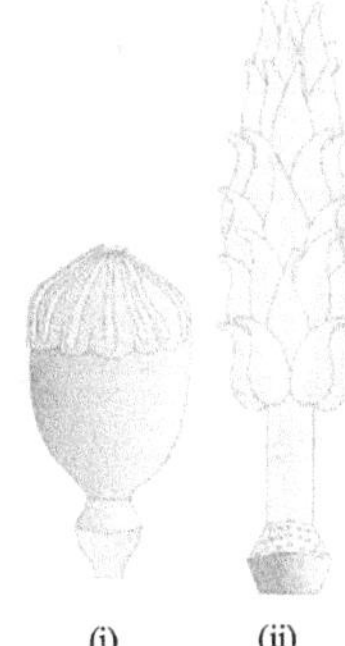

   (a) (i) multicarpellary apocarpous, (ii) multicarpellary syncarpous

   (b) (i) multicarpellary syncarpous, (ii) multicarpellary apocarpous

(c) (i) bicarpellary apocarpous, (ii) bicarpellary syncarpous

(d) (i) bicarpellary syncarpous, (ii) bicarpellary apocarpous

8. Which of the following outbreeding devices are used by majority of flowering plants to prevent inbreeding depression ? **[All India 2022, Term-I, U]**

(i) Pollen release and stigma receptivity are not synchronised.

(ii) Different positions of anther and stigma.

(iii) Production of different types of pollen grains.

(iv) Formation of unisexual flowers along with bisexual flowers.

(a) (i), (ii) and (v) (b) (ii), (iii) and (v)

(c) (i), (iii) and (v) (d) (iii), (iv) and (v)

9. The structure of bilobed anther consists of

[CBSE Sample Paper 2021-22, K]

(a) 2 thecae, 2 sporangia (b) 4 thecae, 4 sporangia

(c) 4 thecae, 2 sporangia (d) 2 thecae, 4 sporangia

10. In the figure of anatropous ovule given below, choose the correct option for the characteristic distribution of cells within the typical embryo sac.

[CBSE Sample Paper, 2021-22, K]

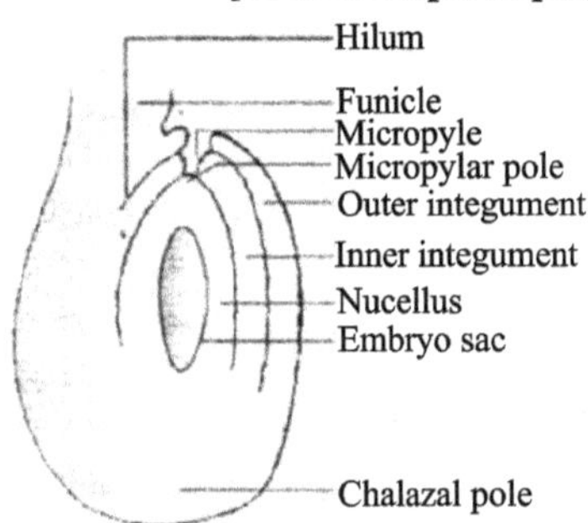

	Number of cells at chalazal end	Number of cells at micropylar end	Number of neclei left in central cell
(a)	3	2	3
(b)	3	3	2
(c)	2	3	3
(d)	2	2	4

11. Pollen grains are well preserved as fossils because of presence of **[CBSE Sample Paper, 2021-22, K]**

(a) sporopollenin (b) cellulose

(c) lignocellulose (d) pectocellulose

12. In the dioecious aquatic plant shown, identify the characteristics of the male flowers that reach the female flowers for pollination:

[CBSE Sample Paper, 2021-22, K]

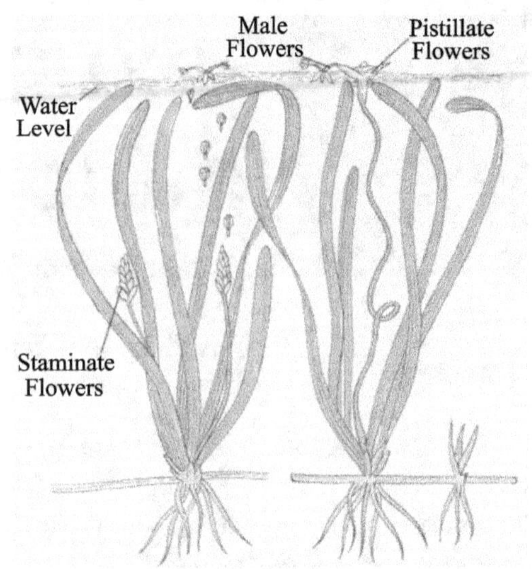

	Size of the flower	Colour of flower	Characteristic feature of pollengrain
(a)	small	brightly coloured	Light wight and non-sticky
(b)	large	colourless	Large and sticky
(c)	small	white	small covered with mucilage
(d)	large	colourless	non sticky

13. In a fertilized ovule, n, 2n and 3n conditions occur respectively in

[CBSE Sample Paper, 2021-22, K]

(a) antipodal, zygote and endosperm

(b) zygote, nucellus and endosperm

(c) endosperm, nucellus and zygote.

(d) antipodals, synergids and integusments

14. A botanist studying Viola (common pansy) noticed that one of the two flower types withered and developed no further due to some unfavorable condition, but the other flower type on the same plant survived and it resulted in an assured seed set. Which of the following will be correct? **[CBSE Sample Paper, 2021-22, K]**

(a) The flower type which survived is Cleistogamous and it always exhibits autogamy

(b) The flower type which survived is Chasmogamous and it always exhibits geitonogamy.

(c) The flower type which survived is Cleistogamous and it exhibits both autogamy and geitonogamy.

(d) The flower type which survived is Chasmogamous and it never exhibits autogamy.

15. Self-pollination is fully ensured if
(a) the flower is bisexual
(b) the style is longer than the filament
(c) the flower is cleistogamous
(d) the time of pistil and anther maturity is different
[All India 2020, K]

4 *Very Short Answer Questions (1 Mark)*

16. (a) Explain the process of the development of a male gametophyte in an angiosperm.
[All India 2023 Set-I, K]

(b) Why is it called a male gametophyte?
[All India 2023 Set-I, K]

17. State the reason why pollen grains lose their viability when the tapetum in the anther is malfunctioning.
[Delhi 2019, U]

5 *Short Answer Questions (2 or 3 Marks)*

18. One of the major approaches of crop improvement programme is Artificial Hybridisation. Explain the steps involved in making sure that only the desired pollen grain pollinate the stigma of a bisexual flower by a plant breeder. **[Delhi 2023 Set-I, U]**

19. (i) Explain the monosporic development of embryo sac in the ovule of an angiosperm. 3

(ii) Draw a diagram of the mature embryo sac of an angiospermic ovule and label any four parts in it. 2
[Delhi 2023 Set-I, U]

20. Draw a schematic transverse section of a mature anther of an angiosperm. Label tis epidermis, middle layers, tapetum, endothecium, sporogenous tissue and the connective.
[All India 2020, U]

21. Explain three different modes of pollination that can occur in a chasmogamous flower.
[Delhi 2020, U]

22. You are conducting artificial hybridization on papaya and potato. Which one of them would require the step of emasculation and why ? However for both you will use the process of bagging. Justify giving one reason.
[All India 2019, U]

23. A mature embryo-sac in a flowering plant may possess 7-cells, but 8-nuclei. Explain with the help of diagram only. **[All India 2017, U]**

24. A pollen grain in angiosperm at the time of dehiscence from an anther could be 2-celled or 3-celled. Explain. How are the cells placed within the pollen grain when shed at a 2-celled stage? **[Delhi 2017, U]**

25. (a) Can a plant flowering in Mumbai be pollinated by pollen grains of the same species growing in New Delhi ? Provide explanations to your answer.

(b) Draw the diagram of a pistil where pollination has successfully occurred. Label the parts involved in reaching the male gametes to its desired destination.
[Delhi 2017, U]

26. Name the organic material exine of the pollen grain is made up of. How is this material advantageous to pollen grain? **[All India 2016, U]**

27. Make a list of any three out breeding devices that flowering plants have developed and explain how they help to encourage cross-pollination. **[All India 2014, U]**

OR

Why are angiosperm anthers called dithecous? Describe the structure of its microsporangium. **[All India 2014, U]**

28. Geitonogamous flowering plants are genetically autogamous but functionally crosspollinated. Justify.
[Delhi 2013, U]

6 *Long Answer Questions (5 Marks)*

29. (i) Describe the arrangement of nuclei and cells in a mature embryo sac of a typical angiosperm.
[All India 2023, Set-I, U]

(ii) Explain the devices the flowering plants have developed to prevent the following types of pollination: **[All India 2023, Set-I, U]**

(1) Prevents both autogamy and geitonogamy

(2) Prevents autogamy, but not geitonogamy

30. (a) Describe the process of megasporogenesis, in an angiosperm. **[Delhi 2020, U]**

(b) Draw a diagram of mature embryo sac of angiosperm, label its any six parts. **[Delhi 2020, U]**

31. (a) Draw the embryo sac of a flowering plant and label the following: **[Delhi 2019, U]**

(i) Central cell   (ii) Chalazal and   (iii) Synergids

(b) Name the cell and explain the process it undergoes to develop into an embryo sac. **[Delhi 2019, U]**

(c) Explain the development of endosperm in coconut.

32. Write down the difference between wind pollination and insect pollination. **[Delhi 2019, K]**

33. (a) Describe any two devices in a flowering plant which prevent both autogamy and geitonogamy. **[All India 2018, U]**

(b) Explain the events upto double fertilization after the pollen tube enters one of the synergids in an ovule of an angiosperm. **[All India 2018, U]**

34. Read the following statement and answer the questions that follow : **[All India 2017, U]**

"A guava fruit has 200 viable seeds".

(a) What are viable seeds?

(b) Write the total number of :

(i) Pollen grains

(ii) Gametes in producing 200 viable guava seeds.

(c) Prepare a flow-chart to depict the post-pollination events leading to viable-seed production in a flowering plant.

35. (a) As a senior biology student you have been asked to demonstrate to the students of secondary level in your school, the prodedure(s) that shall ensure crosspollination in a hermaphrodite flower. List the different steps that you would suggest and provide reasons for each one of them.   [All India 2016, **U**]

(b) Draw a diagram of a section of a megasporangium of an angiosperm and label funiculus, micropyle, embryosac and nucellus.   [All India 2016, **U**]

36. Explain the post-pollination events leading to seed production in angiosperms.   **[Delhi 2016, U]**

37. (a) Plan an experiment and prepare a flow chart of the steps that you would follow to ensure that the seeds are formed only from the desired sets of pollen grains. Name the type of experiment that you carried out.   **[All India 2015, Ap]**

(b) Write the importance of such experiments.   **[All India 2015, Ap]**

38. List the different types of pollination depending upon the source of pollen grain.   **[Delhi 2016, U]**

Topic-2: *Double Fertilisation*

1 *Multiple Choice Questions (1 Mark)*

1. Choose the correct labellings for the parts X, Y and Z in the given figure of the stages in embryo development in a dicot:

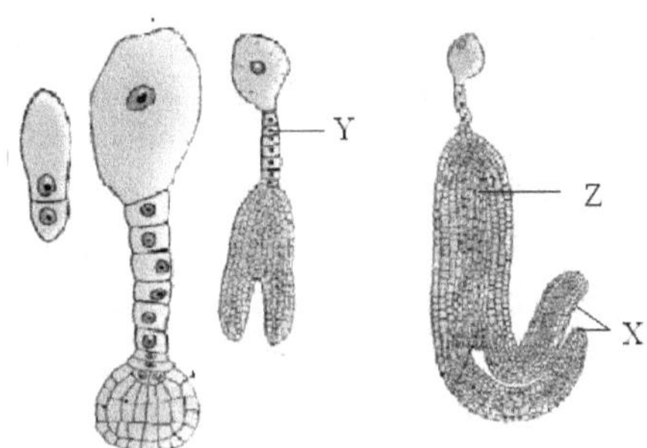

(a) X is suspensor, Y is radicle and Z is cotyledon

(b) X is radicle, Y is cotyledon and Z is suspensor

(c) X is cotyledon, Y is suspensor and Z is radicle

(d) X is zygote, Y is radicle and Z is cotyledon   **[All India 2022, Term-I, U]**

5 *Short Answer Questions (2 or 3 Marks)*

2. The diploid number of chromosomes in an angiospermic plant is 16. What will be the number of chromosomes in its endosperm and antipodal cells?   **[Delhi 2019, U]**

OR

State the reason why pollen grains lose their viability when the tapetum in the anther is malfunctioning.

3. Double fertilisation is reported in plants of both, castor and groundnut. However, the mature seeds of groundnut are non-albuminous and castor are albuminous. Explain the post fertilization events that are responsible for it.   **[Delhi 2015, K]**

Topic-3: *Post-Fertilisation:Structure and Events*

1 *Multiple Choice Questions (1 Mark)*

1. Which of the following structures is well-developed in a mature seed of black pepper? **[All India 2023 Set-I, U]**

(a) Perisperm   (b) Thalamus

(c) Sepals   (d) Peduncle

2. Remnants of nucellus are persistent during seed development in: **[CBSE Sample Paper 2023-24, K]**

(a) pea   (b) groundnut

(c) wheat   (d) black pepper

3. Enclosed within the integuments of a typical anatropous ovule is a diploid mass of cellular tissue known as: **[All India 2022 Term-I, U]**

(a) Megaspore mother cell

(b) Nucellus

(c) Synergids

(d) Embryo sac

4. In a typical dicotyledonous embryo, the portion of embryonal axis above the level of cotyledons is: **[All India 2022 Term-I, U]**

   (a) Plumule   (b) Coleoptile

   (c) Epicotyle   (d) Hypocotyle

5. Which of the following statements are true related to Seed X and Y?   **[CBSE Sample Paper 2021-2022, U]**

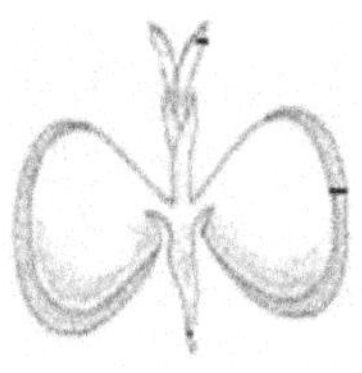 

       Seed X   **Seed Y**

  (i) Seed X is dicot and endospermic or albuminous.

  (ii) Seed X is dicot and non-endospermic or non-albuminous.

  (iii) Seed Y is monocot and endospermic or albuminous.

  (iv) Seed Y is monocot and non-endospermic or non-albuminous.

Choose the correct option with the respect to the nature of the seed

  (a) (i), (iii)   (b) (ii), (iii)

  (c) (i), (iv)   (d) (ii), (iv)

6. The thalamus contributes to the fruit formation in
           [CBSE Sample Paper 2021-2022, K]

  (a) banana   (b) orange

  (c) strawberry   (d) guava.

7. To produce 400 seeds, the number of meiotic divisions required will be   **[CBSE Sample Paper 2021-2022, K]**

  (a) 400   (b) 200   (c) 500   (d) 800

5   *Short Answer Questions (2 or 3 Marks)*

8. For a layman, both apple and banana are fruits. But a biology student categorises fruits as true fruits, false fruits and parthenocarpic fruits. Justify.
              [All India 2020, U]

9. (a) Explain any two ways by which apomictic seed can develop.

(b) List one advantage and one disadvantage of a apomictic crop.

(c) Why do farmers find production of hybrid seeds costly?

10. Draw a diagram of LS of Maize grain and label its any six parts.   **[Delhi 2019, U]**

11. Differentiate between Parthenocarpy and Parthenogenesis. Give one example of each.
              [All India 2018, U]

12. A single pea plant in your kitchen garden produces pods with viable seeds, but the individual papaya plant does not.Explain.   **[All India 2016, K]**

13. (a) Explain the different ways apomictic seeds can develop. Give an example of each.   **[All India 2014, U]**

(b) Mention one advantage of apomictic seeds to farmers.   **[All India 2014, U]**

(c) Draw a labelled mature stage of a dicotyledonous embryo.   **[All India 2014, U]**

14. Explain any three advantages the seeds offer to angiosperms.   **[Delhi 2014, U]**

15. In angiosperms, zygote is diploid while primary endosperm cell is triploid. Explain.   **[All India 2013, K]**

6   *Long Answer Questions (5 Marks)*

16. (a) When a seed of an orange is squeezed, many embryos, instead of one are observed. Explain how it is possible.   **[Delhi 2017, U]**

(b) Are these embryos genetically similar or different ? Comment.   **[Delhi 2017, U]**

17. (a) Draw a L.S. of a pistil showing pollen tube entering the embryo-sac in an angiosperm and label any six parts other than stigma, style and ovary.
              [All India 2013, U]

(b) Write the changes a fertilized ovule undergoes within the ovary in an angiosperm plant.
              [All India 2013, U]

Topic-4: *Apomixis and Polyembryony*

Multiple Choice Questions (1 Mark)

1. Researchers the world over are trying to transfer apomietic genes to hybrid varieties as hybrid characters in the progeny: **[All India 2022 Term-I, U]**

   (a) do not segregate

   (b) segregate

   (c) develop genetic variations

   (d) will remain unexpressed

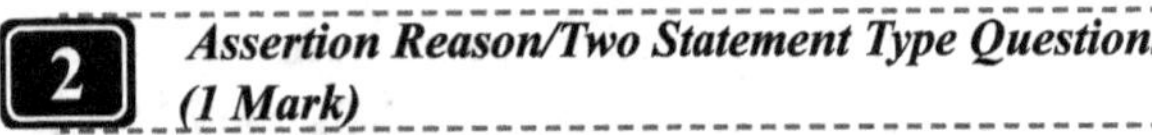
Assertion Reason/Two Statement Type Questions (1 Mark)

2. Consist of two statements–Assertion (A) and Reason (R). Answer these questions selecting the appropriate option given below: **[CBSE Sample Paper 2022-23, U]**

   Assertion: Apomictic embryos are genetically identical to the parent plant.

   Reason: Apomixis is the production of seeds without fertilization.

   (a) Both A and R are true and R is the correct explanation of A.

   (b) Both A and R are true and R is not the correct explanation of A.

   (c) A is true but R is false.

   (d) A is False but R is true.

Very Short Answer Questions (1 Mark)

3. State two advantages of an apomictic seed to a farmer. **[Delhi 2020, K]**

Short Answer Questions (2 or 3 Marks)

4. State what is apomixis. Comment on its significance. How can it be commercially used? **[All India 2015, U]**

Long Answer Questions (5 Marks)

5. (a) Explain any two ways by which apomictic seed can develop. **[All India 2019, U]**

   (b) List one advantage and one disadvantage of a apomictic crop. **[All India 2019, U]**

   (c) Why do farmers find production of hybrid seeds costly ? **[All India 2019, U]**

6. (a) Explain the different ways apomictic seeds can develop. Give an example of each. **[All India 2014, U]**

   (b) Mention one advantage of apomictic seeds to farmers. **[All India 2014, U]**

   (c) Draw a labelled mature stage of a dicotyledonous embryo. **[All India 2014, U]**

Hints & Solutions

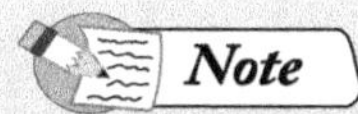

1. **(b)** **(1 Mark)**

2. **(d)** *Zostera* is a submerged marine sea grass that releases long, ribbon-like pollen grains underwater. The pollen grains are carried passively by water and ultimately reach female flowers. **(1 Mark)**

3. **(c)** To overcome incompatible pollination so as to get a desirable hybrid a plant breeder must have the knowledge of pollen pistil interaction. **(1 Mark)**

> **Note**
>
> *Pollination does not guarantee the transfer of right type of pollen C (comptabile pollen) of some species as the stigma.*

4. **(b)** In some members of Rosaceae, Leguminoseae and Solanaceae, they maintain viability of pollen grains for months. **(1 Mark)**

5. **(d)**

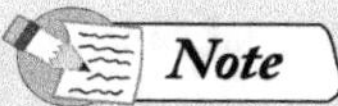

6. **(b)** To sustain animal visits, the flower have to provide rewards to the animals. Nectar and pollen grains are usual floral rewards. **(1 Mark)**

7. **(b)** The gynoecium may consist more than one pistil is called multicarpellary. When there are more than one, the pistils may be fused together (syncarpous) or may be free (apocarpous). **(1 Mark)**

8. **(a)** Flowering plants continued self-pollination result in inbreeding depression. For this it developed many devices to discourage self-pollination and encourage cross-pollination.

   In some species, pollen release and stigma receptivity are not synchronised.

   In some other species, the anther and stigma are placed at different positions so that the pollen cannot come in contact with the stigma of the same flower.

The third device to prevent inbreeding is self-incompatibility. **(1 Mark)**

> **Note**
>
> *Majority of flowering plants prohermaphrodite flowers and pollen grain are likely to come in contact with stigma of same flower.*

9. **(d)** The structure of bilobed anther consists of 2 theca which possess 4 sporangia. **(1 Mark)**

10. **(b)** Chalazal end possess 3 antipodal cells, micropylar end possess 2 synergid cells and 1 egg cell. And central cell have 2 nuclei present in one cell. **(1 Mark)**

11. **(a)** Pollen grains are well preserved as fossils because of presence of sporopollenin. **(1 Mark)**

12. **(c)** small, white, small, covered with mucilage **(1 Mark)**

13. **(a)** antipodal, zygote and endosperm **(1 Mark)**

14. **(a)** The flower type which survived is Cleistogamous and it will always exhibit autogamy **(1 Mark)**

15. **(c)** The process of self-pollination is fully insured if the flower is cleistogamous. The clesitogamous flowers are the type of flower which does not open at all. In such flowers, the anther and stigma lie close to each other and when the anthers dehisce in the flower buds, and then the pollen grains come in contact with the stigma results in self-pollination. **(1 Mark)**

16. **(a)** In angiosperms, the pollen grain is the male gametophyte. Maturation of the male gametophyte or pollen grain includes two mitotic divisions. First divisions form vegetative and generative cell and in the second mitotic division the generative cell forms basically two male gametes and their release occurs from a mature anther. Therefore, it has two male gametes and one vegetative cell. **(½ Marks)**

   (b) In angiosperms, microspores indicate the male gametophyte. Microspores divide mitotically, resulting in two unequal type of cells that are bigger vegetative cell and a small generative cell. The generative cell splits once again resulting in two male gametes or sperms. Microspore in angiosperms is also known as pollen grains. **(½ Marks)**

For fertilization to occur in ongiosperms, pollen has to be transferred to stigma of a flower.

17. Tapetum provides nourishment to the developing pollen grain. When the tapetum in anther is malfunctioning the pollen grain will not get enough nourishment and also loses its viability. **(1 Mark)**

Cleistogamous flowers are autogamous flowers as there are no such chances of cross-pollination.

18. Artificial hybridisation is one of the major approaches of crop improvement programme. In such crossing experiments it is important to make sure that only the desired pollen grains are used for pollination and the stigma is protected from contamination (from unwanted pollen). This is achieved by **emasculation and bagging techniques**. If the female parent bears bisexual flowers, removal of anthers from the flower bud before the anther dehisces using a pair of forceps is necessary. This step is referred to as emasculation. Emasculated flowers have to be covered with a bag of suitable size, generally made up of butter paper, to prevent contamination of its stigma with unwanted pollen. This process is called bagging. When the stigma of bagged flower attains receptivity, mature pollen grains collected from anthers of the male parent are dusted on the stigma, and the flowers are rebagged, and the fruits allowed to develop. **(3 Marks)**

19. (a)

    (i) In a majority of flowering plants, one of the megaspores is functional while the other three degenerate. Only the functional megaspore develops into the female gametophyte (embryo sac). This method of embryo sac formation from a single megaspore is termed monosporic development. The nucleus of the functional megaspore divides mitotically to form two nuclei which move to the opposite poles, forming the 2-nucleate embryo

sac. Two more sequential mitotic nuclear divisions result in the formation of the 4-nucleate and later the 8-nucleate stagesof the embryo sac. It is of interest to note that these mitotic divisions are strictly free nuclear, that is, nuclear divisions are not followed immediately by cell wall formation. After the 8-nucleate stage, cell walls are laid down leading to the organisation of the typical female gametophyte or embryo sac. Observe the distribution of cells inside the embryo sac. Six of the eight nuclei are surrounded by cell walls and organised into cells; the remaining two nuclei, called polar nuclei are situated below the egg apparatus in the large central cell.

(ii) **(2 marks)**

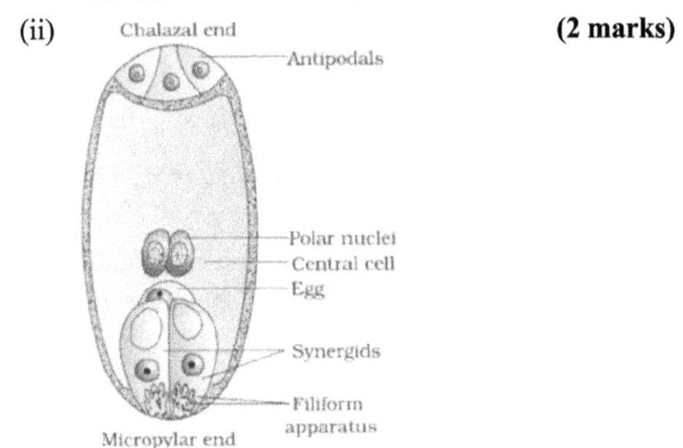

Diagrammatic representation of the mature embryo sac.

20.

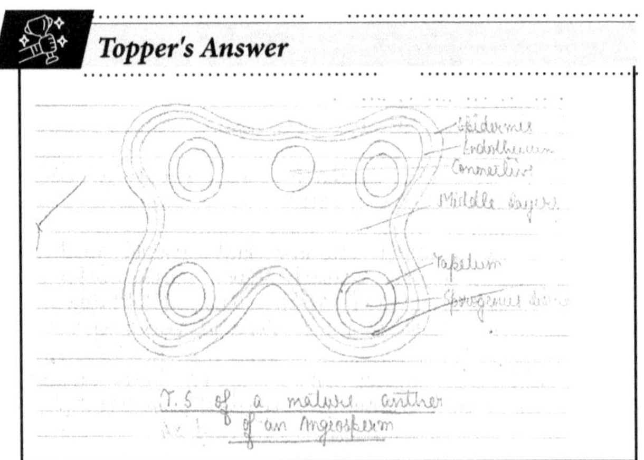

(3 Marks)

Diagrammatic representation of mature anther:

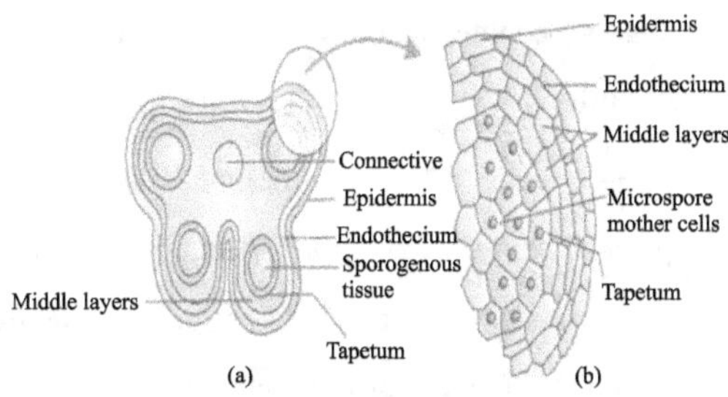

A typical angiosperm anther is bilobed with each lobe having two theca such as they are dithecous. **(3 Marks)**

21. The three types of pollination that takes place in a chasmogamous flower are as follows:

    (a) **Autogamy:** In this type, the process of pollination is achieved within the same flower. It involves the transfer of pollen grains from the anther to the stigma of the same flower. Chasmogamous flowers are type of flowers that are similar to the flowers of other species with exposed anthers and stigma.

    In chasmogamous flowers, the anthers and stigma lie close to each other. When anther dehisces in the flower buds, the pollen grain comes in contact with the stigma to effect pollination. **(1 Mark)**

    (b) **Geitonogamy:** It involves the transfer of pollen grains from the anther to the stigma of another flower of the same plant. It is functionally a type of cross-pollination that involves pollinating agents. But genetically it is similar to autogamy so the pollen grains come from the same plant. **(1 Mark)**

    (c) **Xenogamy:** It involves the transfer of pollen grains from anther to stigma of a different plant. This is the only type of pollination in which pollination brings genetically different types of pollen grains to the stigma. **(1 Mark)**

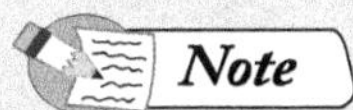

Note

Pollination refers to the process of transfer of pollen grains (shed from the anther) to the stigma of a pistil.

22. Potato require emasculation because it has bisexual flower whereas papaya would require only bagging for artificial hybridisation as papaya has unisexual flowers. After pollinating with the desired pollen grain it is required to bag the plant in order to prevent the plant from pollination by undesirable pollen grains.
(2 Marks)

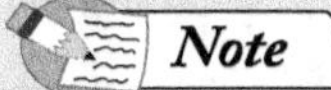

Note

*The process of removal of anthers from the flower bud before the dehiscence of anther by a pair of forceps is called **Emasculation**. The emasculated flower is covered with a bag of suitable size which is made up of butter paper in order to prevent from contamination of stigma with unwanted pollen and this process is called **bagging**.*

23. A mature embryo sac in a flowering plant possess 7 cells, but have 8 nuclei. This can be understood with the help of diagram given below:

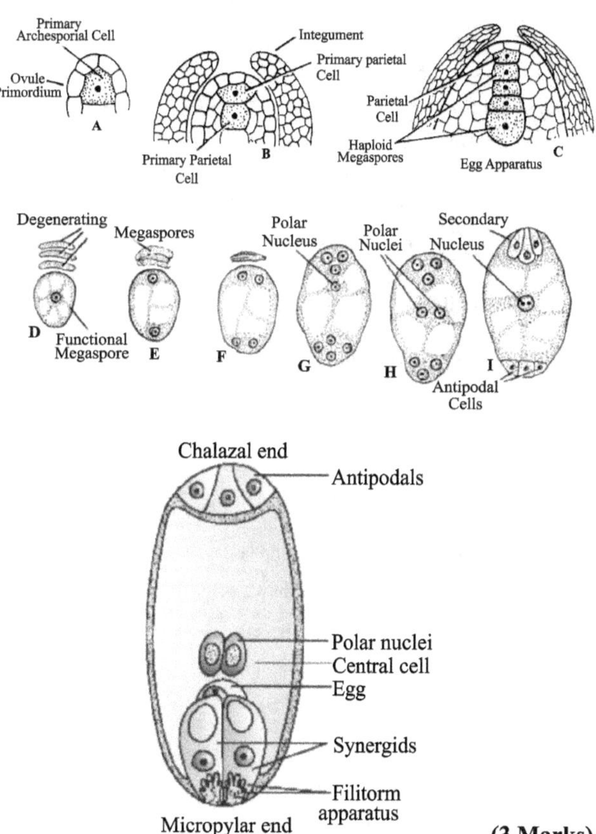

(3 Marks)

Fig.: Development of embryo sac

24. In many angiosperms, pollen grains are released in 2-celled stage while in other plant species, the generative cells are dividing into 2-male gametes and they will form 3-celled stage. When the pollen grain is shed at 2-celled stage then it has two unequal cells such as a bigger vegetative cell and smaller generative cell. **(2 Marks)**

25. (a) Yes, it can be only possible by means of artificial hybridisation in which a pollen grain of one flower is artificially introduced on the stigma of another flower. But it does not involve self-incompatibility of flowers.

- In this, one flower is emasculated and bagged.

- After some time, the bag is removed and then desired pollen grains are introduced on its stigma.

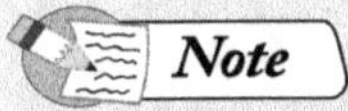

Note

Emasculation refers to the removal of anthers from the floral bud before the anther dehiscence by using a pair of forceps. Whereas bagging refers to the covering of emasculated flower with a bag made of butter paper in order to prevent contamination of stigma with unwanted pollen.

(b) Diagrammatic representation of pistil:

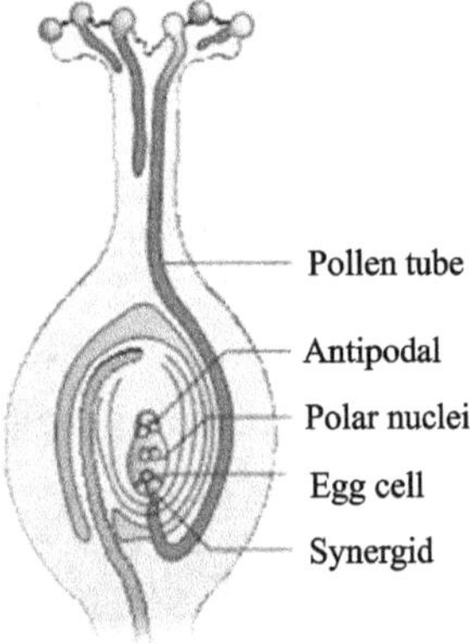

(1 × ½ Marks)

26. The hard outer layer of the pollen grain is called the exine which is made up of sporopollenin. Sporopollenin is one of the most resistant organic material as it tolerate high temperatures and strong acids as well as alkali. It cannot be degraded by enzymatic degradation.

(2 Marks)

27. The outbreeding devices developed by plants are as follows:

- Some species of plants, pollen release an receptivity of stigma are not synchronised. Either the pollen is released before the stigma becomes receptive or

stigma becomes receptive much before the release of pollen.

- Some species of plants, the anther and stigma are placed at different positions so that the pollen cannot come in contact with the stigma of the same flower. Both these devices prevent autogamy.

- The third device helps to prevent inbreeding is self-incompatibility. It is genetic mechanism that prevents self-pollen (from the same flower or other flowers of the same flower) from fertilising the ovules by inhibiting pollen germination or pollen tube growth in the pistil.   **(3 Marks)**

OR

An angiosperm anther is bilobed with each lobe having two theca and because of this is called dithecous.

Structure of microsporangium:

A microsporangium is surrounded by four wall layers such as epidermis, endothecium, middle layer and tapetum. The outer three wall layers provide protection to the microsporangium and also help in dehiscence of anther to release the pollen. The innermost wall layer is the tapetum. It provide nourishment to the developing pollen grains. Cells of the tapetum possess dense cytoplasm and contain more than one nucleus.

(3 Marks)

Note

*The outer hard layer called the exine is made up of **spocropollenin** which is one of the most resistant organic material. It can tolerate high temperature as well as all biochemical and enzymatic degeradation.*

28. Geitonogamy involves the transfer of pollen grains from the anther to the stigma of another flower of the same plant. Geitonogamy is functionally cross-pollination that involves pollinating agent but genetically is similar to autogamy since the pollen grains come from the same plant.   **(2 Marks)**

> **Note**
>
> *Autogamy is a type of self-pollination in which pollination is achieved within the same flower. In this, transfer of pollen grains from the anther to the stigma of the same flower.*

29. (a) (i) In a typical embryo sac of an angiosperm there are seven cells- one central cell, two synergids, one egg cell, and three antipodals. The egg apparatus comprising a group of three cells (two synergids and one egg cell) is found at the micropylar end. Three antipodal cells are located at the chalazal end. Six of the eight nuclei are enclosed by cell walls, whereas, the remaining two nuclei (polar nuclei) are located in the central cell. Hence, a typical angiosperm embryo sac at maturity is 8-nucleate and 7-celled. **(2 × ½ Marks)**

    (ii) (1) Autogamy is a type of pollination is achieved within the same flower. Transfer of pollen grains from the anther to the stigma of the same flower. Geitonogamy involves the transfer of pollen grains from the anther to the stigma of another flower of the same plant. In several species such as papaya, male and female flowers are present on different plants, that is each plant is either male or female (dioecy). This condition prevents both autogamy and geitonogamy.

       (2) In some species, pollen release and stigma receptivity are not synchronised. Either the pollen is released before the stigma becomes receptive or stigma becomes receptive much before the release of pollen. In some other species, the anther and stigma are placed at different positions so that the pollen cannot come in contact with the stigma of the same flower. Both these devices prevent autogamy but not geitonogamy.

(2 × ½ Marks)

> **Note**
>
> *Geitonogamy is a functionally cross pollination involving a pollinating agent.*

30. (a) The process of formation of megaspores from the megaspore mother cell is called megasporogenesis. The megaspore mother cell undergoes the process of meiosis and forms a four haploid tetrad megaspores. The chalazal megaspore remains functional whereas the other 3 will degenerate. So, the functional megaspore is the first cell of the female gametophyte. The cell enlarges and undergoes three free nuclear mitotic divisions.

So the first meiotic division produces two nucleate embryo sac and two nuclei shift to the two ends and again gets divide and forms four nucleate. In this way, eight nucleate structures is formed. One nucleus from each side moves to the middles and they are called polar nuclei. Then the remaining three nuclei form cells at the two ends, 3-celled egg apparatus at the micropylar end and three antipodal cells at the chalazal end. **(2 × ½ Marks)**

(b) Diagrammatic Representation of mature embryo sac in angiosperm:

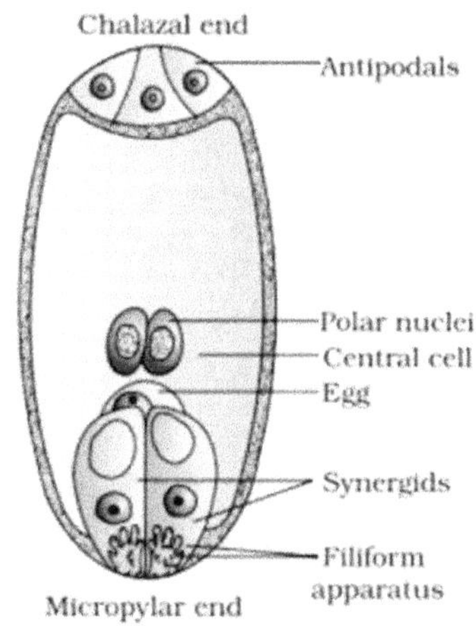

(2 × ½ Marks)

31. (a) Diagrammatic representation of embryo sac:

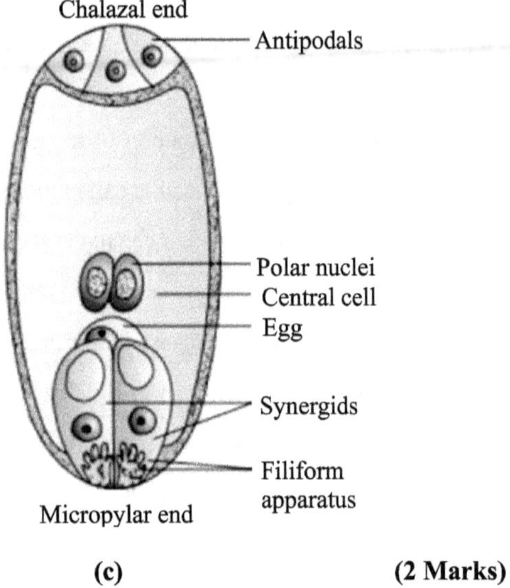

(c) **(2 Marks)**

(b) The process of formation of megaspores from the megaspore mother cell is called megasporogenesis. The megaspore mother cell undergoes the process of meiosis and forms a four haploid tetrad megaspores. The chalazal megaspore remains functional whereas the other 3 will degenerate. So, the functional megaspore is the first cell of the female gametophyte. The cell enlarges and undergoes three free nuclear mitotic divisions.

So the first meiotic division produces two nucleate embryo sac and two nuclei shift to the two ends and again gets divide and forms four nucleate. In this way, eight nucleate structures is formed. One nucleus from each side moves to the middles and they are called polar nuclei. Then the remaining three nuclei form cells at the two ends, 3-celled egg apparatus at the micropylar end and three antipodal cells at the chalazal end. **(2 Marks)**

(c) The Primary Endosperm Nucleus (PEN) is triploid (3n) in nature that undergoes nuclear divisions and give rise to free nuclear endosperm. This free nuclear endosperm is a coconut water whereas its white kernel is the cellular endosperm that is formed when it undergoes cytokinesis. **(1 Mark)**

32.

Topper's Answer

	Wind Pollinated	Insect Pollinated
1.	It is an abiotic mode of pollination also called as anemophily	It is a biotic mode of pollination also called as entomophily.
2.	Pollen grains produced by these flowers are non sticky and light	Pollen grains produced by these flowers are sticky
3.	These flowers are often white and colourless as well as odourless	These flowers are often and generally colourfull with colours to attract their pollinators
4.	These flowers have exposed stamen and pistil with a single ovule	These flowers are of any type and may contain more

Wind pollinated	Insect pollinated
These are small	They are either large or grouped to form large clusters
Usually incospicuous due to dull colours.	The presence of bright colours in corolla, clayx or bracts to attract insects.
They are odourless and devoid of nectar.	Strongly odoured and usually possess nector or edible pollen.
Pollens are produced in large numbers.	Fewer pollen grains are produced.
Examples *Urtica*, Maize, *Parthenium*.	Examples Rose, Snapdragon, Colotropis

33. **(a)** **Autogamy :** Transfer of pollen grains from anther to the stigma of same flower. It is a type of self-pollination.

Geitonogamy : Transfer of pollen grains from anther to the stigma of another flower of same plant. Two devices that prevent both autogamy and geitonogamy are :

(i) **Self - incompatibility :** This is a genetic mechanism & prevents self-pollen from fertilising the ovules by inhibiting pollen germination or pollen tube growth in the pistil.

(ii) **Dioecious plants :** Male and female flowers are present on different plants, that is each plant is either male or female.   **(2 × ½ Marks)**

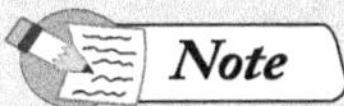

Geitonogamy is functionally cross-pollination that involves a pollinating agent, genetically it is similar to autogamy since the pollen grains come from the same plant.

(b) The events seen after the pollen tube enters one of the synergids in an ovule are as follows :

(i) Pollen tube, after reaching the ovary, enters the ovule through the micropyle and thus enters one of the synergids through filiform apparatus.

(ii) After entering one of synergids, the pollen tube releases the two male gametes into the cytoplasm of the synergid.

(iii) One of the male gametes move towads the egg cell and fuses with its nucleus thus results in formation of zygote (diploid cell). This is Syngamy.

(iv) The other male gamete move towards the two polar nuclei located in the central cell and fuses to form triploid primary endosperm nucleus (PEN). This involves fusion of three haploid nuclei & hence termed as triple fusion.

(v) Two types of fusions, syngamy & triple fusion takes place in an embryosac and hence the phenomenon is termed as double fertilisation.

(vi) After fertilisation, PEN becomes the primary endosperm cell (PEC) & develops into endosperm while zygote develops into an embyo.

(2 × ½ Marks)

34. **(a)** Those seeds that carry a living embryo and are capable of germinating into a seedling under appropriate conditions are termed as viable seeds.

(1 Mark)

(b) **(i)** Number of pollen grams required to form 200 seeds will be 200 only as each pollen grain carries to generative cells or male gametes and only one of the two are involved in zygote formation.

(ii) In total 400 gamete cells are required for production of 200 viable zygotes leading to formation of 200 guava seeds.   **(2 Marks)**

(c) **Flow chart depicting the post pollination events:**

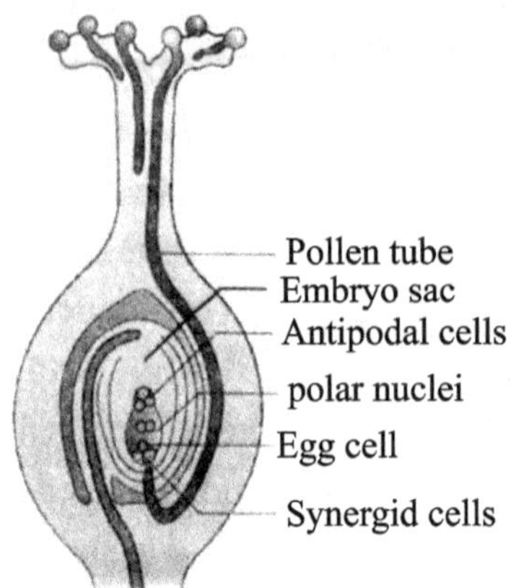

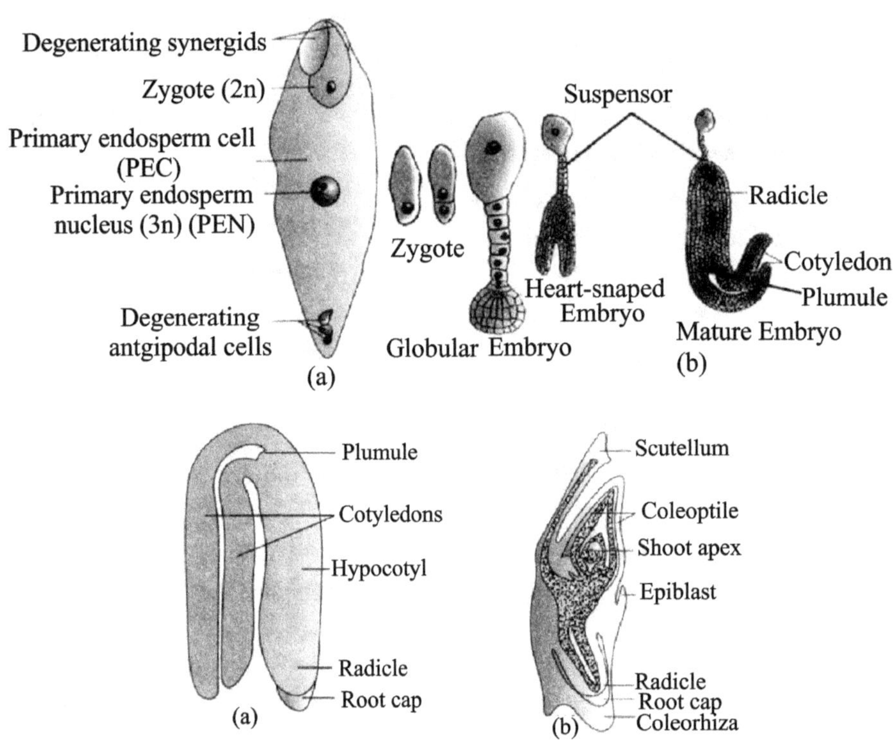

(2 Marks)

35. (a) The procedure used to ensure cross-pollination in hermaphrodite flower are as follows:

- **Emasculation:** If the female parent bears bisexual flowers, removal of anthers from the flower bud before the anther dehisces by using a pair of forceps is called emasculation.

- **Bagging:** Emasculated flower is covered with a bag of suitable size generally made up of butter paper to prevent contamination of its stigma with unwanted pollen and this process is called bagging.

When the stigma of bagged flower attains receptivity, mature pollen grains collected from anthers of the male parent are dusted on the stigma and the flowers are rebagged and the fruits allowed to develop. **(3 Marks)**

The process of transfer of pollen grains to the stigma of a pistil is termed as **pollination.** *The pollination can be divided into three types such as autogamy and geitonogamy are the type of self-pollination whereas xenogamy is a type of cross-pollination.*

(b) Diagrammatic representation of megasporangium of an angiosperm:

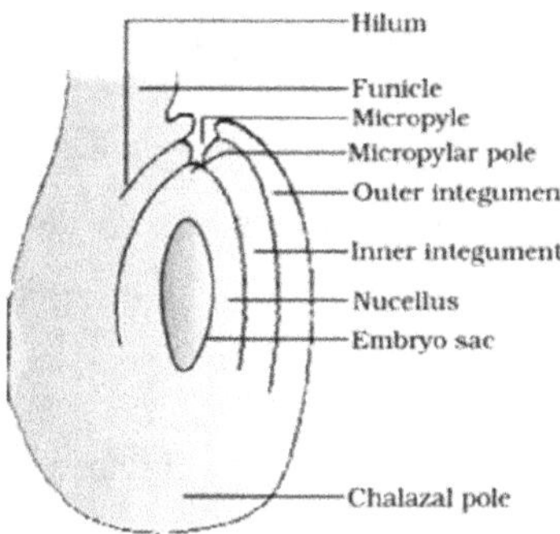

(2 Marks)

36. **(a)** Pollination is a defined as the process of transfer of pollen grains from anthers to stigma. It involves followings steps such as:

- When the pollen grains fall on the stigma, pollen tube is formed and it enters one of the synergids and also releases two male gametes.

- One of the male gametes moves towards the egg and fuse to form a zygote.

- While the other male gamete fuses with polar nuclei and forms a primary endosperm nucleus. This process is termed as triple fusion.

- The central cell becomes the primary endosperm cell after the process of triple endosperm. The primary endosperm nucleus forms endosperm whereas zygote is further developed into the embryo.

- A seed refers to the fertilized ovules that are further inside a fruit.

- The integuments of the ovules are hardened to form the seed coat whereas the micropyle facilitates the entry of oxygen and water into the seeds. **(5 Marks)**

37. **(a)** To obtain seeds formed only from the desired sets of pollen grains one can opt for artificial hybridisation. Following are the steps involved:

A bisexual flower is taken.

↓

Anthers are removed from the flower bud before the anther dehisces (emasculation).

↓

Emasculated flower is covered with butter paper, to prevent contamination of its stigma with unwanted pollen

↓

When the bagged stigma attains receptivity, the desired set of mature pollen grains is dusted (pollination).

↓

Rebagging is done.

↓

Fruits are allowed to develop.

↓

Desired seeds are obtained.

(3 Marks)

(b) Artificial hybridisation is important for the following reasons:

- It helps to improve the crop yield.

- It ensures that the crops produced have the desired characteristics.

- It helps to yield commercially superior varieties.

(2 Marks)

38. There are three different types of pollinations such as:

(i) **Autogamy:** This type of pollination requires transfer of pollen grains from anther to stigma of same flower. In this, the anther and stigma lie close to each other so that self-pollination can occur. Some plants such as *Oxalis, Commeline* and *Viola* produces two types of flowers such as **Chasmogamous flowers:** Such flowers are similar to the flowers of other species with exposed anthers and stigma.

Cleistogamous flowers: Such flowers do not open at all. The anthers and stigma lie close to each other.

(ii) **Geitonogamy:** In this type of pollination, the transfer of pollen grain from anther to the stigma of another flower of same plant. It involves cross-pollination through pollinating agents. But genetically it is similar to autogamy as the pollen grains come from the same plant.

(iii) **Xenogamy:** This type of pollination involves transfer of pollen grains from anther to stigma of a different plant. In this, pollination brings genetically different types of pollen grains to the stigma.

(5 marks)

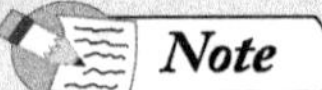

Note

Plants uses one biotic agent such as animals and two abiotic agent such as wind and water for pollination.

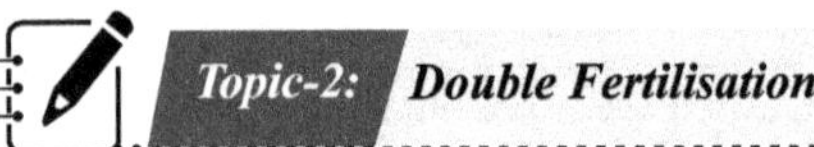

Topic-2: **Double Fertilisation**

1. (c)

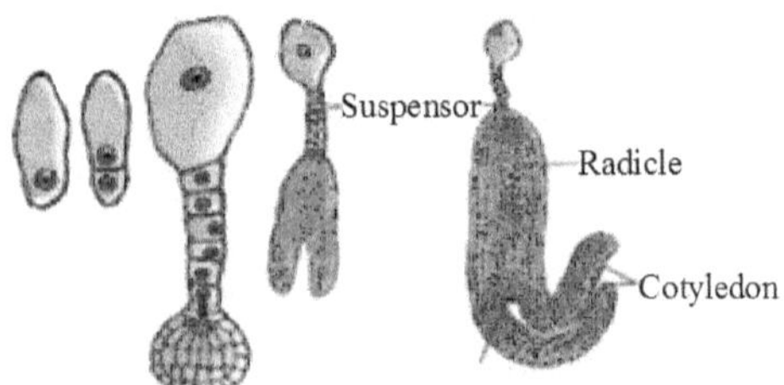

(1 Mark)

2. The diploid number of chromosomes in an angiosperm plant (2n) = 16.

The haploid number (n) will be = 8

Endosperm of an angiosperm is triploid (3n), so the number of chromosome present in endosperm 3n = 8 × 3 = 24.

Whereas antipodal cells are haploid (n) in nature. So, the number of chromosome in antipodal cells will be =8

(2 Marks)

OR

Tapetum provides nourishment to the developing pollen grain. When the tapetum in anther is malfunctioning the pollen grain will not get enough nourishment and will lose its viability. **(2 Marks)**

3. The post fertilisation events that are responsible for the formation of non-albuminous mature seeds of groundnut and albuminous seeds of castor are as follows:

The primary endosperm nucleus divides repeatedly to give rise to free nuclei and this stage is called free nuclear endosperm. The cell wall is formed after the formation of cellular endosperm.

Hence, if the endosperm is consumed fully by the developing embryo before seed maturation results in the formation of non-albuminous seeds such as in groundnut. Whereas if the endosperm persists in the mature seed and can be used up during seed germination then is called as albuminous such as in castor. **(3 Marks)**

Note

*The process of double fertilisation involves the fusion of one gamete with nucleus of egg cell results in the formation of zygote whereas other male gamete move towards the two polar nuclei that is located in the central cell and fuses with polar nuclei to give rise to **primary endosperm nucleus (PEN)**. It is also called triple fusion as it involves the fusion of three haploid nuclei.*

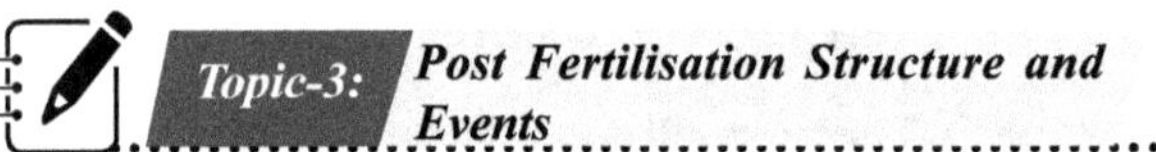

Topic-3: **Post Fertilisation Structure and Events**

1. (a) Perisperm can be defined as the persistant part of nucellus that remain after the embryonic development. It persists in the mature seed of black pepper. **(1 Mark)**

2. (d) black pepper **(1 Mark)**

3. (b) Enclosed within the integuments is a mass of cells called the nucellus. Cells of the nucellus have abundant reserve food materials. In the nucellus, the embryo sac or female gametophyte is present. **(1 Mark)**

> **Note**
>
> *At the time of fertilization, the nucellus consist of a bulky tissue ventral to the embryo sac and a rather thin layer elsewhere.*

4. (c) The portion of embryonal axis above the level of cotyledons is the epicotyl, which terminates with the plumule or stem tip. **(1 Mark)**

5. (b) (ii), (iii) **(1 Mark)**

6. (c) strawberry **(1 Mark)**

7. (c) 500 **(1 Mark)**

8. Fruits that are matured ovaries of flowers are called true fruits and false fruits are develop only from the ovary. Fruits formed as a result of fertilisation, while some species of fruits that are develop without fertilisation and such fruits are called parthenocarpic fruits. Banana is a parthenocarpy and seedless fruit. **(3 Marks)**

9. **(a)** The different ways by which apomictic seeds are developed involved:

(i) Formation of diploid egg as embryo without undergoing reduction division or fertilization for example: *Asteraceae*.

(ii) In several citrus fruits and mango varieties, nuclear cells surrounding the embryo sac start dividing and project into the embryo sac. It gets further developed into the embryos. **(2 Marks)**

(b) **Advantages of apomictic crop:** Apomixis reduces the cost of the hybrid production so that new varieties of seeds are produced more quickly and at a cheaper rate.

Disadvantages of apomictic crop: Apomictic seeds reduce the genetic diversity because of a lack of variations. **(1 Mark)**

(c) Hybrid seeds are produced by cross-pollination of plants and in order to produce desirable hybrid character, plant breeders and scientists are trying thousands of combination to produce such hybrids. So hybrid seeds are produced every years and it requires a lots of scientific research for the production of such hybrid seeds. It is expensive and hence the cost of hybrid becomes too expensive for the farmers. **(2 Marks)**

10. **Diagrammatic Representation of L.S of Maize grain:**

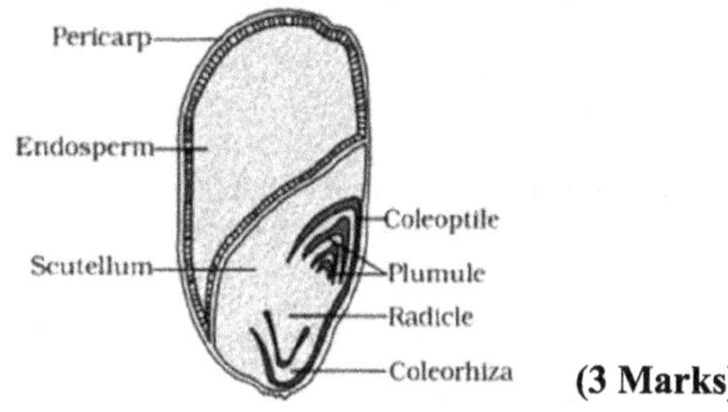

(3 Marks)

11. Parthenogenesis and parthenocarpy are two such processes that results in fruits and individuals from unfertilized ovules or eggs prior to fertilisation.

In most plants, flowers need to be pollinated and fertilized to produce fruits. However, some plants can produce fruits before fertilisation or without fertilisation.

Parthenocarpy is the process which produces fruits from unfertilised ovules in plants. Unfertilised ovules develop into fruits prior to fertilisation. These fruits do not contain seeds. E.g. banana and grapes.

Parthenogenesis is a type of reproduction commonly shown in organisms mainly by some invertebrates and lower plants. It can be described as a process in which unfertilised ovum develops into an individual (virgin birth) without fertilisation. Therefore, it can be considered as a method of asexual reproduction.

The key difference between parthenogenesis and parthenocarpy is, parthenogenesis is shown by animals and plants while parthenocarpy is shown only by plants. Parthenogenesis is seen in organism like rotifers, honeybees and even some lizards and birds (turkey).

(3 Marks)

12. The pea plant is monoecious as the male and female gametes are found on the same plant. So, self pollination takes place in such plants results in the production of seeds. Whereas the papaya plant is dioecious as male and female gametes are found located on the different plants. As only single parent (papaya) is involved according to question so cross pollination will not take place so there will be no seed production. **(2 Marks)**

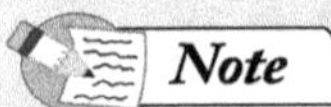

Note

The acrosome of the sperm secretes hyaluronidase enzyme to peneterate the corona radiata layer of the ovum.

13. (a) There are two ways by which the apomitic seeds are produced:

Agamospermy: In this method, the seeds are produced from diploid cells without meiosis and fertilisation. For example: Apple.

Adentive embryony: In this method, the nucellus and integuments extends into the embryo sac and develops into embryo. It involves the formation of more than one embryo. For example: citrus fruit.

(3 Marks)

(b) The main advantage of apomictic seeds is that there is no segregation of characters in the hybrid progeny. The apomictic seeds are cost effective and high yielding. **(1 Mark)**

(c) Diagrammatic Representation of mature stage of dicotyledonous embryo: **(1 Mark)**

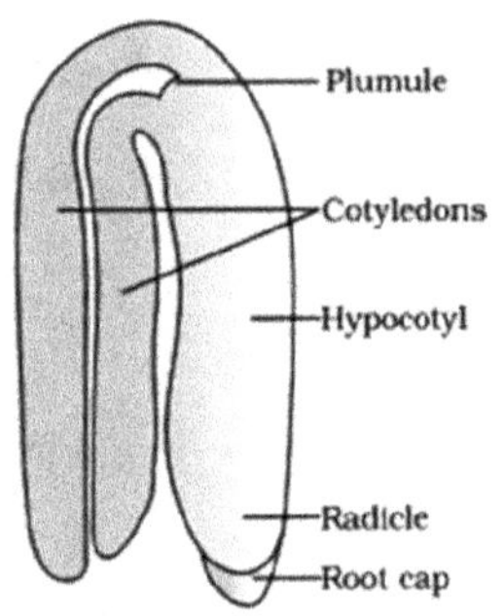

14. The three advantages that seeds offer to angiosperms are as follows:

- The seeds of angiosperms provide protection to the embryo from harsh environmental conditions.

- It provides nourishment and parental care to the developing embryo.

- The dispersal of the seeds to far-off places prevents competition among the members of the same species and prevents their extinction. **(3 Marks)**

Note

In angiosperms, there are two types of seeds albuminous and non-albuminous. Non-albuminous seeds have no residual endosperm as it is completely consumed during embryo development e.g. pea and groundnut whereas albuminous seeds retain a part of endosperm e.g. wheat, maize and castor.

15. The fusion of one haploid male gamete with haploid female gamete (egg cells) results in the formation of a diploid zygote and this process is called sexual reproduction. Whereas endosperm is formed when other male gamete move towards the two polar nuclei which is located in the central cell and its fusion with the two polar nuclei results in the formation of triploid primary endosperm nucleus (PEN). This process is called triple fusion. The central cell after triple fusion becomes the **primary endosperm cell (PEC)** and develops into the **endosperm** whereas the zygote develops into an **embryo**. **(2 Marks)**

16. (a) The occurrence of more than one embryo in a seed in oranges is because of polyembryony. In orange, the nucellar cells, synergids and integument cells are developed into a number of embryos of different sizes. For Example: Citrus. **(2½ Marks)**

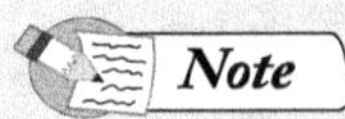

Note

Sometimes the formation of more than one egg in an embryo sac can lead to polyembryony.

(b) Parental characters are maintained in the embryos formed as a result of polyembryony and hence they are genetically similar. As, in this process there is no segregation of characters in the progeny.

(2½ Marks)

17. (a) **Diagrammatic representation of L.S of flower showing growth of a pollen tube:**

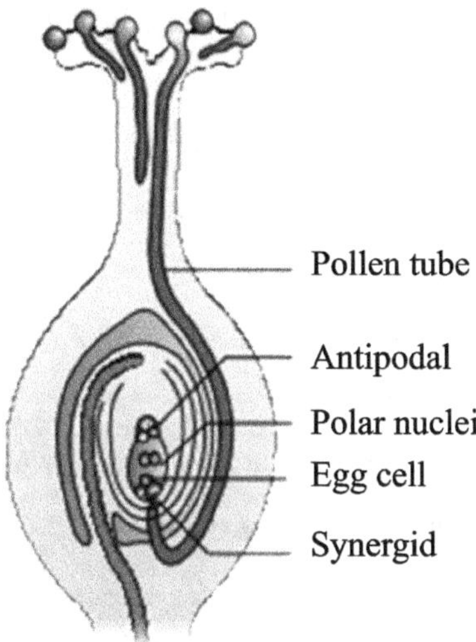

(2 Marks)

(b) When the unfertilized ovule passes through double fertilization and then fertilised ovule is formed which further develops into seed. In this process, the hilum and funiculus are present. Outer integument is developed into texta whereas inner integument is developed into tegman. The chalaza and micropyle are also present while nucellus is absent. In embryo sac, synergids and antipodal cell are degenerate. The central cell then develops into endosperm and egg is developed into the zygote and then into the embryo. **(3 Marks)**

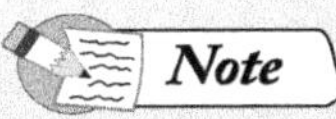
Note

Hilum is the region where the body of the ovule fuses with funicle thus, hilum represents the junction between ovule and funicle.

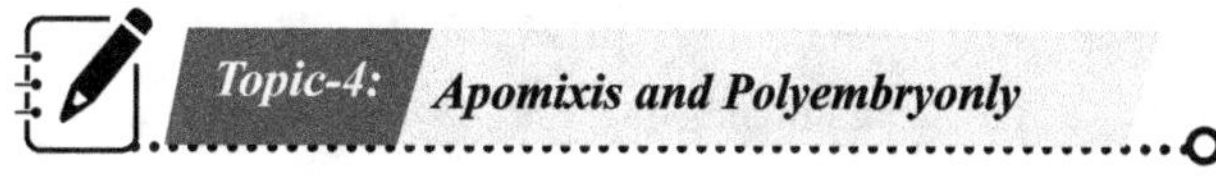

1. (a) Production of hybrid seeds is costly and hence the cost of hybrid seeds becomes too expensive for the farmers. If these hybrids are made into apomicts, there is no segregation of characters in the hybrid progeny. Then the farmers can keep on using the hybrid seeds to raise new crop year after year and he does not have to buy hybrid seeds every year. **(1 Mark)**

2. (a) Both A and R are true and R is the correct explanation of A **(1 Mark)**

3. Apomixis is a form of asexual reproduction that mimics sexual reproduction. As some species of plants such as *Asteraceae* and grasses have evolved special mechanism in order to produce seeds without fertilisation.

Advantage of Apomixis:

Apomixis reduces the cost of hybrid production and helps plant breeders to produce new varieties of seeds more quickly and more cheaply. **(2 Marks)**

4. **Apomixis:** It is a form of asexual reproduction that mimics sexual reproduction, and seeds are produced without fertilisation. It is called apomix is or agamospermy, *e.g.,* Grasses.

Significance: Diploid egg cell is formed without reduction division and develops into embryo without fertilisation, e.g., *Asteraceae* and Grasses.

Commercial applications of apomixis :

(i) By apomixis, hybrid varieties of seeds can be produced, which will provide higher and better yield.

(ii) Apomixis prevents the loss of specific characteristics in the hybrid plants.

(iii) Apomixis is a cost-effective method of producing seeds. **(3 Marks)**

5. **(a)** The different ways by which apomictic seeds are developed involved:

> (i) Formation of diploid egg as embryo without undergoing reduction division or fertilization for example: *Asteraceae.*

> (ii) In several citrus fruits and mango varieties, nuclear cells surrounding the embryo sac start dividing and project into the embryo sac. It gets further developed into the embryos.

(2 Marks)

(b) Advantages of apomictic crop: Apomixis reduces the cost of the hybrid production so that new varieties of seeds are produced more quickly and at a cheaper rate.

Disadvantages of apomictic crop:

Apomictic seeds reduce the genetic diversity because of a lack of variations. **(1 Mark)**

(c) Hybrid seeds are produced by cross-pollination of plants and in order to produce desirable hybrid character, plant breeders and scientists are trying thousands of combination to produce such hybrids. So hybrid seeds are produced every years and it requires a lots of scientific research for the production of such hybrid seeds. It is expensive and hence the cost of hybrid becomes too expensive for the farmers. **(2 Marks)**

6. **(a)** There are two ways by which the apomitic seeds are produced:

Agamospermy: In this method, the seeds are produced from diploid cells without meiosis and fertilization. For example: Apple.

Adentive embryony: In this method, the nucellus and integuments extends into the embryo sac and develops into embryo. It involves the formation of more than one embryo. For example: citrus fruit.

(3 Marks)

(b) The main advantage of apomictic seeds is that there is no segregation of characters in the hybrid progeny. The apomictic seeds are cost effective and high yielding. **(1 Mark)**

(c) Diagrammatic Representation of mature stage of dicotyledonous embryo: **(1 Mark)**

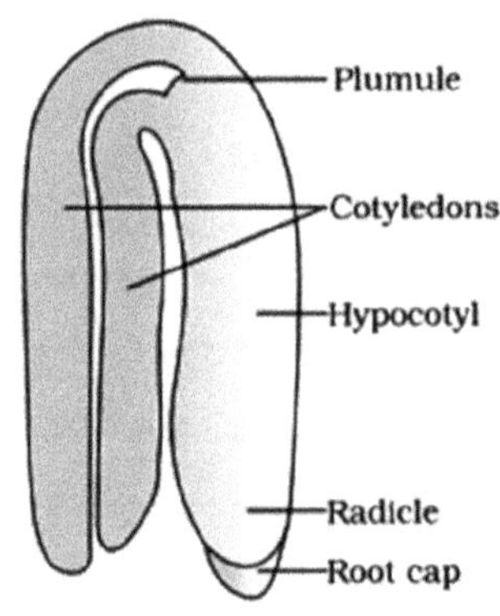

Topic-1: *Male Reproductive System*

1 — *Multiple Choice Questions (1 Mark)*

1. A human male decides to adopt a surgical method for contraception. Identify the point in the diagram where a cut would be made and tied. **[All India 2023, Set-I, U]**

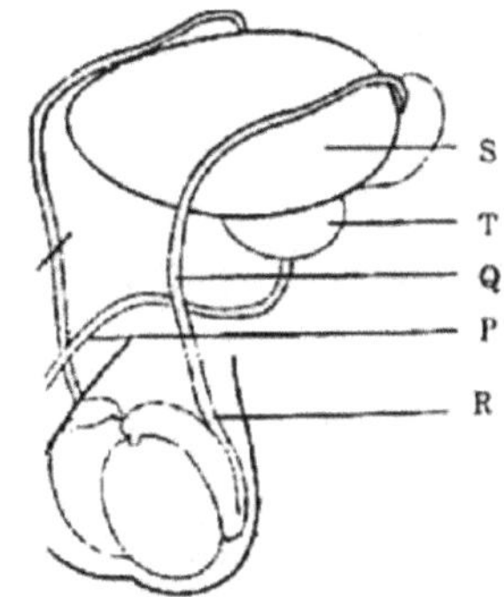

(a) Point S   (b) Point R

(c) Point Q   (d) Point P

2. Given below is a diagramatic view of the human male reproductive system : **[All India 2022, Term-I, U]**

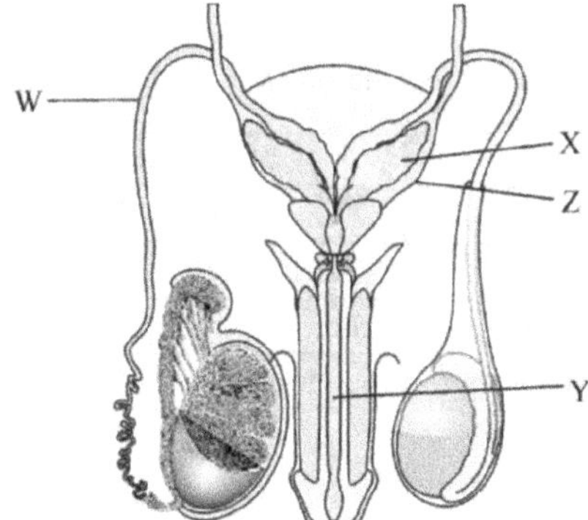

Identify the correct labelling for W, X, Y and Z and choose the correct option from the table below :

	W	X	Y	Z
(a)	Epididymis	Prostrate Gland	Glans Penis	Bulbourethral Gland
(b)	Bulbourethral Gland	Glans Penis	Prostrate Gland	Epididymis
(c)	Vas deferons	Seminal Vesicle	Urethra	Prostrate Gland
(d)	Rete testis	Bulbourethral Gland	Epididymis	Glans Penis

2 — *Assertion Reason/Two Statement Type Questions (1 Mark)*

3. **Assertion (A) :** Interstitial spaces outside the seminiferous tubule have blood vessels and sertoli cells.

   Reason (R) : Sertoli cells provide nutrition to the germ cells. **[All India 2022, Term-I, K]**

   (a) Both Assertion (A) and Reason (R) are true and Reason (R) is the correct explanation of Assertion (A).

   (b) Both Assertion (A) and Reason (R) are true, but Reason (R) is **not** the correct explanation of Assertion (A).

   (c) Assertion (A) is true, but Reason (R) is false.

   (d) Assertion (A) is false, but Reason (R) is true.

4 — *Very Short Answer Questions (1 Mark)*

4. List the four different human male accessory ducts.

   [All India 2020, K]

5 — *Short Answer Questions (2 or 3 Marks)*

5. Explain the functions of the following structures in the human male reproductive system.

   [CBSE Sample Paper 2022-23, U]

   (a) Scrotum

   (b) Leydig cells

   (c) Male accessory glands

6. Draw a labelled diagram to show interrelationship of four accessory ducts in a human male reproductive system.

[All India 2019, U]

7. Draw a diagram of the sectional view of a human seminiferous tubule and label any six of its parts.

[Delhi 2019, U]

8. Draw a diagram of a mature human sperm. Label any three parts and write their functions. **[All India 2018, U]**

9. Draw a labelled diagrammatic sectional view of a human seminiferous tubule. **[All India 2017, U]**

10. Why are the human testes located outside the abdominal cavity? Name the pouch in which they are present.

[All India 2014, U]

11. Draw a diagram of the microscopic structure of human sperm. Label the following parts in it and write their functions. **[Delhi 2013, U]**

(a) Acrosome

(b) Nucleus

(c) Middle piece

6 *Long Answer Questions (5 Marks)*

12. **(i) Write the specific location of the following in the testis in humans:** **[All India 2023, Set-I, U]**

   (1) Sertoli cells

   (2) Leydig cells

(ii) Explain the coordination between Gonadotropins, Leydig cells and Sertoli cells and their role in spermatogenesis. **[All India 2023, Set-I, U]**

Topic-2: *Female Reproductive System*

1 *Multiple Choice Questions (1 Mark)*

1. The uterus opens into the vagina through a narrow :

[All India 2022, Term-I, K]

(a) Ampulla   (b) Isthmus

(c) Cervix   (d) Infundibulum

2. Figure A shows the front view of the human female reproductive system and Figure B shows the development of a fertilized human egg cell

[CBSE Sample Paper 2021-22, Ap]

Figure A   Figure B

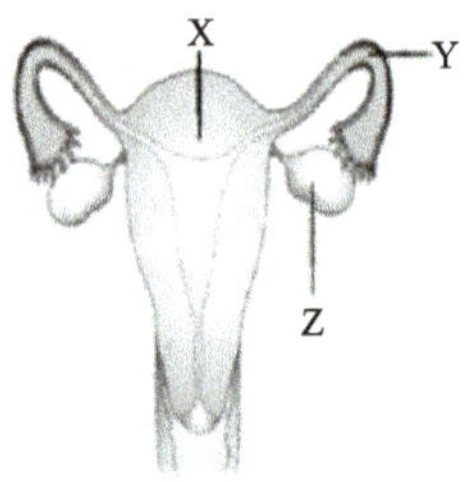

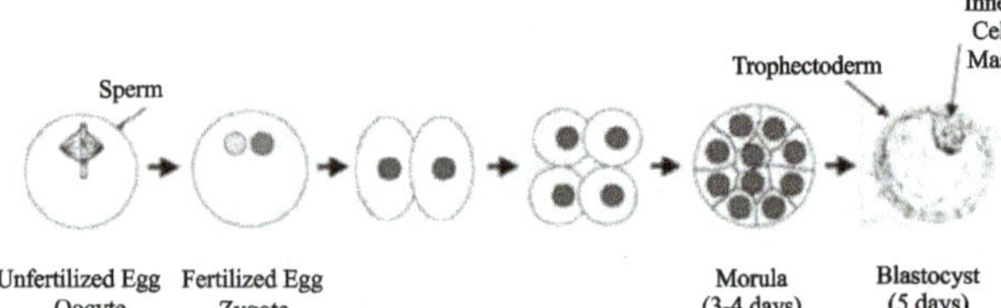

Identify the correct stage of development of human embryo (Figure B) that takes place at the site X, Y and Z respectively in the human female reproductive system (Figure A).

Choose the correct option from the table below:

	X	Y	Z
(a)	Mouth	Fertilized egg	Blastocyst
(b)	Unfertilized egg	Fertilized egg	Morula
(c)	Blastocyst	Fertilized egg	Unfertilized egg
(d)	Fertilized egg	Morula	Blastocyst

Topic-3: *Gametogenesis*

Multiple Choice Questions (1 Mark)

1. The nature of meiotic division during oogenesis in a human female is : **[All India 2022, Term-I, K]**

(a) equal cell division

(b) suspended cell division

(c) continuous cell division

(d) rapid cell division

Very Short Answer Questions (1 Mark)

2. State the fate of a pair of autosomes during gamete formation. **[All India 2017, K]**

Short Answer Questions (2 or 3 Marks)

3. Draw a sectional view of the human ovary showing the different stages of developing follicles, corpus luteum and ovulation. **[All India 2019, U]**

4. Explain the steps in the formation of an ovum from an oogonium in humans. **[All India 2013, U]**

Long Answer Questions (5 Marks)

5. (a) Where and how in the testes process of spermatogenesis occur in humans. **[Delhi 2020, U]**

(b) Draw diagram of human sperm and label four parts. **[Delhi 2020, U]**

6. (a) Draw a sectional view of a human ovary and label primary follicle, tertiary follicle, Graafian follicle and corpus luteum in it. **[All India 2020, U]**

(b) Name the gonadotropins and explain their role in oogenesis and the release of ova. **[All India 2020, U]**

7. (a) Draw a diagrammatic sectional view of a human seminiferous tubule, and label Sertoli cells, primary spermatocyte, spermatogonium and spermatozoa in it. **[All India 2013, U]**

(b) Explain the hormonal regulation of the process of spermatogenesis in humans. **[All India 2013, U]**

8. (a) How 'oogenesis' markedly different from 'spermatogenesis' with respect to the growth till puberty in the humans? **[Delhi 2014, U]**

(b) Draw a sectional view of human ovary and label the different follicular stages, ovum and Corpus luteum. **[Delhi 2014, U]**

Topic-4: *Menstrual Cycle*

Multiple Choice Questions (1 Mark)

1. The correct sequence of hormone secretion from beginning of menstruation is **[All India 2021-22, Term-I, K]**

(a) FSH, progesterone, estrogen.

(b) estrogen, FSH, progesterone.

(c) FSH, estrogen, progesterone.

(d) estrogen, progesterone, FSH.

Matching Based Questions (1 Mark)

2. Observe the following line diagram depicting the 28 days menstrual cycle of a healthy young woman.

[All India 2023, Set-I, K]

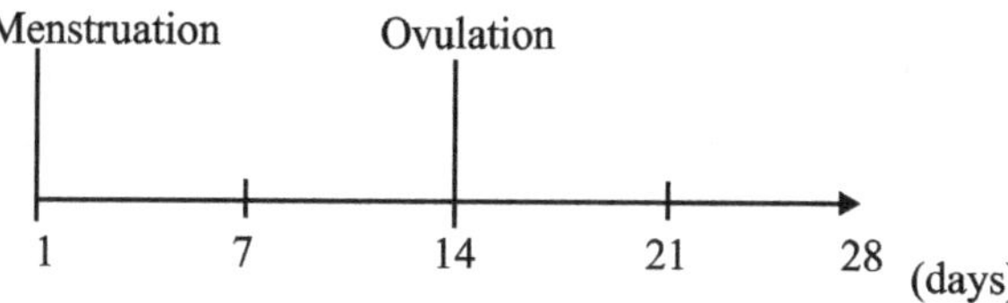

Select the option of days on which this woman would be most and least fertile.

	Most fertile days	Least fertile days
(a)	14-21	1-7
(b)	10-17	21-28
(c)	1-7	14-21
(d)	21-28	7-14

Short Answer Questions (2 or 3 Marks)

3. In the figure given below, parts A and B show the level of hormones which influence the menstrual cycle. Study the figure and answer the questions that follow: **[CBSE Sample Paper 2021-22, A]**

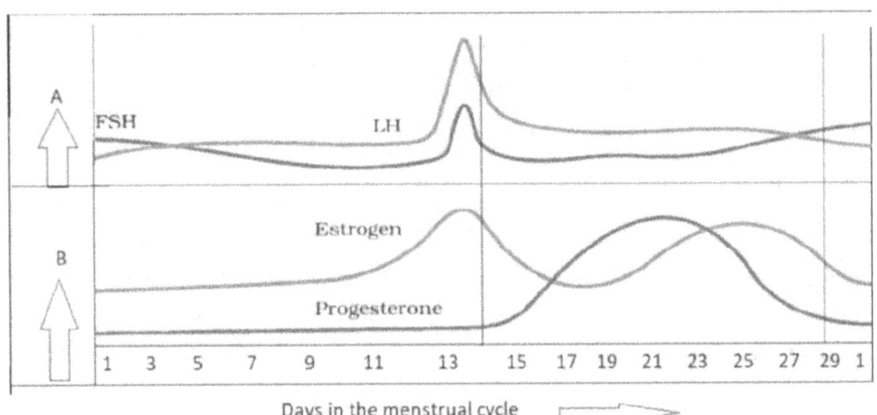

(a) Name the organs which secrete the hormones represented in parts A and B.

(b) State the impact of the hormones in part B on the uterus of the human female during 6 to 15 days of menstrual cycle?

Long Answer Questions (5 Marks)

4. Write the duration and the events that occur in the ovary and the uterus during follicular and luteal phases of the menstural cycle in humans. How do pituitary and ovarian hormones influence these two phases?   **[Delhi 2019, U]**

5. (a) Explain menstrual cycle in human females.

[All India 2018, U]

(b) How can the scientific understanding of the menstrual cycle of human females help as a contraceptive measure?   **[All India 2018, U]**

6. (a) Explain the following phases in the menstrual cycle of a human female :   **[Delhi 2017, U]**

(i) Menstrual phase   (ii) Follicular phase

(iii) Luteal phase

(b) A proper understanding of menstrual cycle can help immensely in family planning. Do you agree with the statement? Provide reasons for your answer.

[Delhi 2017, U]

7. (a) Explain the menstrual phase in a human female. State the levels of ovarian and pituitary hormones during this phase.   **[All India 2016, U]**

(b) Why is follicular phase in the menstrual cycle also referred as proliferative phase? Explain.   **[All India 2016, U]**

(c) Explain the events that occur in a graafian follicle at the time of ovulation and thereafter.   **[All India 2016, U]**

(d) Draw a graafian follicle and label antrum and secondary oocyte.   **[All India 2016, U]**

8. Describe the roles of pituitary and ovarian hormones during the menstrual cycle in a human female.

[All India 2015, U]

9. (a) Draw a diagrammatic sectional view of the female reproductive system of human and label the parts

(i) where the secondary oocytes develop

(ii) which helps in collection of ovum after ovulation

(iii) where fertilization occurs

(iv) where implantation of embryo occurs.

(b) Explain the role of pituitary and the ovarian hormones in menstrual cycle in human females.   **[Delhi 2013, K]**

7   **Case Based Questions**

Case Study: (Qs. 10-15)

A group of medical students carried out a detailed study on the impact of various factors on the different hormones during the menstrual cycle in a human female. They collected the data with different factors. Given below is the graph plotted from the data collected showing the morning temperature and concentration of hormones FSH, LH, estrogen and progesterone during normal menstrual cycle in a woman.

Temperature Graph

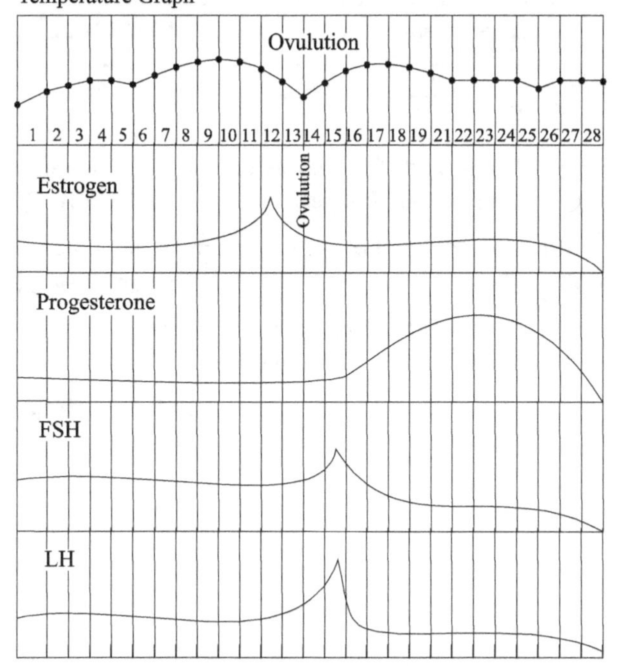

Study the graph and answer the given questions

10. The early morning recording of temperature in the graph during actual and during ovulation respectively are :

(a) low, high   **[All India 2022, Term-I,** **]**

(b) high, low

(c) low, low

(d) high, high

11. The time of ovulation is of importance in cases of :

[All India 2022, Term-I, **]**

(i) couples having difficulty in conception.

(ii) to know the safe period for prevention of pregnancy.

(iii) to inhibit the process of ovulation.

(iv) to stimulate ovarian follicular development.

(a) (i) and (iv)   (b) (ii) and (iv)

(c) (i) and (ii)   (d) (iii) and (iv)

12. The increase in the level of progesterone is maximum under the influence of LH during :

(a) Secretory phase   **[All India 2022, Term-I,** **]**

(b) Follicular phase

(c) Menstruation

(d) Proliferative phase

13. Which of the following hormone/hormones is'are showing rapid surge leading to changes in Graafian follicle just before ovulation ?

(a) LH   **[All India 2022, Term-I, K]**

(b) FSH

(c) FSH and Estrogen

(d) FSH and LH

14. The human corpus luteum starts regressing ________ days after ovulation. (Identify the correct choice for the blank).

[All India 2022, Term-I, K]

(a) 10 – 11   (b) 14 – 15

(c) 16 – 17   (d) 18 – 20

15. As per the data plotted in the graph, in which period of the menstrual cycle is the chance of fertilisation very high in human female ?   **[All India 2022, Term-I, K]**

(a) $3^{rd} – 9^{th}$ days   (b) $10^{th} – 17^{th}$ days

(c) $18^{th} – 23^{rd}$ days   (d) $23^{rd} – 28^{th}$ days

Topic-5: *Fertilisation and Implantation*

1   *Multiple Choice Questions (1 Mark)*

1. Penetration of the sperm in the ovum is followed by

[CBSE Sample Paper 2021-22]

(a) formation of first polar body.

(b) completion of meiosis II.

(c) first meiosis.

(d) dissolution of zona pellucida.

5   *Short Answer Questions (2 or 3 Marks)*

2. Trace the journey of a zygote from the isthmus of the fallopian tube up to its implantation in the uterus of a human female. Highlight the changes the zygote undergoes during the course of its journey up to implantation.

[All India 2023, Set-I, U]

3. The figure given below shows 3 sperms A, B and C.

  (a) Which one of the three sperms will gain entry into the ovum?   **[CBSE Sample Paper 2022-23,** **]**

  (b) Describe the associated changes induced by it on P and Q.   **[CBSE Sample Paper 2022-23,** **]**

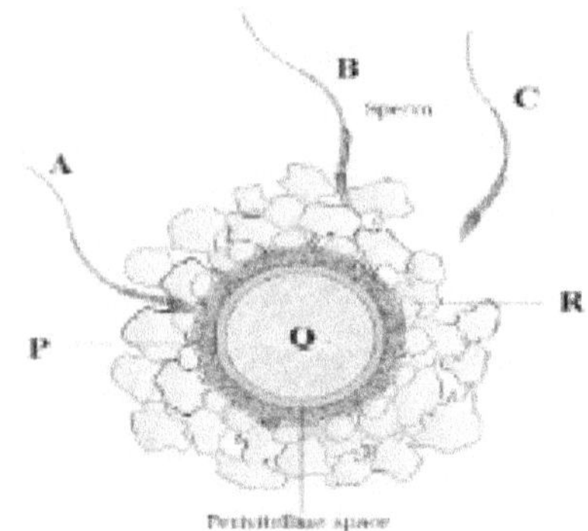

Figure   Ovum surrounded by few sperms

4. Name and explain the role of inner and middle walls of the human uterus.   **[Delhi 2014, U]**

 **6**   *Long Answer Questions (5 Marks)*

5. (a) Briefly explain the events of fertilization and implantation in an adult human female.   **[Delhi 2016, U]**

  (b) Comment on the role of placenta as an endocrine gland.   **[Delhi 2016, U]**

6. Where does fertilization occur in humans? Explain the events that occur during this process.

              [All India 2014, U]

 **Topic-6:**   *Pregnancy and Embryonic Development*

---

1   *Multiple Choice Questions (1 Mark)*

1. During human embryonic development, the heart in the embryo is formed after :   **[All India 2022, Term-I, K]**

  (a) 15 days of pregnancy

  (b) 30 days of pregnancy

  (c) 45 days of pregnancy

  (d) 60 days of pregnancy

2. Which of the following statements are correct with respect to hormones secreted by placenta?

        [CBSE Sample Paper 2021-22, U]

  (i) Placenta secretes relaxin during later stage of pregnancy.

  (ii) Placenta secretes high amount of FSH during pregnancy.

  (iii) Placenta secretes relaxin during initial stage of pregnancy.

  (iv) Placenta secretes hCG and hPL during pregnancy.

  (a) (i) and (iv)

  (b) (i), (ii) and (iv)

  (c) (iii) and (iv)

  (d) (ii), (iii) and (iv)

3. Concentration of which of the following substances will decrease in the maternal blood as it flows from embryo to placenta through the umbilical cord?

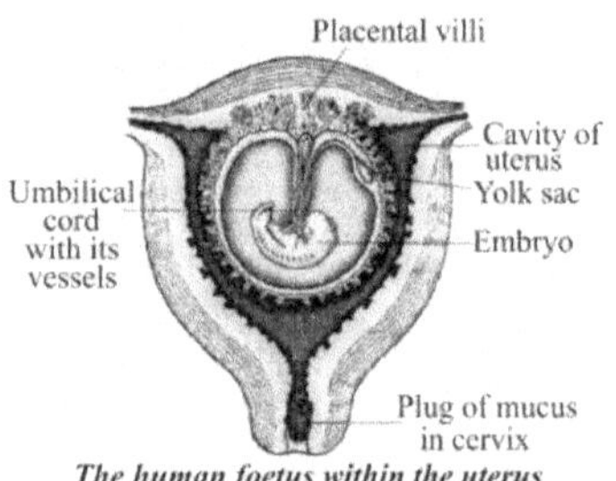

The human foetus within the uterus

        [CBSE Sample Paper 2021-22, U]

  (i) Oxygen   (ii) Amino Acids

  (iii) Carbon dioxide   (iv) Urea

  (a) (i) and (ii)

  (b) (ii) and (iv)

  (c) (iii) and (iv)

  (d) (i) and (iv)

5   *Short Answer Questions (2 or 3 Marks)*

4. Explain the phases in embryonic development from the morula stage till the establishment of pregnancy in a human female.   **[CBSE Sample Paper 2023-24 U]**

5. When and where do chorionic villi appear in humans? State their function. **[Delhi 2013, U]**

6 *Long Answer Questions (5 Marks)*

6. (i) Explain the formation of placenta after the implantation in a human female. **[Delhi 2023, Set-II, U]**

   (ii) Draw a diagram showing human foetus within the uterus and label any four parts in it. **[Delhi 2023, Set-II, U]**

7. (a) Briefly explain the events of fertilization and implantation in an adult human female. **[Delhi 2016, U]**

   (b) Comment on the role of placenta as an endocrine gland. **[Delhi 2016, U]**

8. (a) Arrange the following hormones in sequence of their secretion in a pregnant woman.

   [All India 2017, K]

   (b) Mention their source and the function they perform: hCG, LH, FSH, Relaxin **[All India 2017, K]**

9. During the reproductive cycle of a human female, when, where and how does a placenta develop ? What is the function of placenta during pregnancy and embryo development? **[Delhi 2015, U]**

Topic-7: *Parturition & Lactation*

1 *Multiple Choice Questions (1 Mark)*

1. Choose the correct option for the features of functional mammary gland of all female mammals from the statements below : **[All India 2022, Term-I, U]**

   (i) Glandular tissue with variable amount of fat.

   (ii) Mammary lobes, 30 – 40 in number called alveoli.

   (iii) Mammary ducts joining to form mammary tubules.

   (iv) Mammary ampulla connected to lactiferous duct.

   (a) (i) and (iii)   (b) (ii) and (iii)

   (c) (i) and (iv)   (d) (ii) and (iv)

2 *Assertion Reason/Two Statement Type Questions (1 Mark)*

2. **Assertion:** Parturition is induced by a complex neuro endocrine mechanism.

   [CBSE Sample Paper 2021, Term-I, U]

   Reason: At the end of gestation period, the maternal pituitary releases prolactin which causes uterine contractions.

   (a) If both Assertion and Reason are True and the Reason is a correct explanation of the Assertion.

   (b) If both Assertion and Reason are True but Reason is not a correct explanation of the Assertion.

   (c) If the Assertion is True but Reason is False.

   (d) If both Assertion and Reason are False.

3. During parturition, a pregnant woman is having prolonged labour pains and child birth has to be fastened. It is advisable to administer a hormone that can

   [CBSE Sample Paper 2021, Term-I, U]

   (a) increase the metabolic rate.

   (b) release glucose in the blood.

   (c) stimulate the ovary.

   (d) activate smooth muscles.

5 *Short Answer Questions (2 or 3 Marks)*

4. Medically it is advised to all young mothers that breastfeeding is the best for their newborn babies. Do you agree? Give reasons in support of your answer.

   [All India 2018, U]

5. Why is breast-feeding recommended during the initial period of an infant's growth ? Give reasons.

   [Delhi 2016, U]

6. Describe the process of Parturition in humans.

   [Delhi 2015, K]

Hints & Solutions

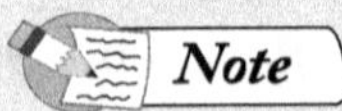
Topic-1: *Male Reproductive System*

1. **(c)** Point Q is vas deferens which is cut and tied during surgical method called vasectomy.   **(1 Mark)**

Note

Vasectomy is a form of male birth control that cuts the supply of sperm to your semen.

2. **(c)**

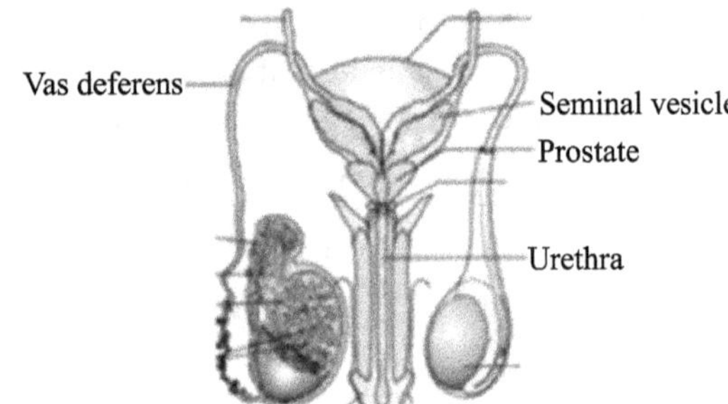

          (1 Mark)

3. **(d)** The regions outside the seminiferous tubules called interstitial spaces, contain small blood vessels and interstitial cells or Leydig cells. The statement in reason is correct.   **(1 Mark)**

4. The human male sex accessory ducts are rete testis, vasa efferentia, vas deferens and epididymis.

Rete testis: The seminiferous tubules of the testis open into the vasa efferentia through rete testis.

Vasa efferentia: It leaves the testis and opens into the epididymis which is located along the posterior surface of each testis.   **(.5 Mark)**

Epididymis: This leads to vas deferns which ascends to the abdomen and loops over the urinary bladder. The epididymis receives a duct from seminal vesicle that opens into urethra as the ejaculatory duct.   **(.5 Mark)**

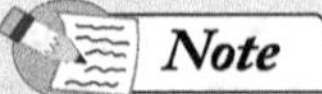
Note

All the male sex accessory ducts plays an important role in the storage and transportation of the sperms from the testis to the outside via urethra.

5. **(a)** Scrotum: The testes are situated outside the abdominal cavity within a pouch called scrotum. The scrotum helps in maintaining the low temperature of the testes (2–2.5 degree celsius lower than the normal internal body temperature) necessary for spermatogenesis.   **(1 Mark)**

(b) Leydig cells: The regions outside the seminiferous tubules called interstitial spaces, contain small blood vessels and interstitial cells or Leydig cells. Leydig cells synthesize and secrete testicular hormones called androgens.   **(1 Mark)**

(c) Male accessory glands: The male accessory glands include paired seminal vesicles, a prostate and paired bulbourethral glands. Secretions of these glands constitute the seminal plasma which is rich in fructose, calcium and certain enzymes. The secretions of bulbourethral glands also help in the lubrication of the penis.   **(1 Mark)**

6. The internal organs of the male reproductive system are called accessory organs. They include the vas deferens, seminal vesicles, prostate gland, and bulbourethral glands.   **(1 Mark)**

Diagrammatic representation of interrelationship of four accessory ducts in a human male reproductive system:

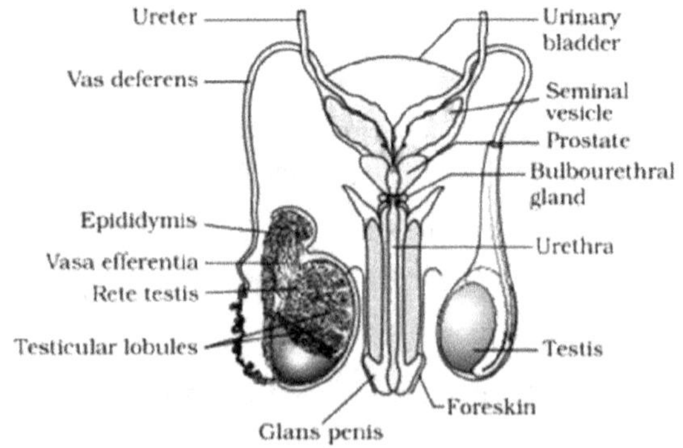

          (1 Mark)

7. Diagrammatic Representation of seminiferous tubules: **(2 Marks)**

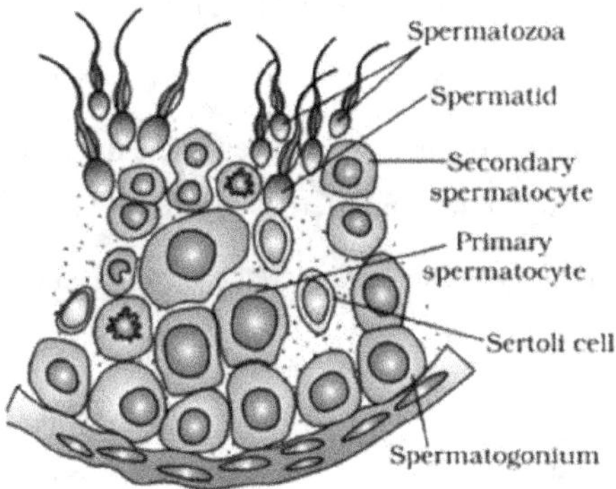

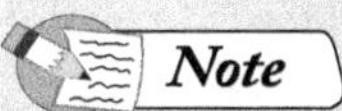
Note

The seminiferous tubules is lined on its inside by two types of cells called male germ cells that undergo meiotic divisions results in sperm formation. Whereas Sertoli cells provide nourishment to the germ cells.

8. Acrosome : It is a cap like structure, filled with hydrolytic enzymes that help in the fertilisation of the ovum.

Middle piece : Possesses numerous mitochondria, which produces energy for the movement of tail and facilitate the movement of tail that facilitates sperm motality essential for fertilization. **(2 Marks)**

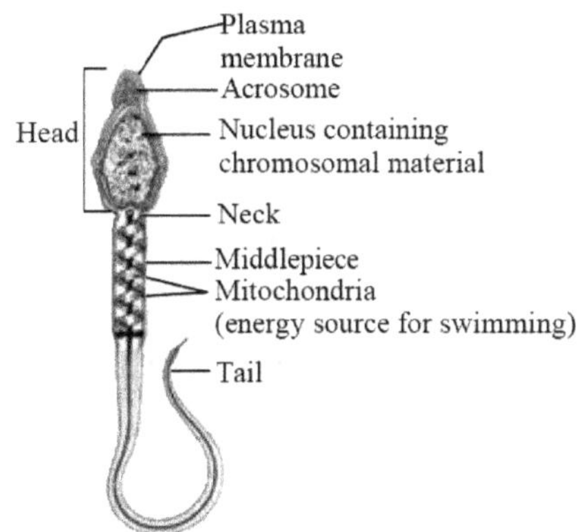

Tail : Facilitate sperm motility essential for fertilisation.

Note

The seminal plasma is rich in fructose, calcium and certain enzymes and seminal plasma alongwith sperms constitute the semen. The secretions of bulbourethral glands also helps in the lubrication of the penis.

9. Diagrammatic sectional view of a seminiferous tubule (enlarged) **(2 Marks)**

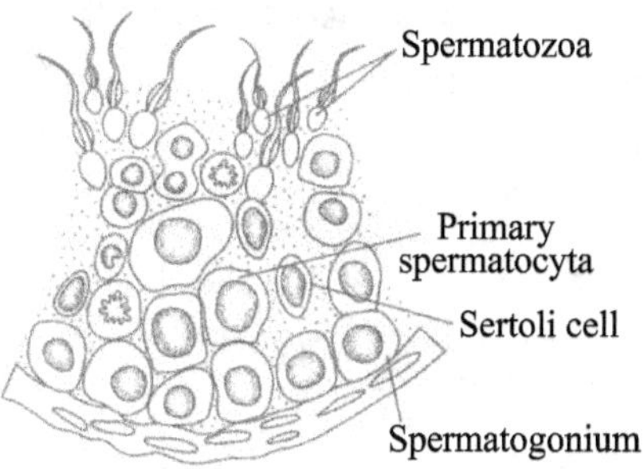

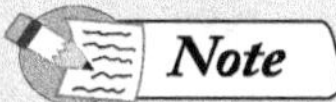
Note

Seminiferous tubules is lined by two types of cells such as sertoli cells and male germ cells. The male germ cells undergo meiotic divisions in sperm formation whereas sertoli cells provide nutrition to the germ cells.

10. The testes are located outside the abdominal cavity in a pouch like structure called scrotum because the process of spermatogenesis or sperm production requires lower temperature (2-2.5°C) than the normal body temperature (37°C).

The scrotum helps in maintaining the low temperature of the testes. **(3 Marks)**

11. Diagrammatic representation of human sperm:

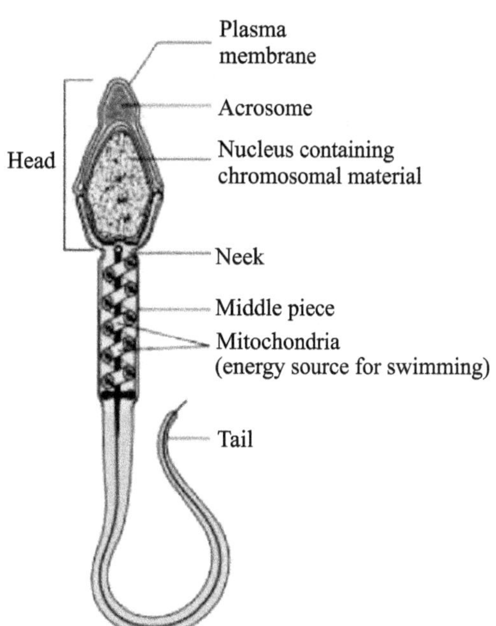

(a) **Acrosome:** The anterior portion of sperm head contains an elongated haploid nucleus and is covered by a cap-like structure called acrosome. It is filled with enzymes that help in fertilisation of the ovum. **(1 Mark)**

Note

The acrosome contains hyaluronidase enzyme that breaks the outer membrane called zona pellucida layer of the ovum and allows the haploid nucleus of the sperm to fuse with the haploid nucleus in the ovum.

(b) **Nucleus:** The nucleus of the sperm cell contains the genetic material such as DNA and during the process of fertilisation; the haploid nucleus of the sperm tends to fuse with haploid nucleus of the egg to form a diploid zygote. **(1 Mark)**

(c) **Middle piece:** The middle piece possesses numerous mitochondria, which produces energy for the movement of tail that facilitates sperm motility which is essential for fertilisation. **(1 Mark)**

12. (i)

(1) Sertoli cells are present in the seminiferous tubules of the male gonads in the testes. **(1 Mark)**

(2) Leydig cells are present in the intertubular/interstitial space. **(1 Mark)**

(ii) The increased levels of GnRH then acts at the anterior pituitary gland and stimulates secretion of two gonadotropins – luteinising hormone (LH) and follicle stimulating hormone (FSH). LH acts at the Leydig cells and stimulates synthesis and secretion of androgens. Androgens, in turn, stimulate the process of spermatogenesis. FSH acts on the Sertoli cells and stimulates secretion of some factors which help in the process of spermiogenesis. Sertoli cells are located within the seminiferous tubules of the testes. **(3 Marks)**

They provide nutrition to the developing sperms.

The Leydig cells are located in the interstitial spaces between the seminiferous tubules.

They synthesize and secrete androgen hormones (like testosterone). **(5 Marks)**

Topic-2: *Female Reproductive System*

1. (c) The uterus opens into vagina through a narrow **cervix** and the cavity of the cervix is called cervical canal. **(1 Mark)**

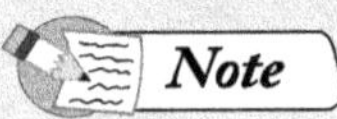
Note

The uterus is single and it is also known as womb.

2. (c) X = Blastocyst, Y = Fertilized egg, Z = Unfertilized egg. **(1 Mark)**

Topic-3: *Gametogenesis*

1. (b) In oogenesis, diploid oogonium go through mitosis until one develops into a primary oocyte, which will begin the first meiotic division, but then arrest; it will finish this division as it develops in the follicle, giving rise to a haploid secondary oocyte and a smaller polar body. **(1 Mark)**

2. The homologous pair of autosomes will separate from each other and will move to different gametes during gamete formation. **(1 Mark)**

3. (2 Marks)

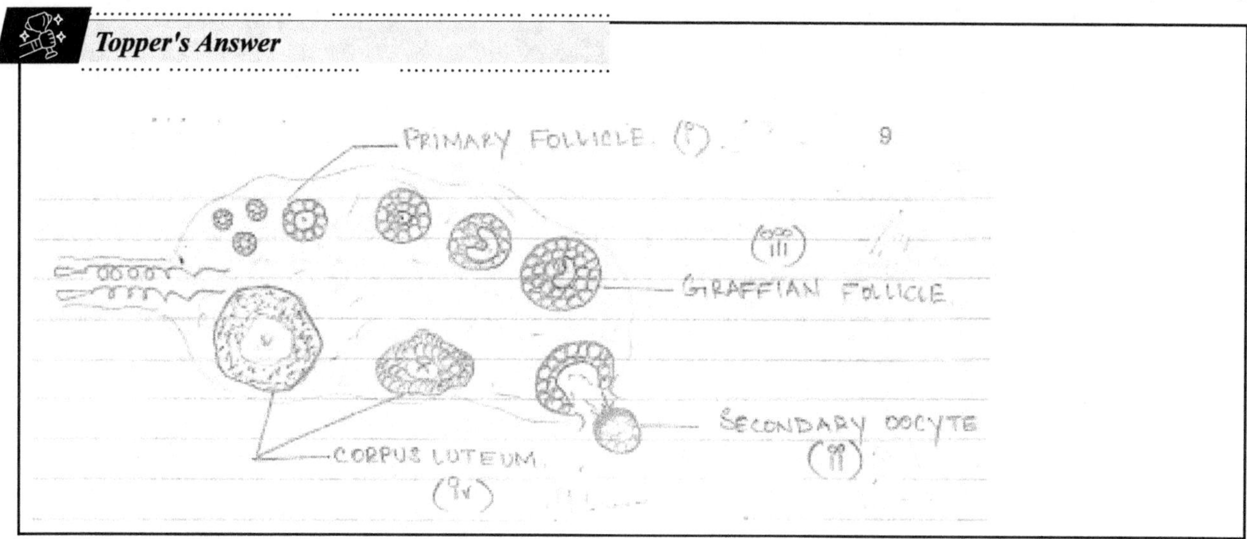

Diagrammatic representation of sectional view of human ovary: (3 Marks)

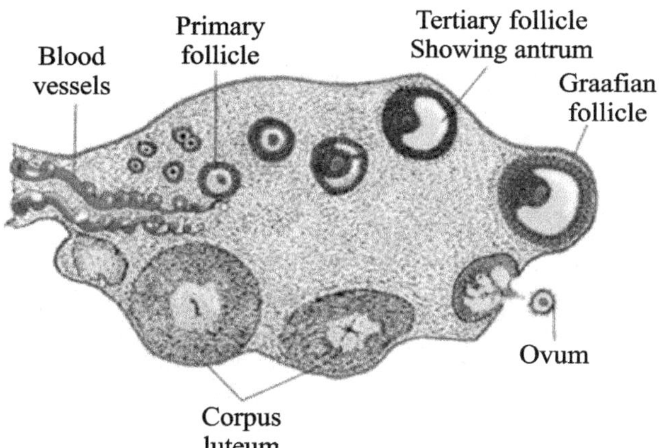

4. The process of formation of a mature female gamete is called **oogenesis.** This process is initiated during the embryonic development stage when a couple of million gamete mother cells or oogonia are formed within each fetal ovary as no more oogonia are formed and added after birth.

Such cells start division and enter into prophase-I of the meiotic division. The cells get temporarily arrested at that stage called **Primary oocytes.**

Each primary oocyte then gets surrounded by a layer of granulosa cells and then called **Primary follicle** and the primary follicles get surrounded by more layers of granulosa cells and a new theca. This is called **secondary follicle.** (1 Mark)

Then the secondary follicle transform into a tertiary follicle which is characterised by a fluid filled cavity called **Antrum.**

The theca layer is organised into an inner theca internal and an outer theca externa. The primary oocyte within the tertiary follicle grows in size and completes its first meiotic division. (1 Mark)

It is an unequal division results in the formation of a large haploid **secondary oocyte** and a tiny first polar body. The tertiary follicle changes into the mature follicle or **Graafian follicle.** The secondary oocyte forms a new membrane called **Zona pellucida.**

The Graafian follicle then ruptures to release the secondary oocyte (ovum) from the ovary by the process called **Ovulation.** (1 Mark)

Diagrammatic representation of steps involved in the process of oogenesis:

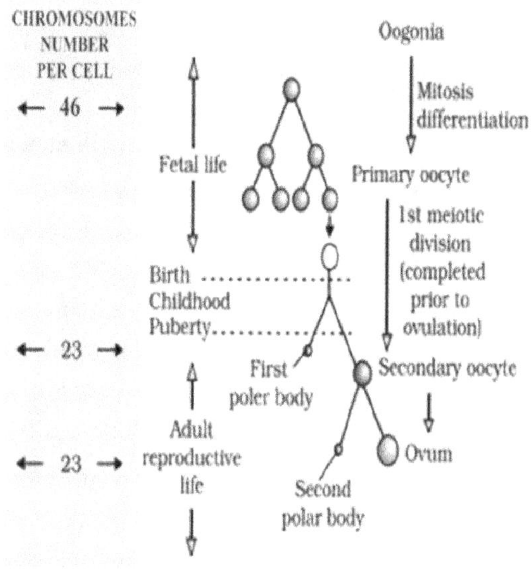

(3 Marks)

5. **(a)** In the testis, the immature male germ cells or spermatogonia produce sperms by spermatogenesis that begins at puberty. The spermatogonia present on the inside wall of seminiferous tubules get multiply by mitotic division and increases in numbers. Each spermatogonium is diploid in nature as it contains 46 chromosomes.

Some of the spermatogonia are called primary spermatocytes that periodically undergo meiosis. A primary spermatocyte completes the first meiotic division results in the formation of two equal, haploid cells called secondary spermatocytes that contains only 23 chromosomes each.

The secondary spermatocytes undergo the second meiotic division to produce four equal, haploid spermatids. The spermatids are then transformed into spermatozoa or sperms by the process called spermiogenesis. After spermiogenesis, sperm heads become embedded in the sertoli cells and then are finally released from the seminiferous tubules by the process called spermiation. **(2½ Marks)**

(b) **Diagrammatic Representation of human sperm:**

(2½ Mark)

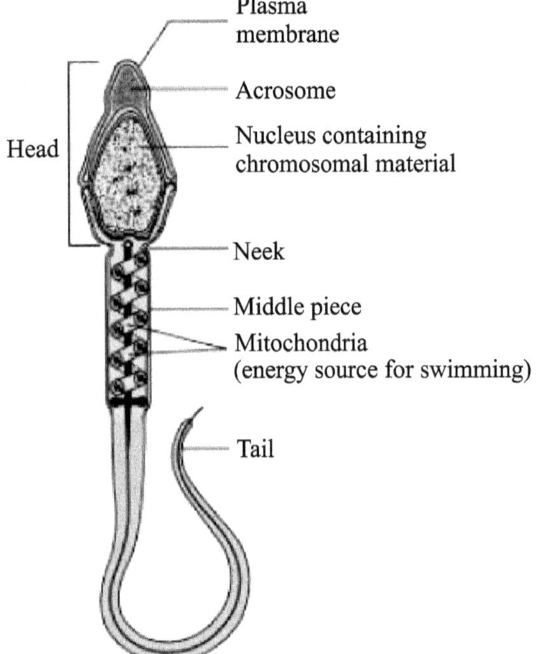

6.

Topper's Answer

(3 + 2 = 5 Marks)

(a) **Diagrammatic representation of sectional view of human ovary:** **(3 Marks)**

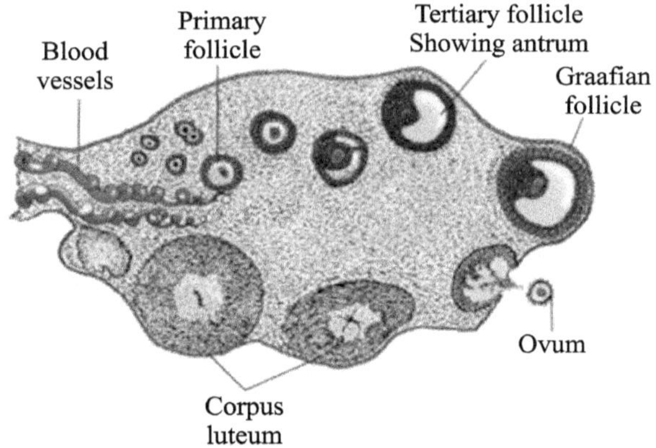

(b) The gonadotropin hormones are luteinizing hormones and follicle stimulating hormones that are secreted by the anterior lobe of the pituitary gland. As, these hormones stimulates ovaries in females and plays an essential role in the process of reproduction. FSH stimulates egg formation in females and LH alongwith FSH helps in the process of ovulation and also prepares the uterus for pregnancy. Whereas estrogen hormone is secreted by the ovaries that induces and also maintains secondary sexual characteristics in females.

(2 Marks)

7. **(a) Diagrammatic representation of sectional view of a seminiferous tubule** **(2 Marks)**

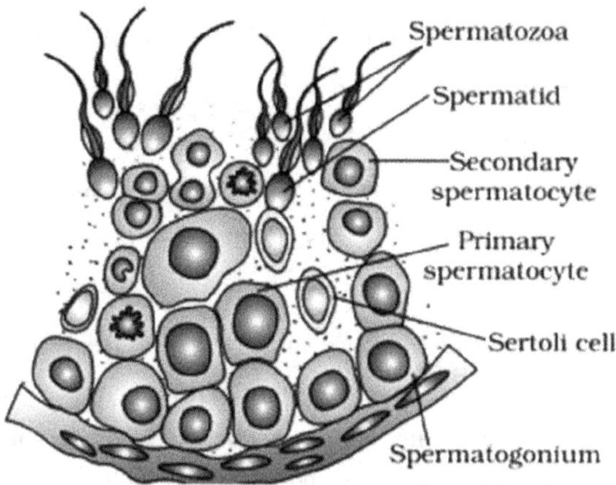

(b) The hormonal regulation of the process of spermatogenesis in humans are as follows:

- The process of spermatogenesis starts at the age of puberty due to significant increase in the secretion of gonadotrophin releasing hormone (GnRH).

- The increase in the level of GnRH acts at the anterior pituitary gland and also stimulates the secretion of two gonadotropins such as luteinising hormone (LH) and follicle stimulating hormone (FSH). **(1.5 Marks)**

- LH acts at the Leydig cells and also stimulates the synthesis and secretion of androgens. Androgen then stimulates the process of spermatogenesis.

- FSH acts on the Sertoli cells and also stimulates the secretion of some factors that help in the process of spermiogenesis. **(1.5 Marks)**

8. **(a)** The process of formation of a mature female gamete is called oogenesis and is different from spermatogenesis. Oogenesis is initiated during the embryonic development stage when a couple

of millions of oogonia or gamete mother cells are formed within each fetal ovary. These cells start division and enter into prophase-I of the meiotic division and get temporarily arrested at that stage called primary oocytes. **(1 Mark)**

Each primary oocyte then gets surrounded by a layer of granulosa cells and then called the primary follicle. A large number of these follicles degenerate during the phase from birth to puberty. So, at puberty only 60,000-80,000 primary follicles are left in each ovary. The primary follicles get surrounded by more layers of granulosa cells and a new theca and this is called secondary follicles. Then secondary follicles transforms into a tertiary follicle that is characterised by a fluid filled cavity called antrum. The theca layer is organised into an inner theca interna and an outer theca externa. **(1 Mark)**

The primary oocyte within the tertiary follicle grows in size and completes its first meiotic division. It is an unequal division that results in the formation of a large haploid secondary oocyte and a tiny first polar body. The secondary oocyte retains bulk of the nutrient rich cytoplasm of the primary oocyte. The tertiary follicle further changes into the mature follicle or Graafian follicle. The secondary oocyte forms a new membrane called zonapellucida surrounding it. Then the Graafian follicle ruptures to release the secondary oocyte from the ovary by the process called ovulation.

Whereas in the process of spermatogenesis, the immature male germ cells or spermatogonia produce sperms in the testis that begins at the puberty.

(1 Mark)

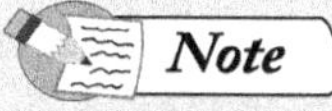

Note

Spermatogenesis starts at the age of puberty due to significant intrease in the secretion of gonadotropin releasing hormone (GnRH).

(b) Diagrammatic Representation of sectional view of ovary and follicular stages of ovum as well as corpus luteum:

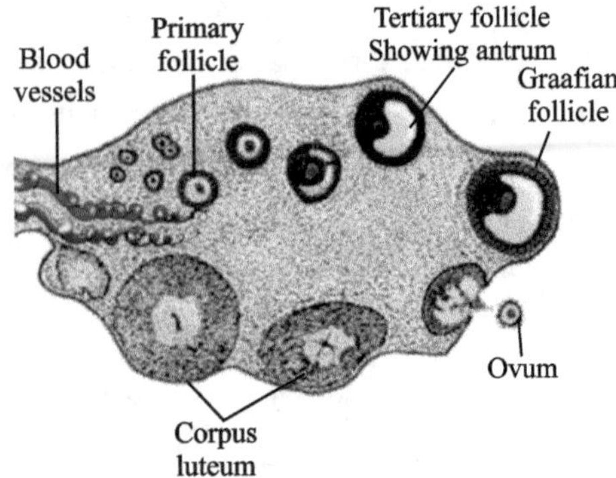

(2 Marks)

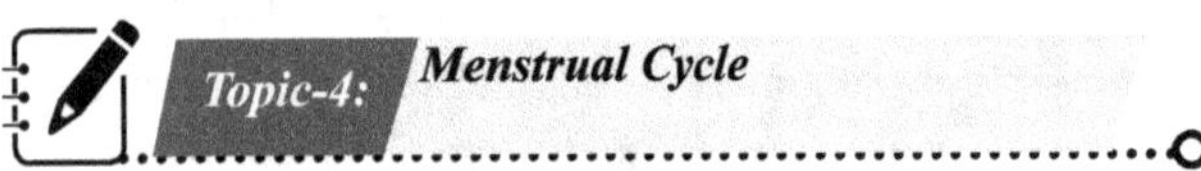

Topic-4: **Menstrual Cycle**

1. **(c)** FSH, estrogen,progesterone. **(1 Mark)**

2. **(b)** 10-17 day of menstrual cycle are most fertile days, because ovulation occurs in which the ovary releases an egg for fertilisation to occur but when this egg does not get fertilised, the endometrium lining sheds causing the release of the egg along with mucus, this occurs in the form of menstruation cycle. This occurs during 21-28 days and the female is in the least fertile stage during 21-28 days.

(1 Mark)

3. (a) A –Pituitary gland; B: Ovary **(1 Mark)**

   (b) Endometrium of the uterus regenerates through proliferation. **(1 Mark)**

4. The menstrual phase is followed by **follicular phase** and during this phase the primary follicles in the ovary grow to become a fully mature Graafian follicle. Then simultaneously the endometrium of uterus regenerates through proliferation. Such changes in the ovary and uterus are induced by changes in the levels of pituitary and ovarian hormones. The secretion of gonadotropins such as luteinizing hormone and follicle stimulating hormone levels gradually increases during follicular phase. **(1 Mark)**

This stimulates follicular development as well as secretion of estrogens hormone by the growing follicles. Both LH and FSH attain a peak level in the middle of cycle that is

about 14th day. The rapid secretion of LH surge induces rupture of Graafian follicle and then induces the release of ovum results in ovulation. **(1 Mark)**

The process of ovulation is followed by luteal phase. During this phase, the remaining parts of the Graafian follicle transforms as the corpus luteum. It secretes a large amount of progesterone hormone that is essential for the maintenance of the endometrium.

As, endometrium is necessary for the process of implantation of fertilised ovum and other events during pregnancy. **(1 Mark)**

If the process of fertilisation does not take place, the corpus luteum degenerates results in the disintegration of the endometrium leading to menstruation. This marks a beginning of new cycle.

A decrease in level of ovarian hormone results in the constriction of arteries that lead to cause shredding of uterine lining and menstruation. The deficit in gonadotropins removes the negative feedback on the hypothalamus and menstrual cycle again begins with the GnRH release. **(1 Mark)**

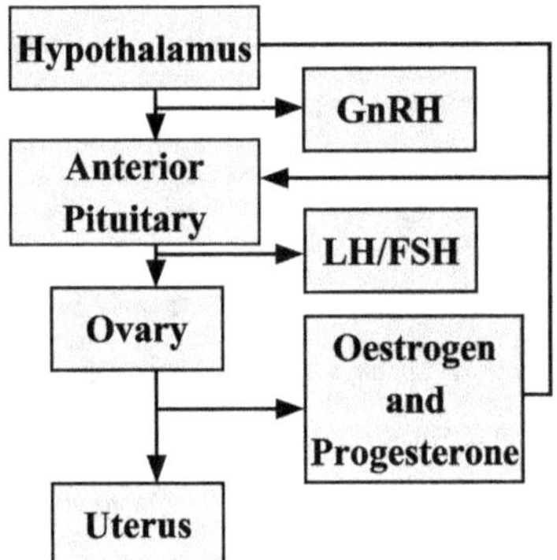

(1 Mark)

Note

*In human females, menstruation is repeated at an average interval of about 28/29 days and the cycle of events starting from one menstruation till the next one is called the **menstrual cycle**.*

5. (a) **Menstrual Cycle :**

   (i) The reproductive cycle in the female primates (e.g. monkeys, apes and humans) is called menstrual cycle.

(ii) The first menstruation begins at puberty and is called **menarche**.

(iii) In human females, menstruation is repeated at an average interval of about 28/29 days and the cycle of events starting from one menstruation till the next one is **menstrual cycle**. **(1 Mark)**

(iv) **The phases of menstrual cycle are as follows:**
Menstrual phase: It lasts for 3-5 days. The menstrual flow results due to breakdown of endometrial lining of the uterus and its blood vessels which forms liquid that comes out through vagina. Menstruation only occurs if the released ovum is not fertilised.

Follicular **phase :** It lasts for 8-10 days. During this phase, the primary follicles in the ovary grow to become a fully mature Grafian follicle and simultaneously the endometrium of uterus regerates through proliferation. The secretion of LH and FSH increases gradually. **(1 Mark)**

Ovulatory **phase :** It lasts for 1 day. There is release of ovum.

Luteal **phase :** It lasts for 13 days. There is LH surge. These induces the remaining parts of Grafian follicle to tranform as corpus luteum and its secretes progesterone for maintenance of the endometriun.

(v) If fertilisation occurs, endomentrium starts preparing for implantation. In the absence of fertilisation, corpus luteum degenerate. **(1 Mark)**

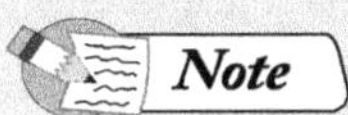

Note

In human beings, menstrual cycles ceases around 50 years of age and is termed as menopause. Cyclic menstruation is an indicator of normal reproductive phase and extends between menarche and menopause.

(b) Scientific understanding of menstrual cycle of human females are very important as a contraceptive measures. It helps in following ways :

(i) Safe period (Rhythm method)

A week before and a week after menstrual bleeding is considered as safe period for sexual intercourse. The idea is based on following facts :

(ii) Ovulation occurs on 14th day of cycle and ovum survives for about 2 days. **(1 Mark)**

(iii) Sperms remain alive for about 3 days.

This method reduces the chances of pregenancy by about 80%.

(iv) Pills used by females are also dependent on menstrual cycle. The pills have to be taken daily for a period of 21 days starting preferably within first five days of menstrual cycle. It is repeated again after period of 7 days. These inhibit ovulation and implantation as well as alter the quality of cervical mucus to prevent/retard entry of sperms. **(1 Mark)**

6. **(a)** The menstrual cycle involves following phases such as:

(i) **Menstrual phase:** This phase takes place when released ovum is not fertilised. This phase occurs within the first 3rd-5th days of cycle where menstrual flow occurs because of the breakdown of endometrial lining of the uterus. **(1 Mark)**

(ii) **Follicular phase:** This phase occurs within the 5th-14th day of the cycle where the primary follicles grow to become a fully mature Graafian follicle, endometrium of uterus regenerates and Graafian follicle ruptures to release ova as ovulation occurs on 14th day. **(1 Mark)**

(iii) **Luteal phase:** This phase occurs within the 15th-28th day. In this phase, the remaining parts of the Graafian follicle transform into Corpus luteum and secretion of progesterone occurs that is essential for the maintenance of endometrium. **(1 Mark)**

(b) Yes, I agree with the statement that taking appropriate precautions between 10th-17th day of menstrual cycle when the chances of fertilisation are high.

(1 Mark)

7. **(a)** The menstrual phase of the menstruation cycle is starts when the menstrual flow occurs and it lasts for

3-5 days. The menstrual flow results because of the breakdown of endometrial lining of the uterus and its blood vessels which forms liquid that comes out through vagina. Menstruation occurs if the released ovum is not fertilised. **(1 Mark)**

> **Note**
>
> *In human females, menstruation is repeated at an average interval of about 28/29 days and the cycle of events starting one menstruation till the next one is called the **menstrual cycle**.*

(b) During the follicular phase, the primary follicles in the ovary grow to become a fully mature Graafian follicle. The endometrium of uterus regenerates through proliferation. This is reason that follicular phase is also called as proliferative phase.

The changes in the ovary and the uterus are induced by changes in the levels of pituitary and ovarian hormones. The secretion of gonadotropins (LH and FSH) increases gradually during this phase and also stimulates follicular development as well as secretion of estrogens by growing follicles.

(1.5 Marks)

(c) The level of both LH and FSH increases and attain a peak level in the middle of cycle (about 14th day). Rapid secretion of LH leads to its maximum level during the mid-cycle called LH surge induces rupture of Graafian follicle and thereby release of ovum (ovulation). The ovulatory phase or ovulation is followed by the luteal phase during which the remaining parts of the Graafian follicle transform as the **corpus luteum.**

The corpus luteum secretes a large amount of progesterone which is essential for maintenance of the endometrium. Endometrium is necessary for implantation of the fertilized ovum and other events of pregnancy. During pregnancy all events of the menstrual cycle stop and there is no menstruation. In the absence of fertilisation, the corpus luteum degenerates and this causes disintegration of the endometrium results in menstruation. **(1.5 Marks)**

(d) Diagrammatic representation of Graafian follicle:

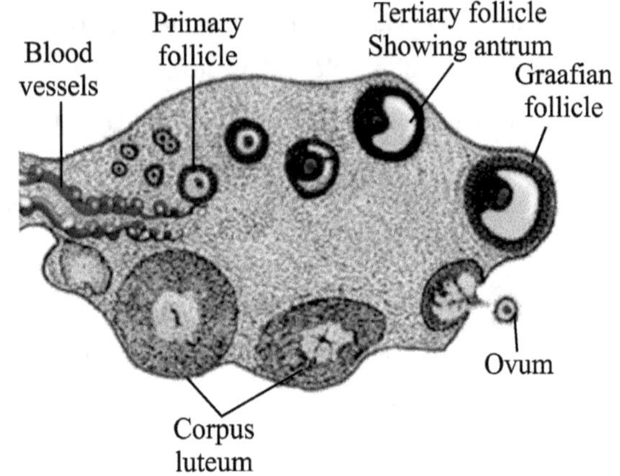

(1 Mark)

8. The rhythmic series of changes that occur in the reproductive organs of female primates (monkeys, apes and human beings) is called **menstrual cycle. (1 Mark)**

- It is repeated at an average interval of about 28/29 days.

- The first appearance of menstruation at puberty is called **menarche.**

- The menstrual cycle has four phases. These are:

(i) Menstrual Phase **(1 Mark)**

- The soft tissue of endometrial lining of the uterus disintegrates causing bleeding.

- The unfertilized egg and soft tissues are discharged.

- It lasts for 3-5days.

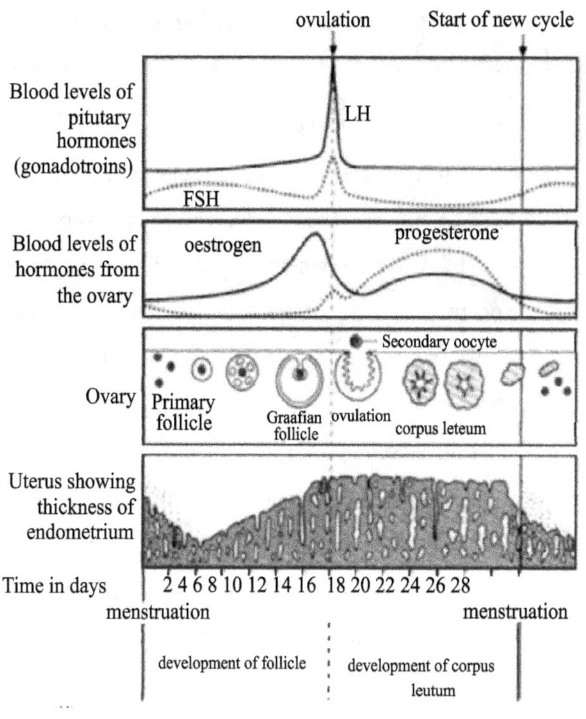

(1 Mark)

(ii) Follicular Phase/Proliferative Phase

- The primary/follicles in the ovary grow and become a fully mature Graafian follicle.

- The endometrium of the uterus is regenerated due to the secretion of LH and FSH from anterior pituitary and ovarian hormone, estrogen.

- It lasts for about 10 to 14 days.

(iii) Ovulatory Phase **(1 Mark)**

- Rapid secretion of LH (LH surge) induced rupture of Graafian follicle, thereby leading to ovulation (released of ovum).

- It lasts for only about 48 hours.

(iv) Luteal Phase/Secretory Phase **(1 Mark)**

- In this phase the ruptured follicle changes into corpus luteum in the ovary and it secrete the hormone progesterone.

- The endometrium thickens further and their glands secrete a fluid into the uterus.

- If ovum is not fertilised, the corpus luteum undergoes degeneration and this causes disintegration of the endometrium leading to menstruation.

- Estrogen and progesterone levels rise during this phase.

- It lasts for only 1 day.

- During pregnancy all events of the menstrual cycle stop and there is no menstruation. The menstrual cycle permanently stops in females at the age of around 50 years. This is called **menopause**.

9. (a) **Diagrammatic representation of section view of female reproductive system:** **(2 Marks)**

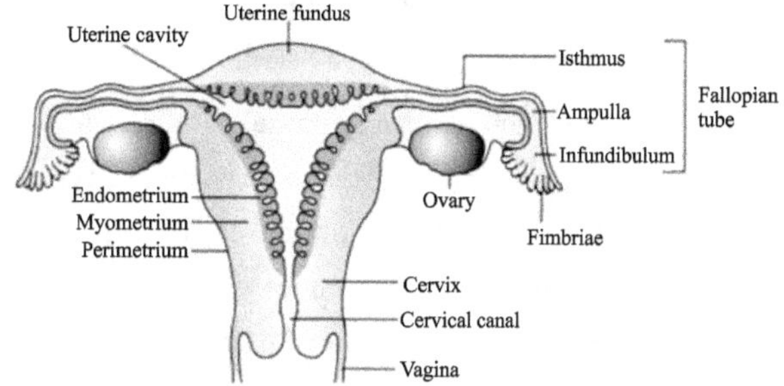

(i) Ovary

(ii) Fimbriae

(iii) Isthmus and ampulla junction

(iv) Endometrium

(b) Changes that takes place in the ovary and uterus during menstrual cycle are caused because of the change in the levels of pituitary and ovarian hormones. After menstrual phase gonadrotropin hormone such as LH (luteinising hormone) and follicular stimulating hormone (FSH) are released from pituitary. Their level gradually increases during follicular phase and it stimulates the development of follicles and secretion of estrogen hormone by growing follicles. So, both LH and FSH attain peak on 13th and 14th day. Rapid secretion of LH causes ovulation on day 14. **(3 Marks)**

During luteal phases, Graafian follicle changes into corpus luteum which secretes progesterone which plays an important role in the maintenance of endometrium that is necessary for implantation.

(5 Marks)

10. **(a)** As per graph during menstrual estrogen is low while during ovulation it reach to its higher peak.

(1 Mark)

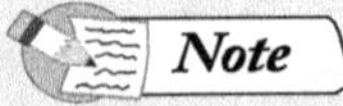

Note

The reproductive cycle in female primates is called menstrual cycle.

11. **(c)** Contraceptive are used to inhibit the ovulation process. Progesterone is important to stimulate ovarian follicular development. Hence only statements i and ii are important for ovulation.

(1 Mark)

12. **(a)** The ovulation (ovulatory phase) is followed by the luteal phase during which the remaining parts of the Graafian follicle transform into the corpus luteum. The corpus luteum secretes large amounts of progesterone which is essential for the maintenance of the endometrium. Hence progesterone level is highest during secretory phase. **(1 Mark)**

13. **(d)** Both LH and FSH attain a peak level in the middle of the cycle (about 14th day). Rapid secretion of LH leading to its maximum level during the mid-cycle called LH surge induces rupture of Graafian follicle and thereby the release of an ovum (ovulation).

(1 Mark)

14. **(c)** In human ovulation followed by 14th to 15th day of menstrual cycle. Then corpus luteum starts regressing at 16th -17th days after ovulation.

(1 Mark)

15. **(b)** The chances of fertilisation is highest during ovulation period hence, 10th -17th period of the menstrual cycle is the chance of fertilisation.

(1 Mark)

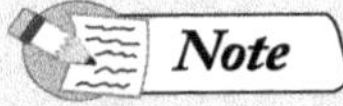

Note

The chances of fertilization is maximum during the period of ovulation.

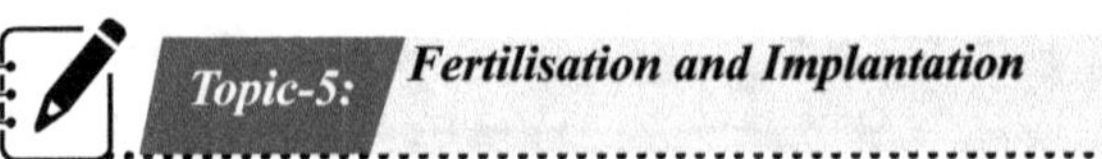

1. **(b)** completion of meiosis II **(1 Mark)**

2. **(a)** The ovaries produce the female egg cells, called the ova or oocytes. The oocytes are then transported to the fallopian tube where fertilisation by a sperm may occur. Then the zygote travels down the fallopian tube, where it becomes a morula. **(1.5 Marks)**

   (b) The fertilised egg then moves to the uterus, where the uterine lining has thickened in response to the normal hormones of the reproductive cycle.

   (c) Once fertilised in the ampullary region of the fallopian tube, the embryo the uterine cavity at the blastocyst stage after 5 days of fertilisation.

   (d) During implantation the embryo adheres to the wall of the uterus. At this step of prenatal development, the conceptus is termed as blastocyst. **(1.5 Marks)**

3. **(a)** Sperm A

   (b) In the figure given Sperm 'A' has come in contact with the zona pellucida layer (P) of the ovum (Q), it will induce changes in the membrane that will block the entry of additional sperms (B and C). Thus, it ensures that only one sperm can fertilise the ovum.

   • The secretions of the acrosome of sperm A will help it to enter into the cytoplasm of the ovum (Q) through the zona pellucid (P) and the plasma membrane, this will induce the completion of the meiotic division of the secondary oocyte (Q). **(1 Mark)**

   • The second meiotic division in Q being unequal will result in the formation of a second polar body and a haploid ovum. Then, the haploid nucleus of the sperm 'A' and that of the ovum (Q) will fuse together to form a diploid zygote. **(1 Mark)**

4. The middle wall of the uterus is called myometrium. It consists of smooth muscles that bring about contraction of uterine muscles during delivery of the baby. **(1.5 Marks)**

The inner wall of the uterus is the inner glandular layer called endometrium and it plays an essential role during menstrual cycle. As it undergoes cyclic changes during menstrual cycle. Endometrium is necessary for implantation of the fertilised ovum and other events of pregnancy. **(1.5 Marks)**

5. (a) **Fertilization:** The process of fertilization is defined as the process of fusion of a sperm with an ovum.

   - Fertilization occurs only if the ovum and sperms are transported simultaneously to the ampullary-isthmic junction.

   - During the process of fertilization, a sperm comes in contact with the *zona pellucida* layer of the ovum and also induces the changes in the membrane in order to block the entry of additional sperms.

   - Sperm secretion help it to enter into the cytoplasm of the ovum through the zona pellucida and the plasma membrane.

   - It induces the completion of the meiotic division of the secondary oocyte.

   - The second meiotic division is unequal results in the formation of a second polar body and a haploid ovum.

   - Zygote is formed by the fusion of haploid nucleus of the sperms and the ovum. **(2 Marks)**

Implantation:

   - The mitotic division starts when the zygote moves through the isthmus of the oviduct called cleavage towards the uterus. It forms 2, 4, 8, 16 daughter cells called blastomeres.

   - Then, the embryo with 8 to 16 blastomeres stages is called morula.

   - It continues to divide and then transforms into blastocyst as it moves further into the uterus.

   - The blastomeres present in the blastocyst are arranged into an outer layer called trophoblast whereas the inner groups of cells are attached to the trophoblast called inner cell mass.

   - After this, the trophoblast layer gets attached to the endometrium whereas the inner cell mass gets differentiated into the embryo.

   - After attachment, the uterine cells rapidly and covers the blastocyst.

   - Now the blastocyst becomes embedded in the endometrium of the uterus and this process is called **Implantation** that results in pregnancy. **(2 Marks)**

(b) Placenta plays an essential role during pregnancy as it facilitates the supply of oxygen and nutrients to the embryo. It also helps in the removal of carbon dioxide and other metabolic waster produced by the embryo. It also acts as an endocrine tissue and produces hormones such as human chorionic gonadotropin (hCG), human placental lactogen(hPL), estrogens, and progestrogens. Relaxin hormone is also secreted by the ovary during the later phase of pregnancy.

(1 Marks)

6. The process of fertilization takes place at only if the ovum and sperms are transported simultaneously to the ampullary-isthmic junction. The process of fusion of a sperm with an ovum at this junction is ampullary-isthmic junction of fallopian tube.

The events involved in the process of fertilisation are as follows:

   - During the process of fertilization, a sperm comes in contact with the *zona pellucida* layer of the ovum and also induces changes in the membrane that block the entry of additional sperms.

   - It ensures that only one sperm can fertilise an ovum.

- The secretions of the acrosome help the sperm enter into the cytoplasm of the ovum through the zona pellucida and the plasma membrane.

- This induces the completion of the meiotic division of the secondary oocyte.

- The second meiotic division is also unequal and results in the formation of second polar body and a haploid ovum.

- The haploid nucleus of the sperms and that of the ovum fuse together to form a diploid zygote.

(5 Marks)

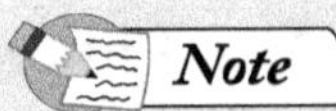

> **Note**
>
> *The acrosome of the sperm secretes hylauronidase enzyme to peneterate the corona radiata layer of the ovum.*

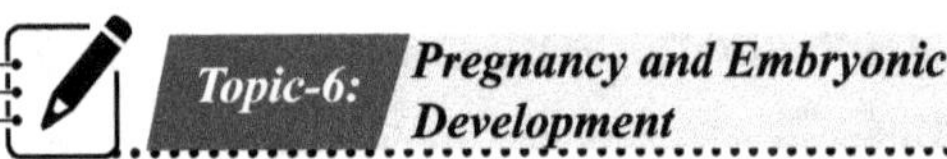

Topic-6: Pregnancy and Embryonic Development

1. **(b)** In human being after one month of pregnancy, the embryo's heart is formed. **(1 Mark)**

> **Note**
>
> *The first sign of growing foetus may be noticed by listening to the heart sound carefully through stethoscope.*

2. **(a)** (i) and (iv) **(1 Mark)**

3. **(a)** (i) and (ii) **(1 Mark)**

4. The embryo with 8 to 16 blastomeres is called a morula.

   - The morula continues to divide and transforms into blastocyst as it moves further into the uterus.

   - The blastomeres in the blastocyst are arranged into an outer layer called trophoblast and

   - An inner group of cells attached to trophoblast called the inner cell mass.

   - The trophoblast layer then gets attached to the endometrium and the inner cell mass gets differentiated as the embryo.

   - After attachment, the uterine cells divide rapidly and covers the blastocyst. **(2.5 Mark)**

   - As a result, the blastocyst becomes embedded in the endometrium of the uterus. This is called implantation and it leads to pregnancy.

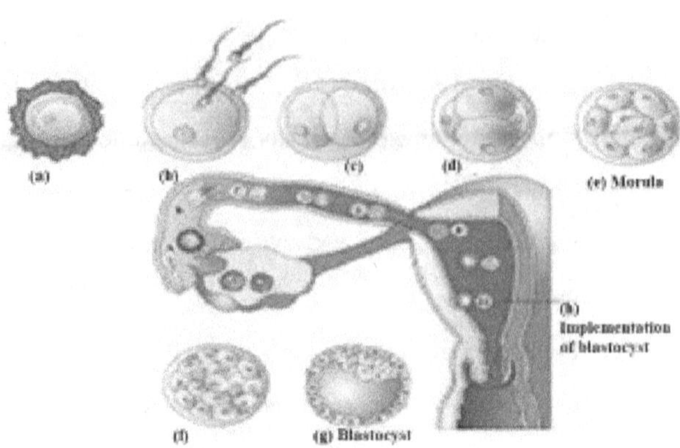

Fig : Fertilisation and passage of growing embryo in fallopian tube

(0.5 Mark)

5. After implantation, finger-like projections appear on the trophoblast called chorionic villi. It is surrounded by the uterine tissue and maternal blood. The chorionic villi and uterine tissue become interdigitated with each other and jointly form a structural and functional unit between the developing embryo or foetus and maternal body called placenta. **(2 Marks)**

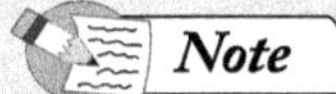

> **Note**
>
> *The placenta is connected with the embryo through umbilical cord which helps in the transportation of substances to and from the embryo.*

6. (i) After implantation, finger-like projections appear on the trophoblast called chorionic villi which are surrounded by the uterine tissue and maternal blood. The chorionic villi and uterine tissue become interdigitated with each other and jointly form a structural and functional unit between developing embryo (foetus) and maternal body called placenta. The placenta facilitates the supply of oxygen and nutrients to the embryo and also removal of carbon dioxide and excretory/waste materials produced by the embryo. The placenta is connected to the embryo through an umbilical cord which helps in the transport of substances to and from the embryo. Placenta also acts as an endocrine tissue and produces several hormones like human chorionic gonadotropin (hCG), human placental lactogen (hPL), estrogens, progestogens, etc. **(3 Marks)**

(ii)

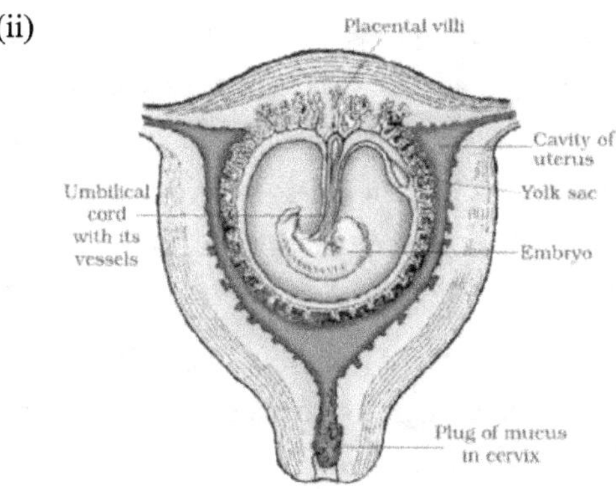

(2 Marks)

7. (a) **Fertilization:** The process of fertilization is defined as the process of fusion of a sperm with an ovum.

   - Fertilization occurs only if the ovum and sperms are transported simultaneously to the ampullary-isthmic junction.

   - During the process of fertilization, a sperm comes in contact with the *zona pellucida* layer of the ovum and also induces the changes in the membrane in order to block the entry of additional sperms.

   - Sperm secretion help it to enter into the cytoplasm of the ovum through the zona pellucida and the plasma membrane.

   - It induces the completion of the meiotic division of the secondary oocyte.

   - The second meiotic division is unequal results in the formation of a second polar body and a haploid ovum.

   - Zygote is formed by the fusion of haploid nucleus of the sperms and the ovum.

Implantation:

   - The mitotic division starts when the zygote moves through the isthmus of the oviduct called cleavage towards the uterus. It forms 2, 4, 8, 16 daughter cells called blastomeres.

   - Then, the embryo with 8 to 16 blastomeres stages is called morula.

   - It continues to divide and then transforms into blastocyst as it moves further into the uterus.

   - The blastomeres present in the blastocyst are arranged into an outer layer called trophoblast whereas the inner groups of cells are attached to the trophoblast called inner cell mass.

   - After this, the trophoblast layer gets attached to the endometrium whereas the inner cell mass gets differentiated into the embryo.

   - After attachment, the uterine cells rapidly and covers the blastocyst.

   - Now the blastocyst becomes embedded in the endometrium of the uterus and this process is called **Implantation** that results in pregnancy. **(3 Marks)**

   (b) Placenta plays an essential role during pregnancy as it facilitates the supply of oxygen and nutrients to the embryo. It also helps in the removal of carbon dioxide and other metabolic waster produced by the embryo. It also acts as an endocrine tissue and produces hormones such as human chorionic gonadotropin (hCG), human placental lactogen(hPL), estrogens, and progestrogens. Relaxin hormone is also secreted by the ovary during the later phase of pregnancy.

(2 Marks)

8. (a) The sequence of secretion of the given hormones in a pregnant woman is as follows:

   (i)   FSH (Follicle Stimulating Hormone)

   (ii) LH (Luteinizing Hormone)

   (iii) hCG (Human Chromic Gonado tropin)

   (iv) Relaxin   **(2 Marks)**

   (b)

Hormone	Source	Functions
FSH	Anterior pituitary lobe	Stimulates the growth of ovarian follicles and maturation of primary oocytes
LH	Anterior pituitary lobe	Induces ovulation and maintains corpus luteum
hCG	Chorionic cells of placenta	Maintains the corpus luteum and stimulates the secretion of progesterone
Relaxin	Ovary	Helps during child birth by relaxing the pelvic muscles as well as muscles of the cervix.

(3 Marks)

9. The placenta develops after the implantation of zygote in the uterus during the reproductive phase of human female. **(1.5 Marks)**

   After implantation, numerous finger-like projections called chorionic villi are formed on the trophoblast. The chorionic villi are surrounded by uterine tissues and maternal blood. Placenta is surrounded by uterine tissues.

   - Placenta plays an essential role during embryonic development as it facilitates the supply of oxygen and nutrients to the embryo.
   - It is also involved in the removal of carbon dioxide and other excretory waste materials by the embryo.
   - The placenta is connected to the embryo through an umbilical cord that helps in the transportation of substances in and out from the embryo.

   (3.5 Marks)

Topic-7: *Parturition and Lactation*

1. **(c)** The mammary glands are paired structures (breasts) that contain glandular tissue and a variable amount of fat. The glandular tissue of each breast is divided into 15-20 mammary lobes containing clusters of cells called alveoli. The cells of alveoli secrete milk, which is stored in the cavities (lumens) of alveoli. The alveoli open into mammary tubules. The tubules of each lobe join to form a mammary duct. Several mammary ducts join to form a wider mammary ampulla which is connected to the lactiferous duct.

   (1 Mark)

2. **(c)** A is true but R is False **(1 Mark)**

3. **(d)** activate smooth muscles **(1 Mark)**

4. Yes, I do agree with the fact that breastfeeding is the best for newborn babies. Mammary glands of the female undergo differentiation during preganancy and starts producing milk. **(1 Mark)**

   The milk produced during the initial few days and lactation is called colostrum which contains IgA antibodies. It helps in developing resistance for newborn baby by providing innate immunity to the developing infant. It helps the baby fight to against viruses and bacteria. Thus breast milk is packed with disease-fighting substances that protect the baby from illness. It also naturally contains many of the vitamins and minerals that a required by newborn. **(2 Mark)**

5. Doctors recommend breast feeding during the initial period of infant's growth to maintain the health of baby. The first yellow milk that comes out from the mammary gland of the mother just after parturition is called colostrum. **(2 Marks)**

   It is rich in protein such as lactalbumin and lactoprotein. It also contains antibody IgA that provide innate immunity to the infant. **(1 Mark)**

6. The process of parturition involves following events:

   - The average duration of human pregnancy is about 9 months and this period is called gestation period.
   - The process of parturition involves vigorous contraction of the uterus at the end of pregnancy results in the expulsion or delivery of the foetus. So, parturition is defined as the process of delivery of the foetus and is also called childbirth. **(1 Mark)**
   - It is induced by a complex neuroendocrine mechanism. As the signals for parturition are originate from the fully developed foetus and the placenta results in induction of mild uterine contractions and this process is called foetal ejection reflex.
   - Foetal ejection reflex triggers the release of oxytocin from the maternal pituitary.
   - Oxytocin hormone acts on the uterine muscle and causes stronger uterine contraction that stimulates the secretion of oxytocin. **(1 Mark)**
   - The stimulatory reflex between the uterine contraction and oxytocin secretion that leads to cause stronger and stronger contractions.
   - It leads to cause expulsion of the baby out of the uterus through the birth canal. **(1 Mark)**

Chapter 3: Reproductive Health

2   *Assertion Reason/Two Statement Type Questions (1 Mark)*

1. **Assertion:** Lactational amenorrhea is the natural method of contraception.   **[CBSE Sample Paper 2021-22, K]**

   Reason: It increases the phagocytosis of sperm.

   (a) Both Assertion (A) and Reason (R) are true and Reason (R) is the correct explanation of Assertion (A).

   (b) Both Assertion (A) and Reason (R) are true, but Reason (R) is **not** the correct explanation of Assertion (A).

   (c) Assertion (A) is true, but Reason (R) is false.

   (d) Assertion (A) is false, but Reason (R) is true.

5   *Short Answer Questions (2 or 3 Marks)*

2. If implementation of better techniques and new strategies are required to provide more efficient care and assistance to people, then why is there a statutory ban on amniocentesis? Write the use of this technique and give reason to justify the ban.   **[All India 2014, Ap]**

1   *Multiple Choice Questions (1 Mark)*

1. An **IUD** recommended to promote the cervix hostility to the sperms is   **[All India 2022, Term-I, K]**

   (a) CuT   (b) Multiload-375

   (c) LNG-20   (d) Cu7

2. The mode of action of the copper ions in an IUD is to   **[CBSE Sample Paper 2021-22, U]**

   (a) increase the movement of sperms.

   (b) decrease the movement of the sperms.

   (c) make the uterus unsuitable for implantation.

   (d) make the cervix hostile to the sperms.

2   *Assertion Reason/Two Statement Type Questions*

   (a) Both Assertion (A) and Reason (R) are true and Reason (R) is the correct explanation of Assertion (A).

   (b) Both Assertion (A) and Reason (R) are true, but Reason (R) is **not** the correct explanation of Assertion (A).

   (c) Assertion (A) is true, but Reason (R) is false.

   (d) Assertion (A) is false, but Reason (R) is true.

3. **Assertion (A) :** Vasectomy is a sterilisation procedure advised for females as a terminal method.

   [All India 2022, Term-I, K]

   Reason (R) : In vasectomy, a small part of the vas deferens is removed or tied by blocking gamete transport therefore preventing conception.

4. **Assertion:** Saheli, an oral contraceptive for females, contains a steroidal preparation.

   Reason: It is a "once a week" pill with very few side effects.   **[CBSE Sample Paper 2021-22, U]**

6   *Long Answer Questions (5 Marks)*

5. Prepare a poster for the school programme depicting the objectives of : "Reproductive and Child Health Care Programme".   **[All India 2019, K]**

6. It is commonly observed that parents feel embarrassed to discuss freely with their adolescent children about sexuality and reproduction. The result of this parental inhibition is that the children go astray sometimes.

   [Delhi 2017, A]

   (a) Explain the reasons that you feel are behind such embarrassment amongst some parents to freely discuss such issues with their growing children.

(b) By taking one example of a local plant and animal, how would you help these parents to overcome such inhibitions about reproduction and sexuality ?

7. Reproductive and Child Healthcare (RCH) programmes are currently in operation. One of the major tasks of these programmes is to create awareness amongst people about the wide range of reproduction related aspects. As this is important and essential for building a reproductively healthy society. **[Delhi 2016, U]**

   (a) "Providing sex education in schools is one of the ways to meet this goal." Give four points in support of your opinion regarding this statement.

   (b) List any two 'indicators' that indicate a reproductively healthy society.

8. Your school has been selected by the Department of Education to organize and host an interschool seminar on "Reproductive Health-Problems and Practices". However, many parents are reluctant to permit their wards to attend it. Their argument is that the topic is "too embarrassing."

   Put forth four arguments with appropriate reasons and explanation to justify the topic to be very essential and timely. **[All India 2015, A]**

9. Given below are certain situations. Analyse the situation and suggest the name of suitable contraceptive device along with mode of action.

Situation	Requirement of contraceptive for –	Name of contraceptive device	Mode of action
1	blocking the entry of sperms through cervix		
2	spacing between children		
3	effective emergency contraceptive		
4	terminal method to prevent any more pregnancy in female		
5	sterilization in male		

[CBSE Sample Paper 2023-24, A]

10. Placed below are case studies of some couples who were not able to have kids. These couples are not ready for adoption or taking gametes from donors. After thoroughly examining the cases, which Assisted Reproductive Technology will you suggest to these couples as a medical expert? Explain briefly with justification of each case.

Couple	Test reports of Female partner	Test reports of male partner
Couple 1	Normal reports	Normal sperms in testes, Missing connection in epididymis and Vas deferens
Couple 2	Blockage in the fallopian tube	Normal reports
Couple 3	Normal reports	Poor semen parameters in terms of count, motility and morphology
Couple 4	low ovarian reserve	Normal reports
Couple 5	Sterilization in male	Morphologically abnormal sperms

[CBSE Sample Paper 2023-24, A]

Topic-3: Medical Termination of Pregnancy

Very Short Answer Questions (1 Mark)

1. Our government has intentionally imposed strict conditions for M.T.P. in our country. Justify giving a reason. **[All India 2017, K]**

Short Answer Questions (2 or 3 Marks)

2. Name and explain a surgical contraceptive method that can be adopted by the male partner of a couple.

   [Delhi 2023, Set-I, K]

3. A pregnant human female was advised to undergo MTP. It was diagnosed that the fetus she was carrying had developed from a zygote having 45 chromosomes with only one X chromosome.

   [CBSE Sample Paper 2023-24, U]

   (a) What is this condition called and how does it arise?

   (b) Why was she advised to undergo MTP?

4. (a) Explain the mode of action of Cu^{++} releasing IUDs as a good contraceptive. How is hormone releasing IUD different from it? **[Delhi 2020, K]**

   (b) Why is 'Saheli' a preferred contraceptive by women (any two reasons)? **[Delhi 2020, K]**

5. (a) Mention the problems that are taken care of by Reproduction and Child Health Care Programme. **[All India 2016, U]**

   (b) What is amniocentesis and why there is a statutory ban on it? **[All India 2016, U]**

Topic-4: *Sexually Transmitted Disease*

1 | *Multiple Choice Questions (1 Mark)*

1. Identify the disease which is *not* a sexually transmitted disease : **[All India 2022, Term-I, K]**
   - (a) Gonnorhoea
   - (b) Syphilis
   - (c) Amoebiasis
   - (d) Chalamydiasis

2 | *Assertion Reason/Two Statement Type Questions (1 Mark)*

2. **Assertion (A) :** Very often persons suffering from Sexually Transmitted Diseases (STD) do not go for timely detection and proper treatment.

   Reason (R) : Absence or less significant symptoms in the early stages of STDs and the social stigma attached to the disease. **[All India 2022, Term-I, U]**
   - (a) Both Assertion (A) and Reason (R) are true and Reason (R) is the correct explanation of Assertion (A).
   - (b) Both Assertion (A) and Reason (R) are true, but Reason (R) is **not** the correct explanation of Assertion (A).
   - (c) Assertion (A) is true, but Reason (R) is false.
   - (d) Assertion (A) is false, but Reason (R) is true.

Topic-5: *Infertility*

1 | *Multiple Choice Questions (1 Mark)*

1. A female undergoing IVF treatment has blocked fallopian tubes. The technique by which the embryo with more than 8 blastomeres will be transferred into the female for further development is

   [CBSE Sample Paper 2021-22, K]
   - (a) ZIFT
   - (b) GIFT
   - (c) IUT
   - (d) AI

2 | *Assertion Reason/Two Statement Type Questions (1 Mark)*

2. **Assertion (A) :** Determining the sex of an unborn child followed by MTP is an illegal practice.

   [Delhi 2023, Set-I, U]

   Reason (R) : Amniocentesis is a practice to test the presence of genetic disorders also.
   - (a) Both (A) and (R) are true and (R) is the correct explanation of (A).
   - (b) Both (A) and (R) are true, but (R) is not the correct explanation of (A).
   - (c) (A) is true, but (R) is false.
   - (d) (A) is false, but (R) is true.

3 | *Matching Based Questions (1 Mark)*

3. Given below are Column A with a list of certain Assisted Reproductive Technologies (ART) and in Column B the procedures followed during ART :

   [Delhi 2023, Set-I, K]

Column A		Column B	
S. No.	Names of ART	S. No.	Procedures
(A)	GIFT	(i)	Transfer of ovum from a donor into the fallopian tube of another female.
(B)	ICSI	(ii)	Transfer of semen from the donor into the vagina of the female.
(C)	ZIFT	(iii)	Injecting sperms directly into the ovum.
(D)	IUI	(iv)	Transfer of early embryos into the fallopian tube.

Choose the option where ART correctly matches with the procedure.
   - (a) (A)-(i), (B)-(ii), (C)-(iii), (D)-(iv)
   - (b) (A)-(iv), (B)-(i), (C)-(ii), (D)-(iii)
   - (c) (A)-(iv), (B)-(iii), (C)-(i), (D)-(ii)
   - (d) (A)-(i), (B)-(iii), (C)-(iv), (D)-(ii)

5 | *Short Answer Questions (2 or 3 Marks)*

4. How can childless couples be helped by the followed assisted reproductive technologies: **[Delhi 2019, K]**
   - (a) GIFT
   - (b) Cytoplasmic Sperm Injection

5. After a brief medical examination a healthy couple came to know that both of them are unable to produce functional gametes and should look for an 'ART' (Assisted Reproductive Technique). Name the 'ART' and the procedure involved that you can suggest to them to help them bear a child. **[Delhi 2015, U]**

6. Suggest and explain any three Assisted Reproducive Technologies (ART) to an infertile couple.

[All India 2013, U]

6   *Long Answer Questions (5 Marks)*

7.   (a) IVF is a very popular method these days that is helping childless couples to bear a child. Describe the different steps that are carried out in this technique. **[All India 2020, U]**

     (b) Would you consider Gamete Intrafallopian Transfer (GIFT) as an IVF? Give a reason in support of your answer. **[All India 2020, U]**

8. A large number of married couples the world over are childless. It is shocking to know that in India the female partner is often blamed for the couple being childless.

[All India 2016, U]

     (a) Why in your opinion the female partner is often blamed for such situations in India? Mention any two values that you as a biology student can promote to check this social evil.

     (b) State any two reasons responsible for the cause of infertility.

     (c) Suggest a technique that can help the couple to have a child where the problem is with male partner

Hints & Solutions

| **Topic-1:** | **Reproductive Health:Problems & Strategies** |

1. (c) A is true but R is false. **(1 Mark)**

2. Aminocentesis is a foetal-sex determination test based on the chromosomal pattern in the amniotic fluid surrounding the developing embryo. This technique is used for the determination of sex and other metabolic disorders of the developing embryo. It is also used for the determination of genetic disorders in the developing foetus. Their will statutory ban on amniocentesis for sex-determination of developing foetus that increases female foeticides, and massive child immunisation. **(1 Mark)**

| **Topic-2:** | **Population Stabilisation and Birth Control** |

1. (c) The hormone releasing IUDs (Progestasert, LNG-20), make the uterus unsuitable for implantation and the cervix hostile to the sperms. **(1 Mark)**

> **Note**
>
> *An IUD is small plastic T-shape device used far birth control.*

2. (b) decrease the movement of the sperms . **(1 Mark)**

3. (d) Sterilisation procedure in the male is called 'vasectomy' and that in the female is called 'tubectomy'. The statement in reason is correct.

   (1 Mark)

4. (d) A is False but R is true **(1 Mark)**

5. (b) Poster presentation on "Reproductive and Child Health Care Programme" **(5 Marks)**

>  **Note**
>
> *The goal of "Reproductive and child Health Care programme" is to provide facilities and support for building up a reproductively healthy society.*

6. (a) The important reasons that parents feel embarrassed to discuss freely with their adolescent children about sexuality and reproduction are illiteracy, conservative attitude, myths and misconceptions among parents. They feel shy to discuss such issues with their children freely. But it is responsibility of every parent to give right information to their children about sexuality, reproduction, adolescence changes and sexual practices so that their children will never be misleaded. **(2½ Marks)**

   (b) An example of male honey bee and orchid *Ophrys* flower represents the sexual attraction phenomena in which the honey bee is attracted towards the *Ophrys* flower. The Mediterranean orchid *Ophrys* employs 'sexual deceit' to get pollination done by a species of one petal of its flower bears an uncanny resemblance to the female of the bee in size, colour and markings. The male bee is attracted to what it perceives as a female, 'Pseudo-copulates' with the flower, and during that process is dusted with pollen from the flower. When this same bee 'Pseudo-copulates' with another flower, it transfers pollen to it and thus pollinates the flower. So, it is a natural phenomenon and similarly parents should openly talk about such matter with their children.

   (2½ Marks)

7. (a) Sex education is one of the best ways in order to create a reproductively healthy society. It also helps people in following ways:

   • Sex education helps to proper knowledge to curious adolescents. It helps them to prevent from being them misguided and also prevents them from believing them about sex-related aspects.

- It helps to create awareness about sexually transmitted disease and its prevention ways.

- Sex education provides proper knowledge about reproductive organs and other changes related to puberty to the adolescents. **(3 Marks)**

(b) The indicators that represent a reproductively healthy society are as follows:

- Increase medical facilities for all sex related problems.

- On time detection and better cure of sexually transmitted diseases. **(2 Marks)**

8. Reproductive health is the total well-being in all aspects of reproduction. It includes the physical, emotional, behavioural and social well-being of an individual. Therefore, there is an urgent need to educate and discuss topics related to the reproductive health.

Following are the topics about reproductive health that should be discussed with the students:

Sexually transmitted diseases, such as AIDS and Gonorrhoea, are transmitted from one individual to another through sexual contact. Therefore, making the students aware about these diseases will help to prevent their spread. Lack of knowledge about there productive status may lead to unwanted pregnancies. Hence, it is necessary to create awareness among people, especially the youth. **(3 Marks)**

Learning about one's sexuality at a proper age may help the students to know about the different changes happening in their body; thereby, leading to a better mental and physical state of health.

Counselling and creating awareness about reproductive health also help to solve the problem related to infertility, birth control, mortality, etc. **(2 Marks)**

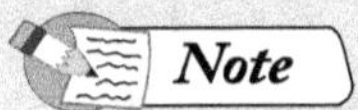

Infertility refers to the inability or failure of a couples to produce children inspite of unprotected sexual co-habitation.

9.

Situation No.	Requirement of contraceptive for–	Name of contraceptive device	Mode of action
1	blocking the entry of sperms through cervix	Diaphragms/cervical caps/ vaults	Cover the cervix during coitus **(1 Mark)**
2	spacing between children	Cu or hormone releasing IUDs such as Cu T/ Cu7/Multiload 375/ Progestasert/LNG 20	Cu ions from Cu containing IUDs increase phagocytosis of sperms within uterus, suppress sperm motility and fertilizing capacity/hormone releasing IUDs make uterus unsuitable for implantation **(1 Mark)**
3	effective emergency contraceptive	Pills containing Progestogens or progestogen–estrogen combination or IUDs within 72 hours of coitus	Pills inhibit ovulation and implantation as well as alter the quality of cervical mucus to prevent the entry of sperms/IUDs – Cu ions increase phagocytosis of sperms within uterus, suppress sperm motility and fertilizing capacity/hormone releasing IUDs make uterus unsuitable for implantation **(1 Mark)**
4	terminal method to prevent any more pregnancy in female	Tubectomy	Block gamete transport and prevent conception. **(1 Mark)**
5	sterilization in male	Vasectomy	Blocks sperm transport. **(1 Mark)**

10. **Couple I:** Normal reports of female, Normal sperms in testes, Missing connection in epididymis and Vas deferens in male.

Assisted Reproductive Technology:

Semen will be devoid of sperms in this case. So, In–vitro fertilization (IVF) by collecting the sperms from epididymis, followed by ZIFT or IUT (Test Tube Baby) is suggested. ZIFT is transfer of zygote or early embryo up to 8 blastomeres in fallopian tube and IUT refers to transfer of embryos with more than 8 blastomeres in uterus. **[1]**

Couple 2: Blockage in the fallopian tube in the female, Normal reports of male.

Assisted reproductive Technology:

Blockage of Fallopian Tube will not allow transfer of sperms to the site of fertilisation. In–vitro fertilization (IVF) followed by IUT (Test Tube Baby). It would involve transfer of embryo with more than 8 blastomeres in uterus. **[1]**

Couple 3: Normal reports of female, Poor semen parameters in terms of count, motility and morphology in male partner

Assisted Reproductive Technology:

Intracytoplasmic sperm injection (ICSI) in which sperm is directly injected into the ovum. Artificial insemination procedure is used mainly when sperms have poor characteristic or low sperm count. **[1]**

Couple 4: Low ovarian reserve in female, Normal reports in male

Assisted Reproductive Technology:

In–vitro–fertilization (IVF) by selection of normal blastocysts from ovary followed by Zygote intra–fallopian transfer involving transfer of zygote or early embryos up to 8 blastomeres (ZIFT) or transfer of embryo with more than 8 blastomeres in the uterus (IUT). **[1]**

Couple 5: Poor ovarian reserve in female, morphologically abnormal sperms in male partner.

Assisted Reproductive Technology:

ICSI intracytoplasmic sperm injection in which selected normal sperms will be injected into the selected blastocyst. Intracytoplasmic sperm injection (ICSI) procedure is used mainly when sperms have poor characteristic or low sperm count. **[1]**

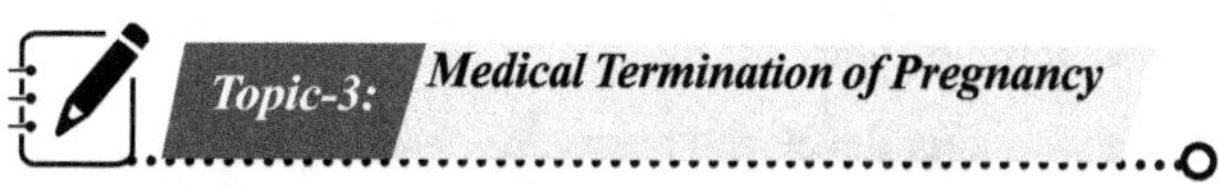

1. Our government has imposed strict conditions for M.T.P. to avoid its misuse. Such restrictions are very important to prevent sex determination before birth of a child and illegal female foeticides in our country. MTP are considered relatively safe during the first trimester, *i.e.,* upto 12 weeks of pregnancy. **(1 Marks)**

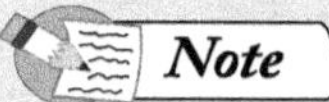

MTP stands for medical termination of pregnancy is defined as the intentional or voluntary termination of pregnancy before full term. It is done to got rid of unwanted pregnancies failure of the controuptius used during coitus or rapes.

2. Surgical methods, also called **sterilisation**, are generally advised for the male/female partner as a terminal method to prevent any more pregnancies. Surgical intervention blocks gamete transport and thereby prevents conception. Sterilisation procedure in the **male** is called 'vasectomy' and that in the **female**, 'tubectomy'.

In vasectomy, a small part of the vas deferens is cut or tied up through a small incision on the scrotum.

(3 Marks)

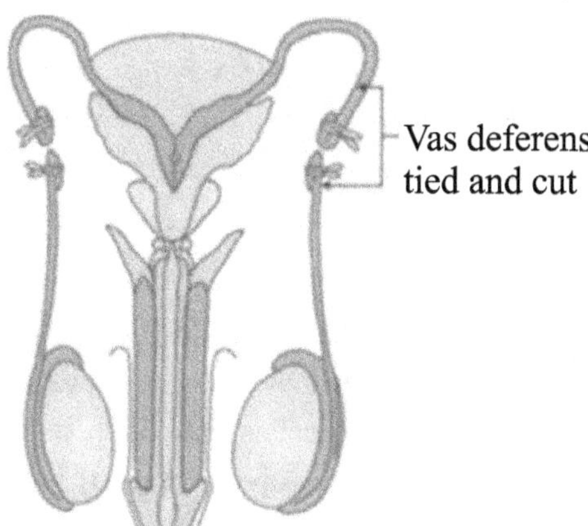

(2 Marks)

3. **(a)** The embryo has Turner's Syndrome [0.5] due to aneuploidy of the sex chromosome. Such a disorder is caused due to the absence of one of the X chromosomes, i.e., 45 with XO. **(3 Marks)**

(b) She was advised MTP as the child will have the following problems:

- rudimentary ovaries
- poorly developed breasts
- lack of other secondary sexual characters
- delayed or no onset of the menstrual cycle and infertile. **(2 Marks)**

4. **(a)** IUDs are Intra Uterine Devices (IUDs) increases phagocytosis of sperms within the uterus and the copper ions are released suppress sperm mortality and the fertilising capacity of sperms.

Example of copper releasing IUDs are cuT, cu7, Multiload 375.

The hormone releasing IUDs make the uterus unsuitable for implantation and the cervix hostile to the sperms. IUDs are ideal contraceptives for the females who want to delay pregnancy.

Example of hormone releasing IUDs is Progestasert, LNG-20. **(1½ Marks)**

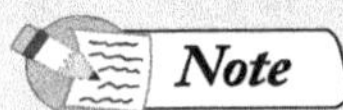

Note

IUDs is one of most widely accepted methods of contraception in India.

(b) Saheli-The new oral contraceptive pill for the females that contains a non-steroidal preparation. It is a 'once a week' pill with very few side effects and high contraceptive value. They inhibit ovulation and implantation as well as alter the quality of cervical mucus to prevent or retard the entry of sperms.

(1½ Marks)

5. **(a)** The "Reproductive and Child Health care (RCH) programmes" create awareness among people about the various reproduction related aspects and also providing facilities as well as support for building up a reproductively healthy society as the major goals of this programmes. **(1½ Marks)**

(b) **Amniocentesis** is a foetal sex determination test based on the chromosomal pattern in the amniotic fluid surrounding the developing embryo for determination of abnormalities in the foetus.

The statutory ban on amniocentesis is because of illegal sex determination that increases female foeticides, massive child immunisation.

(1½ Marks)

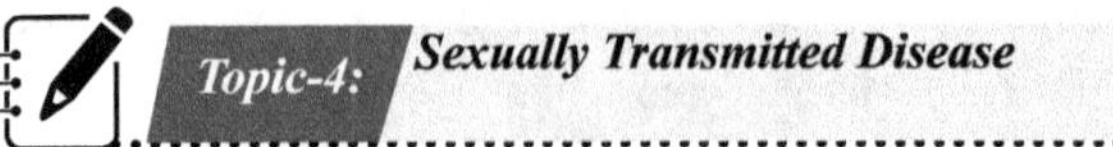

1. **(c)** Amoebiasis caused by protozoan parasites *Entamoeba histolytica* in large intestine of human. The main source of infection is contaminated drinking water and food. **(1 Mark)**

2. **(a)** Infected person may often be asymptomatic and hence, may remain undetected for long. Absence or less significant symptoms in the early stages of infection and the social stigma attached to the STIs, deter the infected persons from going for timely detection and proper treatment. **(1 Mark)**

1. **(b)** GIFT **(1 Mark)**

2. **(b)** Statutory ban on amniocentesis for sex-determination to legally check increasing menace of female foeticides, massive child immunisation, etc., are some programmes that have been mentioned in this connection. In aminocentesis some of the amniotic fluid of the developing foetus is taken to analyse the fetal cells and dissolved substances. This procedure is used to test for the presence of certain genetic disorders such as, Down syndrome, haemoplilia, sickle-cell anemia, etc. to determine the survivability of the foetus. **(1 Mark)**

3. **(d)** Transfer of an ovum collected from a donor into the fallopian tube (**GIFT – gamete intra fallopian transfer**) of another female who cannot produce one, but can provide suitable environment for fertilisation and for further development is another method attempted. **Intra cytoplasmic sperm injection (ICSI)** is another specialised procedure to form an embryo in the laboratory in which a sperm is directly injected into the ovum. The semen collected either from the husband or a healthy donor is artificially introduced either into the vagina or into the uterus (**IUI – intra-uterine insemination**) of the female. The zygote or early embryos (with upto 8 blastomeres) then be transferred into the fallopian tube (**ZIFT–zygote intra fallopian transfer**).

(1 Mark)

4. **(a) GIFT (Gamete Intra Fallopian Transfer):** It is an in vitro fertilisation technique that involves the transfer of ovum collected from a donor into the fallopian tube of another female who is unable to produce eggs. This technique also provide suitable environment for fertilisation and further development. **(1 Mark)**

   (b) Cytoplasmic sperm injection: It is another specialised in vitro technique in which an embyo is formed in a laboratory in which a sperm is directly injected into the ovum. **(1 Mark)**

Assisted Reproductive Technology (ARTs) is used for the treatment of infertility. This technology involves the mating of egg and sperm outside of the body (Invitro) under sterilized condition.

5. The doctor suggests **ZIFT (Zygote intra fallopian transfer)** to those couples who are not able to bear a child. In this procedure, the sperm is collected either from the husband or donor and an ovum is collected from wife or donor. Then sperm and ova are induced to form zygote under controlled conditions in the laboratory. Then the zygote or early embryos upto 8 blastomeres stages are then transferred into the fallopian tube of the female for further development. **(3 Marks)**

6. The ARTs suggested to infertile couples are as follows:

   (i) **In *vitro* fertilisation (IVF)** technique involves collection of ova from the wife/donor (female) and sperms from the husband/donor (male) are collected and are induced to form zygote under stimulated conditions in the laboratory. **(1 Mark)**

   (ii) **Zygote intra fallopian transfer (ZIFT)** involves the transfer of zygote or early embryos upto 8 blastomeres into the fallopian tube of the female.

   (1 Mark)

   (iii) **Gamete intra fallopian transfer (GIFT)** involves the transfer of an ovum which is collected from a donor into the fallopian tube of another female who cannot produce egg but can provide suitable environment for fertilisation and its further development. **(1 Mark)**

ARTs (Assisted reproductive technology) is used for treatment of infertility in couples who are unable to produce offsprings. This method involves fusion of male gamete (sperm) and female gamete (egg) outside the body.

7. **(a)** The technique suggested to the couples who are not able to conceive is IVF (In vitro fertilisation).

   This method involves embryo transfer. In this method, ova from the wife or donor female and sperms from the husband or donor male are collected. The ova and sperm are induced to form zygote under stimulated conditions in the laboratory.

   (2½ Marks)

IVF is the method of fertilization that takes place outside the body in almost the conditions similar to that of body. This technique is also called test tube programme.

   (b) ZIFT (Zygote Intra Fallopian Transfer) is an assisted reproductive technology. The doctor suggests **ZIFT (Zygote intra fallopian transfer)** to those couples who are not able to bear a child. In this procedure, the sperm is collected either from the husband or donor and an ovum is collected from wife or donor. Then sperm and ova are induced to form zygote under controlled conditions in the laboratory. Then the zygote or early embryos upto 8 blastomeres stages are then transferred into the fallopian tube of the female for further development.

   (2½ Marks)

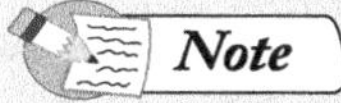

ART (Assisted reproductive technology) involves the treatments and procedures for those couples that are not able to bear child.

8. **(a)** Lack of proper education and unawareness about infertility are the main cause for blaming females in India. **(2 Marks)**

   People should be given knowledge and awareness about several medical techniques that are available to overcome the infertility problems in both male and female. Educate people that not only females are suffering from infertility as males are also suffering from infertility.

(b) Infertility is caused because of physical, congenital, diseases, drugs, immunological problems or even psychological problems. **(1 Mark)**

(c) When infertility is caused because of inability of the male partner to inseminate the female or because of very sperm count in the ejaculates is corrected by **artificial insemination**.

In this technique, the semen collected either from the husband or a healthy donor is artificially introduced either into the vagina or into the uterus (IUI-Intra-uterine insemination) of the female. **(2 Marks)**

Infertility refers to the inability or failure of a couples to produce children in spite of unprotected sexual co-habitation.

4 Chapter — Principles of Inheritance and Variation

Topic-1: *Mendel's Law of Inheritance*

---

1   *Multiple Choice Questions (1 Mark)*

1. According to Mendel, the nature of the unit factors that control the expression of traits were :

[All India 2022, Term-I, K]

- (a) Stable
- (b) Blending
- (c) Stable and discrete
- (d) Discrete

2. The probability of all possible genotypes of offsprings in a genetic cross can be obtained with the help of :

[All India 2022, Term-I, K]

- (a) Test cross
- (b) Back cross
- (c) Punnett square
- (d) Linkage cross

3. In *Pisum sativum*, the flower position may be axial (allele A) or terminal (allele a). What would be the percentage of the offspring with respect to axial flower position, if a cross is made between parents Aa × aa ?

[All India 2022, Term-I, U]

- (a) 25%
- (b) 50%
- (c) 75%
- (d) 100%

4. Given below are the pairs of contrasting traits in *Pisum sativum* as studied by Mendel. Identify the **incorrect** pair of traits :   **[All India 2022, Term-I, U]**

Character	Dominant	Recessive
(a) Stem height	Tall	Dwarf
(b) Seed shape	Round	Wrinkled
(c) Pod colour	Yellow	Green
(d) Flower position	Axial	Terminal

5. A plant breeder crossed a pure breed tall plant having white flowers with a pure breed dwarf plant having blue flowers. He obtained 2002 F_1 progeny and found that they are all tall having blue flowers. Upon selfing these F_1 plants he obtained a progeny of 2160 plants. Approximately how many of these are likely to be short having blue flowers ?

[All India 2022, Term-I, Ap]

- (a) 1215
- (b) 405
- (c) 540
- (d) 135

6. What would be the genotype of the parents if the offspring have the phenotypes in 1:1 proportion?

[CBSE Sample Paper 2021-22, Ap]

- (a) Aa X Aa
- (b) AA X AA
- (c) Aa X AA
- (d) Aa x aa

7. Genotypic ratio of 1:2:1 is obtained in a cross between

[CBSE Sample Paper 2021-22, A]

- (a) AB X AB
- (b) Ab X Ab
- (c) Ab X ab
- (d) ab X ab

8. The gene that controls the ABO blood group system in human beings has three alleles - I^A, I^B and i. A child has blood group O. His father has blood group A and mother has blood group B. Genotypes of other off springs can be:

[CBSE Sample Paper 2021-22, Ap]

- (i) $I^B I^B$
- (ii) $I^A i$
- (iii) $I^B i$
- (iv) $I^A I^B$
- (v) ii

- (a) (i), (ii), (iii), (v)
- (b) (ii), (iii), (iv), (v)
- (c) (iii),(iv), (v)
- (d) (iv), (iii), (i)

---

4   *Very Short Answer Questions (1 Mark)*

9. Name the type of cross that would help to find the genotype of a pea plant bearing violet flowers.

[Delhi 2017, K]

10. A geneticist interested in studying variations and patterns of inheritance in living beings prefers to choose organisms for experiments with shorter life cycle. Provide a reason. **[Delhi 2015, U]**

11. Mention any two contrasting traits with respect to seeds in pea plant that were studied by Mendel.

    [All India 2014, U]

5   *Short Answer Questions (2 or 3 Marks)*

12. State Mendel's law of dominance. How did he deduce the law? Explain with the help of a suitable example.

    [Delhi 2020, Ap]

13. You are given a tall pea plant and asked to find its genotype. How would you find its genotype? Explain.

    [Delhi 2019, Ap]

14. A teacher wants his/her students to find the genotype of pea plants bearing purple coloured flowers in their school garden. Name and explain the cross that will make it possible. **[Delhi 2015, U]**

15. In **Snapdragon**, A cross between true-breeding red flower (RR) plants and true-breeding white flowered (rr) plants showed a progeny of plants with all pink flowers.

    [All India 2014, Ap]

    (a) The appearance of pink flowers is not known as blending. Why?

    (b) What is the phenomenon known as?

16. Mendel published his work on inheritance of characters in 1865, but it remained unrecognized till 1900. Give three reasons for the delay in accepting his work.

    [Delhi 2014, U]

17. In a cross between two tall pea plants some of the offsprings produced were dwarf. Show with the help of Punett square how this is possible. **[Delhi 2013, U]**

18. A true breeding pea plant, homozygous dominant for inflated green podsis crossed with another pea plant with constricted yellow pods (ffgg). With the help of punnett square show the above cross and mention the results obtained phenotypically and genotypically in F_1 generation? **[Delhi 2013, Ap]**

6   *Long Answer Questions (5 Marks)*

19. It is sometimes observed that the F_1 progeny has a phenotype that does not resemble either of the two parents and has intermediate phenotype. Explain by taking a suitable example and working out the cross upto F_2 progeny. **[Delhi 2023 Set-I, Ap]**

20. Explain the genetic basis of blood grouping in human population. **[Delhi 2015, U]**

Topic-2:   *Inheritance of One Gene*

1   *Multiple Choice Questions (1 Mark)*

1. The number of different types of gametes that would be produced from a parent with genotype AABBCc is :

   [All India 2022, Term-I, Ap]

   (a) 1   (b) 2

   (c) 3   (d) 4

2. Possibility of the blood groups of the children in a family where the father is heterozygous for blood group 'A' and the mother is heterozygous for blood group 'B', would be : **[All India 2022, Term-I, A]**

   (a) Blood groups 'A', 'B'

   (b) Blood groups 'A', 'B', 'O'

   (c) Blood group 'AB', 'O'

   (d) Blood groups 'A', 'B', 'AB', 'O'

3. What would be the genotype of the parents if the offspring have the phenotypes in 1:1 proportion?

   [CBSE Sample Paper 2021-22, Ap]

   (a) Aa X Aa   (b) AA X AA

   (c) Aa X AA   (d) Aa x aa

4. In Antirrhinum, RR is phenotypically red flowers, rr is white and Rr is pink. Select the correct phenotypic ratio in F1 generation when a cross is performed between RR X Rr: **[CBSE Sample Paper 2021-22, Ap]**

   (a) 1 red: 2 Pink: 1 white   (b) 2 Pink: 1 white

   (c) 2 Red: 2 Pink   (d) All Pink

2 *Assertion Reason/Two Statement Type Questions (1 Mark)*

5. **Assertion:** When white eyed, yellow bodied *Drosophila* females were hybridized with red eyed, brown-bodied males; and F_1 progeny was intercrossed, F_2 ratio deviated from $9:3:3:1$. **[CBSE Sample Paper 2022-23, Ap]**

Reason: When two genes in a dihybrid are on the same chromosome, the proportion of parental gene combinations is much higher than the non-parental type.

(a) Both (A) and (R) are true and (R) is the correct explanation of (A).

(b) Both (A) and (R) are true, but (R) is not the correct explanation of (A).

(c) (A) is true, but (R) is false.

(d) (A) is false, but (R) is true.

4 *Very Short Answer Questions (1 Mark)*

6. British geneticist R.C. Punnett developed a graphical representation of a genetic cross called "Punnett Square". Mention the possible result this representation predicts of the genetic cross carried. **[All India 2019, K]**

7. State a difference between a gene and an allele. **[Delhi 2016, U]**

5 *Short Answer Questions (2 or 3 Marks)*

8. F_1 progeny of pea plant bearing violet flowers and snapdragon plant bearing red flowers were selfed to produce their respective F_2 progeny. Compare the phenotypes, the genotypes and the pattern of inheritance of their respective F_2 progeny. **[All India 2020, U]**

9. A woman with 'O blood group' marries a man with 'AB blood group'. Work out the cross to show all the possible phenotypes and genotypes of the progeny with respect to blood groups. Explain the pattern of inheritance observed in this cross. **[Delhi 2019, K]**

10. What is a test cross? How can it decipher the heterozygosity of a plant? **[All India 2016, U]**

11. During a monohybrid cross involving at all pea plant with a dwarf pea plant, the off spring populations were tall and dwarf in equal ratio. Work out a cross to show how it is possible. **[All India 2015, Ap]**

12. With the help of one example, explain the phenomena of co-dominance and multiple allelism in human population. **[All India 2014, Ap]**

13. A cross was carried out between two pea plants showing the contrasting traits of height of the plant. The result of the cross showed 50% of parental characters. **[Delhi 2014, Ap]**

(i) Work out the cross with the help of a punnett square.

(ii) Name the type of the cross carried out.

14. How does the gene 'I' control ABO blood groups in humans? write the effect the gene has on the structure of red blood cells. **[Delhi 2014, Ap]**

15. A cross between a red flower bearing plant and a white flower bearing plant of Antirrhinum produced all plants having pink flowers. Work out a cross to explain how this is possible. **[All India 2013, U]**

16. (a) Why is human ABO blood group gene considered a good example of multiple alleles ? **[Delhi 2013, U]**

(b) Work out a cross up to FI generation only. between a mother with blood group A (Homozygous) and the father with blood group B (Homozygous). Explain the pattern of inheritance exhibited. **[Delhi 2013, U]**

6 *Long Answer Questions (5 Marks)*

17. In shorthorn cattle, the coat colours red or white are controlled by a single pair of alleles. A calf which receives the allele for red coat from its mother and the allele for white coat from its father is called a 'roan'. It has an equal number of red and white hairs in its coat.

(a) Is this an example of codominance or of incomplete dominance?

(b) Give a reason for your answer.

(c) With the help of genetic cross explain what will be the consequence phenotype of the calf when

i. red is dominant over white

ii. red is incompletely dominant.

[CBSE Sample Paper 2023-24, A]

18. Differentiate between incomplete dominance and co-dominance. Substantiate your answer with one example of each. **[All India 2019, Ap]**

Topic-3: *Inheritance of Two Genes*

Multiple Choice Questions (1 Mark)

1. In the dihybrid cross that was conducted by Morgan involving mating between parental generation for genes yellow bodied, white eyed female Drosophila and wild type male Drosophila, upto F2 generation is given below:

[All India 2022, Term-I, Ap]

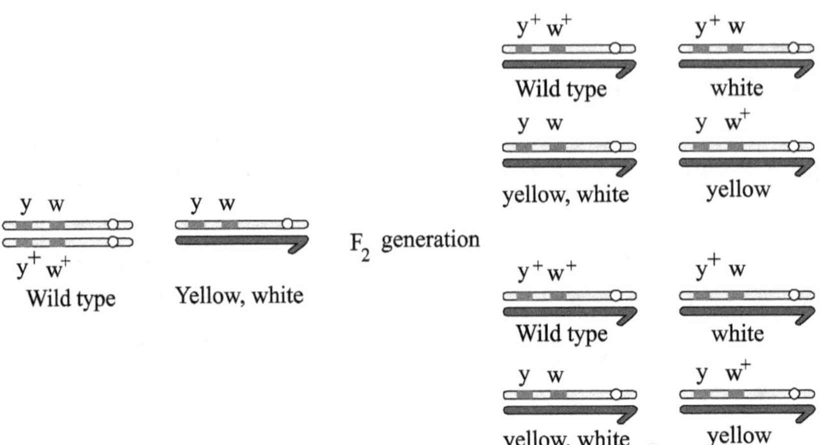

Study the result obtained of the F_2 progeny. Select the correct option from the given choices for the F_2 progeny.

(a) Parental type, 1.3% : Strength of linkage high

(b) Recombinant types, 1.3% : Strength of linkage low

(c) Parental type 98.7% : Strength of linkage high

(d) Recombinant types, 98.7% : Strength of linkage low.

2. Which of the following statements indicates parallelism in genes and chromosomes?

[CBSE Sample Paper 2021-22, U]

(i) They occur in pairs

(ii) They segregate during gamete formation

(iii) They show linkage

(iv) Independent pairs segregate independently

(a) (i) and (iii)　　(b) (ii) and (iii)

(c) (i), (ii) and (iii)　　(d) (i), (ii) and (iv)

3. A cross is made between tall pea plants having green pods and dwarf pea plants having yellow pods. In the F2 generation, out of 80 plants how many are likely to be tall plants? **[CBSE Sample Paper 2021-22, Ap]**

(a) 15　　(b) 20　　(c) 45　　(d) 60

4. Given below is a dihybrid cross performed on Drosophila.

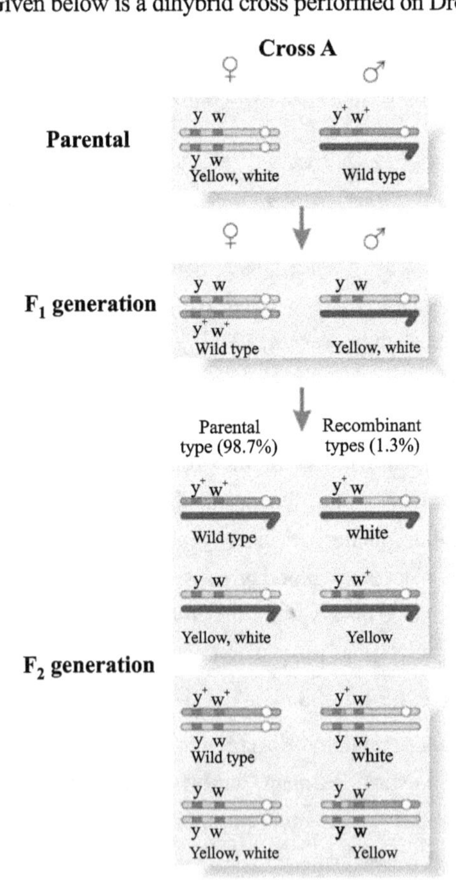

[CBSE Sample Paper 2021-22, A]

Which of the following conclusions can be drawn on the basis of this cross?

When yellow bodied (y), white eyed (w) Drosophila females were hybridized with brown bodied (y+), red eyed males (w+) and F1 progenies were intercrossed, F2 generation would have shown the following ratio:

(a) 1:2:1 because of linkage of genes

(b) 9:3:3:1 because of recombination of genes

(c) Deviation from 9:3:3:1 ratio because of segregation of genes

(d) Deviation from 9:3:3:1 ratio because of linkage of genes

2 *Assertion Reason/Two Statement Type Questions (1 Mark)*

5. **Assertion:** When the two genes in a dihybrid cross are situated on the same chromosome, the proportion of parental gene combinations is much higher than nonparental type. **[CBSE Sample Paper 2021-22, A]**

Reason: Higher parental gene combinations can be attributed to crossing over between two genes.

(a) Both (A) and (R) are true and (R) is the correct explanation of (A).

(b) Both (A) and (R) are true, but (R) is not the correct explanation of (A).

(c) (A) is true, but (R) is false.

(d) (A) is false, but (R) is true.

4 *Very Short Answer Questions (1 Mark)*

6. By using Punnett square depict the genotypes and phenotypes of test crosses (where green pod colour (G) is dominant over yellow pod colour (g)) in Garden pea with unknown genotype. **[Delhi 2023 Set-I, A]**

5 *Short Answer Questions (2 or 3 Marks)*

7. By using Punnett square depict the genotypes and phenotypes of test crosses (where green pod colour (G)

is dominant over yellow pod colour (g) in Garden pea with unknown genotype. **[Delhi 2023 Set-II, U]**

8. Compare in any three ways the chromosomal theory of inheritance as proposed by Sutton and Bovery with that of experimental results on pea plant presented by Mendel. **[All India 2019, U]**

OR

(a) Explain linkage and recombination as put forth by T.H. Morgan based on his observations with Drosophila melanogaster crossing experiment. **[All India 2019, U]**

(b) Write the basis on which Alfred Sturtevant explained gene mapping. **[All India 2019, U]**

9. Write the scientific name of the fruit-fly. Why did Morgan prefer to work with fruit-flies for his experiments? State any three reasons. **[All India 2014, Ap]**

6 *Long Answer Questions (5 Marks)*

10. Describes the dihybrid cross upto F2 generation as conducted by Gregor Mendel using pure lines of Garden Pea for characters seed shape and seed colour.

[Delhi 2023 Set-III, K]

11. (a) Why did T.H. Morgon select *Drosophila melanogaster* for his experiments? **[Delhi 2020, Ap]**

(b) How did he disprove Mendelian dihybrid F2 phenotypic ratio of 9 : 3 : 3 : 1? Explain giving reasons. **[Delhi 2020, Ap]**

12. (a) Write the scientific name of the organism Thomas Hunt Morgan and his colleagues worked with for their experiments. Explain the correlation between linkage and recombination with respect to genes as studied by them. **[All India 2018, U]**

(b) How did Sturtevant explain gene mapping while working with Morgan ? **[All India 2018, U]**

13. State and explain the "Law of independent assortment" in a typical Mendelian dihybrid cross.

[All India 2017, U]

Topic-4: *Polygenic Inheritance and Pleiotropy*

1 *Multiple Choice Questions (1 Mark)*

1. The number of different types of gametes that would be produced from a parent with genotype AABBCc is :

(a) 1   (b) 2   (c) 3   (d) 4   **[All India 2022 Term-I, Ap]**

2. How many types of gametes would be produced if the genotype of a parent is AaBB?

[CBSE Sample Paper 2021-22, U]

(a) 1   (b) 2   (c) 3   (d) 4

3. In human beings, where genotype AABBCC represents dark skin colour, aabbcc represents light skin colour and AaBbCc represents intermediate skin colour; the pattern of genetic inheritance can be termed as:

[CBSE Sample Paper 2021-22, U]

(a) Pleiotropy and codominance

(b) Pleiotropy and incomplete dominance

(c) Polygenic and qualitative inheritance

(d) Polygenic and quantitative inheritance

4   *Very Short Answer Questions (1 Mark)*

4. At a particular locus, the frequency of allele A is 0.8 and that of allele a is 0.2. What would be the frequency of heterozygotes in a random mating population at equilibrium?   **[CBSE Sample Paper 2023-24, U]**

(a) 0.32   (b) 0.16

(c) 0.24   (d) 0.48

Topic-5:   *Sex Determination*

1   *Multiple Choice Questions (1 Mark)*

1. Which of the following animals exhibit male heterogamety?   **[All India 2022, Term-I, K]**

(i) Fruit fly   (ii) Fowl

(iii) Human   (iv) Honey bee

(a) (i) and (iii)   (b) (ii) and (iv)

(c) (ii) and (iii)   (d) (i) and (iv)

2. Which of the following combination of chromosome numbers represents the correct sex determination pattern in honey bees?   **[CBSE Solve Paper 2021-22, U]**

(a) Male 32, Female 16   (b) Male 16, Female 32

(c) Male 31, Female 32   (d) Female 32, Male 31

3. A couple has two daughters. What is the probability that the third child will also be a female?

[CBSE Solve Paper 2021-22, A]

(a) 25%   (b) 50%   (c) 75%   (d) 100%

4   *Very Short Answer Questions (1 Mark)*

4. A male honeybee has 16 chromosomes whereas its female has 32 chromosomes. Give one reason.

[All India 2016, U]

5. How many chromosomes do drones of honeybee possess? Name the type of cell division involved in the production of sperms by them.   **[All India 2015, U]**

5   *Short Answer Questions (2 or 3 Marks)*

6. The cytological observations made in a number of insects led to the development of the concept of genetic/chromosomal basis of sex-determination mechanism. Honey bee is an interesting example to study the mechanism of sex-determination. Study the schematic cross between the male and the female honey bees given below and answer the questions that follow:

[All India 2020, U]

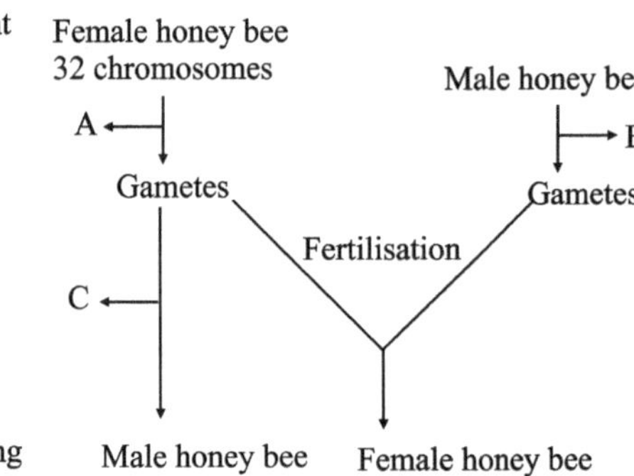

(a) Identify the cell divisions 'A" and 'B' that lead to gamete formation in female and male honey bees respectively.

(b) Name the process 'C' that leads to the development of male honey bee (drone).

7. Explain the mechanism of 'sex determination' in birds. How does it differ from that of human beings?

[All India 2018, U]

8. Differentiate between male and female heterogamety.

[Delhi 2015, **U**]

9. Write the types of sex-determination mechanisms the following crosses show. Give an example of each type.

(i) Female XX with Male XO [Delhi 2014, **Ap**]

(ii) Female ZW with Male ZZ [Delhi 2014, **Ap**]

10. Women are often blamed for producing female children. Consequently, they are ill-treated and ostracized. How will you address this issue scientifically if you were to conduct an awareness programme to highlight the values involved? [Delhi 2014, **U**]

6 *Long Answer Questions (5 Marks)*

11. (a) Explain the mechanism of sex-determination in humans. [All India 2013, **U**]

(b) Differentiate between male heterogamety and female heterogamety with the help of an example of each. [All India 2013, **U**]

Topic-6: *Mutation*

1 *Multiple Choice Questions (1 Mark)*

1. What is the smallest part of a DNA molecule that can be changed by a point mutation?

(a) Oligonucleotide (b) Codon

(c) Gene (d) Nucleotide

[CBSE Sample Paper 2023-24, **K**]

Topic-7: *Genetic Disorders*

1 *Multiple Choice Questions (1 Mark)*

1. The cause of Klinefelter's syndrome in humans is :

[All India 2022, Term-I, **K**]

(a) Absence of Y-chromosome

(b) Absence of X-chromosome

(c) Extra copy of an autosome

(d) Extra copy of an X-chromosome

2. In humans rolling of tongue is an autosomal dominant trait (R). In a family both the parents have the trait of rolling tongue but their daughter does not show the trait, whereas the sons have the trait of rolling of tongue.

The genotypes of the family would be :

[All India 2022, Term-I, **U**]

	Mother	Father	Daughter	Son
(a)	Rr	Rr	rr	rr
(b)	Rr	Rr	rr	RR
(c)	rr	Rr	RR	rr
(d)	RR	rr	Rr	Rr

3. Study the pedigree analysis of human given below and identify the type of inheritance along with an example :

[All India 2022, Term-I, **A**]

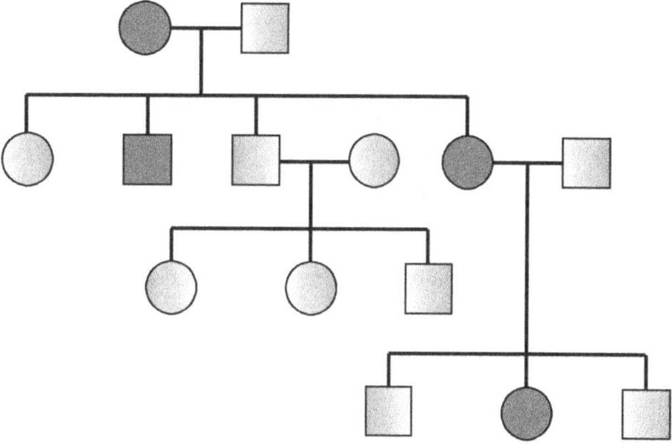

(a) Sex-linked recessive, Haemophilia

(b) Sex-linked dominant, Vitamin D resistant rickets

(c) Autosomal recessive, Sickle-cell anaemia

(d) Autosomal dominant, Myotonic Dystrophy

4. The correct statement with respect to Thalassemia in humans is : **[All India 2022, Term-I, K]**

(a) α-Thalassemia is controlled by a single gene HBB.

(b) The gene for α-Thalassemia is located on chromosome-16.

(c) β-Thalassemia is controlled by two closely linked genes HBA-1 and HBA-2.

(d) In β-Thalassemia the production of α-globin chain is affected.

5. Given below is a Karyotype of a human foetus obtained for screening to find any probable genetic disorder : **[All India 2022, Term-I, Ap]**

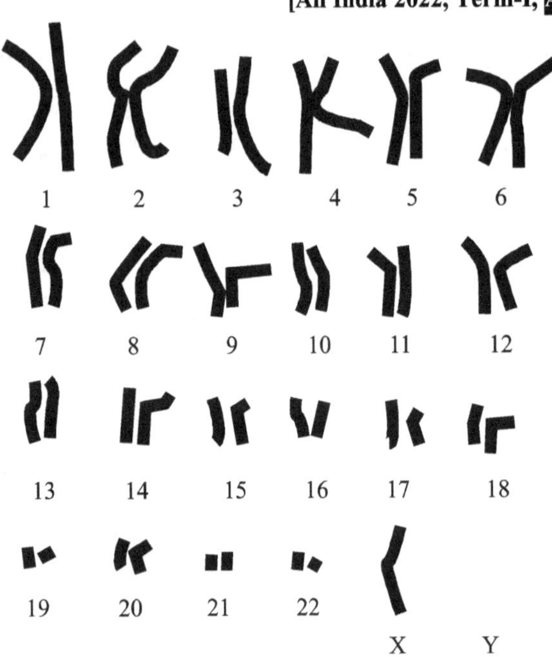

Based on the Karyotype, the chromosomal disorder detected in unborn foetus and the consequent symptoms the child may suffer from are :

(a) Turner's syndrome : Sterile ovaries, short stature

(b) Down's syndrome : Gynaecomastia, overall masculine stature

(c) Turner's syndrone : Small round head, flat back of head

(d) Down's syndrome : Furrowed tongue, short stature.

6. Which of the following amino acid substitution is responsible for causing sickle cell anemia? **[CBSE Sample Paper 2021-22, K]**

(a) Valine is substituted by Glutamic acid in the α – globin chain at the sixth position

(b) Valine is substituted by Glutamic acid in the α – globin chain at seventh position

(c) Glutamic acid is substituted by Valine in the α – globin chain at the sixth position

(d) Glutamic acid is substituted by Valine in the α – globin chain at the sixth position

7. What is the pattern of inheritance in the above pedigree chart? **[CBSE Sample Paper 2021-22, A]**

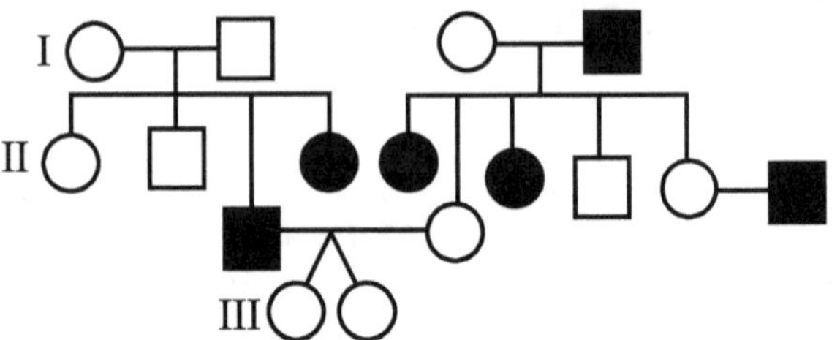

(a) Autosomal dominant (b) Autosomal recessive

(c) Sex -linked dominant (d) Sex -linked recessive

8. Placed below is a karyotype of a human being. **[CBSE Sample Paper 2021-22, A]**

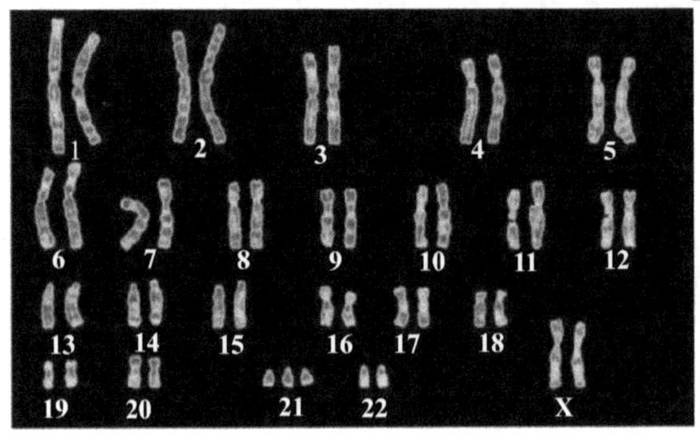

On the basis of this karyotype, which of the following conclusions can be drawn:

(a) Normal human female

(b) Person is suffering from Colour Blindness

(c) Affected individual is a female with Down's syndrome

(d) Affected individual is a female with Turner's syndrome

9. Rajesh and Mahesh have defective haemoglobin due to genetic disorders. Rajesh has too few globin molecules while Mahesh has incorrectly functioning globin molecules. Identify the disorder they are suffering from. **[CBSE Sample Paper 2021-22, U]**

	Rajesh	Mahesh
(a)	Sickle cell anaemia- an autosome linked recessive trait	Thalassemia - an autosome linked dominant trait
(b)	Thalassemia - an autosome linked recessive blood disorder	Sickle cell anaemia - an autosome linked recessive trait
(c)	Sickle cell anaemia - an autosome linked recessive trait	Thalassemia - an autosome linked recessive blood disorder
(d)	Thalassemia - an autosome linked recessive blood disorder	Sickle cell anaemia - an autosome linked dominant trait

10. What should be the genotype of the indicated member?

[CBSE Sample Paper 2023-24, U]

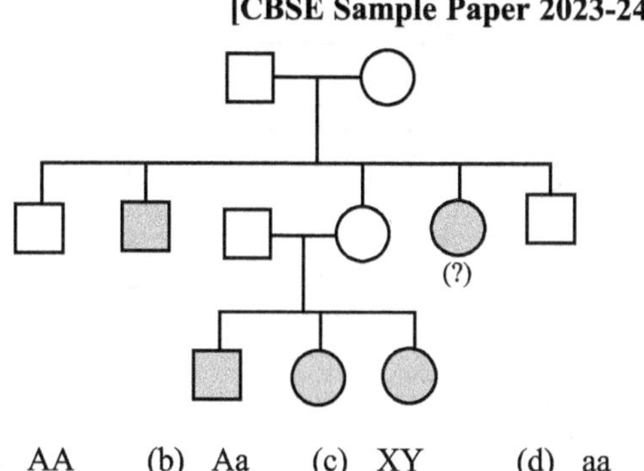

(a) AA   (b) Aa   (c) XY   (d) aa

2   *Assertion Reason/Two Statement Type Questions (1 Mark)*

(a) Both (A) and (R) are true and (R) is the correct explanation of (A).

(b) Both (A) and (R) are true, but (R) is not the correct explanation of (A).

(c) (A) is true, but (R) is false.

(d) (A) is false, but (R) is true.

11. Assertion (A) : In Thalassemia an abnormal myoglobin chain is synthesized due to a gene defect.

Reason (R) : α-Thalassemia is controlled by genes HBA1 and HBA2 on chromosome 16.

[Delhi 2023 Set-I, U]

12. Assertion (A) : Accumulation of phenylalanine in the brain results in metal retardation in Phenylketonuria.

Reason (R) : The affected person lacks phenylalanine which is therefore not converted to tyrosine.

[All India 2022, Term-I, U]

4   *Very Short Answer Questions (1 Mark)*

13. The diagram below shows the sequence of amino acids in part of a haemoglobin molecule.

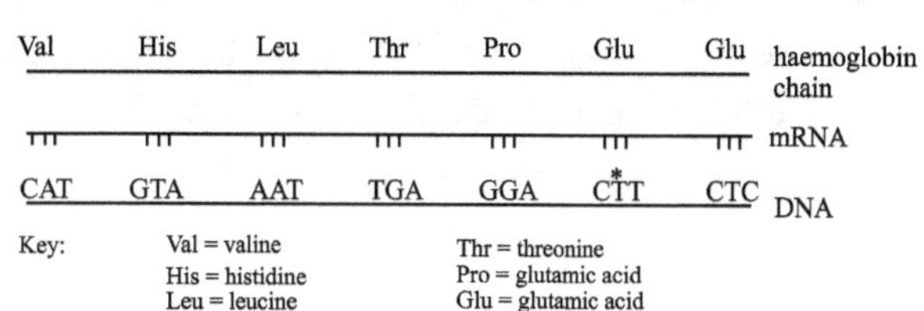

(a) If the base T* was substituted with A, how would it affect the haemoglobin chain?

(b) Name the condition and the effects associated with the above substitution.

[CBSE Sample Paper 2023-24, A]

14. Name the disorder in humans with the following karyotype: **[Delhi 2019, K]**

(a) 22 pairs of autosomes + XO

(b) 22 pairs of autosomes + 21st chromosome + XY

15. Following are the features of genetic codes. What does each one indicate? Stop codon; Unambiguous codon; Degenerate docon; Universal codon **[All India 2016, U]**

5   *Short Answer Questions (2 or 3 Marks)*

16. The chromosome number is fixed for all normal organisms leading to species specification whereas any abnormality in the chromosome number of the fixed number of chromosomes both in male and female. In male it is '44 + XY' and in female it is '44 + XX'. Thus the human male is heterogametic, in other words produces two different types of gametes one with '22 + X' chromosomes and the other with '22 + Y' chromosomes respectively. Human female, on the other hand is homogametic i.e. produces only one type of gamete with '22 + X' chromosomes only.

Sometimes an error may occur during meiosis of cell cycle, where the sister chromatids fail to segregate called nondisjunction, leading to the production of abnormal gametes with altered chromosome number. On fertilisation such gametes develop into abnormal individuals. **[Delhi 2023 Set-I, A]**

(a) State what is aneuploidy.

(b) If during spermatogenesis, the chromatids of sex chromosomes fail to segregate during meiosis, write only the different types of gametes with altered chromosome number that could possibly be produced.

(c) A normal human sperm (22 + Y) fertilises an ovum with karyotype '22 + XX'. Name the disorder the offspring thus produced would suffer from and write any two symptoms of the disorder.

OR

(c) Name a best known and most common autosomal aneuploid abnormality in human and write any two symptoms. **[Delhi 2023 Set-I, A]**

17. Generally it is observed that human males suffer from hemophilia more than that of human females who rarely suffer from it. Explain giving reason. **[All India 2020, U]**

18. Two children, A and B aged 4 and 5 years respectively visited a hospital with a similar genetic disorder. The girl A was provided enzyme-replacement therapy and was advised to revisit periodically for further treatment. The girl, B was, however, given a therapy that did not require revisit for further treatment. **[All India 2019, U]**

(a) Name the ailments the two girls were suffering from?

(b) Why did the treatment provided to girl A required repeated visits ?

(c) How was the girl B cured permanently ?

19. Give names of Mendalian disorder along with their symptoms? **[All India 2019, U]**

20. Write down a short note on genetic disease known as Thalassmeia? **[All India 2019, K]**

21. During a medical investigation, an infant was found to possess an extra chromosome-21. Describe the symptoms the child is likely to develop later in the life. **[All India 2017, U]**

22. Give an example of an autosomal recessive trait in humans. Explain its pattern of inheritance with the help of a cross. **[Delhi 2016, U]**

23. Why is pedigree analysis done in the study of human genetics? State the conclusions that can be drawn from it. **[All India 2014, U]**

24. Identify 'a', 'b', 'c', 'd', 'e' and 'f' in the table given below: **[All India 2014, U]**

No.	Syndrome	Cause	Characteristics of **affected** individuals	Sex Male/Female/Both
1.	Down's	Trisomy of 21	'a' (i), (ii)	'b'
2.	'c'	XXY	Overall masculine development	'd'
3.	Turner's	45 with OX	'e' (i), (ii)	'f'

25. A colourblind child is born to a normal couple. Work out a cross to show how it is possible. Mention the sex of this child. **[Delhi 2014, Ap]**

26. Why are human females rarely haemophilic?

Explain. How do haemophilic patients suffer?

[All India 2013, U]

 **Long Answer Questions (5 Marks)**

27. (a) Why are thalassemia and haemophilia categorized as Mendelian disorders? Write the symptoms of these diseases. Explain their pattern of inheritance in humans. **[All India 2015, Ap]**

(b) Write the genotypes of the normal parents producing a haemophilic son.

28. A child suffering from Thalassemia is born to a normal couple. But the mother is being blamed by the family for delivering a sick baby. **[Delhi 2013, A]**

(a) What is Thalassemia?

(b) How would you counsel the family not to blame the mother for delivering a child suffering from this disease? Explain.

(c) List the values your counselling can propagate in the families.

7   *Case Based Questions*

29. Study the Pedigree chart given below and answer the questions that follow:

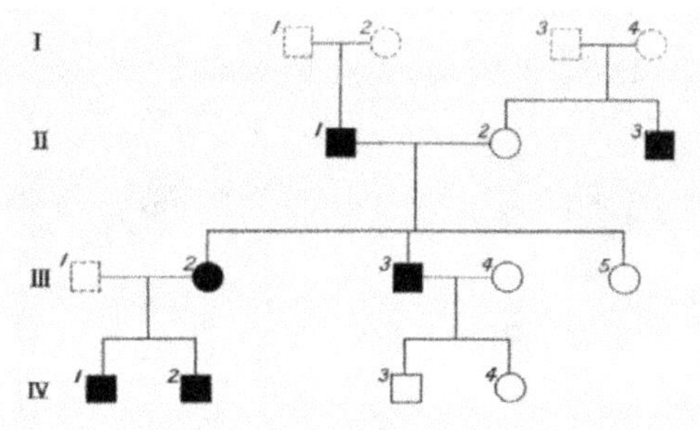

Symbols used in the given Pedigree Chart are as follows:

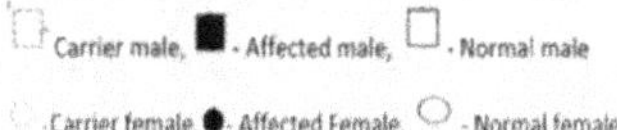

(a) On the basis of the inheritance pattern exhibited in this pedigree chart, what conclusion can you draw about the pattern of inheritance?

(b) If the female is homozygous for the affected trait in this pedigree chart, then what percentage of her sons will be affected ?

(c) Give the genotype of offsprings 1,2,3 and 4 in III generation.

OR

(c) In this type of inheritance pattern, out of male and female children which one has less probability of receiving the trait from the parents. Give a reason.

[CBSE Sample Paper 2022-23, A]

Hints & Solutions

 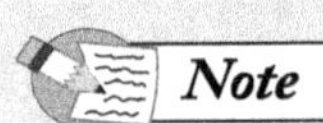

Topic-1:   *Mendel's Law of Inheritance*

1. **(c)** According to Mendel, the natures of unit factor that control the expression of trait were stable and discrete. **(1 Mark)**

2. **(c)** Reginald Punnett, an English geneticist, established one of the simplest methods for calculating the mathematical chance of inheriting a given feature. Punnett square became popular as a result of his technique. It's the simplest graphical method for determining all conceivable genotype combinations in children. **(1 Mark)**

> **Note**
>
> *Test-cross involves mating of an unknown genotypic individual with a known homozygous recessive.*

3. **(b)** when cross is occur between axial (Aa) and terminal (aa) then, **(1 Mark)**

Parent	Aa	aa
	(Axial)	(Terminal)

F1 Gen.

	A	a
a	Aa	aa
a	Aa	aa

as shown in punnett square the phenotype ratio of Axial flower is 50 % and terminal flower is 50 %.

4. **(c)** The dominant pod colour of *Pisum sativum* is green colour while recessive pod colour is yellow in colour. **(1 Mark)**

5. **(b)** The cross between pure breed of tall plant with write colour flower (TTbb) with pure breed with short plant and blue flower (ttBB). Then the F_2 progeny will be :

Tall plant with blue flower: 9

Tall plant with white flower: 3

Dwarf plant with blue flower: 3

Dwarf plant with white flower: 1

Therefore, the probability of short plant with blue flower is

3/16 of 2160 = 405 **(1 Mark)**

6. **(d)** Aa × aa **(1 Mark)**

7. **(b)** Ab × Ab **(1 Mark)**

8. **(b)** (ii), (iii), (iv), (v) **(1 Mark)**

9. Test cross is used for the determination of genotype of pea plant bearing violet flowers. **(1 Mark)**

> **Note**
>
> *Test cross helps the students to determine whether the genotype of the plant is heterozygous dominant (Ww) or homozygous dominant (WW).*

10. A geneticist prefers to choose organisms for experiments with shorter life cycle because it helps the geneticist to study many generations in the shorter life spans of those organisms. **(1 Mark)**

11. The two contrasting traits related to the seeds of pea plant that were studied by Mendel are as follows:

Seed shape- Round seeds and Wrinkled seeds

Seed colour- Yellow and Green **(1 Mark)**

12. Mendal's law of dominance states that characters are controlled by discrete unit called factors. They occur in pair. In a dissimilar pair of factors one member of the pair dominates (dominant) over the other (recessive).

This law is used to explain the expression of only one of the parental characters in a monohybrid cross in the F1 generation. The expression of both alleles in the F2 generation. He also explained the proportion of 3:1 obtained at the F2 generation. **(3 Mark)**

Diagrammatic Representation of an Example of Mendel's law of Dominance:

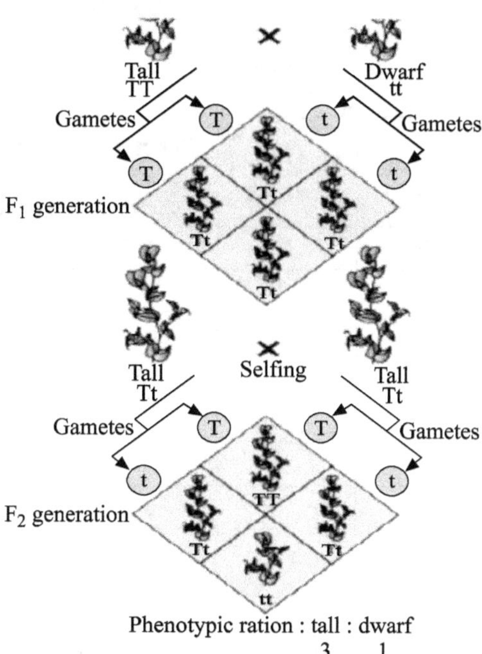

13. A test cross is used to determine the genotype of pea plant. In this a tall plant is crossed with dwarf plant. In the F1 generation, all the progeny obtained are tall. So the genotype of the tall plant is TT. In the F2 generation, 50% tall plants and 50% dwarf plants are obtained and the genotype of the tall plant is Tt.

Diagrammatic Representation of Test cross:

	Male			Female
Parents	TT	X		tt
Gametes	(T) (T)	X		(t) (t)
F₁ generation	Tt	Tt	Tt	Tt

	Male			Female
Parents	Tt		X	tt
Gametes	(T) (t)		X	(t) (t)
F₂ generation	Tt	Tt	tt	tt

(3 Marks)

14. Purple colour is a dominant phenotype in pea plant and the genotype of the pea plant with purple flowers can be determined by test cross.

In test cross, the pea plant whose genotype is to be determined is crossed with a homozygous recessive parent (ww) having white flowers. It helps the students to determine whether the genotype of the plant is heterozygous dominant (Ww) or homozygous dominant (WW).

Diagrammatic representation of a test cross is as follows:

Parents:	WW (purple)	X	ww (white)
Gametes:	W W		w w

F₁ generation : Ww   Ww   Ww   Ww

Result: All flower are voilet

Interpretation: Unknown flower is homozygous dominant

Parents:	Ww (Purple)	X	ww (white)
	(Dominant phenotype)		(Homozygous recessive)

Gametes :   Ww   ww

F₂ generation : Ww   Ww   ww   ww

Result: 50% flowers are violet and 50% flowers are white.

Interpretation: Unknown flower is heterozygous

(3 Marks)

15. (a) The appearance of pink colour in a Snapdrgon flower or *Antirrhinum sp.* is not considered as blending because the process of blending involves intermixing of two characters but in Snapdragon flower, the alleles do not mix with each other. So, they tends to maintain their originality and reappear in F2 generation. The development of pink colour is because the dominant allele is not completely dominant over the recessive allele.   **(2 Marks)**

(b) This phenomena is called incomplete dominance

(1 Marks)

16. Three reasons that are responsible for the delay in accepting Mendel's work:

- Lack of communication and publicity.
- His concept of factors or gene as discrete units that did not blend with each other was not accepted in the terms of variations that occur naturally in nature.
- Mendel's approach to explain biological phenomena with the help of mathematics was also not accepted.

(3 Marks)

17. The given cross represents in a form of Punett square are as follows:

Parents: Tt X Tt

Gametes: Tt Tt

F$_1$ generation: Tt Tt Tt tt

  (Tall plant) (Tall plant)(Tall plant) (Dwarf)

When two heterozygous tall parents are crossed, three heterozygous tall and one dwarf plant is obtained.

  (2 Marks)

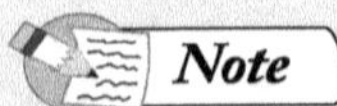

Note

Punett square was developed by a British geneticist, Reginald C.Punnett and is defined as a graphical representation for calculation of probability of all the possible genotypes of offsprings in a genetic cross.

18.

Parents (Inflated, green pods) × (Constricted, yellow pods)

Genotypes FFGG ffgg

Gametes (FG) (fg)

F$_1$ generation FfGg (All Inflated green pods)

Making the correct punnett square **(1 Mark)**

Phenotype - All Inflated green pods **(½ Mark)**

Genotype –FfGg **(½ Mark)**

19. If the F$_1$ progeny has a phenotype that does not resemble either of the two parents, this could due to incomplete dominance. For example, Incomplete dominance is seen in cross-pollination experiments between red and white snapdragon plants. The allele that produces the red color (R) is not completely expressed over the recessive allele that produces the white color (r). The resulting offspring are pink. **(5 Marks)**

20. The inheritance of human blood group is an example of codominance and multiple alleles. ABO blood grouping in human beings are controlled by *I* gene. The plasma membrane of the red blood cells has sugar polymers that are found on the surface of RBCs and is controlled by this gene.

The *I* gene has three alleles I^A, I^B and *i*. The gene I^A and I^B are dominant over *i* and both I^A and I^B express their own types of sugars. This phenomenon is called **codominance.** Hence, red blood cells have both A and B types of sugars. There are three different alleles and there are six different genotypes of the human ABO blood types. **(2½ Marks)**

Tabular representation of genetic basis of Blood Groups in Human population:

Allele from Parent 1	Allele from Parent 2	Genotype of offspring	Blood types of offspring
I^A	I^A	$I^A I^A$	A
I^A	I^B	$I^A I^B$	AB
I^A	*i*	$I^A i$	A
I^B	I^A	$I^A I^B$	AB
I^B	I^B	$I^B I^B$	B
I^B	*i*	$I^B i$	B
i	*i*	*i i*	O

  (2½ Marks)

Topic-2: *Inheritance of One Gene*

1. **(d)** Three genes A, B, and C control skin colour in humans with the dominant forms A, B and C responsible for dark skin colour and the recessive forms 'c' for light skin colour. Hence, The type of gametes produced by the parent with genotype AABBCc is 4. **(1 Mark)**

2. **(d)** If the Father is with heterozygous A blood group ($I^A I^O$) and mother with heterozygous B blood group ($I^B I^O$) then the progeny of such parents are,

	I^A	I^O
I^B	$I^A I^B$	$I^B I^O$
I^O	$I^A I^O$	$I^O I^O$

Phenotype blood group of $I^A I^B$ – AB blood group

  $I^B I^O$ – B blood group

  $I^A I^O$ – A blood group

  $I^O I^O$ – O blood group

Therefore, progeny is with blood group A,B,AB, and O.

  (1 Mark)

3. **(d)** Aa × aa **(1 Mark)**

4. **(c)** 2 Red : 2 Pink **(1 Mark)**

5. **(a)** Both A and R are true and R is the correct explanation of A. **(1 Mark)**

6. The Punnett square helps in understanding the production of gametes by the parents, and formation of the zygotes in F_1 and F_2 generation. The Punnett square is a graphical representation for the calculation of probability of all the possible genotypes of offsprings in a genetic cross.

(1 Mark)

7. The difference between gene and allele are as follows:

Gene		Allele	
(i)	Gene is a segment of DNA that controls a specific trait.	(i)	Allele is defined as specific form of a gene.
(ii)	They are responsible for the expression of specific traits.	(ii)	Alleles are responsible for variation as a specific trait can be expressed.
(iii)	They are not found in pairs.	(iii)	They are always found in pairs.

(1 Mark)

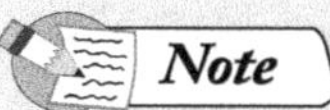

Note

The Punnett square was developed by a British geneticist, Reginald C. Punnett. Phenotypes refer to the observable characteristics of organisms that involve appearance, development and behaviour of organisms. Genotypes refer to the genetic constitution of organisms.

8. The pattern of inheritance is Incomplete dominance in which the none of the two alleles are dominant over each other. So, when both the alleles are present together intermediate or new phenotypes are formed. Intermediate formed is intermediate between the independent expressions of two alleles.

The phenotypic ratio and genotypic ratio such as 1:2:1 are same in case of incomplete dominance. **(2 Marks)**

9. The inheritance of ABO blood grouping in humans is an example of Co-dominance and multiple alleles. ABO blood grouping in human beings are controlled by I gene. The plasma membrane of the red blood cells has sugar polymers that are found on the surface of RBCs and is controlled by this gene. **(3 Marks)**

Diagrammatic representation of a Cross:

Parents	Father	X	Mother	
	$I^A I^B$	X	ii	
Gametes	I^A I^B	X	i i	
F_1 genration	$I^A i$	$I^A i$	$I^B i$	$I^B i$

The above cross represents that in F1 generation blood A and B are dominant over blood O group. So, the children's have 50 % chances of getting A and B blood group.

Note

Co-dominance is a type of inheritance in which the alleles of a gene pair in a heterozygote are independently expressed themselves. Multiple alleles refer to the more than three alternative forms of allele of a gene.

10. A test cross is a cross between the F1 progeny and its homozygous recessive parents. Test cross is used for the determination of dominant character which is coming from the homozygous dominant genotype or heterozygous genotype. For example: TT and Tt for tallness.

Representation of genetic cross:

Parents:	Tt (tall)	X	tt (dwarf)	
Gametes:	Tt		tt	
F_1 generation :	Tt	Tt	Tt	Tt

Result: All the progeny obtained are tall.

When Heterozygous tall (Tt) plant is crossed with homozygous dwarf (tt) plant:

Parents:	Tt (tall)	X	tt (dwarf)	
Gametes:	Tt		tt	
F_2 generation :	Tt	Tt	tt	tt

Result: 50% tall and 50% dwarf progenies are obtained in F_2 generation. **(3 Marks)**

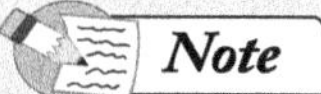

Note

Test cross is used for the determination of the heterozygosity of the plant.

11. When a cross is made between tall pea plant which is heterozygous and dwarf (small) pea plant which is homozygous. This cross can be represented as follows :

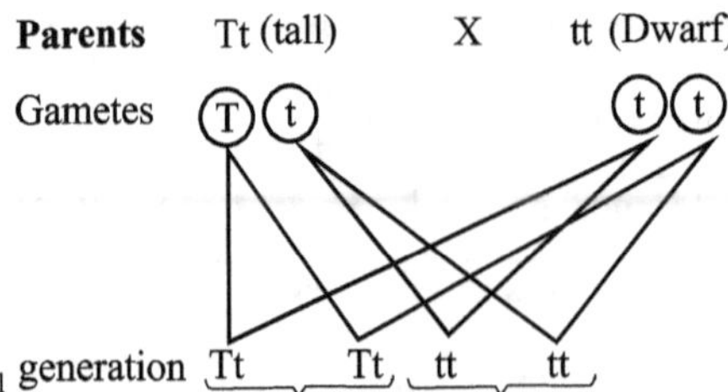

The ratio will be 50% dominant and 50% recessive incase of hybrid or heterozygous individual.   **(3 Marks)**

12. The phenomena of multiple allelism and co-dominance are represented by ABO blood group in human beings. The gene i for the blood group contains three alleles such as I^A, I^B and i. These alleles represent the phenomena of multiple allelism as it contain more than two alleles that controls the same characters. The alleles I^A and I^B are co-dominant and express themselves independently in a next generation. The presence of both the blood group I^A and I^B produces blood group AB and this is an example of co-dominance.   **(3 Marks)**

Note

Co-dominance is a form of inheritance in which the alleles of a gene pair in a heterozygote are independently expressed themselves in a hybrid.

13. (i) **Diagrammatic Representation of Cross:**

Parents	*Tt(male)*	*X*	*tt Female*
Gametes	(T) (t)	X	(t) (t)
F₁ generation	Tt Tt	tt	tt
Results		50% tall and 50% dwarf offsprings	

    In the above cross, 50% progeny is tall (dominant) and 50% progeny is dwarf (recessive). **(1½ Marks)**

    (ii) The type of cross carried out is called test cross. In test cross, an unknown dominant phenotype is crossed with an individual homozygous recessive for that specific trait.   **(1½ Marks)**

14. The inheritance of human blood group is an example of codominance and multiple alleles. ABO blood grouping in human beings are controlled by I gene. The plasma membrane of the red blood cells has sugar polymers that are found on the surface of RBCs and is controlled by this gene.

The I gene has three alleles I^A, I^B and i. The gene I^A and I^B are dominant over i and both I^A and I^B express their own types of sugars. This phenomenon is called co-dominance. Hence, red blood cells have both A and B types of sugars. While i allele do not produce any sugar. There are three different alleles and there are six different genotypes of the human ABO blood types. **(1½ Marks)**

Tabular representation of genetic basis of Blood Groups in Human population:

Allele from Parent 1	Allele from Parent 2	Genotype of offspring	Blood types of offspring
I^A	I^A	I^{A}I^A	A
I^A	I^B	I^{A}I^B	AB
I^A	i	I^{A}i	A
I^B	I^A	I^{A}I^B	AB
I^B	I^B	I^{B}I^B	B
I^B	i	I^{B}i	B
i	i	ii	O

(1½ Marks)

15. A cross between a red flower bearing plant and white flower bearing plant of Antirrhinum produces all plants having pink flowers is an example of incomplete dominance.

P generation:	RR (red)	X	rr (white)
	↓		↓
Gametes:	R		r
F₁ generation:		Rr (all pink)	
Gametes:	Rr (male)	X	Rr (female)
F2 generation:	RR (Red)	Rr (pink) R r (pink)	rr (white)
	1	1 1	1

The phenotypic and genotypic ratio obtained in incomplete dominance is 1:2:1   **(3 Marks)**

Note

Incomplete dominance states that a form of gene interaction in which two alleles that controls a trait is dominant over each other and the progeny obtained is the intermediate of the two alleles.

16. (a) The inheritance of human blood group is an example of codominance and multiple alleles. ABO blood grouping in human beings are controlled by I

gene. The plasma membrane of the red blood cells has sugar polymers that are found on the surface of RBCs and is controlled by this gene.

The I gene has three alleles I^A, I^B and i. The gene I^A and I^B are dominant over i and both I^A and I^B express their own types of sugars. This phenomenon is called **Codominance**. Hence, red blood cells have both A and B types of sugars. While i allele do not produce any sugar. There are three different alleles and there are six different genotypes of the human ABO blood types.   **(1½ Marks)**

Tabular representation of genetic basis of Blood Groups in Human population:

Allele from Parent 1	Allele from Parent 2	Genotype of offspring	Blood types of offspring
I^A	I^A	$I^A I^A$	A
I^A	I^B	$I^A I^B$	AB
I^A	i	$I^A i$	A
I^B	I^A	$I^A I^B$	AB
I^B	I^B	$I^B I^B$	B
I^B	i	$I^B i$	B
i	i	$i\,i$	O

(1½ Marks)

(b) Genetic Cross:

Parents: $I^A I^A$ X $I^B I^B$

                        (Mother)   (Father)

Gametes: I^A I^A X $I^B I^B$

F_1 **generation:** $I^A I^B$ $I^A I^B$ $I^A I^B$ $I^A I^B$

The above cross indicates that, if the mother has A blood group (homozygous) and father has B blood group (homozygous) conditions, then, all the offsprings will have AB blood group.   **(3 Marks)**

17. (a) Codominance   **(1 Mark)**

(b) Codominance is a condition in which two different alleles for a genetic trait are expressed. Individuals receive one version of a gene, called an allele, from each parent.   **(1 Mark)**

(c) (i) If pure breeding red coated cattles are represented as 'RR' and pure breeding white coated as 'rr'. If Red is dominant over White. A cross between 'RR' and 'rr' would produce red coated cattles (RR) and white coated cattle (rr) in the ratio of 3:1

Parents: RR (Red) X rr (White)

Gametes: R   r

	R	r
R	RR Red coat	Rr Redcoat
r	Rr Red coat	rr White coat

F 1 generation– 3:1   **(1½ Marks)**

(ii) If the red and white coated cattles produce pink colour on a cross then, they exhibit incomplete dominance in the inheritance of coat colour due to which they produce pink coloured coat upon hybridisation.

If pure breeding red coated cattles are represented as 'RR' and pure breeding white coated as 'rr', then the pink coated cattles are 'Rr'.

A cross between 'RR' and 'rr' would produce pink coated cattles (Rr) and white coated cattle (rr) in the ratio of 1:2:1

Parents: RR (Red) X rr (White)

Garments: R   W

	R	r
R	RR Red coat	Rr Pink coat
r	Rr Pink coat	rr (White)

F1 Generation – 1:2:1   **(1½ Marks)**

18. The difference between incomplete and co-dominance are as follows:

	Incomplete dominance		Codominance
(i)	It is a phenomena in which none of the alleles of a gene is dominant over each other and a new phenotype is formed. The new phenotype is intermediate between the independent expression of two alleles.	(i)	Codominance is a phenomena in which both the alleles of a gene ex-presses themselves independently in a heterozygote.
(ii)	New phenotypes are always formed as a result of incomplete dominance.	(ii)	In case of codominance, no new phenotype is formed.
(iii)	Examples are snapdragon and mirabilis jalapa	(iii)	Examples are Roan character in cattles and blood grouping in humans.

(5 Marks)

1. **(c)**

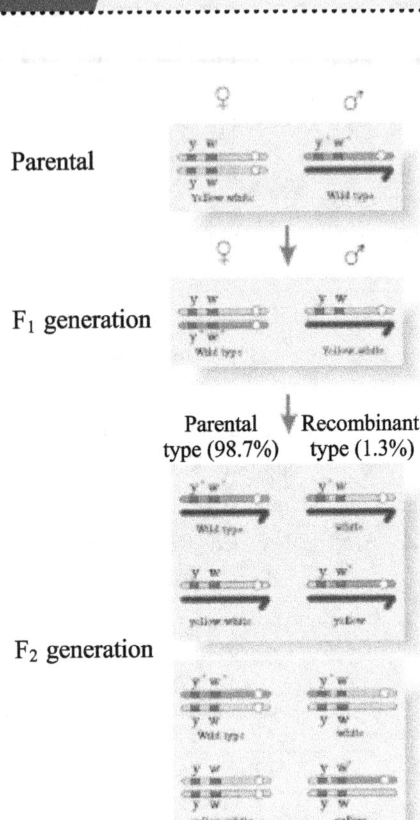

(1 Mark)

2. **(d)** (i), (ii) and (iv) **(1 Mark)**

3. **(d)** 60 **(1 Mark)**
Out of 9 : 3 : 3 : 1 = 16
9 + 3 will be tall.
Therefore, $12/16 \times 80 = 60$

4. **(d)** Deviation from 9:3:3:1 ratio because of linkage of genes. **(1 Mark)**

5. **(c)** A is true but R is false **(1 Mark)**

6. The tests cross between green pod colour (GG) and yellow pod colour (gg) in garden pea.

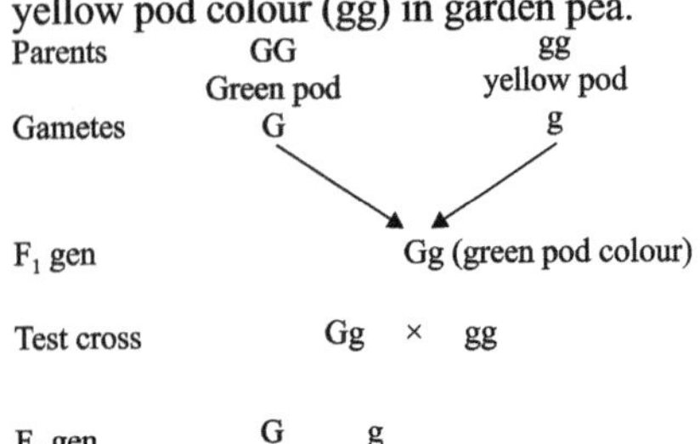

	G	g
g	Gg	gg
g	Gg	gg

(1 Mark)

Hence, the genotype and phenotype of this test cross is 1:1

7.

	G	g
G	GG	Gg
g	gg	gg

In this example, the unkown genotype is crossed with a homozygous.

In this example, the unknown genotype is crossed with a homozygous recessive (gg) individual. The dominant allele G represents green pod color, while the recessive allele g represents yellow pod color. The genotypes of the resulting offspring can be read from the boxes in the Punnett square.

The possible genotypes of the offspring are GG and Gg. GG individuals will have green pods, while Gg individuals will also have green pods because the G allele is dominant. Only gg individuals will have yellow pods.

The phenotype ratio of the offspring from this test cross will be 1:1, meaning half of the offspring will have green pods and half will have yellow pods. The genotype ratio will be 1:1, meaning half of the offspring will be homozygous dominant (GG) and half will be heterozygous (Gg). **(3 Marks)**

8. The chromosomal theory of inheritance given by Sutton and Boveri and experimental results presented by Mendel can be compared in the following ways:

(i) In a diploid organism, the factors (genes) and chromosomes occur in pairs.

(ii) Both chromosomes as well as genes segregate at the time of gamete formation such that only one of each pair is transmitted to a gamete. So, a gamete contains only one chromosome of a type and only one of the two alleles of a trait.

(iii) Each pair of chromosome and gene segregates independent of another pair.

(iv) The paired condition of both chromosomes as well as Mendelian factors is restored during fertilisation. **(3 Marks)**

> **Note**
>
> *The chromosomal theory of inheritance was proposed by Sutton and Boveri states that the genes are located at specific loci on the chromosome that segregate and assort independently during the process of meiosis and then recombine at the time of fertilization in the zygote.*

OR

(a) T.H. Morgan studied X-linked genes in *Drosophila* and observed that when the two genes in a dihybrid cross were situated on the same chromosome, the proportion of parental gene combinations is much higher than the non-parental type. He attributed this due to the physical association or linkage of the two genes on a chromosome and coined the term linkage and the term recombination describes the generation of non-parental gene combinations. **(1½ Marks)**

(b) Alfred Sturtevant used the frequency of recombination between gene pairs on the same chromosome as a measure of distance between them and mapped their position on the chromosome.

(1½ Marks)

> **Note**
>
> *Genes present on the same chromosome are separated during meiosis and the new combination of the gene could be formed and this phenomenon is called recombination of the gene. They are attached to one another like beads on a string in a linear organisation. The distance between the linked genes indicates the strength of linkage.*

9. The scientific name of the fruit fly is called *Drosophilla melanogaster.* Morgan prefers to work with fruit-flies for his experiment because of the following reasons such as:

- They are easily grown on a simple synthetic medium in a laboratory.

- They complete their life cycle in about two weeks and a single mating could produce a large number of offsprings.

- There was a clear differentiation of sexes as male and female flies are easily distinguishable.

(2 Marks)

10. **(b)** In the dihybrid cross with pea plants, Mendel crossed two pea plants with a set of two contrasting characteristics, for example- the seed color as well as seed shape. He crossed a pea plant with round, green sees with one having yellow, wrinkled seeds. The plants obtained in the F1 generation were then self-crossed and the phenotypic ratio of the plants obtained in the F2 is known as Mendel's dihybrid ratio, which resulted in 9:3:3:1. **(2½ Marks)**

(2½ Marks)

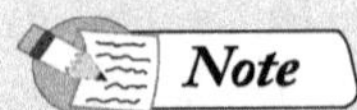

There are many types of RNA found in eukaryotic and prokaryatic cells. Three main tyhpe of RNA are mRNA, tRNA, rRNA.

11. **(a)** T.H Morgan selected *Drosophila melanogaster* for his experiments because he found that fruit flies are suitable for studies as they could be easily grown on simple synthetic medium in the laboratory.

- They tend to complete their life cycle in about two weeks and a single mating could produce a large number of progeny flies.

- Sexes are clearly differentiated between male and female flies.

- They exhibit several types of hereditary variations that can be observed with low power microscope.

(2½ Marks)

(b) Morgan carried out many dihybrid crosses in *Drosophilla* to study the genes that were sex-linked. These crosses were similar to the dihybrid cross performed by Mendel in peas. He hybridised yellow-bodied, white-eyed females to brown-bodied, red-eyed males and intercrossed their F1 progent.

Then he observed that the two genes did not segregate independently to each other and the F2 ration deviated very significantly from the 9:3:3:1 ratio.

He observed that the genes were located on the X-chromosome and they saw quickly that when the two genes in a dihybrid cross were situated on the same chromosome, the proportion of parental gene combinations were much higher than the non-parental type. According to Morgan, this is because of physical association or linkage of the two genes and coined the term linkage. It used to describe this physical association of genes on a chromosome and is called recombination. It is term used to describe the generation of non-parental gene combinations.

(2½ Marks)

12. **(a)** *Drosophila melanogaster* : Morgan carried out several dihybrid crosses in *Drosophila* to study gens that were sex-lined. Morgan and his group knew that the genes were located on the X chromosome and saw quickly that when the two genes in a dihybrid cross were situated on the same chromosome, the proportion of parental gene combinations were much higher than the non-parental type. Morgan attributed this due to the physical association or linkage of the two genes and coined the term linkage to describe this physical association of genes on a chromosome and the term recombination to describe the generation of non- parental gene combination. Morgan and his group also found that even when genes were grouped on the same chromosome, some genes were very tightly linked (showed very low recombination) while others were loosely linked.

Morgans student Alfred Sturtevant used the frequency of recombination between gene pairs on the same chromosome as a measure of the distance between genes and 'mapped' their position on the chromosome. (2½ Marks)

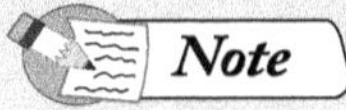

Genetic maps are extensively used as a starting point in the sequencing of whole genomes.

(b) Alfred Sturtevant expressed the frequency of recombination between gene pairs present on the same chromosome as the distance between those genes. He then mapped the positions of the genes on the chromosome. Today, gene maps are used as a starting point in the genome sequencing.

(2½ Marks)

13. The law of independent assortment that "when two pairs of traits are combined in a hybrid segregation of one pair of chardeters is independent of other pair of characters". This law was proposed by Mendel based on the results of dihybrid crosses, where inheritance of two traits were considered simultaneously. Independent assortment is not applicable for the genes located on the same chromosomes i.e. linked genes. The following cross between a pure-breeding plant with yellow, round seeds and another pure breeding plant with green, wrinkled seeds, can be taken as an example to explain this law.

(2½ Marks)

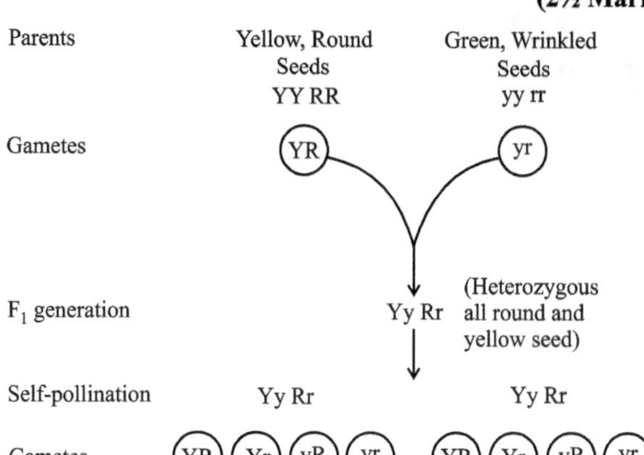

The Phenotypic ratio is : 9 : 3 : 3 : 1

9 round yellow : 3 round green : 3 wrinkled yellow : 1 wrinkled green

Wrinkled yellow and round green are recombinants.

Round yellow and wrinkled green are parental combinations.

The genotypic ratio is :

YY RR	:	YY Rr	:	Yy RR	:	Yy Rr	:	YY rr
1	:	2	:	2	:	4	:	1

Yy rr	:	yy RR	:	yy Rr	:	yy rr
2	:	1	:	2	:	1

In this cross, the factors for colour of seeds and those for shape of seeds have segregated independently and each gamete has one factor for each of these two traits.

(2½ Marks)

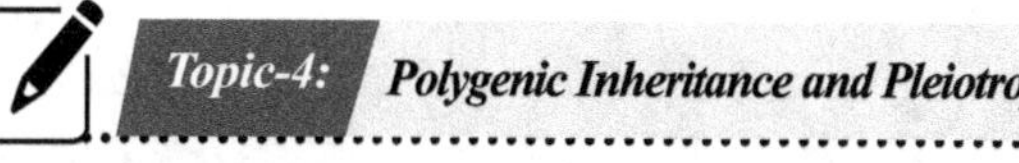

1. **(d)** Three genes A, B, and C control skin colour in humans with the dominant forms A, B and C responsible for dark skin colour and the recessive forms 'c' for light skin colour. Hence, The type of gametes produced by the parent with genotype AABBCc is 4. **(1 Mark)**

2. **(b)** 2 **(1 Mark)**

3. **(d)** Polygenic and quantitative inheritance **(1 Mark)**

4. **(a)** 0.32 **(1 Mark)**

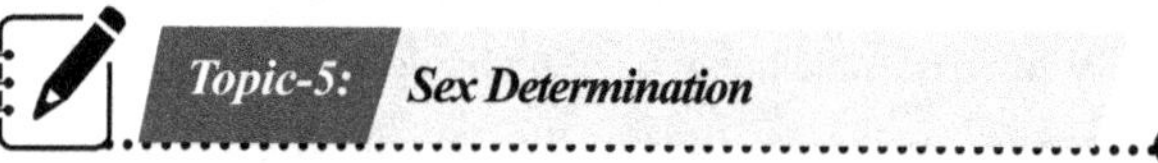

1. **(a)** Males produce two different types of gametes, (a) either with or without X chromosome or (b) some gametes with X-chromosome and some with Y-chromosome. Such types of sex determination mechanisms are designated to be an example of male heterogamety. e.g.- Human beings, *Drosophila*

(1 Mark)

2. **(b)** Male 16, Female 32 **(1 Mark)**

3. **(b)** 50% **(1 Mark)**

4. Male honeybees are formed by the process of parthenogenesis which involves development from unfertilized eggs. The unfertilised eggs carry only half number of chromosome such as 16 chromosomes (haploid). While female honeybees are developed from unfertilized eggs and has 32 chromosomes. **(1 Mark)**

5. In honeybees, the females are diploid and males are haploid as they have total 16 chromosomes.

The males are developed from unfertilized eggs and these eggs chromosome are multiply mitotically to produce more haploid cells. **(1 Mark)**

6.

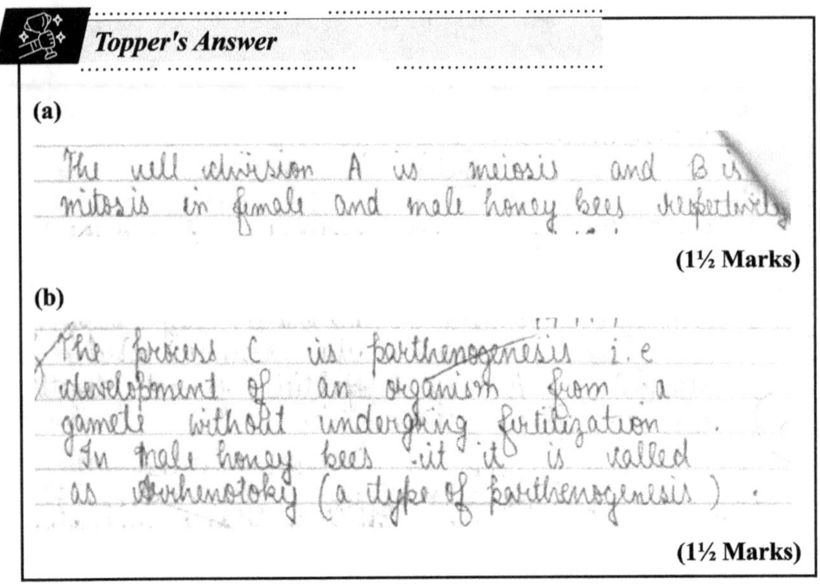

(a) 'A' Female honeybees are diploid so, the process of meiosis takes place for the gamete formation in female honeybees. While 'B' male honeybees are haploid so, mitosis takes place for the gamete formation in male honeybees. **(1½ Marks)**

(b) Honeybees are classified into three categories such as queen, drone and workers. So, the male honey bees are called drones. The male honey bees or drones are developed from the unfertilized female eggs and this phenomenon is called arrhenotoky. Arrhenotoky is a type of parthenogenesis in which unfertilized eggs are develop into males.

(1½ Marks)

7. In birds, sex determination is of ZW - ZZ type.

In this type the males are homogametic and have ZZ sex chromosomes, and females are heterogametic with ZW pair of sex chromosomes.

Parents :	Male	X	Female
	ZZ		ZW
Gametes:	(Z)(Z)		(Z)(W)
F₁:	ZW		ZZ
	Female		Male

whereas, in human beings, the chromosomal mechanism of sex determination is of XX - XY type. The human male is heterogametic and have XY sex chromosomes and human female is homogametic with XX sex chromosomes. **(2 Marks)**

8. The difference between male and female heterogamety are as follows:

Male heterogamety	Female heterogamety
(i) In male heterogamety, male produces two different types of gametes.	(i) In female heterogamety, female (human) produces two similar types of gametes or in case of insects, two types of gametes.
(ii) Gametes produced are XY and XO.	(ii) ZW is the only one type of heterogamete produced by female.
(iii) Examples: Grasshoppers, bugs	(iii) Example: Birds, reptiles, fishes.

(3 Makrs)

 **Note**

The term heterogamety refers to the sex of a species in which the chromosomes are not same.

9. (i) The type of sex determination mechanism shown in female XX with male XO is male heterogamety such as in Humans. **(1 × ½ Marks)**

(ii) The type of sex determination mechanism shown in female ZW with male ZZ is female heterogamety such as in Birds. **(1½ Marks)**

10. The sex of the child is determined by father as the type gametes child receives from the father. As, the father contains two types of chromosomes such as XY whereas the mothers contains only XX chromosomes. When X chromosome from father fuses with the X chromosome from mother then the child will be girl while if the Y chromosome from father fuses with X chromosome of mother then the child will be boy. So, the female or mother is not responsible for the sex determination of child. Women should not be ill-treated for giving birth to a girl child, as both males and females are equally important for the balance of nature and continuity of species. **(3 Marks)**

11. (a) The chromosome pattern in the human female is XX and that in the male is XY. So, all the haploid gametes produced by the female (ova) have the sex chromosome X while in the male gametes (sperms) the sex chromosome could be either X or Y. Hence, 50 % of the sperms carry the X chromosome whereas the other 50 % carry the Y. After the fusion of the male and female gametes the zygote carries either XX or XY depends on whether the sperm carrying X or Y chromosome fertilized the ovum.

Zygote carrying XX would develop into a female baby and XY would become male baby. It is concluded that the sex of a child is dependent on father not on mother. **(2 × ½ Marks)**

(b) The difference between male and female heterogamety are as follows:

Male heterogamety: Male heterogamety in human males is XY while males of insects such as grasshopper and bugs are XO.

Female heterogamety: Female heterogamety is observed in some species of birds, fishes and insects. Females of butterfly and moth consists of ZO sex chromosomes and females of fish, reptiles and birds consist of ZW sex chromosome.

(2½ Marks)

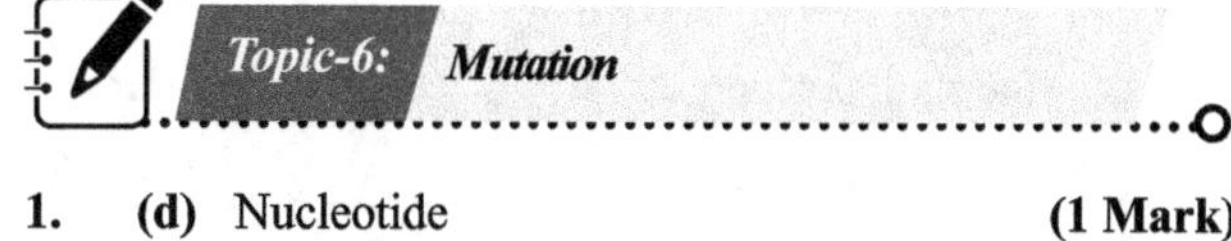

1. (d) Nucleotide **(1 Mark)**

1. (d) Klinefelter's Syndrome is a genetic disorder that is also caused due to the presence of an additional copy of the X chromosome resulting in a karyotype of 47, XXY. **(1 Mark)**

2. (b)

Parent	R r	×	R r
	(Mother)		(Father)

F1 generation

	R	r
R	RR	Rr
r	Rr	rr

Mother and father have autosomal dominant traits with Rr and Rr respectively. After crossing between these two traits, the son is born with this autosomal dominant trait RR whereas the daughter is born with the recessive trait rr. **(1 Mark)**

3. (d) Representative pedigree analysis is the example of Autosomal dominant trait Myotonic dystrophy. **(1 Mark)**

4. (b) α Thalassemia is controlled by a single gene HBB on chromosome 11 of each parent and occurs due to mutation of one or both the genes.

α Thalassemia, production of â globin chain is affected.

α Thalassemia is controlled by two closely linked genes HBA1 and HBA2 on chromosome 16 of each parent. **(1 Mark)**

5. (a) Turner's Syndrome is a disorder is caused due to the absence of one of the X chromosomes, i.e., 45 with X0, Such females are sterile as ovaries are rudimentary. **(1 Mark)**

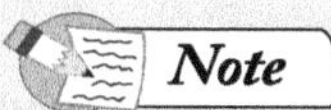

Symptoms of Turner syndrome include short stature, heart defects and certain learning disabilities.

6. **(d)** Glutamic acid is substituted by Valine in β chain at the sixth position   **(1 Mark)**

7. **(b)** Autosomal recessive   **(1 Mark)**

8. **(c)** Affected individual is a female with Down's syndrome   **(1 Mark)**

9. **(b)**

Rajesh	Mahesh
Thalassemia - an autosome linked recessive blood disorder	Sickle cell anaemia - an autosome linked recessive trait

     (1 Mark)

10. **(d)** aa   **(1 Mark)**

11. **(d)** In thalassemia, the formation of abnormal haemoglobin molecules resulting into anaemia which is characteristic of the disease. A thalassemia is controlled by two closely linked genes HBA1 and HBA2 on chromosome 16 of each parent and it is observed due to mutation or deletion of one or more of the four genes.   **(1 Mark)**

12. **(c)** The affected individual lacks an enzyme that converts the amino acid phenylalanine into tyrosine. As a result of this phenylalanine is accumulated and converted into phenylpyruvic acid and other derivatives. Accumulation of these in brain results in mental retardation.   **(1 Mark)**

Note

Untreated phenylketouria can lead to brain damage, intellectual disabilities, behavioural symptoms or seizures.

13. **(a)** CTT would become CAT which codes for valine. Thus, valine would replace glutamic acid at that point.   **(½ Mark)**

(b) Sickle cell anaemia, the mutant haemoglobin molecule undergoes polymerization leading to the change in the shape of the RBC from biconcave disc to elongated sickle like structure.   **(½ Mark)**

14. **(a)** 22 pairs of autosome + XO occurs in case of turner syndrome. The total number of chromosomes is 45 with XO. Females with turner syndrome are sterile as their ovaries are rudimentary. Such females also lack other secondary sexual characters.   **(½ Mark)**

(ii) 22 pairs of autosomes +21st chromosome+ XY occurs in Klinefelter's syndrome. It is a genetic disorder that is caused due to the presence of an additional copy X-chromosome results in 47 + XXY chromosome. Such males have overall masculine development but they have feminine development such as breast development. Such males are sterile.   **(½ Mark)**

15. **Stop codon:** There are 64 codons out of which 61 codons codes for 20 amino acids and three are stop codon that terminates the process of protein synthesis (translation). Stop codons are UAA, UGA and UAG.

Unambiguous codon: One codon codes only for one amino acid and hence is called unambiguous and specific.

Degenerate codon: The codon is read in mRNA in a contiguous fashion as there are no punctuations.

Universal codon: The code is nearly universal. For example: from bacteria to human UUU would code for phenylalanine (Phe) amino acid.   **(1 Mark)**

16. **(a)** Failure of segregation of chromatids during cell division cycle results in the gain or loss of a chromosome, called aneuploidy.   **(1 Mark)**

(b) If sister chromatids fail to separate during meiosis II, the result is one gamete that lacks that chromosome, two normal gametes with one copy of the chromosome, and one gamete with two copies of the chromosome.   **(1 Mark)**

(c) Klinefelter's Syndrome is genetic disorder is also caused due to the presence of an additional copy of X chromosome resulting into a karyotype of 47, XXY. Such an individual has overall masculine development, however, the feminine development (development of breast, i.e., Gynaecomastia) is also expressed. Such individuals are sterile.   **(1 Mark)**

OR

(c) Down's Syndrome is autosomal aneuploid abnormality causes due to genetic disorder. It is the presence of an additional copy of the chromosome number 21 (trisomy of 21). The symptoms shows in individual is short statured with small round head, furrowed tongue and partially open mouth Palm is broad with characteristic palm crease. Physical, psychomotor and mental development is retarded.   **(1 Mark)**

17.

Human males suffer from haemophillia more than human females because haemophillia is a sex linked recessive disease.

The genes which causes haemophilia are located on X sex chromosome and are recessive. As a male contains one X and one Y sex chromosome thus even only presence of one X^h (or infected gene carrying X chromosome) is enough to cause infection in man and does thus it affects the man/male.

Whereas for a female who carries XX chromosome as its sex chromosome has to carry $X^h X^h$ to be infected as for such a sufferer the mother would be the carrier and father should be a haemophilic (later unviable). Hence, the chances of female to be sufferer is very rare.

P - $\quad X^h X \qquad . \qquad X Y$

Gametes - Ⓧʰ Ⓧ $\quad$ X $\quad$ Ⓧ Ⓨ

F₁ generation — $X^h X$ / $X^h Y$ / $X Y$ / $X X$

1 Carrier Female + 1 infected male, 1 non infected male & 1 non infected female

Hence, the chances of a female to be a haemophilic is very rare and the chances of a man to be sufferer is quite high. This haemophilia is caused due to absence of the Anti haemophilic factor and christmas factor from the cascades of protein which cause clotting of blood.

These disease used to run in the family line of Queen Victoria as she was the carrier of it.

(3 Marks)

Hemophilia is a recessive X-linked genetic disorder. Hemophilia is more common among males than females because males only inherit one X-chromosome. Humans have 22 pairs of autosomal chromosomes and one pair of sex chromosome. There are 46 chromosomes in humans. Females have XX chromosome while males have X and Y chromosome. So, male offspring inherit X-chromosome from their mother and Y-chromosome from their father. Males only have one X-chromosome and if the X-chromosome and this is the reason that males are suffering from haemophilia as the X-chromosome carries mutation. While in females, as they have two X chromosomes, and this is a recessive disorder so females are carrier of this disease and can pass this disorder to male offsprings. **(3 Marks)**

> **Note**
>
> *Hemophilia is caused because of the absence of blood clotting factor VIII (Hemophilia-A) and IX (haemophilia-B).*

18. **(a)** The two girls are suffering from a genetic disorder resulting in adenosine deaminase (ADA) deficiency due to deletion of its gene that codes for adenosine deaminase enzyme **(1 Mark)**

(b) Girl A was treated by enzyme replacement therapy, in which functional ADA is given to the patient by injection. This technique is not completely curative as it requires repeated infusion. **(1 Mark)**

(c) Girl B was treated using gene therapy where the gene isolate from marrow cells producing ADA was introduced into cells at an early embryonic stage in order to provide permanent cure. **(1 Mark)**

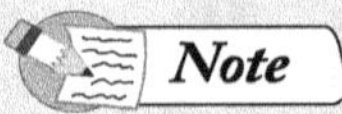

> **Note**
>
> *ADA deficiency is caused because of the deletion of the gene that codes for adenosine deaminase enzyme. Severe combined Immunodeficiency disorder (SCID) is caused because of the defect in gene which codes for adenosine deaminase enzyme.*

19.   **(3 + 2 = 5 Marks)**

Topper's Answer

a) Phenylketonuria (Disease) [Mendelian Disorder]
- Reduction in mental abilities development / Retardation
- Reduction in hair & skin pigmentation.

b) Klinefelter's Syndrome [Chromosomal Disorder]
- The male is sterile.
- Development of female feminine character (Development of Breasts → Gynaecomastia).

According to Mendalian genetics, inheritance pattern follows inheritance from two carrying parents. **(3 + 2 = 5 Marks)**

Phenylektonuria

This genetic disorder is autosomal recessive in nature.

It is an inborn error caused due to the decreased metabolism level of the amino acid phenyalanine.

In this disorder, the affected person does not have the enzyme that converts phenylalanine to tyrosine. As a result, phenylalanine acumulation takes place in the body and is converted into many derivaties which result in mental retardation.

Haemophilia

Haemophilia is a X-linked recessive disorder. Being a recessive disorder, it is expressed only in homozygous recessive conditions. Human males have one copy of the affected gene in males in each cell is sufficient to cause the disorder (X^cY). Hence, being X-linked recessive mutation, it is more frequent in males. Females carry two X-chromosomes and this females with two copies of the affected gene show the disorder (X^cX^c). Females heterozygous (X^cX) for this trait be normal but serve as a carrier of the disease. If it would have been a Y-linked disorder, It would have been expressed more in males because males carry one copy of Y-chromosome and can express both recessive and dominant Y-linked genes.

20. (3 Marks)

> **Topper's Answer**
>
> B) Thalassemia → Autosomal recessive trait
> → The parents should be heterozygous for the gene (carriers) for the offspring to be affected.
>
> Genotype : $A^T A^t$ ♀ × $A^T A^t$ ♂ (Parents)
>
> T → Dominant gene
> t → Recessive gene
> A → Autosomes
>
> Cause :– Mutation (OR) Deletion of one (OR) more genes responsible for production of globin chains that constitute haemoglobin molecules.
>
> This results in reduced synthesis of either α (OR) β globin chains.
>
> α Thalassemia → Mutation (OR) Deletion of HBA1 and HBA2 on chromosome 16 genes
> β Thalassemia → Mutation of HBB gene on chromosome 11.

This is a type of disorder in which the body makes an abnormal amount of haemoglobin. As a result, a large number of red blood cells are destroyed that leads to anaemia.

(3 Marks)

It is an autosomal recessive disease.

Facial bone deformities, abdominal swelling, dark urine are some of the symptoms of thalassemia.

21. Down's syndrome is a genetic disorder caused due to the presence of an additional copy of chromosome number 21 (trisomy of 21). The affected individual will have:

(i) short statured with small round head

(ii) furrowed tongue

(iii) partially open mouth

(iv) Simian crease is prominent in the middle of the palm and b road palm

(v) retarded physical, psychomotor and mental development

(vi) IQ is less than 25. (3 Marks)

> **Note**
>
> *Down's syndrome was first described by Langdon Down in 1866.*

22. **Sickle cell anaemia** is an example of autosomal recessive hereditary disorder. In this disorder, the erythrocytes become sickle shaped due to deficiency of oxygen. This disorder is caused due to the formation of abnormal haemoglobin-S. Genes for sickle cell erythrocytes is represented by **HbS** whereas normal genes are represented by **HbA**.

Representation of cross of sickle cell anaemia:

Parents	Carrier man		Carrier women
Gametes	Hb^A Hb^S	X	Hb^A Hb^S
	(Hb^A) (Hb^S)		(Hb^A) (Hb^S)
Offspring	$Hb^A Hb^A$ $Hb^A Hb^S$	$Hb^A Hb^S$	Hb^S Hb^S
ratio	1 : 2 : 1		

(3 Marks)

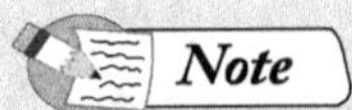

In case of sickle cell anaemia, abnormal haemoglobin HbS is differ from normal haemoglobin HbA only by one amino acid at 6th amino acid of beta-globin chain of haemoglobin. The glutamic acid is replaced by valine due to substitution mutation of Thymine (T) by Adenine (A) at the second position of triplet codon such as CTC into CAC. The substitution mutation occurs at 11th chromosome. Codon CTC is transcribed into GAG that codes for amino acid glutamic acid. Whereas CAC is transcribed into GUG that codes amino acid valine.

23. Pedigree analysis is done to study the human genetics because it provides all essential information that can be utilised to trace the inheritance of a specific trait such as abnormality or disease. Several disorders are inheritable and depend on the genetics of the families. They inherit the genes from such families. So pedigree analysis is done to trace such inheritance patterns.

The conclusions that can be drawn from the pedigree analysis are:

- The pattern of inheritance and tracing of Mendelian disorders.
- The trait in question is dominant or recessive.
- The trait is linked to the sex chromosomes or autosomes. **(3 Marks)**

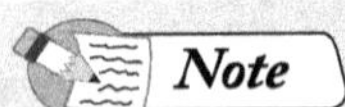

In the pedigree analysis the inheritance of a specific terait is represented in the family tree over generations.

24.

S. No	Syndrome	Cause	Characteristics of affected individuals		Sex Male/ Female/ Both
1.	Down's	Trisomy of 21	(i)	The affected individual is short statured with small round head.	Commonly occurs in males.
			(ii)	They have furrowed tongue and partially open mouth.	
2.	Klinefelter's syndrome	XXY	**Overall masculine development**		This disorder occurs in males.
3.	Turner's	45 with XO	(i)	Such females are sterile as there ovaries are rudimentary	Commonly occurs in females.
			(ii)	They also lacks secondary sexual characters.	

(3 Marks)

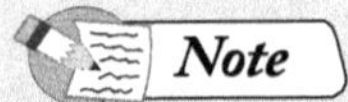

The chromosomal disorders are caused due to absence or excessive or abnormal arrangement of one or more chromosomes.

25. Colour blindness is a sex-linked disease. The gene for this disorder is present is on X chromosome. As males have only one X chromosome while females have two X chromosomes. If a colour blind child is born from a normal couple then in this case, the mother will be carrier for colour blindness and colour blind child will be male.

Diagrammatic Representation Cross of Colour blindness:

Parents	$X^C X$ (Mother)	X	XY (Father)
Gametes	X^C X	X	X Y
F_1 generation	X^C X	X^C Y	XX XY
Results	Carrier female	Colour blind male	Normal child (male and female

(3 Marks)

26. Haemophilia is a sex linked recessive disorder which is transmitted from unaffected carrier female to male progeny. This disorder is more common among males than females. Humans have 22 pairs of autosomal chromosomes and one pair of sex chromosome. There are 46 chromosomes in humans. Females have XX chromosome while males have X and Y chromosome. So, male offspring inherit X-chromosome from their mother and Y-chromosome from their father. Males only have one X-chromosome if the X-chromosome carries mutation and this is the case of reason that males are suffering from haemophilia, While in females, as they have two X chromosomes, and this is a recessive disorder so females are only the carrier of this disease and can pass this disorder to male offsprings. Genetic cross for haemophilia:

Parents: XX^h **(female)**   X X^hY **(male)**

Gamtes: X X^h X^h Y

F_1 generation: X X^h XY $X^h X^h$ X^hY

            (Carrier (normal   **(haemophilic**

(haemophilic

           female)   male)   female)   male)

Hemophilia is caused because of the absence of blood clotting factor VIII (Hemophilia-A) and IX (haemophilia B) and impairs the ability of the body to control blood clotting and coagulation even by a simple cut.**(3 Marks)**

27. (a) Thalassaemia and haemophilia are categorised as Mendelian disorders because they occur by mutation in a single gene.Their mode of inheritance follows the principles of Mendelian genetics. Mendelian disorders can be autosomal dominant (muscular dystrophy) autosomal recessive (thalassaemia), sex linked (haemophilia)

Symptoms of Thalassaemia:

Thalassaemia minor results only in mild anaemia, characterised by low haemoglobin level.

Thalassaemia major is also known as Cooley's anaemia. In this disease, affected infants are normal but as they reach 6 to 9 months of age, they develop severe anaemia, skeletal deformities, jaundice, fatigue, etc.

Symptoms of Hemophilia:

Person suffering from this disease does not develop a proper blood clotting mechanism.

A haemophilic patient suffers from non-stop bleeding even on a simple cut, which may lead to death.

Pattern of Inheritance of Thalassaemia:

Pair of alleles Hb^A and Hb^T controls the expression of this disease.

Conditions for thalassemia :

Hb^A and Hb^A : Normal

Hb^A and Hb^T : Carrier

Hb^T and Hb^T : Diseased

Let us assume that both father and mother are the carriers (Hb^AHb^T) of beta thalassaemia.

Parents	Hb^AHb^T		Hb^AHb^T	
	(Father)	×	(Mother)	
Offsprings	Hb^AHb^A	Hb^AHb^T	Hb^AHb^T	Hb^THb^T
	Normal	Carrierchild	Carrierchild	Child with

Pattern of Inheritance of Haemophilia:

Haemophilia is an X-linked genetic disorder. Compared to females, males have higher chances of getting affected because females have two XX chromosomes while males have only one X and Y chromosome. Thus, for a female to get affected by one haemophilia, she have the mutant allele on both the X chromosomes while males can be affected if they carry it on the single X chromosome.

Conditions for haemophilia:

XY; XX: Normal

X^hY:

HaemophilicX^hX:

Carrier

X^hX^h :Haemophilic

Let us assume that a carrier female (X^hX) is married to a normal male.

Parents		XY	X^hX	
		(Male)	×	(Female)
	X^hX	XX	X^hX	XX
Offsprings	Carrier	Normal	Haemophilic	Normal
Figenuation	female	female	male	male

(2 × ½ Marks)

> *Note*
>
> *Hemophilia is caused because of the absence of blood clotting factor VIII (Hemophilia-A) and IX (hemophilia-B)*

(b) When a normal male marries a carrier female (she is considered normal as she contains the mutant gene on one of her X chromosomes), they can produce a haemophilic son. So, the genotype of the parents would be XY and X^hX.

Parents		XY	×	X^hX	
		(Male)		(Female)	
	X^hX	XX	X^hY	XY	
Offsprings	Carrier	Normal	Haemophilic	Normal	
	daughter	daughter	son	son	

(2 × ½ Marks)

28. (a) Thalassemia is an autosomal recessive disorder. It is caused due to the mutation or deletion of gene that controls the formation of globin chain of haemoglobin. This results in anaemia. **(1 Mark)**

(b) Thalassemia is an autosomal recessive disorder as in this disorder the mutation is carried on one of the autosomes, so the carrier can be any one of the two parents and has an equal probability for coming from both mother and father. So, to just blame the mother for the child's abnormality is unjustified.

(2 Marks)

(c) The following values can be given to the families such as:

- provide a healthy diet to the children
- accepting their child with all the positives and negatives
- neither of the parents are responsible for giving birth to a sick child
- the defect is caused because of a random change in the genes of the child
- provide emotional support to child to overcome his/her anxiety, depression and fear about the disorder. **(2 Marks)**

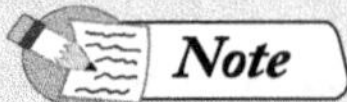

Thalassemia is a type of Mendelian disorder.

29. (a) X- linked, Recessive trait **(2 Mark)**

   (b) 100% **(½ × 1 Mark)**

   (c) XY OR XY, 2. X X, 3. XY, 4. XX **(½ × 1 Mark)**

OR

The possibility of the female getting the trait is less.

(½ × 1 Mark)

The female will get the trait only if the mother is at least a carrier and the father is affected. **(½ × 1 Mark)**

5 | Molecular Basis of Inheritance

Chapter

Topic-1: *The DNA*

---

1 **Multiple Choice Questions (1 Mark)**

1. A short piece of DNA, having 20 base pairs, was analyzed to find the number of nucleotide bases in each of the polynucleotide strands. Some of the results are shown in the table. **[CBSE Sample Paper 2023-24, Ap]**

	Number of nucleotide bases			
	Adenine	Cytosine	Guanine	Thymine
Strand 1	4	4		
Strand 2		5		

How many nucleotides containing Adenine were present in strand 2?

(a) 2   (b) 4   (c) 5   (d) 7

2. In a certain species of insects, some have 13 chromosomes, and the others have 14 chromosomes. The 13 and 14 chromosome bearing organisms are

[CBSE Sample Paper 2023-24, Ap]

(a) males and females, respectively

(b) females and males, respectively

(c) all males

(d) all females

3. The correct feature of Double-helical structure of DNA as given by Waston and Crick is :

[All India 2022, Term-I, U]

(a) Right-handed helix, pitch is 3.4 nm

(b) Left-handed helix, pitch is 3.8 nm

(c) Right-handed helix, pitch is 3.8 nm

(d) Left-handed helix, pitch is 3.4 nm

4. Histone proteins that help in forming the nucleosomes in the nucleus are rich in basic amino acids such as :

[All India 2022, Term-I, K]

(a) Arginine and tyrosine

(b) Lysine and histidine

(c) Arginine and lysine

(d) Histidine and tryptophan

5. A DNA molecule is 160 base pairs long. If it has 20% adenine, how many cytosine bases are present in this DNA molecule ? **[All India 2022, Term-I, Ap]**

(a) 48   (b) 64   (c) 96   (d) 192

6. Which of the following amino acid residues will constitute the histone core?

[CBSE Sample Paper 2022-23, K]

(a) Lysine and Arginine

(b) Asparagine and Arginine

(c) Glutamine and Lysine

(d) Asparagine and Glutamine

7. Total number of nucleotide sequences of DNA that codes for a hormone is 1530. The proportion of different bases in the sequence is found to be Adenine=34%, Guanine=19%, Cytosine = 23%, Thymine = 19%.

[CBSE Sample Paper 2021-22, Ap]

Applying Chargaff's rule, what conclusion can be drawn?

(a) It is a double stranded circular DNA.

(b) It is a single stranded DNA.

(c) It is a double stranded linear DNA.

(d) It is a single stranded DNA coiled on Histones.

8. A stretch of an euchromatin has 200 nucleosomes. How many bp will there be in the stretch and what would be the length of the typical euchromatin?

[CBSE Sample Paper 2021-22, Ap]

(a) $20,000$ bp and $13,000 - 10^{-9}$ m

(b) $10,000$ bp and $10,000 - 10^{-9}$ m

(c) $40,000$ bp and $13,600 \times 10^{-9}$ m

(d) $40,000$ bp and $13,900 \times 10^{-9}$ m

9. Observe structures A and B given below. Which of the following statements are correct?

[CBSE Sample Paper 2021-22, Ap]

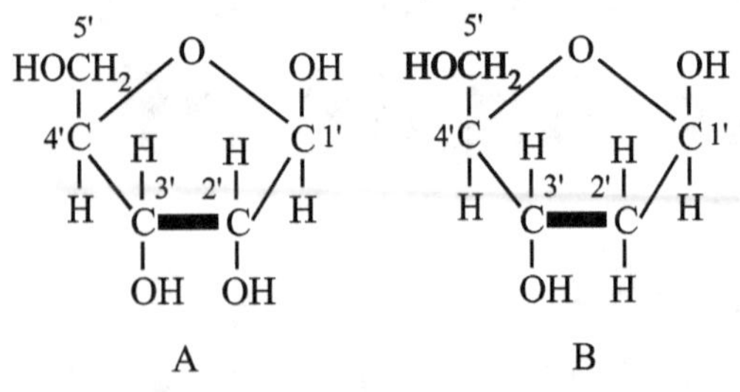

A   B

(a) A is having 2'-OH group which makes it less reactive and structurally stable, whereas B is having 2'-H group which makes it more reactive and unstable.

(b) A is having 2'-OH group which makes it more reactive and structurally unstable, whereas B is having 2'-H group which makes it less reactive and structurally stable.

(c) A and B both have -OH groups which make it more reactive and structurally stable.

(d) A and B both are having -OH groups which make it less reactive and structurally stable

 **4**   *Very Short Answer Questions (1 Mark)*

10. Write the dual purpose served by Deoxyribonucleoside triphosphates in polymerisation. **[All India 2018, K]**

5   *Short Answer Questions (2 or 3 Marks)*

11. Although a prokaryotic cell has no defined nucleus, yet DNA is not scattered throughout the cell. Explain.
[All India 2018, U]

12. Describe the structure of a nucleosome.

13. (a) A DNA segment has a total of 1000 nucleotides, out of which 240 of them are adenine containing nucleotides. How many pyrimidine bases this DNA segment possesses ? **[Delhi 2015, Ap]**

(b) Draw a diagrammatic sketch of a portion of DNA segment to support your answer. **[Delhi 2015, Ap]**

6   *Long Answer Questions (5 Marks)*

14. (a) Write the features that a biomolecule must fulfill to be able to act as a genetic material. **[All India 2020, K]**

(b) DNA and RNA are both genetic materials. Which one of the two is more stable and why?
[All India 2020, K]

15. (a) State the 'Central dogma' as proposed by Francis Crick. Are there any exceptions to it ? Support your answer with a reason and an example.
[All India 2018, K]

(b) Explain how the biochemical characterization (nature) of "Transforming Principle' was determined, which was not defined from Griffith's experiments.

16. (a) How are the following formed and involved in DNA packaging in a nucleus of a cell ? **[Delhi 2016, U]**

(i) Histone octomer

(ii) Nucleosome

(iii) Chromatin

(b) Differentiate between Euchromatin and Heterochromatin. **[Delhi 2016, U]**

17. (a) Explain the process of DNA replication with the help of a schematic diagram. **[Delhi 2014, U]**

(b) In which phase of the cell cycle does replication occur in Eukaryotes ? What would happen if cell-division is not followed after DNA replication ?
[Delhi 2014, U]

 **Topic-2:**   *The Search for Genetic Material*

1   *Multiple Choice Questions (1 Mark)*

1. Identify the element used by Hershey and Chase to label the protein in their experiment, from the following options: **[All India 2023, Set-I, K]**

(a) P^{32} (b) S^{32} (c) S^{35} (d) P^{35}

6   *Long Answer Questions (5 Marks)*

2. (a) Describe the various steps of Griffith's experiment that led to the conclusion of the 'Transforming Principle'. **[All India 2014, U]**

(b) How did the chemical nature of the 'Transforming Principle' get established?

3. (a) Write the conclusion drawn by Griffith at the end of his experiment with *Streptococcus pneumoniae*.

(b) How did O. Avery, C MacLeod and M. McCarty prove that DNA was the genetic material? Explain.
[All India 2013, U, Delhi 2013, U]

Topic-3: *RNA World*

[1] Multiple Choice Questions (1 Mark)

1. The reactive hydroxyl group in the nucleotide of RNA is:
   [All India 2022, Term-I]
   (a) $5'$ OH   (b) $4'$ OH
   (c) $3'$ OH   (d) $2'$ OH

[5] Short Answer Questions (2 or 3 Marks)

2. (a) (i) How many types of RNA polymerases are there in a eukaryote cell? Mention which one of them transcribes hnRNA.
   [All India 2023 Set-I, U]

   (ii) Write the changes that hnRNA undergoes before it leaves the nucleus as mRNA.
   [All India 2023 Set-I, U]

   OR

   (b) The length of DNA in any cell is far greater than the dimension of its nucleus. Explain how this enormous DNA is packaged in a eukaryotic cell.

3. Describe the structure of a RNA polynucleotide chain having four different types of nucleotides.
   [Delhi 2013, U]

[6] Long Answer Questions (5 Marks)

4. How did Hershey and Chase established that DNA is transferred from virus to bacteria ?   **[Delhi 2015, K]**

Topic-4: *Replication — The Experimental Proof*

[1] Multiple Choice Questions (1 Mark)

1. If *E.* coli were allowed to grow in the culture medium for 80 minutes by Matthew Meselson and Franklin Stahe in their experiments, the proportion of light and hybrid density DNA molecule would have been :
   [All India 2022, Term-I, U]
   (a) 87.5% of light density DNA and 12.5% of hybrid density DNA
   (b) 75.0% of light density DNA and 25% of hybrid density DNA.
   (c) 50% of light density DNA and 50% of hybrid density DNA.
   (d) 12.5% of light density DNA and 87.5% of hybrid density DNA.

2. If Meselson and Stahl's experiment is continued for sixth generations in bacteria, the ratio of Heavy strands 15N/15N :Hybrid15N/14N : light 14N/14N containing DNA in the sixth generation would be
   [CBSE Sample Paper, 2021-22, U]
   (a) 1:1:1   (b) 0:1:7   (c) 0:1:15   (d) 0:1:31

[6] Long Answer Questions (5 Marks)

3. Hershey and Chase carried out their experiment under three steps: **[Delhi 2019, U]**
   (a) Infection, (b) Blending, and (c) Centrifugation. Explain each one of these steps that helped them to prove that DNA is the hereditary material.

4. Describe Meselson and Stahl's experiment that was carried in 1958 on E. Coli. Write the conclusion they arrived after the experiment.   **[All India 2016, U]**

Topic-5: *Replication — The Machinery and the Enzymes*

[1] Multiple Choice Questions (1 Mark)

1. Taylor and colleagues performed experiments on _________ using radioactive _________ to prove that the DNA is chromosomes replicate semi-conservastively. (Select the correct option for the blanks)
   (a) *Vicia faba*, Uridine   **[All India 2022, Term-I, U]**
   (b) *E. coli*, Uridine
   (c) *Vicia faba*, Thymidine
   (d) *E. coli*, Thymidine

2. Which one of the following diagram correctly represents DNA replication in eukaryotes ?
   [All India 2022, Term-I, U]

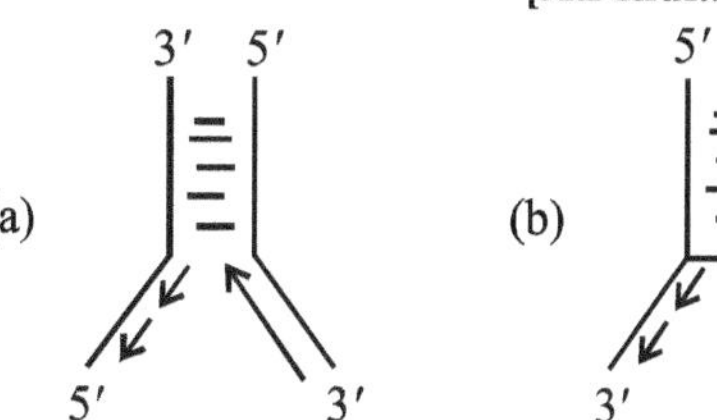

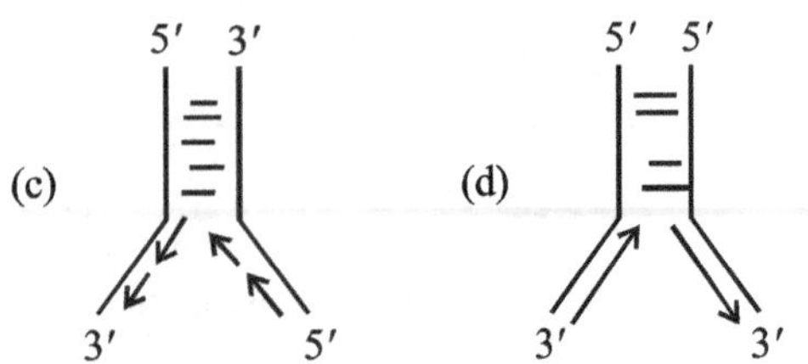

3. Origin of replication of DNA in E. coli is shown below, Identify the labelled parts (i), (ii), (iii) and (iv)

[CBSE Paper, 2021-22, K]

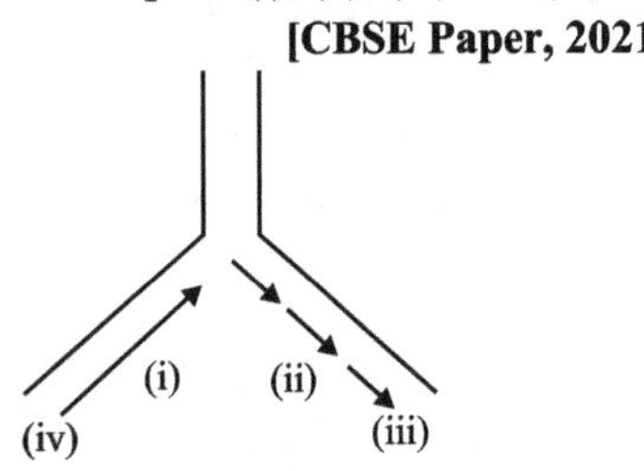

(a) (i)- discontinuous synthesis , (ii)- continuous synthesis (iii) 3' end (iv) 5'end

(b) (i)- continuous synthesis , (ii)- discontinuous synthesis (iii) 5' end (iv) 3'end

(c) (i)- discontinuous synthesis, (ii)- continuous synthesis (iii) 5' end (iv) 3'end

(d) (i)- continuous synthesis , (ii)- discontinuous synthesis (iii) 3' end (iv) 5'end

 **4** *Very Short Answer Questions (1 Mark)*

4. Name the enzyme and state its property that is responsible for continuous and discontinuous replication of the two strands of a DNA molecule.

[Delhi CBSE Board 2013, K]

 **5** *Short Answer Questions (2 or 3 Marks)*

5. Explain the mechanism of DNA replication with the help of a replication fork. What role does the enzyme DNA-ligase play in a DNA replication fork? **[All India 2019, K]**

OR

Construct and label a transcription unit from which the RNA segment given below has been transcribed. Write the complete name of the enzyme that transcribed this RNA. **[All India 2019, Ap]**

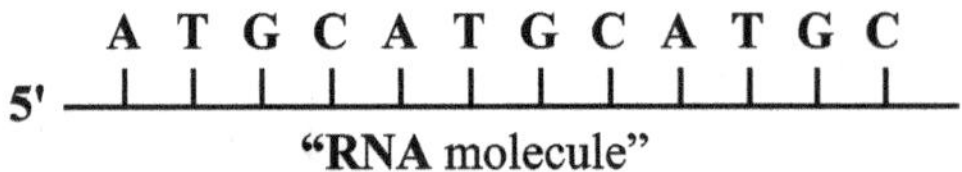

6. (a) Why does DNA replication occur within a replication fork and not in its entire length simultaneously?

[Delhi 2019, U]

(b) "DNA replication is continuous and discontinuous on the two strands within the replication fork." Give reasons. **[Delhi 2019, U]**

7. Discuss the role the enzyme DNA ligase plays during DNA replication. **[Delhi 2016, U]**

8. Describe the experiment that helped demonstrate the semi-conservative mode of DNA replication.

[Delhi 2016, U]

Topic-6: *Transcription*

 **1** *Multiple Choice Questions (1 Mark)*

1. A diagrammatic illustration of the process of transcription by RNA polymerase-II in eukaryote is given below. Choose the most appropriate statement with respect to the fate of the precursor of mRNA transcribed that will be: **[All India 2022, Term-I, U]**

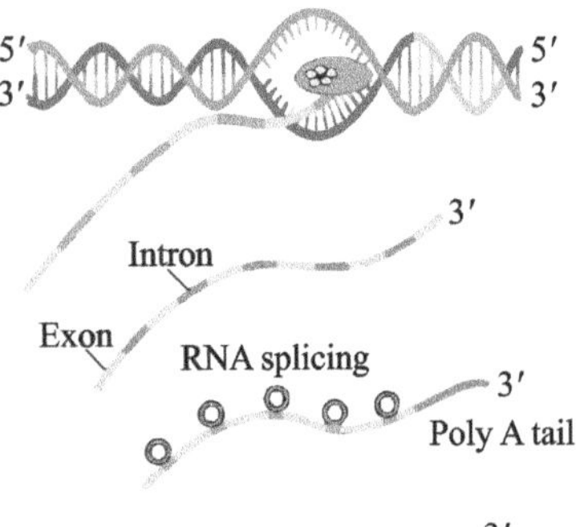

(a) Translation will take place once the precursor of mRNA leaves the nucleus.

(b) Translation on mRNA will not take place once the precursor of mRNA leaves the nucleus.

(c) Translation will take place in the nucleus.

(d) The precursor of mRNA has to be processed further in next step before being translated.

2. A template strand in a bacterial DNA has the given base sequence: :5' – AGGTTTAACG – 3'

[All India 2022, Term-I, Ap]

What would be the RNA sequence transcribed from this template strand ?

(a) 5' – CGUUAAACCU – 3'

(b) 5' – AGGUUUUUCG – 3'

(c) 5' – TCCAAATTGC – 3'

(d) 5' – AGGTTTAACG – 3'

3. The promoter site and the terminator site for transcription are located at

[CBSE Sample Paper 2021-22, ]

(a) 3' (downstream) end and 5 Œ (upstream) end, respectively of the transcription unit

(b) 5' (upstream) end and 3 Œ (downstream) end, respectively of the transcription unit

(c) the 5' (upstream) end of the transcription unit

(d) the 3' (downstream) end of the transcription unit

4. In a bacterium when RNA-polymerase binds to the promoter on a transcription unit during transcription, it

(a) terminates the process **[Delhi 2020, K]**

(b) helps remove introns

(c) initiates the process

(d) inactivates the exons

4 *Very Short Answer Questions (1 Mark)*

5. In a bacterium when RNA-polymerase binds to the promoter on a transcription unit during transcription, it

(a) terminates the process **[Delhi 2020, K]**

(b) helps remove introns

(c) initiates the process

(d) inactivates the exons

6. Given below is one of the strands of a DNA segment:

[All India 2020, U]

$$3' \xrightarrow{TACGTACGTACGTACG} G'$$

(a) Write its complementary strand.

(b) Write a possible RNA strand that can be transcribed form the above DNA molecule formed.

7. What do 'X' and 'Y' represent in the transcription unit of the DNA molecule shown? **[Delhi 2019, U]**

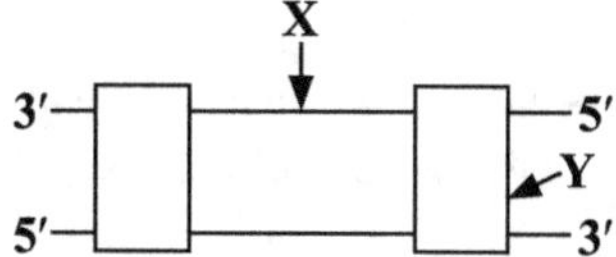

8. What is a cistron? **[All India 2015, K]**

9. Name the transcriptionally active region of chromatin in a nucleus. **[Delhi 2015, K]**

6 *Long Answer Questions (5 Marks)*

10. (a) Describe the process of transcription in bacteria.

[All India 2016, U]

(b) Explain the processing the hnRNA needs to undergo before becoming functional mRNA eukaryotes.

[All India 2016, U]

 **Topic-7:** *Genetic Code*

1 *Multiple Choice Questions (1 Mark)*

1. Given below is a sequence of bases in mRNA of a bacterial cell. Identify the amino acid that would be incorporated at codon position 3 and codon position 5 during the process of its translation.

[Delhi 2023 Set-I, Ap]

2. A codon is a 'triplet of bases' was suggested by :

(a) Marshall Nirenberg **[All India 2022, Term-I, U]**

(b) Har Gobind Khorana

(c) Georgee Gamow

(d) Francis Crick

3. Identify the correct pair of codon with its corresponding pair of amino acid : **[All India 2022, Term-I, U]**

(a) UAA : Leucine

(b) UGA : Serine

(c) AUG : Histidine

(d) UUU : Phenylalanine

4. A region of coding strand of DNA has the following nucleotide sequence : **[All India 2022, Term-I, K]**

5' – TACGCCG – 3'

The sequence of bases on mRNA transcribed by this would be :

(a) 5' – UACGCCG – 3'

(b) 3' – UACGCCG – 3'

(c) 5' – ATGCGGC – 3'

(d) 3' – ATGCGGC – 3'

5   *Short Answer Questions (2 or 3 Marks)*

5. CTTAAG

GAATTC   **[CBSE Sample Paper 2022-23, Ap]**

(a) What are such sequences called? Name the enzyme used that recognizes such nucleotide sequences.

(b) What is their significance in biotechnology?

6. Differentiate between the genetic codes given below :

[Delhi 2017, U]

(a) Unambiguous and Universal

(b) Degenerate and Initiator

Topic-8: **Translation**

1   *Multiple Choice Questions (1 Mark)*

1. Charging of tRNA during translation is necessary for :

[All India 2022, Term-I, U]

(a) Binding of anticodons of tRNA to the respective codons of mRNA

(b) Peptide bond formation between two amino acids

(c) Movement of ribosomes from codon to codon

(d) Binding of ribosomes to the mRNA

2. In the given figure of translation machinery of eukaryotes, select the correct labellings for (i), (ii), (iii) and (iv) :

[All India 2022, Term-I, A]

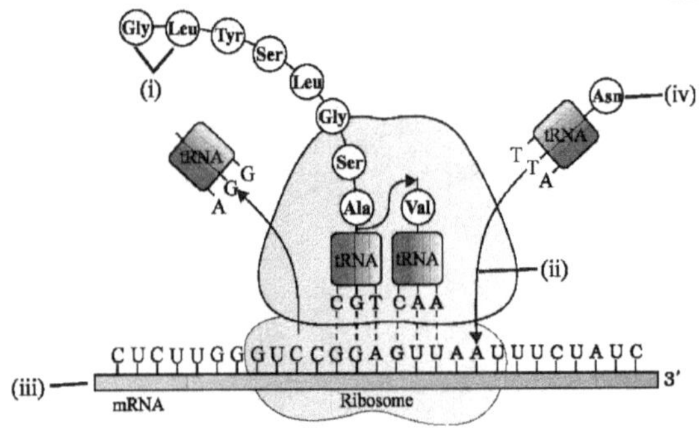

(a) (i) Codon, (ii) Anticodon, (iii) tRNA, (iv) 3' end of mRNA

(b) (i) Anticodon, (ii) Codon, (iii) 3' end of mRNA, (iv) 5' end of mRNA

(c) (i) Polypeptide chain, (ii) Large subunit of ribosome, (iii) 5' end of mRNA, (iv) tRNA.

(d) (i) Ribozyme, (ii) Polypeptide chain, (iii) tRNA, (iv) 5' end of tRNA.

3. Which of the following is correct about mature RNA in eukaryotes?

7. (i) Name the scientist who suggested that the genetic code should be made of a combination of three nucleotides. **[Delhi 2014, U]**

(ii) Explain the basis on which he arrived at this conclusion. **[Delhi 2014, U]**

6   *Long Answer Questions (5 Marks)*

8. (a) Write the contributions of the following scientists in deciphering the genetic code. George Gamow ; Hargobind Khorana ; Marshall Nirenberg ; Severo Ochoa **[All India 2019, U]**

(b) State the importance of a Genetic code in protein biosynthesis. **[All India 2019, U]**

(a) Exons and introns do not appear in the mature RNA.

(b) Exons appear, but introns do not appear in the mature RNA.

(c) Introns appear, but exons do not appear in the mature RNA.

(d) Both exons and introns appear in the mature RNA.

[CBSE Paper 2021-22, K]

4. Two important RNA processing events lead to specialized end sequences in most human mRNAs: ____ (i)____ at the 5' end, and ____(ii)____ at the 3' end. At the 5' end the most distinctive specialized end nucleotide, ____(iii)____ is added and a sequence of about 200 (iv) is added to the 3' end.

(a) (i) Initiator codon (ii) Promotor (iii) Terminator codon (iv) Release factors

(b) (i) Promotor (ii) Elongation (iii) Regulation (iv) Termination.

(c) (i) Capping (ii) Polyadenylation (iii) mGppp (iv) Poly(A).

(d) (i) Repressor (ii) Co repressor (iii) Operon (iv) sRelease factors

[CBSE Sample Paper 2021-22, U]

5. Transcription unit is represented in the diagram given below.

Identify site (i), factor (ii) and Enzyme (iii) responsible for carrying out the process.

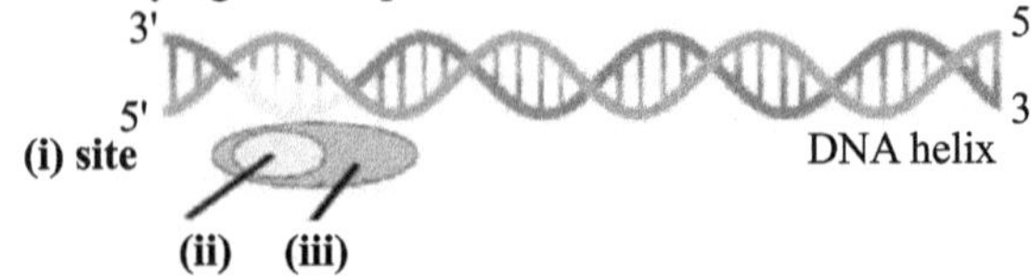

(a) (i) Promoter Site, (ii) Rho factor (iii) RNA polymerase

(b) (i) Terminator Site, (ii) Sigma factor (iii) RNA polymerase

(c) (i) Promoter Site, (ii) Sigma factor (iii) RNA polymerase

(d) (i) Promoter Site, (ii) Sigma factor (iii) DNA polymerase

[CBSE Sample Paper 2021-22, U]

6.

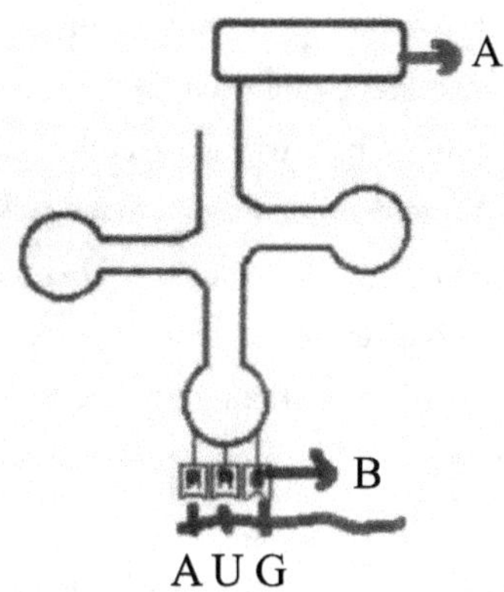

A U G

AUG on the mRNA will result in the activation of which of the following RNA having correct combination of amino acids:

	Site A	Site B
(a)	UAC	Methionine
(b)	Methionine	UAC
(c)	Methionine	AUG
(d)	AUG	Methionine

[CBSE Sample Paper 2021-22, Ap]

7. Which cellular process is shown below?

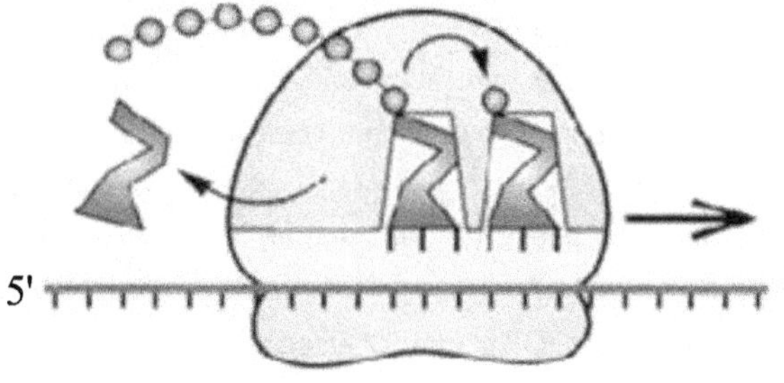

(a) DNA Replication

(b) Translation - Initiation

(c) Translation - Elongation

(d) Translation – Termination

[CBSE Sample Paper 2021-22, K]

 **5** *Short Answer Questions (2 or 3 Marks)*

8. (a) Identify the polarity of x to x' in the diagram below and mention how many more amino acids are expected to be added to this polypeptide chain.

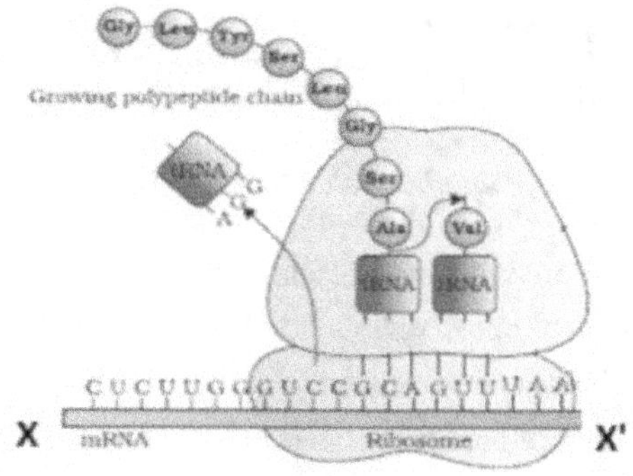

(b) Mention the codon and anticodon for alanine.

(c) Why are some untranslated sequences of bases seen in mRNA coding for a polypeptide? Where exactly are they present on mRNA?

[CBSE Sample Paper 2022-23, U]

9. Why the process of transcription & translation are coupled in prokaryotes but not in eukayotes?

[Delhi 2019, K]

6 *Long Answer Questions (5 Marks)*

10. Protein synthesis requires the services of all three types of RNAs, namely t-RNA, m-RNA and r-RNA. Explain the role of each of them during the process of protein synthesis in prokaryotes.

[All India 2023 Set-I, U]

11. (a) Describe the structure and function of a t-RNA molecule. Why is it referred to as an adapter molecule? **[Delhi 2017, K]**

(b) Explain the process of splicing of hn-RNA in a eukaryotic cell. **[Delhi 2017, K]**

12. How do m-RNA, t-RNA and ribosomes help in the process of translation? **[All India 2015, Ap]**

13. Observe the segment of mRNA given below.

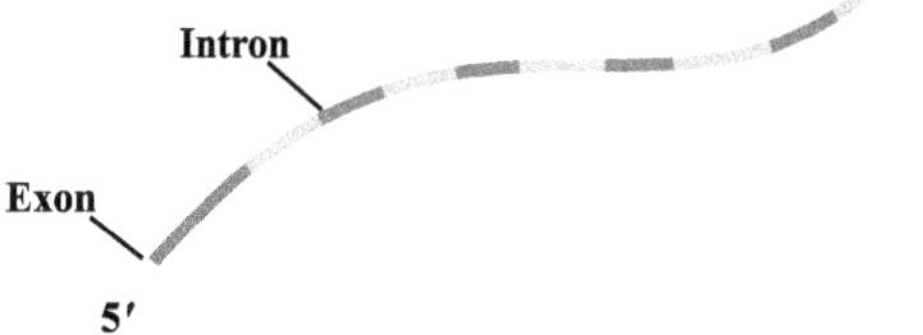

[CBSE Sample Paper 2022-23, U]

(a) Explain and illustrate the steps involved to make fully processed hnRNA?

(b) Gene encoding RNA Polymerase I and III have been affected by mutation in a cell. Explain its impact on the synthesis of polypeptide, stating reasons.

Topic-9: *Regulation of gene expression*

1 *Multiple Choice Questions (1 Mark)*

| p | i | p | o | z | y | a |

1. In the presence of allolactose, the lac repressor in the operon of *E. coli* :   **[All India 2022, Term-I, K]**
   (a) binds to the operator
   (b) cannot bind to the operator
   (c) binds to the promoter
   (d) binds to the regulator.

2. In *E.coli*, the lac operon gets switched on when   **[CBSE Sample Paper 2021-22, U]**
   (a) lactose is present and it binds to the repressor.
   (b) repressor binds to operator.
   (c) RNA polymerase binds to the operator.
   (d) lactose is present and it binds to RNA polymerase.

6 *Long Answer Questions (5 Marks)*

3. Study the schematic representation of the genes involved in the lac operon given below and answer the questions that follow: **[CBSE Sample Paper 2022-23, U]**

   (a) The active site of enzyme permease present in the cell membrane of a bacterium has been blocked by an inhibitor, how will it affect the lac operon?
   (b) The protein produced by the i gene has become abnormal due to unknown reasons. Explain its impact on lactose metabolism stating the reason.
   (c) If the nutrient medium for the bacteria contains only galactose; will operon be expressed? Justify your answer.

4. Write the different components of a lac-operon in *E.coli*. Explain its expression while in an 'open' state.   **[Delhi 2017, K]**

5. Explain the role of lactose as an inducer in a lac operon.   **[Delhi 2016, U]**

6. Describe how the lac operates, both in the presence and absence of an inducer in *E.coli*.   **[All India 2014, U]**

Topic-10: *Human Genome Project*

1 *Multiple Choice Questions (1 Mark)*

1. Select the important goals of HGP from the given options: **[All India 2022, Term-I]**
   (i) Store the information for data analysis
   (ii) Cloning and amplification of human DNA
   (iii) Identify all the genes present in human DNA
   (iv) Use of DNA information to trace human history
   (a) (i) and (ii)
   (b) (ii) and (iii)
   (c) (i) and (iii)
   (d) (ii) and (iv)

5 *Short Answer Questions (2 or 3 Marks)*

2. Human Genome Project (HGP) was a mega project launched in the year 1990 with some important goals.   **[Delhi 2023 Set-I, K]**
   (a) Enlist any four prime goals of HGP.
   (b) Name any one common non-human animal model organism which has also been sequenced thereafter.

3. (a) List the two methodologies which were involved in human genome project. Mention how they were used.   **[Delhi 2017, U]**
   (b) Expand 'YAC' and mention what was it used for.   **[Delhi 2017, U]**

4. (a) What do 'Y' and 'B' stand for in 'YAC' and 'BAC' used in Human Genome Project (HGP). Mention their role in the project.   **[All India 2016, U]**
   (b) Write the percentage of the total human genome that codes for proteins and the percentage of discovered genes whose functions are known as observed during HGP.   **[All India 2016, U]**

5. Write a detail description of Human genome project?   **[All India 2013, K]**

6. List salient features of Human genome?   **[Delhi 2013, K]**

Topic-11:   DNA Fingerprinting

1   Multiple Choice Questions (1 Mark)

1. DNA profiles of the child and three individuals 1, 2 and 3 who claim to be the parents of the child are given below. Select the option that shows the correct actual parent/parents of the child.   **[All India 2023 Set-I, A]**

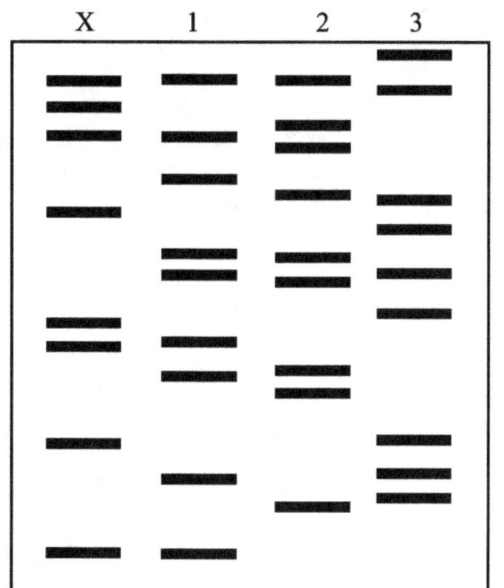

Child Individual   Individual   Individual
  X   1   2   3

(a) Individual 1 and 3   (b) Individual 1 and 2

(c) Individual 2 and 3

(d) Individual 1 is the only parent of the child amongst 1, 2 and 3

2. Short stretches of DNA used to identify complementary sequence in a sample are called
          [CBSE Sample Paper 2021-22, U]

(a) probes   (b) markers

(c) VNTRs   (d) primers

3. What are minisatellites?
          [CBSE Sample Paper 2021-22, K]

(a) 10-40 bp sized small sequences within the genes

(b) Short coding repetitive region on the eukaryotic genome

(c) Short non-coding repetitive sequence forming large portion of eukaryotic genome

(d) Regions of coding strands of the DNA

4. There was a mix-up at the hospital after a fire accident in the nursery division. Which of these children belong to the parents?

          [CBSE Sample Paper 2021-22, A]

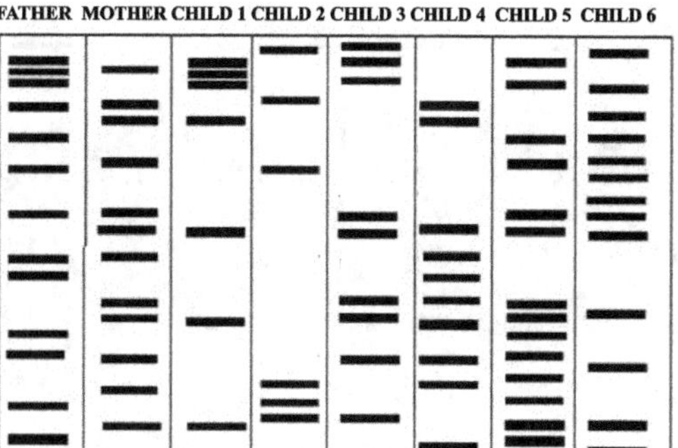

FATHER MOTHER CHILD 1 CHILD 2 CHILD 3 CHILD 4 CHILD 5 CHILD 6

LANE 1 LANE 2 LANE 3 LANE 4 LANE 5 LANE 6 LANE 7 LANE 8

(a) All of the children   (b) Children 2, 3 & 6

(c) Children 1 & 3   (d) Children 2 & 4

5. How many types of gametes would be produced if the genotype of a parent is AaBB?
          [CBSE Sample Paper 2021-22, A]

(a) 1   (b) 2   (c) 3   (d) 4

5   Short Answer Questions (2 or 3 Marks)

6. What are 'SNPs'? Where are they located in a human cell? State any two ways the discovery of SNPs can be of importance to humans.   **[Delhi 2020, K]**

7. A number of passengers were severely burnt beyond recognition during a train accident. Name and describe a modern technique that can help hand over the dead to their relatives.   **[All India 2017, U]**

8. Explain the significance of satellite DNA in DNA fingerprinting technique.   **[All India 2015, Ap]**

9. Following the collision of two trains a large number of passengers are killed. A majority of them are beyond recognition. Authorities want to hand over the dead to their relatives. Name a modern scientific method and write the procedure that would help in the identification of kinship.   **[Delhi 2015, U]**

10. In a maternity clinic, for some reasons the authorities are not able to hand over the two new-borns to their respective real parents. Name and describe the technique that you would suggest to sort out the matter.
          [All India 2013, U]

6   Long Answer Questions (5 Marks)

11. Name and describe the steps involved in the technique widely used in forensics that serves as the basis of paternity testing in case of disputes.   **[Delhi 2023, Set II, U]**

12. Write down a short note on DNA fingerprinting, & its steps?   **[All India 2020, U]**

13. (a) Why did T.H. Morgon select *Drosophila melanogaster* for his experiments?   **[Delhi 2020, Ap]**

   (b) How did he disprove Mendelian dihybrid F2 phenotypic ratio of 9 : 3 : 3 : 1? Explain giving reasons.   **[Delhi 2020, Ap]**

Hints & Solutions

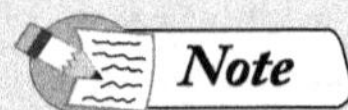

Topic-1: **The DNA**

1. **(d)** 7 **(1 Mark)**

2. **(a)** males and females, respectively **(1 Mark)**

3. **(a)** The two chains are coiled in a right-handed fashion. The pitch of the helix is 3.4 nm and there is roughly 10 bp in each turn. **(1 Mark)**

Note

The structure of DNA is reffered to as a double helix as it resembles a twisted staircase.

4. **(c)** Histones are rich in the basic amino acid residues lysine and arginine. Both the amino acid residues carry positive charges in their side chains.

(1 Mark)

Note

As in this question, only one trait is considered, it is an example of mono-hybrid cross.

5. **(a)** As per Chargaff rule ratio of Adenine is equal to Thymine and Guanine is equal to Cytosine.

Therefore, if Adenine is of 20 % then Thymine is also 20% whereas Guanine is of 30% then cytosine is also of 30%.

Hence, if DNA molecule with 160 bp then amount of cytosine is 30% of 160 = 48

(1 Mark)

6. **(a)** Lysine and Arginine **(1 Mark)**

7. **(b)** It is a single stranded DNA **(1 Mark)**

8. **(c)** 40,000 bp and $13,600 \times 10^{-9}$ m **(1 Mark)**

9. **(b)** A is having 2'-OH group which makes it more reactive and structurally unstable whereas B is having 2'-H group which makes it less reactive and structurally stable

(1 Mark)

10. Deoxyribonucleoside triphosphates (DTPs) serves as substrates i.e. nucleotides during replication and also supply energy for polymerisation reaction by breaking of high energy terminal phosphates bond. **(1 Mark)**

Note

DNA replication is the process by which a double stranded DNA molecule is copied to produce two identical DNA molecules. DNA replication takes place in the cytoplasm of prokaryotes and in the nucleus of eukaryotes.

11. In prokaryotes, the DNA (negatively charged) is scattered in the cytoplasm means that it is naked and is not covered by any membrane. The prokaryotes use an arrangement that helps to pack genetic material tightly into a specific region, positively charged protein hold it in large loops known as nucleoid because prokaryote does not have a well defined nucleus. So, the DNA is not scattered but present in the form of membrane less structure called nucleoid. This nucleoid floats in the cytoplasm and can be found anywhere in the cytoplasm. Also the DNA in form of single chromosomes is attached to mesosome at a point. **(3 Marks)**

12. DNA is organized into bead structure called nucleosome. There is a set of positively charged, basic proteins called histones, which are rich in basic amino acids – lysine and arginine. They have positively charged side chains. Histones organize into unit of 8 molecules called histone octamer. Negatively charged DNA is wrapped around this positively charged octamer to form nucleosome. One histone octamer has 8 histones. One nucleosome (DNA + histone octamer) attaches to other nucleosome with the help of linker DNA associated with H1 protein.

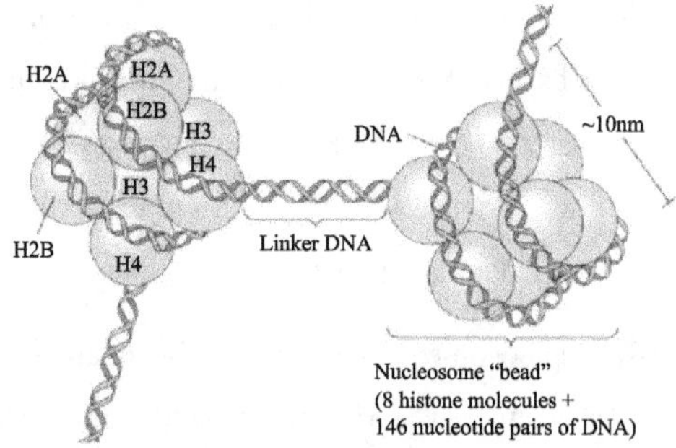

Fig.: Nucleosome structure

A typical nucleosome contains 200 bp of DNA helix. Nucleosome forms chromatin in the form of bead on string. Chromatin condense/super coil at metaphase stage to form chromosomes. Packaging of chromatin to chromosomes occurs with the help of additional set of proteins called NHC (non-histone chromosomal) proteins. **(3 Marks)**

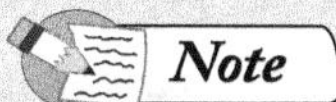

Note

*In a nucleus, some of the region of **chromatin** are loosely packed (and stains light) and are referred to as **euchromatin**. The chromatin that is more densely packed and stains dark are called **heterochromatin***

13. (a) According to chargaff's rule, the ratio of purine (adenine and guanine) and pyrimidine is equal.

As, the ratio of adenine + thymine and guanine + cytosine = 1

If a DNA contains 1000 nucleotides and out of this, 240 are adenine.

Then, the ratio of adenine and thymine are same = 240

So, number of pyrimidine bases = 1000-240

$$= 520$$

Ratio of cytosine $= \dfrac{520}{2} = 260$

Ratio of guanine $= \dfrac{520}{2} = 260$

Hence, the number of pyrimidine nitrogenous bases = Cytosine + Thymine

= 260 + 240 = 500 **(2 Marks)**

(b) Diagrammatic representation of structure of DNA:

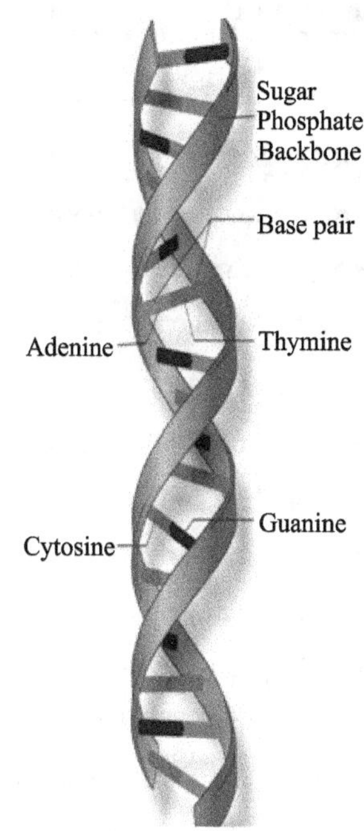

(1 Mark)

14. (a) The features that biomolecules must fulfill as a genetic material are as follows: **(3 Marks)**

- Ability to replicate means a biomolecule should have an ability to generate replica.

- Stability means a biomolecule should be chemically and structurally stable.

- Mutation means a biomolecule should provide a scope for slow changes which is required for evolution.

- Expression means a biomolecule should be able to express itself in the form of 'Mendelian characters'.

(b) DNA is more stable because of the presence of thymine that provides extra stability to the DNA.

(2 Marks)

15. (a) Francis Crick proposed the central dogma, which states that the genetic information flows from DNA to RNA and then to protein.

replication

$$DNA \xrightarrow{\text{transcription}} mRNA \xrightarrow{\text{translation}} protein$$

Central dogma

There are few exceptions to this as observed in the case of some viruses (retrovirus). In retro virus, DNA is synthesized from RNA with the help of reverse transcriptase which is known as reverse transcription. **(2 Marks)**

(b) Transforming Principle : In 1928, Frederick Griffith, in a series of experiments with Streptococcus pneumoniae (bacterium responsible for pneumonia), witnessed a transformation in the bacteria. During the cource of his experiment, a living organism (bacteria) had changed in physical form. He concluded that the R strain bacteria had somehow been tranformed by the heat - killed S strain bacteria. Some 'transforming principle', transferred from the heat - killed S strain, had enabled the R strain to synthesise a smooth polysaccharide coat and become virulent. This must be due to the transfer of the genetic material. However, the biochemical nature of genetic material was not defined from his experiments. Oswald Avery, Colin MacLeod and Maclyn McCarty worked to determine the biochemical nature of 'tranforming principle' in Griffith's experiment. They purified biochemicals (proteins , DNA, RNA, etc.) from the heat - killed S cells to see which ones could transform live R cells into S cells. They discoveredf that DNA alone from S bacteria caused R bacteria to become transformed. They also discovered that protein - digesting enzymes (proteases) and RNA - digesting enzymes (RNases) did not affect transformation, so the transforming substance was not a protein or RNA. Digestion with DNase did inhibit transformation, suggesting that the DNA caused the transformation. They concluded that DNA is the hereditary material, but not all biologist were convinced. **(3 Marks)**

16. (a) (i) Histone octomer: The histones are positively charged basic proteins. They are rich in basic amino acid such as lysine and arginines. They are organised to form a unit of eight molecules called a histone octomer.

(ii) Nucleosome: The negatively charged DNA molecule is wrapped around the positively charged histone octomer in order to form a structure called nucleosome. In a typical nucleosome, 200 bp of DNA helix are present.

(iii) Chromatin: The nucleosomes are unit together to form a chromatin. The nucleosome appears like beads-on-strings on the chromatin. It is packed to form chromatin fibres that further coil and condense at the metaphasic stage of cell division in order to form chromosome. It involves non- histone proteins for packaging called non-histone chromosomal protein (NHC). **(3 Marks)**

(b) The difference between euchromatin and hetero chromatin are as follows:

Euchromatin	Heterochromatin
(i) It is region of chromatin that is loosely packed.	(i) It is region of chromatin that is densely packed.
(ii) It stains light.	(ii) It stains dark
(iii) Euchromatins are transcriptionally active	(iii) Heterochromatin are transcriptionally inactive.

(2 Marks)

17. (a) DNA replication is the biological phenomenon in which a duplicate copy of DNA is synthesised. It involves following steps:

- The process of DNA replication takes place in the S-phase of the cell cycle.

- DNA dependent DNA polymerase enzyme is required for the process of replication.

- Deoxyribonucleoside triphosphate (DNTPs) plays dual role such as it acts as substrate as well as provides energy for polymerisation reaction.

- It originates at specific regions in DNA called the origin of replication because of the requirement of the origin of replication that a piece of DNA if needed to be propagated during recombinant DNA that requires a vector.

- DNA polymerase enzyme polymerises a large number if nucleotides in a very short time.

- For long DNA molecules, since the two strands of DNA cannot be separated in its entire length because of very high energy requirement.

- So the replication takes place within a small opening of the DNA helix called replication fork. The DNA-dependent DNA polymerase catalyse the polymerisation only in one direction such as 5'→3'.

- One strand called as template strand having polarity 3'→5', so the replication is continuous while the other strand having polarity 5'→3', so the replication is discontinuous.

- The discontinuously synthesised fragments are called okazaki fragment are later joined by the DNA ligase enzyme. **(2 × ½ Marks)**

Diagrammatic Representation of replication fork during replication:

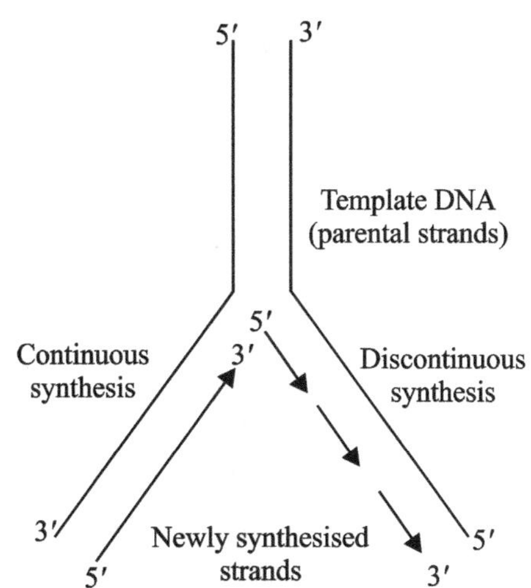

(b) In eukaryotes, the replication of DNA takes place at S-phase of the cell-cycle. The replication of DNA and cell division cycle should be highly coordinated. If cell division is not followed after DNA replication then the replicated chromosome would not be distributed to daughter nuclei. A repeated replication of DNA without any cell division results in the accumulation of DNA inside the cell. This would increase the volume of the cell nucleus causes cell expansion. **(2 × ½ Marks)**

Topic-2: *The search for Gentic Material*

1. **(c)** Hershey and Chase wanted to check if it was the DNA or the protein of the bacteriophage that was injected as genetic material into the bacterial cells. For this, they cultured bacteriophage in two different media - One containing radioactive sulphur (sulphur being a constituent of certain amino acids) to label the protein coat of the bacteriophage, and another containing radioactive phosphorus to label their DNA core. **(1 Mark)**

2. **(a)** The transforming principle was proposed by Frederick Griffith in 1928. He performed his experiment with *Streptococcus pneumonia* a bacteria which is responsible for causing pneumonia.

(3 Marks)

The following steps are involved in his experiment:

- When *Streptococcus pneumonia* bacteria are grown on a culture plate, some bacteria produces smooth shiny colonies (s) whereas other produce rough colonies (R).

- It is because the S strain bacteria have a mucous polysaccharide coating whereas the R strain bacteria lack this coating.

- When the mice infected with the S strain or virulent strain, the mice die because of pneumonia infection.

- When the mice infected with the R strain do not develop pneumonia.

- Then, Griffith was able to kill bacteria by heating. He observed that heat-killed S strain bacteria injected into mice did not kill them.

- When he injected a mixture of heat-killed S and live R bacteria, the mice died. He recovered living S bacteria from the dead mice.

After this experiment, he concluded that the R strain bacterium has been transformed by the heat-killed S strain bacteria. As some 'transforming principle' was transferred from the heat-killed S strain and enabled the R strain to synthesise a smooth polysaccharide coating and become virulent. This is because of the transfer of the genetic material.

(b) The biochemical characterisation of Transforming principle was determined by Oswald Avery, Colin Macleod and Maclyn McCarty. Prior it was thought that the genetic material was protein.

The following steps are involved in his experiment:

- They purified biochemicals such as proteins, DNA and RNA from the heat-killed S cells to determine which one could transform live R cells into S cells.

- They discovered that DNA alone from S bacteria caused R bacteria to become transformed.

- They also discovered that protein-digesting enzymes such as proteases and RNA-digesting enzymes such as RNases did not affect the transformation.

- Hence, it was proved that the transforming substance was not protein and RNA.

- Digestion with DNase did inhibit transformation and the DNA caused the transformation.

- So, they concluded that DNA is the hereditary material. **(2 Marks)**

3. (a) Griffith concluded that the R-strain bacteria had somehow been transformed by the heat-killed S strain bacteria. Some 'transforming principle,' transferred from the heat killed S-strain that had enabled the R strain to synthesise a smooth polysaccharide coat and become virulent. This is because of the transfer of the genetic material.

(2 Marks)

(b) The biochemical characterisation of Transforming principle was determined by Oswald Avery, Colin Macleod and Maclyn McCarty. Prior it was thought that the genetic material was protein.

The following steps are involved in his experiment:

- They purified biochemicals such as proteins, DNA and RNA from the heat-killed S cells to determine which one could transform live R cells into S cells.

- They discovered that DNA alone from S bacteria caused R bacteria to become transformed.

- They also discovered that protein-digesting enzymes such as proteases and RNA-digesting enzymes such as RNases did not affect the transformation.

- Hence, it was proved that the transforming substance was not protein and RNA.

- Digestion with DNase did inhibit transformation and the DNA caused the transformation.

So, they concluded that DNA is the hereditary material.

(3 Marks)

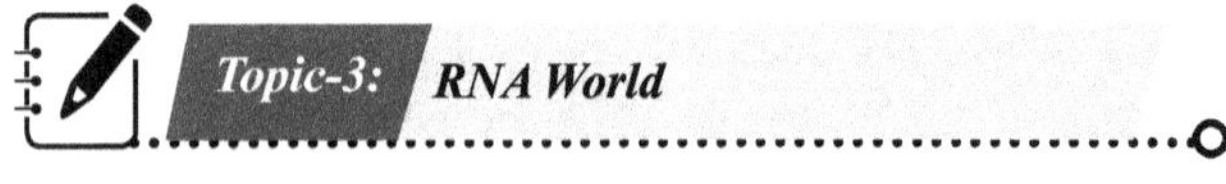

1. (d) The 2'-OH hydroxyl protons are responsible for differences in conformation, hydration, and thermodynamic stability of RNA and DNA oligonucleotides. Additionally, the 2'-OH group plays a central role in RNA. **(1 Marks)**

2. **(a)** **(i)** Eukaryotes have three RNA polymerases which are structurally distinct complexes, though share certain subunits in common, and have a specific function and specific promoter sequence. RNA polymerase I synthesize preribosomal RNA (pre-rRNA), which contains the precursor for the 18S, 5.8S, and 28S rRNAs. RNA polymerase II is synthesized mRNAs and some specialized RNAs. RNA polymerase III makes tRNAs, the 5S rRNA, and some other small specialized RNAs. The enzyme RNA Polymerase II is responsible for the transcription of eukaryotic hnRNA.   **(1½ Marks)**

(ii) hnRNA is required to undergo spicing process before becoming functional mRNA in eukaryotes. hnRNA have both coding and non coding sequences and thus it undergoes splicing where all the non coding (introns) are removed and all the coding (exons) are bind together and forms functional mRNA.   **(1½ Marks)**

OR

(b) In eukaryotes, the length of the chromatin material is large so it is required to be packed in a manner so that it can be condensed in a single nucleus. There is a set of positively charged, basic proteins called histones. A protein acquires charge depending upon the abundance of amino acids residues with charged side chains. Histones are rich in the basic amino acid residues lysine and arginine. Both the amino acid residues carry positive charges in their side chains. Histones are organised to form a unit of eight molecules called histone octamer. The negatively charged DNA is wrapped around the positively charged histone octamer to form a structure called nucleosome. A typical nucleosome contains 200 bp of DNA helix. Nucleosomes constitute the repeating unit of a structure in nucleus called chromatin, threadlike stained (coloured) bodies seen in nucleus. The nucleosomes in chromatin are seen as 'beads-on-string' structure when viewed under electron microscope (EM). The beads-on-string structure in chromatin is packaged to form chromatin fibers that are further coiled and condensed at metaphase stage of cell division to form chromosomes. The packaging of chromatin at higher level requires additional set of proteins that collectively are referred to as Non-histone Chromosomal (NHC) proteins. In a typical nucleus, some region of chromatin are loosely packed (and stains light) and are referred to as euchromatin. The chromatin that is more densely packed and stains dark are called as Heterochromatin. Euchromatin is said to be transcriptionally active chromatin, whereas heterochromatin is inactive.   **(3 Marks)**

3. RNA (Ribonucleic acid) is a single stranded nucleic acid. It is a polymer of ribonucleotides that contains four nitrogenous bases such as adenine, guanine, uracil and cytosine.

Nucleoside = Nitrogenous base + Pentose sugar –ribose sugar (linked by N-glycosidic bond)

Nucleotide = Nucleoside + phosphate group (linked by phosphodiester bond)

Nucleotides are linked together by 3'-5' phosphodiester bond for the formation of polynucleotide chain of RNA.

In a polynucleotide chain, a phosphate moiety remains free at 5' end of ribose sugar (5' end of polymer chain) and one –OH group remains free at 3' end of ribose (3' end of polymer chain).   **(3 Marks)**

Diagrammatic representation of RNA polynucleotide:

4.

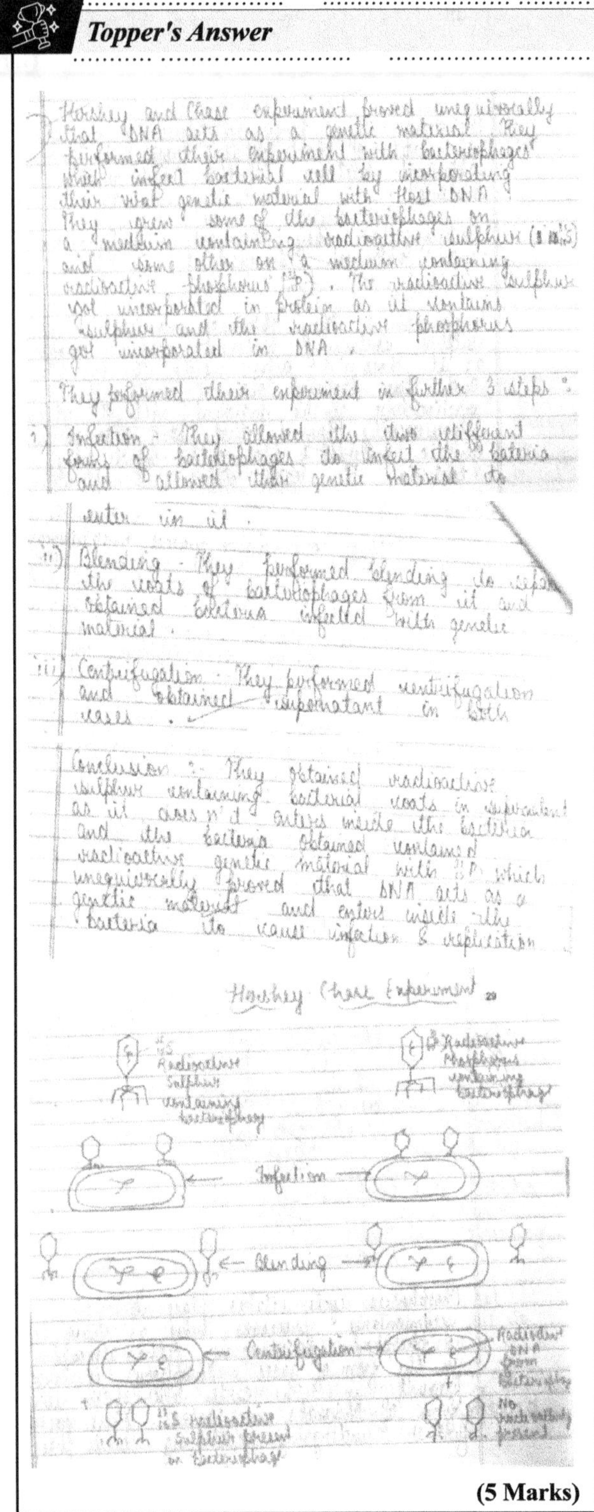

To proof that DNA is the genetic material an experiment was performed by Alfred Hershey and Martha Chase in 1952. They worked with viruses that infect bacteria called bacteriophage.

Following steps are involved in Hershey and Chase experiment:

- They grow viruses on a different medium containing radioactive phosphorus and radioactive sulphur.

- Viruses grown in the presence of radioactive phosphorus contained radioactive DNA but not protein because DNA contains phosphorus but is absent in protein.

- Whereas virus grown in a medium containing radioactive sulphur contained radioactive protein but not radioactive DNA because sulphur is absent is DNA.

- Radioactive phages were allowed to attach to *E.coli* bacteria.

- As the infection proceeded, the viral coats were removed from the bacteria by agitating them in a blender.

- Then the virus particles were separated from the bacteria by spinning them in a centrifuge.

- So the bacteria that infected with viruses that contain radioactive DNA were radioactive.

- This indicates that DNA was the material that can be passed from the virus to bacteria.

- Bacteria that were infected with viruses that contain radioactive proteins were not radioactive.

- This indicates that proteins did not enter the bacteria from the viruses.

- Hence, it is proved that DNA is the genetic material that is passed from virus to bacteria.

Diagrammatic representation of Hershey and Chase experiment:

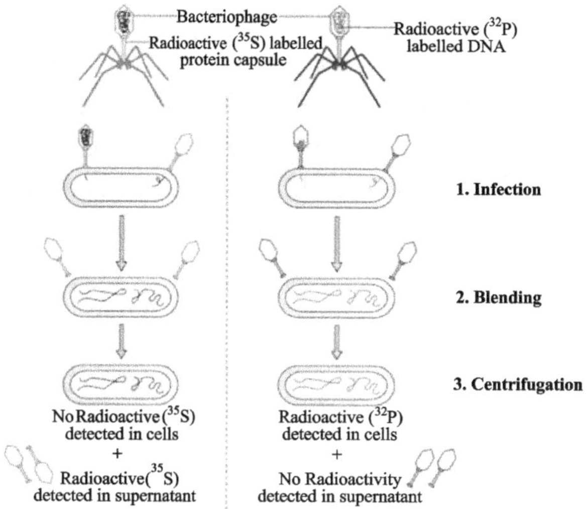

(5 Marks)

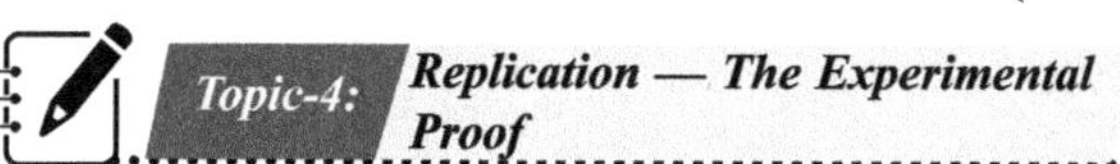

Topic-4: Replication — The Experimental Proof

1. (a) *E. coli* divides in 20 minutes. So, after 80 minutes there will be 4 generations. In the first generation all the strands will be hybrid (as the heavy isotope will be incorporated in the newly synthesised strand of DNA) i.e the two DNA will be of intermediate nature. In the second generation, 50% the DNA will be light and 50% will be hybrid. In the 3rd generation, 25% will be hybrid and 75% will be light and in the fourth generation 12.5% will be hybrid and 87.5% will be light strand. **(1 Mark)**

2. (d) $0 : 1 : 31$ **(1 Mark)**

3. To proof that DNA is the genetic material an experiment was performed by Alfred Hershey and Martha Chase in 1952. They worked with viruses that infect bacteria called bacteriophage.

    Following steps are involved in Hershey and Chase experiment:

(a) **Infection**

- They grow viruses on a different medium containing radioactive phosphorus and radioactive sulphur.

- Viruses grown in the presence of radioactive phosphorus contained radioactive DNA but not protein because DNA contains phosphorus but is absent in protein.

- Whereas virus grown in a medium containing radioactive sulphur contained radioactive protein but not radioactive DNA because sulphur is absent in DNA.

- Radioactive phages were allowed to attach to *E.coli* bacteria.

(b) **Blending:**

- As the infection proceeded, the viral coats were removed from the bacteria by agitating them in a blender.

(c) **Centrifugation:**

- Then the virus particles were separated from the bacteria by spinning them in a centrifuge.

- So the bacteria that infected with viruses that contain radioactive DNA were radioactive.

- This indicates that DNA was the material that can be passed from the virus to bacteria.

- Bacteria that were infected with viruses that contain radioactive proteins were not radioactive.

- This indicates that proteins did not enter the bacteria from the viruses.

- Hence, it is proved that DNA is the genetic material that is passed from virus to bacteria.

(3 Marks)

Diagrammatic representation of Hershey and Chase experiment:

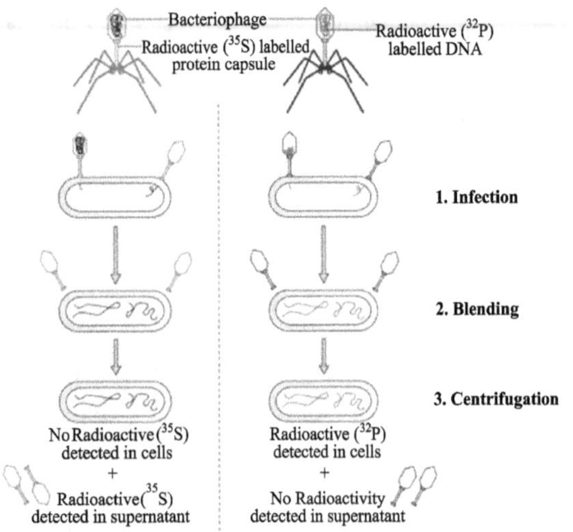

(2 Marks)

4. Matthew Meselson and Franklin Stahl performed the following experiment in 1958 to prove that DNA replicates semiconservatively:

   (i) They grwo *E.coli* in medium containing 15NH4Cl (15N is the heavy isotope of nitrogen) as the only nitrogen source for many generations. This result was that 15N was incorporated into newly synthesised DNA.

   (ii) This heavy DNA molecule could be distinguished from the normal DNA by centrifugation in a cesium chloride (CsCl) density gradient.

   (iii) Then they transferred the cells into a medium with normal 14NH4Cl and took samples at different time intervals as the cells multiplied and extracted the DNA that remained as double-stranded helices. The different samples were separated independently on CsCl gradients to measure the densities of DNA.

   (iv) Thus, the DNA that was extracted from the culture one generation after the transfer from 15N to 14N medium had a hybrid or intermediate density. DNA extracted from the culture after another generation was composed of equal amounts of this hybrid DNA and of 'light' DNA. **(5 Marks)**

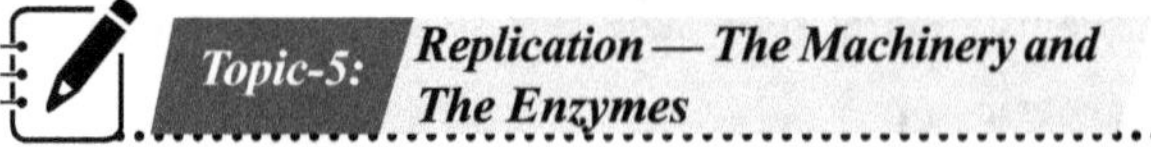

1. **(c)** The experiments involving use of radioactive thymidine to detect distribution of newly synthesised DNA in the chromosomes was performed on *Vicia faba* (faba beans) by Taylor and colleagues in 1958. The experiments proved that the DNA in chromosomes also replicate semiconservatively.

   (1 Mark)

2. **(d)**

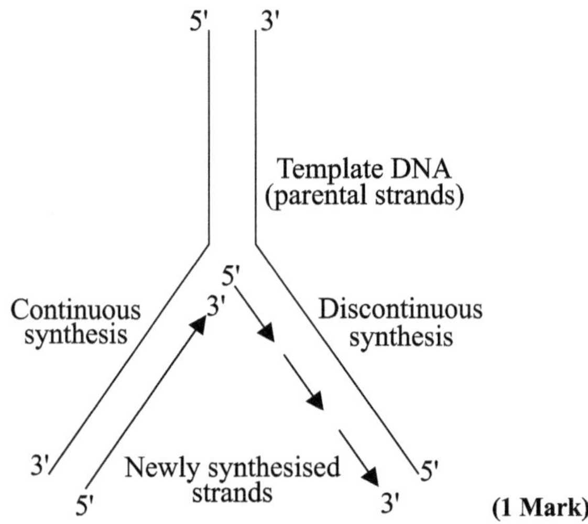

(1 Mark)

3. **(d)** (i)- continuous synthesis , (ii)- discontinuous synthesis (iii) 3' end (iv) 5' end

   (1 Mark)

4. An enzyme DNA-dependent DNA polymerase is responsible for the continuous and discontinuous replication of the DNA strand. DNA-dependent DNA polymerase enzyme catalyses the polymerisation of DNA in only direction such as from 5'→3' and is called coding strand and is discontinuous. Whereas the complementary strand having polarity 3'→5' is called antisense strand and is continuous.

   (1 Mark)

5. DNA replication is semiconservative. The replication occurs at origin of replication within a small opening of DNA helix called as 'replication fork'. It requires helicase, topoisomerase, single strand binding proteins,

DNA-dependent DNA polymerase for polymerisation of deoxyribonucleotides, deoxyribonucleotides as substrate and source of energy for polymerisation reaction, primase for the synthesis of RNA primer, and DNA ligase to join DNA fragments.   **(1 Mark)**

The various steps of DNA replication are as follows:

(i) Helicase unwinds the double helix by breaking the hydrogen bonds between complementary base pairs, while single strand binding proteins helps to stabilize the single strands prevent them from rejoining. The enzyme topoisomerase enzyme releases tension generated due to unwinding and super coiling at the end of DNA opposite to the replication fork.

(ii) The DNA-dependent DNA polymerases cannot initiate the process of replication on their own. So, primase enzyme forms short sequences of RNA called primers that provide a starting point for elongation.

(iii) DNA polymerase catalyses polymerisation only in one direction i.e. 5'→ 3' so on one strand (the template with polarity 3' 5') the replication is continuous while on other (the template with polarity 5' 3'), it is discontinuous. These discontinuously synthesised fragments are called 'Okazaki fragments'. Okazaki fragments are later joined by enzyme DNA ligase.   **1 Mark)**

Diagrammatic representation of replication fork:

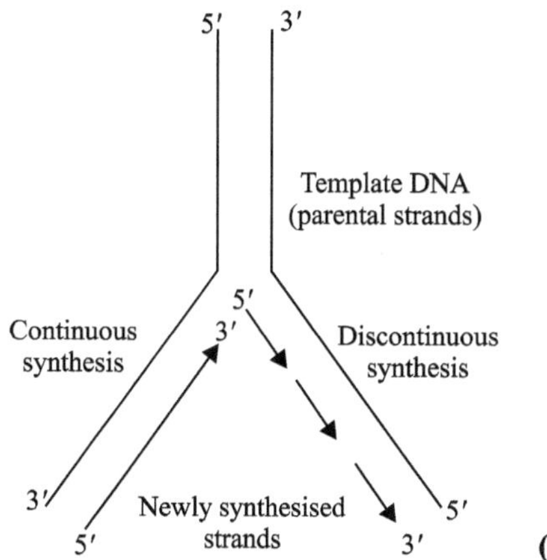

(1 Mark)

DNA (Deoxyribonucleic acid) is a biological process the formation of two identical copies of DNA from parent DNA.

OR

The process of copying genetic information from one strand of DNA into RNA is called transcription. The enzyme catalyse the polymerisation only in one direction that is 5'→3', the strand that has polarity 3'→5' acts as a template and is called template strand. Whereas the other strand is called coding strand and has polarity 3'→5'. The promoter is located towards 5'-end (upstream) of the structural gene. Promoter provides binding site for RNA polymerase. Terminator is located towards 3'-end (downstream) of the coding strand and terminates the process of transcription. For the given RNA, the transcription unit will be:

Diagrammatic representation of transcription unit:

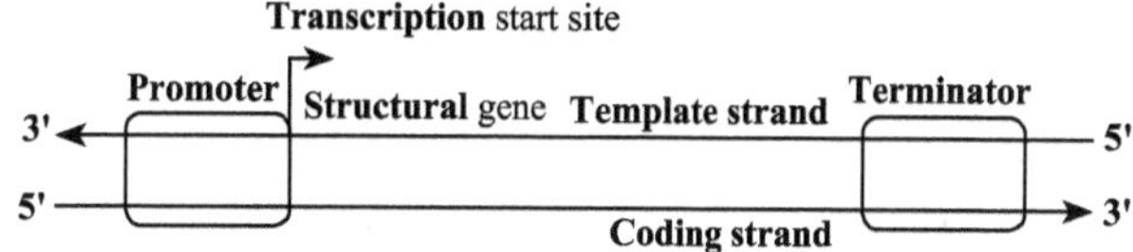

DNA dependent RNA polymerase enzyme is required for the process of transcription.   **(3 Marks)**

The mRNA molecule have uracil (U) in place of thymine (T).

6.   (a) DNA is a large and double helical molecule. The process of DNA replication occurs only in small region of DNA not in its entire length in one time. As large amount of energy is required for opening a whole double helical DNA.   **(1 Mark)**

DNA is more stable than RNA due to absence of $2^1 - OH$ group and presence of thymine in place of uracil in DNA.

(b) In DNA replication, DNA-dependent DNA polymerase is involved in the process of DNA replication. This enzyme catalyses the polymerisation of deoxynucleotides in $5' \rightarrow 3'$ direction, this is called lagging strand of the DNA and replication is discontinuous whereas when the replication takes place in $3' \rightarrow 5'$, this strand is called leading strand and replication is continuous.

(2 Marks)

Note

The discontinuously synthesised strand of the fragments are joined together by DNA ligase enzyme and such fragments are called OKAZAKI fragments.

7. During DNA replication, the lagging strand of template DNA is discontinuous ($5' \rightarrow 3'$). The formed segments are short segments of replicated DNA ($3' \rightarrow 5'$) are called **OKAZAKI** fragments. The OKAZAKI fragments of DNA **are joined together by DNA ligase enzyme.**

(2 Marks)

8. The semiconservative nature of DNA replication was experimentally proved by Matthew Meselson and Franklin stahl in 1958 by using heavy nitrogen (^{15}N) in *E.coli*. It involves following steps such as:

(1) They grow *E.coli* in a medium containing ^{15}NH$_4$Cl. As nitrogen serves as the only source for many generations. ^{15}N is the heavy isotope of nitrogen. So, the ^{15}N was incorporated into newly synthesized DNA.

(2) This heavy DNA molecule is distinguished from normal DNA molecule by cesium chloride (CsCl) density gradient centrifugation. Then they transfer the cells into another medium containing normal ^{14}NH$_4$Cl. They took the samples at different time interval as the cells multiplied and then DNA was extracted from the cells. In this ways, different samples were separated independently on CsCl gradients in order to measure the densities of DNA.

(3) The DNA was extracted from the culture medium one generation after the transfer from ^{15}N to ^{14}N medium had a hybrid or intermediate densities.

The DNA extracted from the culture medium after another generation was composed of equal amounts of this hybrid and of light DNA. **(3 Marks)**

Diagrammatic representation of semiconservative DNA replication:

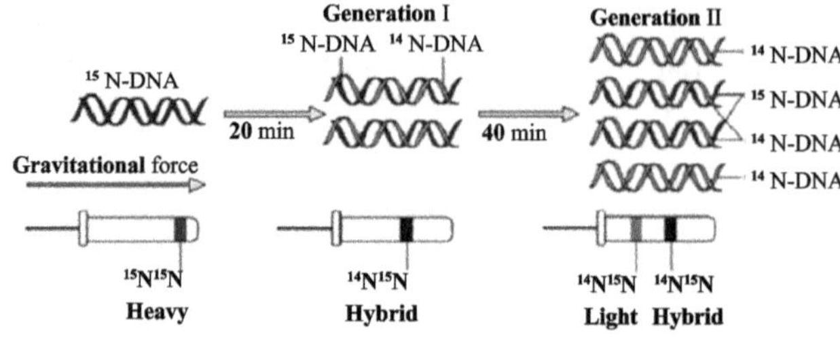

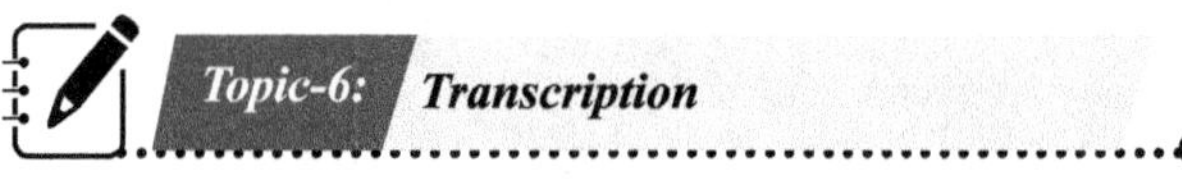

(Separation of DNA by Centrifugation) **(3 Marks)**

Topic-6: *Transcription*

1. (a) The fully processed hnRNA, now called mRNA, that is transported out of the nucleus for translation.

(1 Mark)

2. (a) 5'- AGGTTTAACG -3'   Template strand

As template strand code from 3' to 5'

Then the strand will become   **3'- GCAATTTGGA- 5'**

Therefore the mRNA strand for this template is-

5'- CGUUAAACCU -3'

(1 Mark)

3. (b) 5' (upstream) end and 3' (downstream) end, respectively of the transcription unit   **(1 Mark)**

4. (c) When the RNA polymerase in bacteria get binds with the promoter in order to initiates the process of transcription. Promoter is a sequence of DNA that provides a binding site for RNA polymerase enzyme. It is located towards 5'-end (upstream) of a structure gene.   **(1 Mark)**

5. (c) When the RNA polymerase in bacteria get binds with the promoter in order to initiates the process of transcription. Promoter is a sequence of DNA that provides a binding site for RNA polymerase enzyme. It is located towards 5'-end (upstream) of a structure gene.   **(1 Mark)**

6. **(a)** The complementary strand formed is: **(1 Mark)**

Given strand-

3'-TACGTACGTACGTACG-5'

Complementary strand-

5'-ATGCATGCATGCATGC-3'.

(b) The RNA strand that can be transcribed from the given DNA segments 3'-TACGTACGTACGTACG-5' is

5'-AUGCAUGCAUGCAUGC-3'.   **(1 Mark)**

7. The 'X' and 'Y' in the given figure represents template strand and terminator region. **(1 Mark)**

Template strand: The strand that has polarity 3' $\rightarrow$ 5' acts as a template strand.

Terminator region: The terminator region is located towards 3'-end (downstream) of the coding strand and it terminates the process of transcription.

8. Cistron is that segment of DNA which specifies synthesis of a polypeptide.   **(1 Mark)**

9. Euchromatin is the transcriptionally active region of chromatin in a nucleus.   **(1 Mark)**

10. (a) (i) In bacteria, there are three major types of RNAs such as mRNA, tRNA and rRNA.

(ii) A single DNA-dependent RNA polymerase synthesises all three types of RNA in prokaryotes.

(iii) **Initiation:** RNA polymerase binds to promoter and initiates the process of transcription. It uses nucleoside triphosphate as substrate and polymerises in a template depended manner.

(iv) **Elongation:** This is the second step involved in bacterial transcription that facilitates the opening of the helix and continues elongation of DNA duplex.

(v) **Termination:** Once the RNA polymerase reaches the terminator region, the nascent RNA and RNA polymerase enzyme falls off, results in the termination of transcription.

The bacterial RNA polymerase requires initiation factor (sigma factor) to initiate the process of transcription and termination factor (Rho factor) to terminate the process of transcription.

Diagrammatic representation of transcription in bacteria:

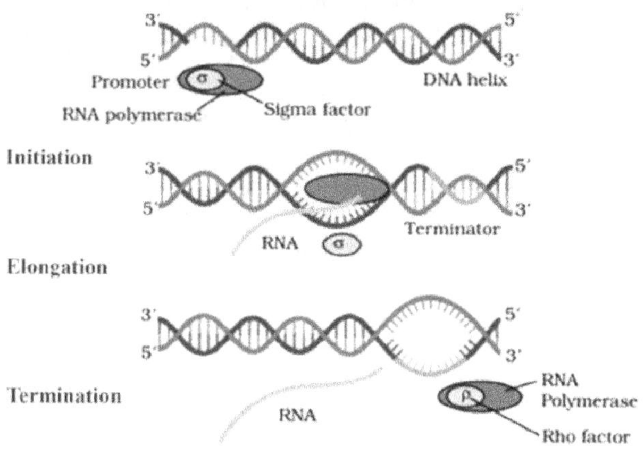

(3 Marks)

(b) The hnRNA or heterogeneous nuclear RNA (hnRNA) is a precursor of mRNA transcribed by RNA polymerase II enzyme in eukaryotes.

The hnRNA is also called primary transcript and it contains both the exons and the introns. It is non-funtional.

So, the process of removal of introns from the exons in a hnRNA is called **splicing** and the exons are joined together by DNA ligase enzyme.

The process of **capping** involves addition of unusual nucleotide (methyl guanosine triphosphate) to the 5'-end of the hnRNA.

The process of **tailing** involves the addition of adenylate residues (200-300) are added at 3'-end in a template independent manner.

The fully processed hnRNA is called mRNA which is transported out of the nucleus for translation.

(2 Marks)

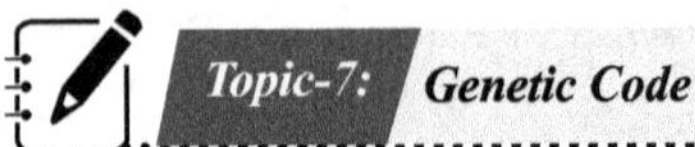
Topic-7: *Genetic Code*

1. (a) In the given sequence of bases of bacterial cell, the 3rd codon position is **UUU** which codes for **Phenylalanine** and the 5th codon position is **AUG** that codes for **Methionine**. **(1 Mark)**

2. (c) **George Gamow** suggested that the genetic code should be made up of a combination of three nucleotides. He proposed that If 20 amino acids are to be coded by 4 bases, then the code should be made up of three nucleotides. **(1 Mark)**

3. (d) The code is nearly universal: for example, from bacteria to human UUU would code for Phenylalanine (phe). **(1 Mark)**

4. (a) 5' - TACGCCG – 3'   Coding strand   **(1 Mark)**

3' – ATGCGGC – 5'   Template strand

Therefore mRNA strand transcribed by template strand is

5'- UACGCCG -3'

5. (a) Palindromic sequences (0.5), endonuclease enzyme

(½ × 2 = 1 Mark)

(b) Restriction enzymes can make complementary cut counterparts forming sticky ends for recombination DNA / RDNA technology/ to facilitate ligation of vector and foreign DNA. **(1 Mark)**

6. (a) Difference between unambiguous and universal:

Unambiguous	Universal
Unambiguous means code is specific as one codon codes for only one amino acid.	**Universal** means codon is same in all organisms.

(1 Mark)

(b) Difference between degenerate and initiator:

Degenerate	Initiator
Degenerate means when an amino acid is coded by more than one codon.	**AUG** is an initiator codon as it initiates the process of translation and codes for amino acid methionine.

(1 Mark)

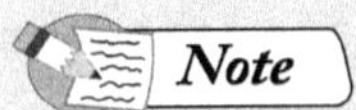
Note

In prokaryotes, GUG acts as a initiation codon and codes for amino acid Valine.

7. (i) George Gamow was scientist who suggested that the genetic code should be made of a combination of three nucleotides. **(1 Mark)**

(ii) According to George Gamow, there are only 4 nitrogenous bases and if they have to code for 20 amino acids, the code should constitute a combination of bases. He also suggested that in order to code for all the 20 amino acids, the code should be made up of three nucleotides. This was a very bold proposition, because a permutation combination of 4^3 ($4×4×4$) that would generate 64 codons. He provide an evidence that the codon was triplet in nature. **(1 Mark)**

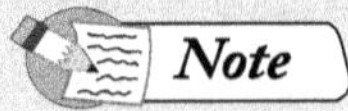
Note

A codon is a sequence of three DNA or RNA nucleotides. There are 64 codon out which 61 codes for 20 aminoacides and 3 codons are stop codon that terminates the process of translation.

8. (a) **George gamow:** He worked on radioactive decay that affects the nucleus of atomon a stellar nucleosynthesis and star formation.

Hargobind Khorana: He synthesized copolymers of nucleotides such as UGUGUGUG. They observed that they have stimulated the formation of polypeptides having alternatively similar amino acid sequence such as cysteine-valine-cysteine.

Marshall Nirenberg: He discovered the first "triplet"-a sequence of three bases of DNA that codes for one of the twenty amino acids which serves as the building blocks of the proteins.

Severo Ochoa: He investigated how DNA and RNA are formed as well as which enzymes control this process. He discovered polynucleotide phosphorylase enzyme which helps in polymerization of ribonucleotides in template independent manner. **(2½ Marks)**

(b) Genetic code is the biochemical basis of heredity consisting of codons in DNA and RNA that determine the specific amino acid sequence in proteins and appear to be uniform for nearly all known forms of life.

Importance of genetic code in protein biosynthesis:

- Genetic code is important because it provides information encoded in genetic material (DNA or RNA sequences) to be translated into proteins (amino acid sequences) by living cells.

- All organisms on Earth utilise proteins in chemical reactions to facilitate physiological functions.

- Differences in genetic code result in coding of different proteins, and it leads to cause genetic variations in organisms. **(2½ Marks)**

Topic-8: *Translation*

1. **(b)** Charging of tRNA during translation process is called amino-acylation of tRNA. When two such charged tRNAs are brought close enough the formation of peptide bond between the corresponding amino acids would be favoured energetically. The presence of a catalyst would enhance the rate of peptide bond formation. **(1 Mark)**

9.

2. **(c)**

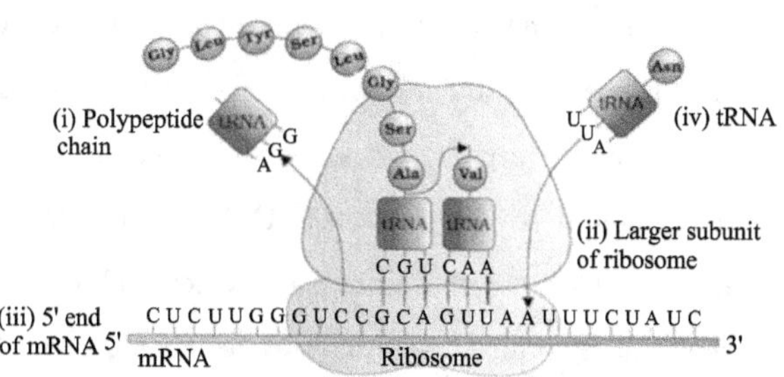

(1 Mark)

3. **(b)** exons appear but introns do not appear in the mature RNA **(1 Mark)**

4. **(c)** (i) Capping (ii) Polyadenylation (iii) $^{m}G_{ppp.}$ (iv) Poly(A). **(1 Mark)**

5. **(c)** (i) Promotor Site, (ii) Sigma factor (iii) RNA polymerase **(1 Mark)**

6. **(b)** **(1 Mark)**

7. **(c)** Translation- Elongation **(1 Mark)**

8. **(a)** x to x' is 5' _______ > 3' **(½ Mark)**

No more amino acids will be added **(½ Mark)**

(b) GCA Anticodon is CGU **(1 Mark)**

(c) The untranslated regions are required for an efficient translation process. **(½ Mark)**

They are present before the initiation codon at the 5' – end and after the stop/termination codon, at the 3' – end **(½ Mark)**

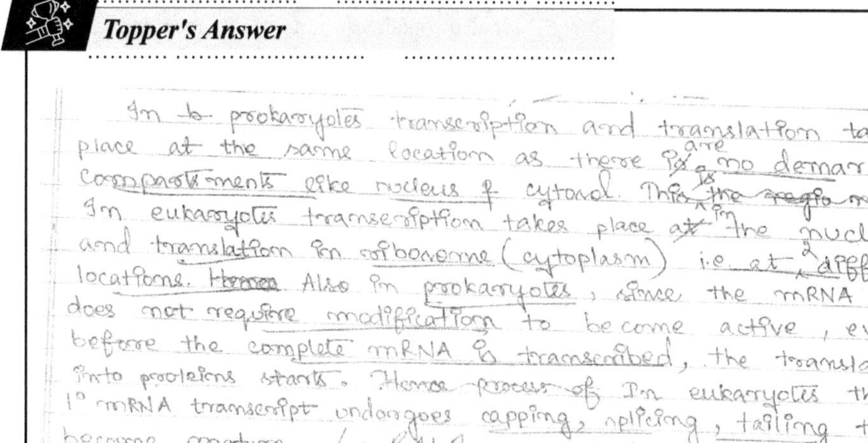

Topper's Answer

In prokaryotes transcription and translation take place at the same location as there is no demarcated compartments like nucleus & cytosol. This the are new In eukaryotes transcription takes place at the nucleus and translation in ribosome (cytoplasm) i.e. at 2 diff locations. Also in prokaryotes, since the mRNA does not require modification to become active, even before the complete mRNA is transcribed, the translation into proteins starts. Hence In eukaryotes the 1° mRNA transcript undergoes capping, splicing, tailing to become mature. mRNA Due to all these reasons, process of transcription & translation are coupled in prokaryotes but not in eukaryotes.

(3 Marks)

Prokaryotes don't have a nucleus. In eukaryotic cells, transcription happens inside the nucleus and translation can't happen until the mRNA is transported out into the cytoplasm. But in prokaryotes, everything is happening in the cytoplasm so as soon as the mRNA molecule starts to be made, there are ribosomes ready to hop on board and start making protein. And this may be when the mRNA is only 1% made, the other 99% is still only coded in the DNA. **(3 Marks)**

10. The role of t-RNA, m-RNA and r-RNA during the process of protein synthesis in prokaryotes is as follows:

t-RNA: tRNA functions as an adapter molecule during the translation process. It was earlier known as soluble RNA or sRNA. As an adapter, it links the amino acids to nucleic acids. It carries the amino acid to be added in the peptide chain and also deciphers the codon for the same in the mRNA molecule.

m-RNA: Messenger RNAs are required for converting the genetic information in the DNA into functional proteins. More than one protein can be encoded in a single mRNA. In prokaryotes mRNAs must have a ribosome binding site in order to be translated. **(2½ Marks)**

r-RNA: Ribosomal RNA (rRNA) is the RNA component of a ribosome and helps in protein synthesis. These structures physically move along an mRNA molecule and catalyse the assembling of amino acids into protein chains. They also bind tRNAs and various accessory molecules needed for the synthesis of protein. **(2½ Marks)**

11. **(a) Structure of t-RNA:**

   - The structure of t-RNA looks like a clover-leaf but its 3-D structure is inverted L-shaped

   - It has an anticodon loop that has bases complementary to the code.

   - It also contains amino acid acceptor end to which it gets bind with an amino acids.

   - They are specific for each amino acid.

   - The T-loop of t-RNA helps in binding to ribosome.

   - D-loop help in binding of amino acyl synthetase.

   - It also contains a variable loop.

Diagrammatic Representation of structure of t-RNA:

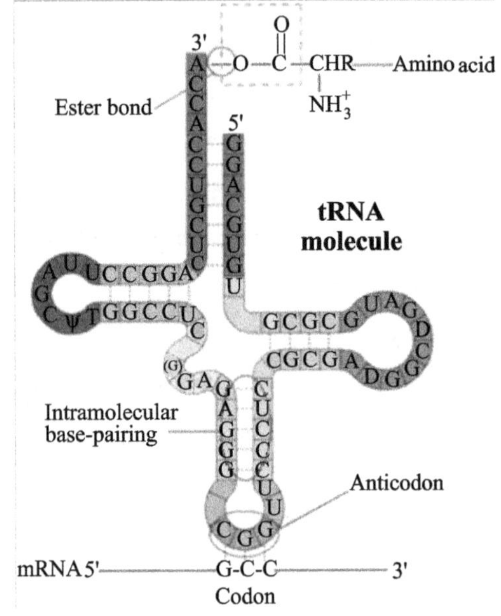

Function of t-RNA:

   - It has anticodon loop that has bases complementary to the code.

   - It also contains an amino acid acceptor end to which it gets binds with amino acid.

   - t-RNA are specific for each amino.

   - It is an adaptor molecule because it reads the code and on the another hand it binds with the specific amino acid. **(3 Marks)**

(b) The primary transcript contains both coding and non-coding sequences called as exon and introns. So, the non-coding sequences or introns are removed by the process of splicing and exons are joined together in a specific manner. Primary transcript after splicing is called hnRNA. It undergoes two additional processes called capping and tailing. In capping, an unusual nucleotide called methyl guanosine triphosphate is added to the 5'-end of hnRNA whereas in tailing, adenylate residues contains 200-300 bp are added at the 3'-end in a template independent manner. The fully processed hnRNA or primary transcript is called mRNA which is further transported into the nucleus for the process of translation. **(2 Marks)**

12. Translation is the process of polymerising amino acid to form a polypeptide chain.

The triplet sequence of base pairs in mRNA defines the order and sequence of amino acids in a polypeptide chain.

The process of translation involves the following three steps:

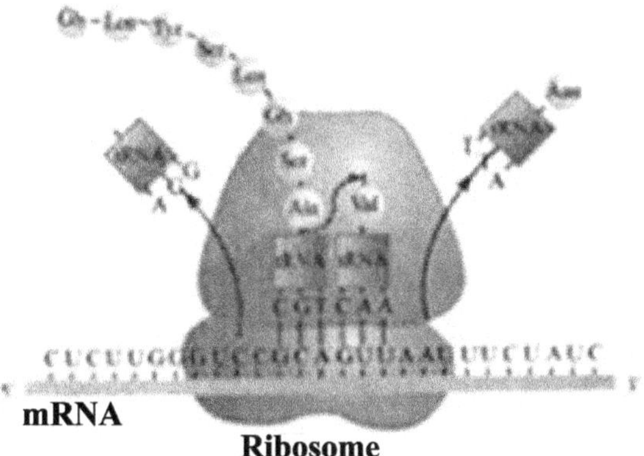

(i) Initiation

(ii) Elongation

(iii) Termination

During the initiation of the translation, tRNA gets charged when the amino acid binds to it using ATP.

The start (initiation) codon (AUG) present on mRNA is recognised only by the charged tRNA.

The ribosome acts as an actual site for the process of translation and contains two separate sites in a large subunit for the attachment of subsequent aminoacids.

The small subunit of ribosome binds to mRNA at start codon (AUG) followed by the large subunit. Then, it initiates the process of translation.

During the elongation process, the ribosome moves one codon downstream along with mRNA so as to leave the space for binding of another charged tRNA.

The amino acid brought by tRNA gets linked with the previous amino acid through a peptide bond and this process continues result in the formation of a polypeptide chain.

When the ribosome reaches one or more stop codon (VAA, UAG and UGA), the process of translation gets terminated. The polypeptide chain is released and the ribosomes get detached from mRNA. **(5 Marks)**

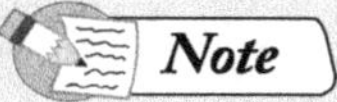

Note

Codon AUG codes for amino acid Methionine that serves as an initiation codon in eukaryotes. Whereas GUG codes for aminoacid valine and acts as initiation codon in prokaryotes.

13. (a) The hnRNA undergoes processes called capping and tailing **followed by splicing**. In capping, an unusual nucleotide is added to the 5'-end of hnRNA methyl guanosine triphosphate. In tailing, adenylate residues (about 200–300) are added at 3'-end in a template independent manner. Now the hnRNA undergoes a process where the introns are removed and exons are joined to form mRNA called splicing.

$(½ × 6 = 3 \textbf{ Marks})$

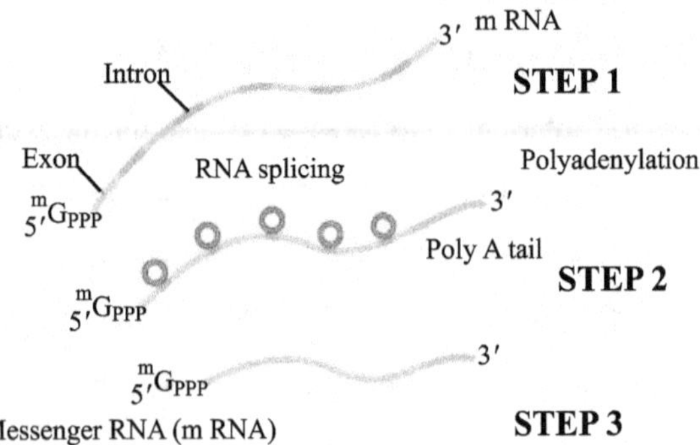

(b) The process of translation will not happen, thus the polypeptide synthesis is stopped/ hampered.

(1 Mark)

The reason for the above is:

RNA polymerase I transcribes rRNAs which is the cellular factory for protein synthesis. **(½ Mark)**

RNA polymerase III helps in transcription of tRNA which is the adaptor molecule/ that transfers amino acids to the site of protein synthesis. **(½ Mark)**

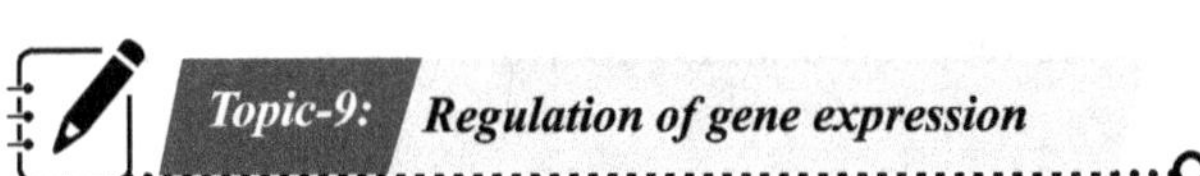
Topic-9: *Regulation of gene expression*

1. **(b)** In the presence of allolactose, a binary complex is formed between allolactose and the repressor that makes binding of the repressor to the operator region impossible. **(1 Mark)**

2. **(a)** lactose is present, and it binds to the repressor

(1 Mark)

3. **(a)** When the active site of enzyme permease present in the cell membrane of a bacterium has been blocked by an inhibitor, the lactose is not transported into the cell . As lactose is the inducer, the lac operon will not be switched on.

(b) Since the repressor protein synthesized by the i gene is abnormal, it will not bind to the operator region

of the operon, resulting in a continuous state of transcription process

(c) No, because galactose is not an inducer/ it is a product of lactose metabolism **(2 + 2 + 1 Mark)**

4. *Lac* operon was proposed by Jacob and Monad in 1961. It contains following components such as:

(i) **Structural gene:** There are three types of structural genes that codes for different enzymes and facilitates the process of transcription in the presence of inducer (lactose).

- The **z gene** codes for enzyme beta-galactosidase that regulates the switching on and is responsible for the hydrolysis of disaccharide, lactose into its monomeric unit's glucose.

- **y gene** codes for enzyme permease that increases the permeability of the cell to beta-galactosides.

- **a gene** codes for enzyme transacetylase.

(ii) **Promoter:** It is the sequence of DNA at which the RNA polymerase enzyme get binds and initiates the process of transcription.

(iii) **Operator:** It is sequence of DNA that is adjacent to promoter.

(iv) **Regulator gene:** A gene that codes for repressor protein and binds with the operator and because of it operon is switched "off".

(v) **Inducer:** Lactose is inducer that helps in switching "on" of operon.

Lactose acts as the substrate for enzyme beta-galactosidase. This enzyme regulates the switching on and off the operon because of this it is termed as inducer. So, in the absence of glucose (carbon source), if lactose is added in the growth medium of the bacteria. The lactose is transported into the cells by the action of permease enzyme that increases permeability of the cell to beta-galactosides.

Lactose induces the operon in following manner:

- In a lac operon, the repressor protein is synthesised from the *i gene.*

- This repressor protein gets bind with the operator region of the operon and prevents RNA polymerase enzyme from transcribing the operon.

- In the absence of lactose, the repressor gene produces repressor protein and get binds with the operator gene. It prevents the RNA polymerase enzyme to get binds with the operon.

Diagrammatic Representation of lac operon in the absence of lactose:

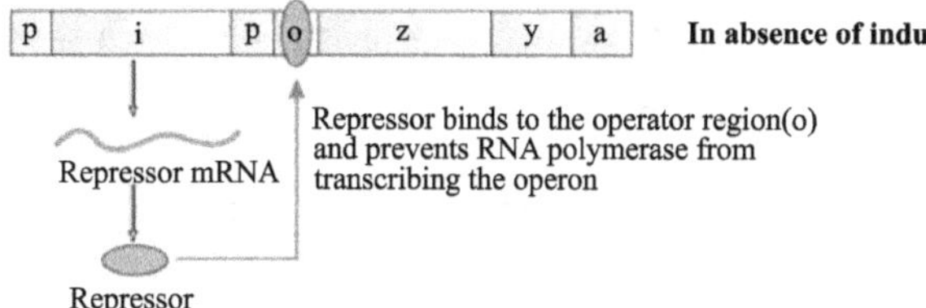

- In the presence of lactose as an inducer, the repressor protein is inactivated. It allows RNA polymerase enzyme to activate the promoter and initiates the process of transcription by structural genes.

Diagrammatic Representation of lac operon in the presence of inducer:

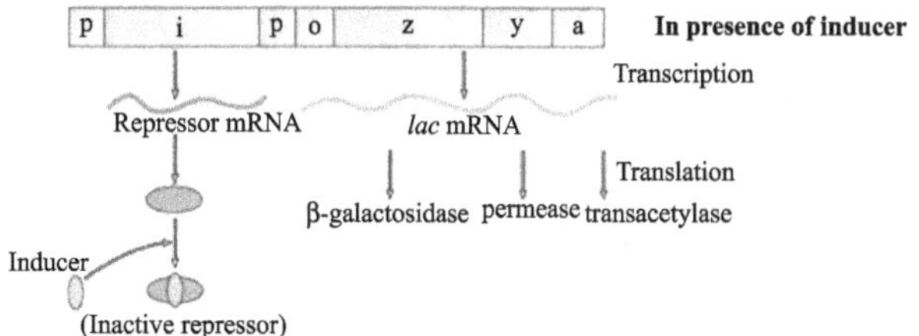

(5 Marks)

5. Lactose acts as the substrate for enzyme beta-galactosidase. This enzyme regulates the switching on and off the operon because of this it is termed as inducer.

So, in the absence of glucose (carbon source), if lactose is added in the growth medium of the bacteria. The lactose is transported into the cells by the action of permease enzyme that increases permeability of the cell to beta-galactosides.

Lactose induces the operon in following manner:

- In a *lac* operon, the repressor protein is synthesised from the *i* gene.

- This repressor protein gets bind with the operator region of the operon and prevents RNA polymerase enzyme from transcribing the operon.

- In the presence of lactose as an inducer, the repressor protein is inactivated. It allows RNA polymerase enzyme to activate the promoter and initiates the process of transcription. **(5 Marks)**

6. *Lac* operon was proposed by Jacob and Monad in 1961. It contains following components such as: **(5 Marks)**

(i) **Structural gene:** There are three types of structural genes that codes for different enzymes and facilitates the process of transcription in the presence of inducer (lactose).

- The **z gene** codes for enzyme beta-galactosidase that regulates the switching on and is responsible for the hydrolysis of disaccharide, lactose into its monomeric unit's glucose.

- **Y gene** codes for enzyme permease that increases the permeability of the cell to beta-galactosides.

- **a gene** codes for enzyme transacetylase.

(ii) **Promoter:** It is the sequence of DNA at which the RNA polymerase enzyme get binds and initiates the process of transcription.

(iii) **Operator:** It is sequence of DNA that is adjacent to promoter.

(iv) **Regulator gene:** A gene that codes for repressor protein and binds with the operator and because of it operon is switched "off".

(v) **Inducer:** Lactose is inducer that helps in switching "on" of operon.

Lactose acts as the substrate for enzyme beta-galactosidase. This enzyme regulates the switching on and off the operon because of this it is termed as inducer. So, in the absence of glucose (carbon source), if lactose is added in the growth medium of the bacteria. The lactose is transported into the cells by the action of permease enzyme that increases permeability of the cell to beta-galactosides.

Lactose induces the operon in following manner:

- In a *lac* operon, the repressor protein is synthesised from the *i* gene.

- This repressor protein gets bind with the operator region of the operon and prevents RNA polymerase enzyme from transcribing the operon.

- In the absence of lactose, the repressor gene produces repressor protein and get binds with the operator gene. It prevents the RNA polymerase enzyme to get binds with the operon.

Diagrammatic Representation of lac **operon in the absence of lactose:**

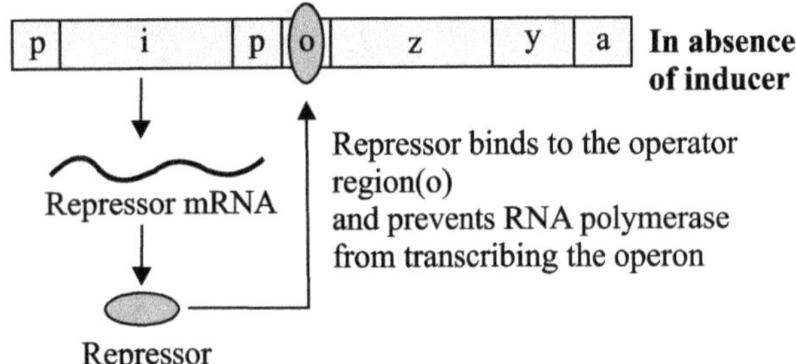

- In the presence of lactose as an inducer, the repressor protein is inactivated. It allows RNA polymerase

enzyme to activate the promoter and initiates the process of transcription by structural genes.

Diagrammatic Representation of lac **operon in the presence of inducer:**

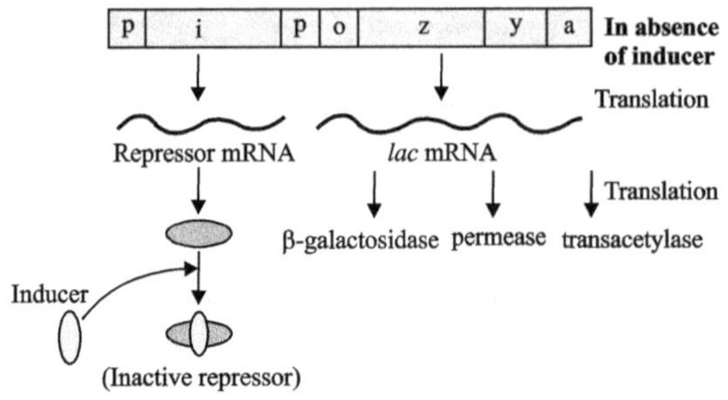

(5 Marks)

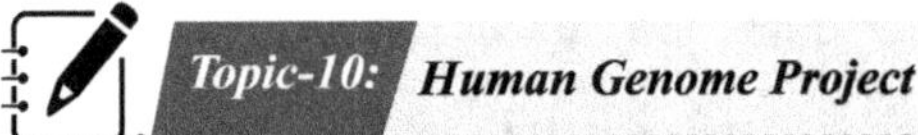

Topic-10: **Human Genome Project**

1. **(c)** Some of the important goals of HGP were as follows:

(i) Identify all the approximately 20,000-25,000 genes in human DNA;

(ii) Determine the sequences of the 3 billion chemical base pairs that make up human DNA;

(iii) Store this information in databases;

(iv) Improve tools for data analysis;

(v) Transfer related technologies to other sectors, such as industries;

(vi) Address the ethical, legal, and social issues (ELSI) that may arise from the project. **(1 Marks)**

2. **(a)** The prime goals of HGP are :

(i) Identify all the approximately 20,000-25,000 genes in human DNA;

(ii) Determine the sequences of the 3 billion chemical base pairs that make up human DNA;

(iii) Store this information in databases;

(iv) Improve tools for data analysis. **(2 Marks)**

(b) There are many non-human model organisms, such as bacteria, yeast, *Caenorhabditis elegans* (a free living non-pathogenic nematode), *Drosophila* (the fruit fly), plants (rice and *Arabidopsis*), etc., have also been sequenced. **(1 Mark)**

3. (a) Human Genome Project was also called mega project that has approximately 3×10^9 bp. Human Genome Project involves two major approaches such as ESTs and Sequence Annotation and The two approaches are ESTs and Sequence Annotation.

(1½ Marks)

- **Expressed sequence Tags:** This approach aims identifying all the genes that expressed as RNA.

- **Sequence Annotations:** This approach involves sequencing of the entire set of genome either coding or non-coding sequences or later assigning different region with functions.

(b) **YAC** stands for Yeast Artificial Chromosome. It is used as cloning vectors for cloning DNA fragments in suitable host to carry out the process of DNA sequencing. **(1½ Marks)**

4. (a) BAC stands for Bacterial artificial chromosomes and YAC stands for Yeast artificial chromosomes.

BAC and YAC are commonly used host cells for cloning of DNA fragments using specialised vectors. **(1 Mark)**

(b) Less than 2 percent of the genome codes for proteins and the function of over 50 percent of the discovered genes are unknown. **(1 Mark)**

5. Human Genome Project (HGP) was called a mega project. You can imagine the magnitude and the requirements for the project if we simply define the aims of the project as follows:

Human genome is said to have approximately 3×10^9 bp, and if the cost of sequencing required is US $ 3 per bp (the estimated cost in the beginning), the total estimated cost of the project would be approximately

9 billion US dollars. Further, if the obtained sequences were to be stored in typed form in books, and if each page of the book contained 1000 letters and each book contained 1000 pages, then 3300 such books would be required to store the information of DNA sequence from a single human cell. The enormous amount of data expected to be generated also necessitated the use of high speed computational devices for data storage and retrieval, and analysis. HGP was closely associated with the rapid development of a new area in biology called **Bioinformatics**.

Goals of HGP

Some of the important goals of HGP were as follows:

(i) Identify all the approximately 20,000-25,000 genes in human DNA;

(ii) Determine the sequences of the 3 billion chemical base pairs that make up human DNA;

(iii) Store this information in databases;

(iv) Improve tools for data analysis;

(v) Transfer related technologies to other sectors, such as industries;

(vi) Address the ethical, legal, and social issues (ELSI) that may arise from the project.

The Human Genome Project was a 13-year project coordinated by the U.S. Department of Energy and the National Institute of Health. During the early years of the HGP, the Wellcome Trust (U.K.) became a major partner; additional contributions came from Japan, France, Germany, China and others. The project was completed in 2003. Knowledge about the effects of DNA variations among individuals can lead to revolutionary new ways to diagnose, treat and someday prevent the thousands of disorders that affect human beings. Besides providing clues to understanding human biology, learning about non-human organisms DNA sequences can lead to an understanding of their natural capabilities that can be applied toward solving challenges in health care, agriculture, energy production, environmental remediation. Many non-human model organisms, such as bacteria, yeast, Caenorhabditis elegans (a free living non-pathogenic nematode), Drosophila (the fruit fly), plants (rice and Arabidopsis), etc., have also been sequenced. **(3 Marks)**

6. Some of the salient observations drawn from human genome project are as follows:

   (i) The human genome contains 3164.7 million bp.

   (ii) The average gene consists of 3000 bases, but sizes vary greatly, with the largest known human gene being dystrophin at 2.4 million bases.

   (iii) The total number of genes is estimated at 30,000– much lower than previous estimates of 80,000 to 1,40,000 genes. Almost all (99.9 per cent) nucleotide bases are exactly the same in all people.

   (iv) The functions are unknown for over 50 per cent of the discovered genes.

   (v) Less than 2 per cent of the genome codes for proteins.

   (vi) Repeated sequences make up very large portion of the human genome.

   (vii) Repetitive sequences are stretches of DNA sequences that are repeated many times, sometimes hundred to thousand times. They are thought to have no direct coding functions, but they shed light on chromosome structure, dynamics and evolution.

   (viii) Chromosome 1 has most genes (2968), and the Y has the fewest (231).

   (ix) Scientists have identified about 1.4 million locations where singlebase DNA differences (SNPs – single nucleotide polymorphism, pronounced as 'snips') occur in humans. This information promises to revolutionise the processes of finding chromosomal locations for disease-associated sequences and tracing human history. **(3 Marks)**

Topic-11: *DNA Fingerprinting*

1. **(d)** Individual 1 exhibit largest number of common bands with the child X that are band 1, 3,6 and 8 are common so individual 1 is expected to be the parent of child X. **(1 Mark)**

2. **(a)** Probes **(1 Mark)**

3. **(c)** Short non-coding repetitive sequence forming large portion of eukaryotic genome **(1 Mark)**

4. **(c)** A. Children 1 & 3 **(1 Mark)**

5. **(b)** 2 **(1 Mark)**

6. SNPs are single nucleotide polymorphism that occurs in humans. These are the most common form of genetic variation among people. Each SNPs represents a difference in a single nucleotide sequence of DNA. SNPs are located in a DNA between the genes such as promoters, exons, introns or 5' and 3' untranslated regions. Basically they are located within a gene or in a regulatory region near a gene.

   They act as biological markers that helps scientist to locate the genes that are associated with diseases. It helps to measure the genetic variations among individuals.

   (3 Marks)

7. The technique that will help the authorities to establish the identity of the dead is known as DNA fingerprinting.

Basis of DNA Fingerprinting - DNA fingerprinting is a method for comparing the DNA sequences of any two individuals. 99.9% of the base sequences in all human beings are identical. It is the remaining 0.1% that makes every individual unique. In this, certain specific regions called repetitive DNA sequences that are different in every individual, that are used for comparative study. This repetitive DNA is separated from the bulk DNA as different peaks during density gradient centrifugation in which, bulk DNA forms major peak and the other small peaks are referred to as **satellite DNA**. These sequences show high degree of polymorphism and form the basis of DNA fingerprinting.

Methodology of DNA fingerprinting- The DNA fingerprinting technique involves following steps

(i) Extraction –DNA is extracted from cells in a centrifuge

(ii) Amplification - Many copies of extracted DNA are made by polymerase chain reaction.

(iii) Restriction Digestion – DNA is cut into fragments with enzymes into precise sequences.

(iv) Separation of DNA sequences – The cut DNA fragments are passed though electrophoresis set up containing agarose gel and the separated fragments can be seen under UV radiation.

(v) Southern Blotting- The separated sequences are transferred onto a nylon membrane.

(vi) Hybridisation- The nylon membrane is immersed in a bath and radioactive labelled VNTR probes are added.

(vii) Autoradiography- The membrane is pressed onto an X-ray film and dark bands develop the probe sites which resemble bar codes.

After autoradiography, different bands are obtained which are characteristics of an individual. The presence of similarities between the casualties and their relatives determines their relatedness on the basis of which the dead bodies can be handed over to their respective relatives. **(3 Marks)**

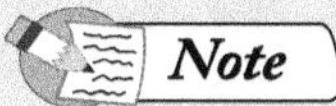

The VNTR belongs to a class of satellite DNA referred to as mini-satellite. A small DNA sequence which is arranged tandenly in many copy numbers the copy number varies from chromosome to chromosome in an individual.

8. Short nucleotide repeats in the DNA are very specific in each individual and vary in number from person to person but are inherited. These are called the **'Variable Number Tandem Repeats' (VNTRs)**. These are also called **"minisatellites"**.

Role of VNTR in DNA fingerprinting: DNA fingerprinting technique for identifying individuals generally using repeated sequences in the human genome that produces a pattern of bands that is unique for every individuals. Each individual inherits these repeats from his/her parents which are used as genetic markers in a personal identity test. For example, a child might inherit a chromosome with six tandem repeats from the mother and the same tandem repeats four times in the homologous chromosome inherited from the father. The half of VNTR alleles of the child resemble that of the mother and half that of the father. **(3 Marks)**

9. DNA fingerprinting is the molecular biology technique and a modern scientific method which is used for the kinship analysis.

Procedure used in DNA fingerprinting:

- Variable Number Tandem Repeats (VNTRs) are satellite DNAs that shows higher degree of polymorphism.

- In DNA fingerprinting, VNTRs probes are used.

- DNA from an individual is collected from every tissue such as blood, hair-follicle, skin, bone and so on.

- Isolated DNA sample from an individual is then cut with the help of restriction endonucleases.

- Then, the fragments are separated through gel electrophoresis on the basis of their size.

- Then, the separated DNA fragments are immobilised on a synthetic nylon or nitrocellulose membrane.

- Immobilised DNA fragments are hybridised with the help of VNTRs probe.

- The hybridised DNA fragments can be detected by autoradiography.

- VNTRs probes vary in sizes from 0.1-20kb.

- So, in the autoradiogram, a band of different sizes will be obtained.

- Such bands are serves as the characteristics of an individual.

- VNTRs are different in every individual.**(3 Marks)**

10. DNA fingerprinting technique is used to describe the parental identification of two newborns in a maternity clinic.

    The steps involved in the process of DNA fingerprinting are as follows:

    - Isolation of DNA from the new borns and parents.

- DNA digestion by restriction endonucleases

- DNA fragments are separated by electrophoresis technique.

- Separated DNA fragments are transferred (blotting) to synthetic membranes such as nitrocellulose or nylon membrane.

- Hybridisation using labelled VNTR probe and,

- Hybridised DNA fragments are detected by using autoradiography. **(3 Marks)**

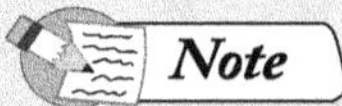

*The DNA fingerprinting technique was developed by Alec Jeffreys and he used a satellite DNA as probe that represents a very high degree of polymorphism called **VNTR (Variable Number of Tandem Repeats)**. **VNTRs** are repetitive units of 10-60 bp and show a higher degree of polymorphism as these base pair sequences are different in different individuals.*

11. **(a)** DNA finger printing is a technique to identify a person on the basic of his / her DNA specificity.

    DNA of the human is almost the same for all individuals but very small amount differs from person to person and forensic science analysis this DNA to identify people.

    The steps involve in DNA finger printing are:

    (i) Isolation of DNA,

    (ii) Digestion of DNA by restriction endonucleases,

    (iii) Separation of DNA fragments by electrophoresis,

    (iv) Transferring (blotting) of separated DNA fragments to synthetic membranes, such as nitrocellulose or nylon,

    (v) Hybridisation using labelled VNTR probe, and

    (vi) Detection of hybridised DNA fragments by autoradiography. **(5 Marks)**

12.

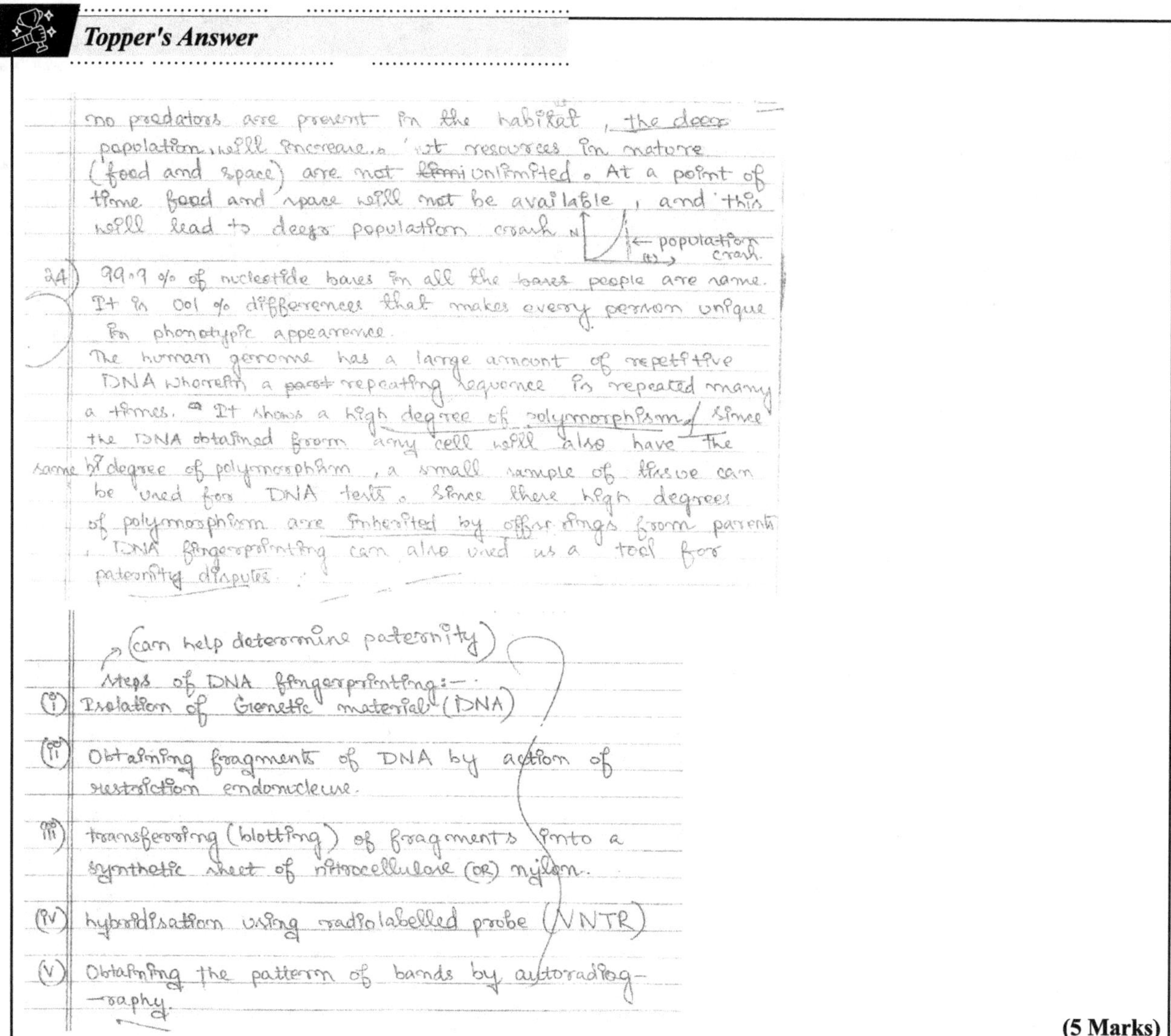

(5 Marks)

DNA fingerprinting involves identifying differences in some specific regions in DNA sequence called as repetitive DNA, because in these sequences, a small stretch of DNA is repeated many times. These repetitive DNA are separated from bulk genomic DNA as different peaks during density gradient centrifugation. The bulk DNA forms a major peak and the other small peaks are referred to as satellite DNA. Depending on base composition (A : T rich or G:C rich), length of segment, and number of repetitive units, the satellite DNA is classified into many categories, such as micro-satellites, mini-satellites etc. These sequences normally do not code for any proteins, but they form a large portion of human genome. These sequence show high degree of polymorphism and form the basis of DNA fingerprinting. Since DNA from every tissue (such as blood, hair-follicle, skin, bone, saliva, sperm etc.), from an individual show the same degree of polymorphism, they become very useful identification tool in forensic applications. Further, as the polymorphisms are inheritable from parents to children, DNA fingerprinting is the basis of paternity testing, in case of disputes.   **(5 Marks)**

The technique of DNA Fingerprinting was initially developed by Alec Jeffreys. He used a satellite DNA as probe that shows very high degree of polymorphism. It was called as Variable Number of Tandem Repeats (VNTR). The technique, as used earlier, involved Southern blot hybridisation using radiolabelled VNTR as a probe. It included

(i) isolation of DNA,

(ii) digestion of DNA by restriction endonucleases,

(iii) separation of DNA fragments by electrophoresis,

(iv) transferring (blotting) of separated DNA fragments to synthetic membranes, such as nitrocellulose or nylon,

(v) hybridisation using labelled VNTR probe, and

(vi) detection of hybridised DNA fragments by autoradiography. A schematic.

representation of DNA fingerprinting

13. **(a)** T.H Morgan selected *Drosophila melanogaster* for his experiments because he found that fruit flies are suitable for studies as they could be easily grown on simple synthetic medium in the laboratory.

- They tend to complete their life cycle in about two weeks and a single mating could produce a large number of progeny flies.

- Sexes are clearly differentiated between male and female flies.

- They exhibit several types of hereditary variations that can be observed with low power microscope.

(2 Marks)

(b) Morgan carried out many dihybrid crosses in *Drosophilla* to study the genes that were sex-linked. These crosses were similar to the dihybrid cross performed by Mendel in peas. He hybridised yellow-bodied, white-eyed females to brown-bodied, red-eyed males and intercrossed their F1 progent.

Then he observed that the two genes did not segregate independently to each other and the F2 ration deviated very significantly from the 9:3:3:1 ratio.

He observed that the genes were located on the X-chromosome and they saw quickly that when the two genes in a dihybrid cross were situated on the same chromosome, the proportion of parental gene combinations were much higher than the non-parental type. According to Morgan, this is because of physical association or linkage of the two genes and coined the term linkage. It used to describe this physical association of genes on a chromosome and is called recombination. It is term used to describe the generation of non-parental gene combinations.

(3 Marks)

6 | Evolution

Chapter 6

Topic-1: Origin of Life

1 — Multiple Choice Questions (1 Mark)

1. The hypothesis that "Life originated from pre-existing non-living organic molecules was proposed by
   [Delhi 2020, K]

   (a) Oparin and Haldane (b) Louis Pasteur

   (c) S.L. Miller (d) Hugo de Vries

4 — Very Short Answer Questions (1 Mark)

2. State the two principal outcomes of the experiments conducted by Louis Pasteur on origin of life.
   [All India 2019, K]

3. State two postulates of Oparin and Haldane with reference to origin of life. **[Delhi 2017, K]**

5 — Short Answer Questions (2 or 3 Marks)

4. (a) Darwin's theory of Natural Selection is widely accepted but some limitations have been identified by modern biologists. Mention the limitations identified. **[All India 2023, Set-I, U]**

   (b) Name and state the most accepted theory of evolution in modern times. **[All India 2023, Set-I, U]**

   (c) Mention any two ways the limitations identified in Darwin's theory of evolution are explained in modern biology. **[All India 2023, Set-I, U]**

5. List the two main propositions of Oparin and Haldane.
   [All India 2013, K]

Topic-2: What are the Evidences for Evolution?

1 — Multiple Choice Questions (1 Mark)

1. Evolutionary convergence is development of a
   [CBSE Sample Paper 2022-23, U]

   (a) common set of functions in groups of different ancestry.

   (b) dissimilar set of functions in closely related groups.

   (c) common set of structures in closely related groups.

   (d) dissimilar set of functions in unrelated groups.

4 — Very Short Answer Questions (1 Mark)

2. What role does an individual organism play as per Darwin's theory of natural selection? **[All India 2017, U]**

3. State a reason for the increased population of dark coloured moths coinciding with the loss of lichens (on tree barks) during industrialization period in England.
   [Delhi 2015, U]

4. Identify the examples of convergent evolution from the following: **[Delhi 2013, U]**

   (i) Flippers of penguins and dolphins

   (ii) Eyes of octopus and mammals

   (iii) Vertebrate brains

5 — Short Answer Questions (2 or 3 Marks)

5. Industrial melanism in England after 1850 is an excellent example of Natural selection. Explain how?
   [Delhi 2023, Set-I, U]

6. Wings of birds and wings of butterflies contribute to locomotion. Explain the type of evolution such organs are a result of. **[All India 2020, K]**

7. "Abingdon tortoise in Galapagos islands became extinct within a decade on introduction of goats in the island." Explain giving reason. **[Delhi 2023 (Set-II), K]**

8. (a) Differentiate between analogous and homologous structures. **[All India 2018, K]**

(b) Select and write analogous structures from the list given below: **[All India 2018, K]**

(i) Wings of butterfly and birds

(ii) Vertebrate hearts

(iii) Tendrils of *Bougainvillea* and *Cucurbita*

(iv) Tubers of sweet potato and potato

9. Differentiate between homology and analogy. Give one example of each. **[All India 2016, U]**

10. Explain the increase in the numbers of melanic (dark winged) moths in the urban areas of post-industrialization period in England. **[All India 2013, U]**

11. With the help of any two suitable examples explain the effect of anthropogenic actions on organic evolution.

[Delhi 2013, U]

12. The graphs below show three types of natural selection. The shaded areas marked with arrows show the individuals in the population which are not selected. The dotted vertical lines show the statistical means.

[CBSE Sample Paper 2023-24, A]

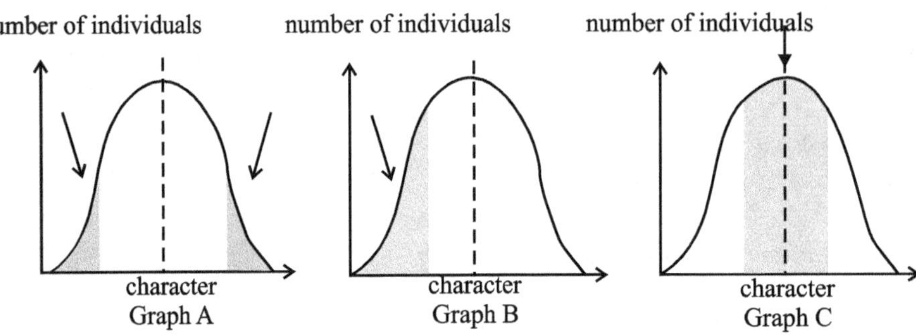

(a) What names are given to the types of selection shown in graphs A, B

(b) After the selection has operated for several generations in the above populations indicated as Graph A, B and C, graphically illustrate the probable results.

6 *Long Answer Questions (5 Marks)*

13. (a) How do the observations made during moth collection in pre and post industrialized era in England support evolution by Natural Selection? **[All India 2017]**

(b) Explain the phenomenon that is well represented by Darwin's finches other than natural selection. **[All India 2017]**

Topic-3: **What is Adaptive Radiation?**

1 *Multiple Choice Questions (1 Mark)*

1. Identify the option that gives the correct type of evolution exhibited by the two animals shown, living in the same habitat in Australia. **[All India 2023, Set-I, U]**

Mouse   Marsupial mouse

(a) Convergent Evolution

(b) Disruptive Selection

(c) Divergent Evolution

(d) Homologous Ancestry

5 *Short Answer Questions (2 or 3 Marks)*

2. Mention Darwin's observations made on finches during his visit to Galapagos Islands. Write the explanation given by Darwin on his observations. **[Delhi 2023, Set-III, U]**

3. (a) Select the homologous structures from the combinations given below: **[All India 2015, U]**

(i) Forelimbs of whales and bats

(ii) Tuber of potato and sweet potato

(iii) Eyes of octopus and mammals

(iv) Thorns of *Bougainvillea* and tendrils of *Cucurbita*

(b) State the kind of evolution they represent.

4. Explain adaptive radiation with the help of a suitable example. [Delhi 2015, U]

5. How does marsupials represent the examples of adaptive radiation? [Delhi 2014, U]

 **Topic-4:** **Biological Evolution and Mechanism of Evolution**

4 *Very Short Answer Questions (1 Mark)*

1. According to de-Vries what is saltation ? [Delhi 2016, K]

5 *Short Answer Questions (2 or 3 Marks)*

2. Compare the mechanism of evolution as put forth by Charles Darwin and de Vries. [Delhi 2019, U]

6 *Long Answer Questions (5 Marks)*

3. Explain Darwinian theory of evolution with the help of one suitable example. State the two key concepts of the theory. [Delhi 2014, U]

4. What are the observation that led to the discovery of natural selection? [Delhi 2013, U]

 **Topic-5:** **Hardy-Weinberg Principle**

5 *Short Answer Questions (2 or 3 Marks)*

1. (a) How is Hardy-Weinberg's expression "(p2 + 2pq+q2) = 1"derived? [CBSE Sample Paper 2022-23, U]

   (b) List any two factors that can disturb the genetic equilibrium. [CBSE Sample Paper 2022-23, U]

2. How would the gene flow or genetic drift affect the population in which either of them happen to take place ? [All India 2019, K]

3. With the help of an algebraic equation, how did Hardy-Weinberg explain that in a given population the frequency of occurrence of alleles of a gene is supposed to remain the same through generations? [All India 2018, U]

4. $p^2 + 2pq + q^2 = 1$, Explain this algebraic equation on the basis of Hardy Weinberg's principle. [All India 2017, U]

5. What does the following equation represent? Explain $p^2 + 2pq + q^2 = 1$ [All India 2015, Ap]

 **6** *Long Answer Questions (5 Marks)*

6. (a) Explain Hardy-Weinberg Principle on the basis of the algebraic equation p2 + 2pq + q2 =1. [All India 2020, K]

   (b) How do gene migration and genetic drift affect this genetic equilibrium? [All India 2020, K]

 **Topic-6:** **A Brief Account of Evolution**

1 *Multiple Choice Questions (1 Mark)*

1. Which one of the following was not present during the Mesozoic Era of the geological time scale? [All India 2023, U]
   (a) Ferns (b) Horsetails
   (c) Ginkgos (d) Bryophytes

 **4** *Very Short Answer Questions (1 Mark)*

2. Rearrange the following from early to late geologic periods: [All India 2019, U]
   Carboniferous, Silurian, Jurassic.

 **5** *Short Answer Questions (2 or 3 Marks)*

3. (a) State what does the study of Fossils indicate. [Delhi 2020, U]

   (b) Rearrange the following group of plants according to their evolution from Palaeozoic to Cenozoic periods: [Delhi 2020, U]

   Rhynia; Arborescent Lycopods; Conifers; Dicotytedon.

Topic-7:   *Origin and Evolution of Man*

 **1**   *Multiple Choice Questions (1 Mark)*

1. At which stage during evolution did human use hides to protect their bodies and buried their dead?

   [Delhi 2023, Set-I, ]

   (a) *Homo habilis*   (b) Neanderthal man

   (c) Java man   (d) *Homo erectus*

4   *Very Short Answer Questions (1 Mark)*

2. Write the probable differences in eating habits of (*Homo habilis*) and (*Homo erectus*).   [All India 2016, U]

 **5**   *Short Answer Questions (2 or 3 Marks)*

3. Write two differences between *Homo erectus* and *Homo habilis*.   [All India 2019, K]

4. Mention the evolutionary significance of the following organisms :   [All India 2017, U]

   (a) Shrews   (b) Lobefins

   (c) Homo habilis (d) Homo erectus

5. Write the characteristics of *Ramapithecus, Dryopithecus* and Neanderthal man.   [Delhi 2017, K]

6. Mention any three characteristics of Neanderthal man that lived in near east and central Asia.

   [Delhi 2014, U]

7. Mention some important characteristics of Dryophithecus and Ramapithecus.   [Delhi 2013, U]

Hints & Solutions

Topic-1:	*Origin of Life*

1. **(a)** "Life originated from pre-existing non-living organic molecules (RNA, protein and so on)" was proposed by Oparin and Haldane. He also stated that the formation of life was preceded by chemical evolution such as the formation of diverse organic molecules from inorganic constituents. The conditions on earth were-high temperature, volcanic storms, reducing atmosphere containing CH_4, NH_3 and so on. **(1 Mark)**

2. The two principle outcomes of the experiments conducted by Louis Pasteur on origin of life are as follows:

(1 Mark)

- He showed that in pre-sterilised flasks, life did not come from killed yeast.

- Whereas in another flask open to air, new living organisms arose from 'killed yeast'.

3. Oparin and Haldane proposed that the first form of life could have been evolved from pre-existing non-living organic molecules such as RNA, protein and so on.

They also state that the formation of life was preceded by chemical evolution such as the formation of diverse organic molecules from inorganic constituents.

The conditions on the earth for survival were high temperature, volcanic storms and reducing atmosphere contains CH_4, NH_3 and so on. **(1 Mark)**

4. **(a)** **(i)** The theory of evolution could not explain how and where variations have arisen.

(ii) It also could not explain how the variations are inherited. **(1 Mark)**

(b) Theory given by Hugo de Vries is the most accepted theory of evolution in modern times. In the first decade of twentieth century, Hugo deVries based on his work on evening primrose brought forth the idea of mutations – large difference arising suddenly in a population. He believed that it is mutation which causes evolution and not the minor variations (heritable) that Darwin talked about. Mutations are random and directionless while Darwinian variations are small and directional. Evolution for Darwin was gradual while deVries believed mutation caused speciation and hence called it saltation (single step large mutation). **(1 Mark)**

(c) The two ways the limitations identified in Darwin's theory of evolution are explained in modern biology are as follows:

1. According to Darwin evolution is a gradual process caused by minor variation this was contradicted by de Vries who proposed that evolution is an outcome of mutations that appear suddenly. He called it saltation (single step large mutation).

2. According to Darwin evolution is a slow directional process whereas according to deVries evolution is caused by random chance events or mutations resulting in sudden evolution of characters in a single or few generation.

(1 Mark)

5. Oparin of Russia and Haldane of England proposed the following:

(i) The first form of life could come from pre-existing non-living organic molecules such as RNA, proteins, etc. and the formation of life was preceded by chemical evolution such as formation of diverse organic molecules from inorganic constituents.

(1 Mark)

(ii) The conditions on Earth were - high temperature, volcanic storms, reducing atmosphere containing CH_4, NH_3, and so on. **(1 Mark)**

Topic-2: **What are the Evidences for Evolution?**

1. **(a)** Common set of characters in groups of different ancestry. **(1 Mark)**

2. As per Darwin's theory of natural selection, an individual organism in a population is responsible for passing on the variation and favourable mutations to the next generations by taking part in a successful event of sexual reproduction. **(1 Mark)**

3. Before industrialization, it was observed that there were more white-winged moths or melanised moths were found on the trees than dark-winged moths. But after industrialization in 1920s, it was observed that there were more dark-winged moths were found in the same area. It occurs because during post-industrialisation period, the tree trunks became dark due to industrial smoke and soots. In this condition, the white-winged moth did not survive because of predators. Hence dark-winged or melanised moth survived. **(1 Mark)**

Before industrialisation, the tree trunks are covered by white-coloured lichen and in the background the white winged moth survived.

4. (i) Flippers of penguins and Dolphin is an example of convergent evolution and are analogous structures.

(ii) Eyes of octopus and mammals are also an example of convergent evolution as the structures are analogous structures.

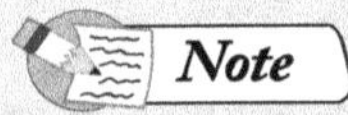

Analogous structures are those that are not anatomically similar structures but perform similar functions.

(iii) Vertebrate brain is an example of divergent evolution and is homologous organ. **(1 Mark)**

5. In a collection of moths made in 1850s, i.e., before industrialisation set in, it was observed that there were more white-winged moths on trees than dark-winged or melanised moths. However, in the collection carried out from the same area, but after industrialisation, i.e., in 1920, there were more dark-winged moths in the same area, i.e., the proportion was reversed. The explanation put forth for this observation was that 'predators will spot a moth against a contrasting background'. During post industrialisation period, the tree trunks became dark due to industrial smoke and soots. Under this condition the white-winged moth did not survived due to predators, dark-winged or melanised moth survived. Before industrialisation set in, thick growth of almost white-coloured lichen covered the trees - in that background the white winged moth survived but the dark-coloured moth were picked out by predators. They will not grow in areas that are polluted. Hence, moths that were able to camouflage themselves, i.e., hide in the background, survived. This understanding is supported by the fact that in areas where industrialisation did not occur e.g., in rural areas, the count of melanic moths was low. This showed that in a mixed population, those that can better-adapt, survive and increase in population size. Remember that no variant is completely wiped out. **(3 Marks)**

6.

Topper's Answer

Wings of birds and wings of butterflies are not anatomically similar but contribute to the same function i.e locomotion Which exactly represents how organisms with different structures adapt to similar functions $\frac{1}{2}$ $\frac{1}{2}$ in common habitat and converge in a same direction Hence they represent convergent type of evolution though having analogous organs and no common ancestors

(2 Marks)

The wings of butterfly and wings of birds are look alike but are not anatomically similar structures but they perform similar functions. Such organs are called analogous organs. Analogous organs are the results of convergent evolution. **(2 Marks)**

7. The Abingdon Tortoise in Galapagos Islands became extinct within a decade only when the goats entered on the Island. It is an example of competitive exclusion this occurred due to the greater browsing efficiency of the goats. **(2 Marks)**

8. (a) **Difference between homologous and analogous organs:**

Homologous organ	Analogous organ
(i) Homology is based on divergent evolution.	(i) Analogy is based on convergent evolution.
(ii) In homology, the structures are evolved from the same origin and have common ancestors but they have different functions.	(ii) In analogy, the structures are evolved from different origin and have different ancestors but have similar functions.
Eg. Wings of birds and forelimbs of human.	Eg. Wings of birds and wings insects.

(1½ Marks)

(b) These are the analogous structure from the given list:

(i) Wings of butterfly and birds.

(ii) Tubers of sweet potato and potato. **(1½ Marks)**

9. Difference between homology and analogy:

Homology	Analogy
(i) Homologous organs are those organs that are anatomically similar but perform different functions.	(i) Analogous organs are those that are anatomically not similar but perform same function.
(ii) This type of evolution is called divergent evolution.	(ii) This type of evolution is called convergent evolution.
(iii) Homology indicates common ancestry.	(iii) Analogy do not share common ancestry.
For example: Thorn and tendrils of *Bougainvillea* and *Cucurbita*.	**For example:** Flippers of penguins and Dolphins.

(3 Marks)

10. During post-industrialisation period, the tree trunks became dark due to industrial smoke and soots. So under this condition, the white winged moth did not survive due to predators, dark-winged or melanised moth survived. Whereas before industrialisation, thick growth of almost white-coloured lichen covered the trees-in that background the white winged moth survived but the dark-coloured moth were picked out by predators. **(3 Marks)**

11. The effect of anthropogenic actions on organic evolution:

(i) **Industrial melanism:** Before industrialization, it was observed that there were more white-winged moths or melanised moths were found on the trees than dark-winged moths. But after industrialization in 1920s, it was observed that there were more dark-winged moths were found in the same area. It occurs because during post-industrialisation period, the tree trunks became dark due to industrial smoke and soots. In this condition, the white-winged moth did not survive because of predators. Hence dark-winged or melanised moth survived. **(1½ Marks)**

(ii) Use of herbicides and pesticides results in the selection of resistant varieties in very short time scale. It also leads to the development of microbes resistant to several antibiotics in a shorter time period because of anthropogenic actions. **(1½ Marks)**

12. (a) A – stabilising; B – directional; C – disruptive; **(1½ Marks)**

(b) Graph A – Stabilising

Graph B – Directional

Graph C – Disruptive **(1½ Marks)**

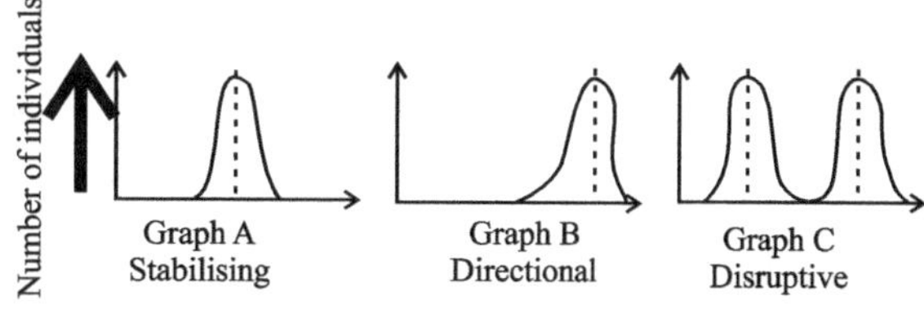

13. **(a)** **Industrial mechanism** is an example of the natural selection of a particular form of an organism in an environment which has changed due to the ill effects of pollution created by industrial activities. *Biston betularia* is commonly called peppered moth because of the presence of black dots on creamy–white body. These moths during 1850, were mostly gray (*Biston betularia typica*) and during day time used to rest on tree-trunks which had lichens grown on them. They resembled with the background and could not be detected by their predators, mainly birds. During industrial revolution in England, the coal was burnt and the soot got deposited on the tree-trunk. Moreover, sulphur dioxide killed lichens. In such polluted areas all the moths of white coloured now could be spotted by birds. A few black individuals which had mutant gene were selected by nature. Such individuals got more chances of reproduction and the white moth were reduced in number.

After about 100 years (by 1950), more than 90% of the individuals had become black, 'Melanic form' (*Biston betularia carbonaria*). Here biologists could see the evolution occurring before their eyes. This evolution from white to black (Melanic) forms was not due to mutation but due to selection of pre-existing mutant allele by nature (Natural selection). Now, when electricity is being used in industries, the number of white moths is again increasing. This also indicates that industrial pollution has not eliminated the genes responsible for light colour of the moth. The above hypothesis was also tested by Dr. H. B. D. Kettlewell after releasing equal number of dark and light moths. **(2½ Marks)**

(b) 'Darwin's Finches' illustrated adaptive radiation. In this, the species, all deriving from a common ancestor, have overtime successfully adapted to their environment via natural selection. Previously, the finches occupied the South American mainland, but somehow managed to occupy the Galapagos islands, over 600 miles away. They occupied an ecological niche with little competition. As the population began to flourish in these advantageous conditions, intraspecific competition became a factor, and resources on the islands were squeezed and could not sustain the population of the finches for long. Due to the mechanisms of natural selection, and changes in the gene pool, the finches became more adapted to the environment. As competition grew, the finches managed to find new ecological niches, that would present less competition and allow them and their genome to be continued. Thus the finches adapted to take advantage of the various food sources available on the island, which were being used by other species. Over the long term, the original finch species may have disappeared, but by diversifying, would stand a better chance of survival. All in all, the finches had adapted to their environment via natural selection, which in turn, has allowed the species to survive in the longer term, the prime directive of any species.

(2½ Marks)

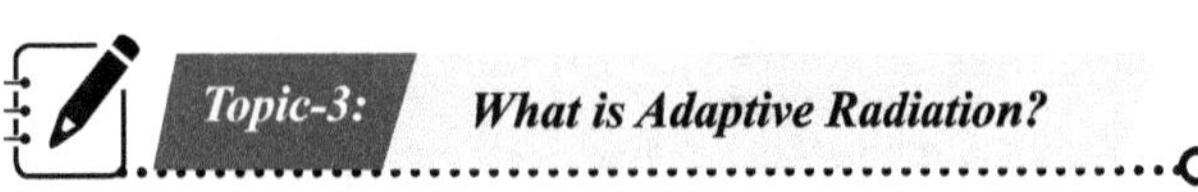

Topic-3: *What is Adaptive Radiation?*

1. **(a)** The changes in characteristics occur in consequence to adapt to a new environment. It can be in structures that serve the same function. Adaptive radiation is a convergent pattern of evolution and results in the formation of analogous structures like the fins of whales and fishes. The given figure is showing the transformation of mouse to marsupial mouse resulting into convergent evolution due to adaptive radiation.

(1 Mark)

2. On his visit to the Galapagos Islands, Charles Darwin discovered several species of finches that varied from island to island which helped him to develop his theory of natural selection. He observed that the shape of the beak of the birds varied according to the type of food they consume. The finches that ate large nuts had strong beaks for breaking the nuts open. Finches that ate small nuts and seeds had beaks for cracking nuts and seeds. **(2 Marks)**

3. **(a)** Homologous organs are the organs having similar structure and origin but performing different functions.

   From the given options, following are homologous structures:

   Forelimbs of whales and bats are similar in structure but perform different functions of swimming and flying, respectively.

   Thorns of *Bougainvillea* and tendrils of *Cucurbita* are both modifications of a stem arising from axillary bud but perform different functions of protection and climbing, respectively. **(1 Mark)**

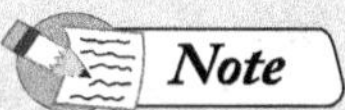

Note

Homology indicates common anastory and is based on divergent evolution.

   (b) The evolution represented by homologous organs or structures is divergent evolution as they have common origin but have diverged (became dissimilar) with evolution due to adaptations to different needs. **(1 Mark)**

4. Adaptive radiation is defined as the process of evolution of different species in a specific geographical area starting from a point and literally radiating to another areas of geography or habitat. Darwin finches and Australian marsupials are examples of adaptive radiation.

   (2 Marks)

5. A number of marsupials, each different from the other evolved from an ancestral stock, but all within the Australian island continent. When more than one adaptive radiation appeared to have occurred in an isolated geographical area (representing different habitats), one can call this convergent evolution.

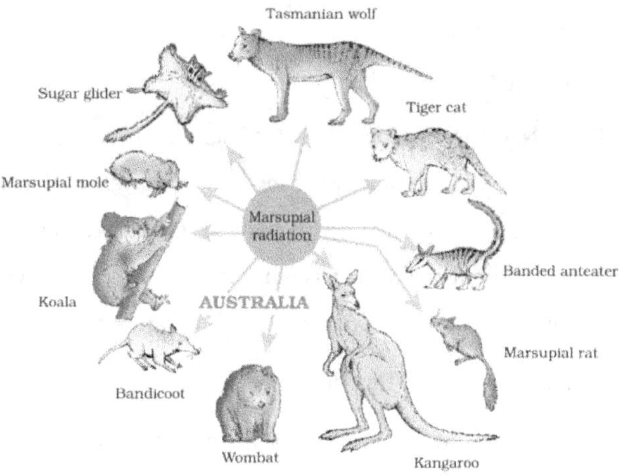

Fig : Adaptive radiation of marsupials of Australia

(3 Marks)

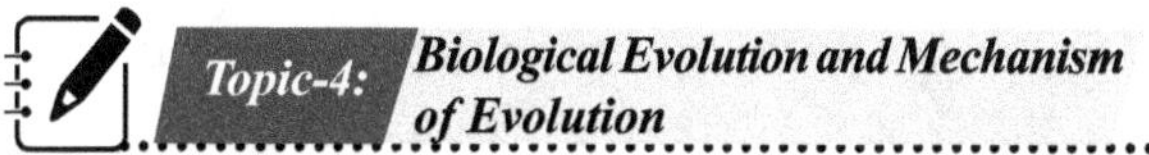

Topic-4: *Biological Evolution and Mechanism of Evolution*

1. According to Hugo de Varies saltation is a single step large mutation. He said that speciation is caused due to mutation. Saltation is responsible for speciation.

   (1 Mark)

Note

Mutation is defined as the sudden and permanant alteration in the nucleotide sequence of DNA.

2. The Darwin's theory of evolution is based on **Natural selection.** According to Darwin's, variation results in evolution. Variations are inheritable and were small as well as directional. Natural selection favours survival of the fittest one as nature selects individuals that are fit and able to adapt as well as survive in changing environment.

   The theory of Hugo de Varies is based on mutation. He believed that large differences occurs suddenly in a population. He also said that mutation results in evolution. According to Hugo de Varies mutation are random and directionless. Mutation leads to cause speciation and hence is called as **saltation or single step large mutation.** **(3 Marks)**

3. Branching descent and natural selection are the two key concepts of Darwinian theory of Evolution.

    According to the concept of Branching descent, various species have come into existence from a common ancestor.

    In Natural selection, the nature selects the individuals that are most fit to adapt to their environment. It occurs because of availability of limited natural resources, variations in the characters of the members of population and inheritance of variations to next generation.

    According to the Darwin theory of evolution:

    *   New forms keep on gradually evolving with time in the history.

    *   Those organisms that adapt themselves better to the surrounding survive and reproduce whereas other die and promotes the survival of the fittest one.

    *   There is always variation in characteristics of populations that help them to adapt better to the surroundings.

    Example of natural selection is industrial melanism in which before industrialization, it was observed that there were more white-winged moths or melanised moths were found on the trees than dark-winged moths. But after industrialization in 1920s, it was observed that there were more dark-winged moths were found in the same area. It occurs because during post-industrialisation period, the tree trunks became dark due to industrial smoke and soots. In this condition, the white-winged moth did not survive because of predators. Hence dark-winged or melanised moth survived. **(5 Marks)**

Note

Evolution is defined as the change in the characteristics of a species over several generations and is responsible for natural selection.

4. Natural selection is based on certain observations which are factual. For example, natural resources are limited, populations are stable in size except for seasonal fluctuation, members of a population vary in characteristics (infact no two individuals are alike) even though they look superficially similar, most of variations are inherited etc. The fact that theoretically population size will grow exponentially if everybody reproduced maximally (this fact can be seen in a growing bacterial population) and the fact that population sizes in reality are limited, means that there had been competition for resources. Only some survived and grew at the cost of others that could not flourish. The novelty and brilliant insight of Darwin was this: he asserted that variations, which are heritable and which make resource utilisation better for few (adapted to habitat better) will enable only those to reproduce and leave more progeny. Hence for a period of time, over many generations, survivors will leave more progeny and there would be a change in population characteristic and hence new forms appear to arise. **(5 Marks)**

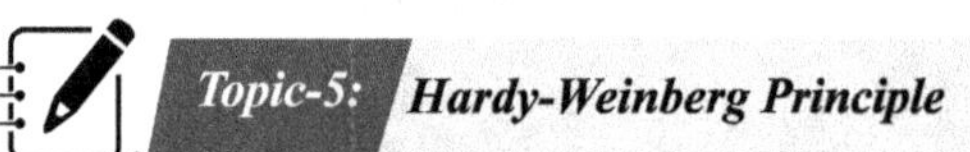

Topic-5: *Hardy-Weinberg Principle*

1. (a) Sum Total of All the Allele Frequencies is 1: Let there be two alleles A and a in a population. The frequencies of alleles A and a are 'p' and 'q' respectively. **(½ Mark)**

    The frequency of AA individuals in a population is p^2 and it can be explained that the probability that an allele A with a frequency of p would appear on both the chromosomes of a diploid individual is simply the product of the probabilities, i.e., p^2.

    Similarly, the frequency of aa is q^2 and that of Aa is 2pq. **(½ Mark)**

    $p^2 + 2pq + q^2) = 1$, where p^2 represents the frequency of homozygous dominant genotype, 2pq represents the frequency of the heterozygous genotype and q^2 represents the frequency of the homozygous recessive. **(1 Mark)**

(b) Factors that affect Hardy–Weinberg equilibrium:

   (i)   Gene migration or gene flow

   (ii) Genetic drift

   (iii) Mutation

   (iv) Genetic recombination

   (v)   Natural Selection (Any 2)   **(½ + ½ = 1 Mark)**

2. If gene migration occurs multiple times then it is known as gene flow. The Hardy-Weinberg law states that the gene pool remains constant. Gene flow is the transfer of genetic information from one population to another. If the same change takes place by chance then it is called genetic drift. When migration of a section of population to another place and population occurs, gene frequencies change in the original as well as in the new population. New genes or alleles are added to the new population and are lost from old population. There would be a gene flow if this gene migration happens multiple times. If the same change occurs by chance, then it is called genetic drift.

(2 Marks)

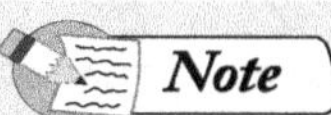
Note

Gene pool refers to the total number of genes and their alleles in a population.

3. In a given population, one can find out the frequency of occurrence of alleles of a gene or a locus. This frequency is supposed to remain fixed and even remain the same through generations. Hardy-Weinberg principle stated it using algebraic equations.

This principle states that the allele frequencies in a population are stable and is constant from generation to generation. The gene pool (total genes and their alleles in a population) remains a constant. This is called genetic equilibrium. Sum total of all the allelic frequencies is 1. Individual frequencies, for example, can be named p, q, etc. In a diploid, p and q represents the frequency of allele A and allele a. The frequency of AA individuals in a population is simply p^2.

This is simply stated in another ways, i.e., the probability that an allele A with a frequency of p appear on both the chromosomes of a diploid individual is simply the product of the probabilities, i.e., p^2. Similarly of aa is q^2, of Aa 2pq.

Hence, $p^2 + 2pq + q^2 = 1$. This is a binomial expansion of $(p + q)^2$. When frequency measured, differs from expected values, the difference (direction) indicates the extent of evolutionary change. Disturbance in genetic equilibrium, or Hardy-Weinberg equilibrium, i.e., change of frequency of alleles in a population would then be interpreted as resulting in evolution.   **(2 Marks)**

4. Hardy Weinberg's principle states that allele frequencies are stable and is constant from one generation to other generation. The gene pool remains constant called genetic equilibrium. Sum total of all the allele frequencies is one. Suppose there are two alleles '*A*' and '*a*' in a population. Their frequencies are *p* and *q*, respectively. The frequency of *AA* individual in a population is P^2. It can be explained that the probability that an allele A with a frequency of *p* appear on both the chromosomes of a diploid individual is simply the product of the probabilities, *i.e.*, p^2. In the same way, the frequency *aa* is q^2 and for *Aa* is *pq*.

$$p^2 + 2pq + q^2 = 1$$

where, p^2 represents frequency of homozygous dominant genotype,

2pq represents the frequency of the heterozygous genotype and represents the frequency of homozygous recessive.

In population genetics studies, the Hardy-Weinberg equation can be used to measure whether the observed genotype frequencies in a population differ from the frequencies predicted by the equation. If there is any difference in the frequencies, it indicates the extent of evolutionary change.   **(3 Marks)**

5. Hardy Weinberg's principle states that allele frequencies are stable and is constant from generation to generation. The gene pool remains constant called **genetic equilibrium**. Sum total of all the allele frequencies is one. Suppose there are two alleles '*A*' and '*a*' in a population. Their frequencies are *p* and *q*, respectively. The frequency of *AA* individual in a population is P^2. It can be explained that the probability that an allele *A* with a frequency of *p* appear on both the chromosomes of a diploid individual is simply the product of the probabilities, *i.e.*, p^2. In the same way, the frequency *aa* is q^2 and for *Aa* is *pq*.

$p^2 + 2pq + q^2 = 1$

where, p^2 represents frequency of homozygous dominant genotype,

$2pq$ represents the frequency of the heterozygous geno type and represents the frequency of homozygous recessive. **(3 Marks)**

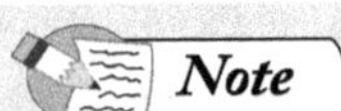
Note

VNTRs (Variable Number Tandem Repeats) are repetitive units of 10-60bp and show a higher degree of polymorphism as these base pairs sequences are different in different individuals.

6. (a) The algebraic equation $p^2 + q^2 + 2pq = 1$ is a binomial expansion of $(p + q)^2$. This algebraic equation represents the Hardy-Weinberg's principle that is used to calculate the genetic variation of a population at equilibrium. The Hardy-Weinberg principle states that the allele frequencies in a population are stable and which is remains constant from one generation to another generation.

So, p represents the frequency of allele A, q represents the frequency of allele a, p^2 represents the frequency of AA (homozygous) individuals in a population. Whereas q^2 represents the frequency of aa and 2pq represents the frequency of Aa (heterozygous) individuals. It also indicates that the sum of all the allelic frequencies is equal to one.

(3 Marks)

(b) Gene migration refers to the movement of the alleles from one population to another that result in inbreeding between the members of the two population. So, the removal of alleles from one population or addition of alleles into another population is called gene migration. While genetic drift which is also called 'Swell Wright Effect'. Genetic drift is random in allele frequencies. It results in elimination of alleles or fixation of the other alleles in the population. **(2 Marks)**

Topic-6: *A Brief Account of Evolution*

1. (d) Bryophytes were the part of cenozoic era. **(1 Mark)**

2. (b) The correct sequence from early to late geological period is: Silurian period Carboniferous period and Jurassic period. **(1 Mark)**

3. (a) The study of fossils is considered as the important evidence for evolution because it represents that the life on the earth was once different from the life that is found on earth today. The study of fossils is important because it helps to determine and study the physical structure of extinct organisms. With the help of fossils, one can determine that how long life has existed on earth and how the different plants as well as animals are evolved and are related to each other. **(2 Marks)**

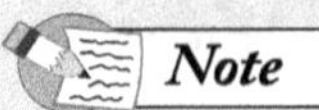
Note

Fossils are the dead remains impression or trace of an animal on plant of are preserved in Earth's rust from a past geological age.

(b) Paleozoic – Rhynia

Arborescent Lycopods

Mesozoic – Conifers

Dicotyledons **(1 Mark)**

Topic-7: *Origin and Evolution of Man*

1. (b) The Neanderthal man with a brain size of 1400cc lived in near east and central Asia between 1,00,000-40,000 years back. They used hides to protect their body and buried their dead. **(1 Mark)**

2. Difference between eating habits of *Homo habilis* and *Homo erectus* are as follows:

Characteristics	*Homo habilis*	*Homo erectus*
Eating habits	They did not eat meat.	They ate meat.

(1 Mark)

3. Difference between *Homo erectus* and *Homo habilis*.

(2 Mark)

S. No.	Character	*Homo erectus*	*Homo habilis*
(i)	**Brain capacity**	900 cc	650–800 cc
(ii)	**Eating habit**	They probably ate meat	They probably did not eat meat

4. (a) Shrews were the first mammals. These were the long-tailed insectivorous, squirrel-like creatures, which gave rise to the primitive primates, namely lemurs and tarsiers in the beginning of the tertiary period (Palaeocene epoch).

(b) The discovery of Coelacanth (lobefins) first amphibians is significant as they prove that amphibian have evolved from fish-like organisms. Lobefins were the ancestors of modern day frogs and salamanders.

(c) *Homo habilis* were the first human-like primate who lived in Africa about 2 million years ago. Their brain capacities were between 650- 800cc and they had bipedal locomotion, moved erect and probably didn't eat meat.

(d) *Homo erectus* were the next primates evolved from *Homo habilis* about 1.5 mya. They had a large brain capacities around 900cc and they had an erect posture. They probably ate meat. **(3 Marks)**

5.

Characteristics of *Ramapithecus*	Characteristics of *Dryopithecus*	Characteristics of Neanderthal man
Ramapithecus walked like gorillas and chimpanzees.	*Dryopithecus* has hairy arms and legs of same length.	Nenderthal man has brain capacity of 1400cc
They had dental structure more similar to man.	They walked like gorillas, chimpanzees, and apes.	They hide in order to protect their bodies and also buried their dead ones.

(3 Marks)

6. The three characteristics of Neanderthal man are as follows:

- They have brain capacity 1400cc and lived near east and central Asia between 1,00,000-40,000 years back. **(1)**

- They used hides to protect their body. **(1)**

- They buried their dead. **(1)**

(3 Marks)

7. (i)   About 15 mya, primates called Dryopithecus and Ramapithecus were existing. They were hairy and walked like gorillas and chimpanzees.

    (ii) Ramapithecus was more man-like while Dryopithecus was more ape-like. Few fossils of man-like bones have been discovered in Ethiopia and Tanzania.

    (iii) These revealed hominid features leading to the belief that about 3-4 mya, man-like primates walked in eastern Africa. They were probably not taller than 4 feet but walked up right.

    (iv) Two mya, Australopithecines probably lived in East African grasslands. Evidence shows they hunted with stone weapons but essentially ate fruit.

    (v)   Some of the bones among the bones discovered were different.   **(3 Marks)**

7 Chapter — Human Health and Disease

 **Topic-1:** *Common Diseases in Humans*

 **1**   *Multiple Choice Questions (1 Mark)*

1. Select the pathogen mismatched with the symptoms of disease caused by it from the list given below :

   [Delhi 2023, Set-I, U]

   (a) Entamoeba histolytica : Constipation, abdominal pain.

   (b) Epidermophyton : Dry scaly lesions on nail.

   (c) Wuchereria bancrofti : Chronic inflammation of lymphatic vessels of lower limb.

   (d) Haemophilus influenzae : Blockage of the intestinal passage.

2. Interferons are proteins. In human they are secreted by:

   [Delhi 2023, Set-II, K]

   (a) Thymus gland

   (b) B-lymphocytes

   (c) Viral infeced cells

   (d) Tonsils

2   *Assertion Reason/Two Statement Type Questions (1 Mark)*

3. **Assertion (A):** Mary Mallon continued to spread typhoid for many years.   **[All India 2023 Set-I, A]**

   Reason (R): *Salmonella typhi* generally enters the small intestine through food and water contaminated with it.

   (a) Both Assertion (A) and Reason (R) are true and Reason (R) is the correct explanation of the Assertion (A).

   (b) Both Assertion (A) and Reason (R) are true, but Reason (R) is not the correct explanation of the Assertion (A).

   (c) Assertion (A) is true, but Reason (R) is false.

   (d) Assertion (A) is false, but Reason (R) is true.

4   *Very Short Answer Questions (1 Mark)*

4. It is often observed that the chances of a person suffering from measles in his or her lifetime are low if he or she has suffered from the disease in their early childhood. Justify the statement.   **[All India 2020, U]**

5. Name two diseases whose spread can be controlled by the eradication of *Aedes* mosquitoes.   **[All India 2018, K]**

5   *Short Answer Questions (2 or 3 Marks)*

6. (a) "Plasmodium protozoan needs both a mosquito and a human host for its continuity." Explain.

   [Delhi 2023, Set-I, U]

   OR

   (b) We all must work towards maintaining good health because 'health is wealth'. Enlist any six ways of achieving good health.   **[Delhi 2023, Set-I, U]**

7. When a microorganism invades a host, a definite sequence of events usually occur leading to infection and disease, causing suffering to the host. This process is called pathogenesis. Once a microorganism overcomes the defense system of the host, development of the disease follows a certain sequence of events as shown in the graph. Study the graph given below for the sequence of events leading to appearance of a disease and answer the questions that follow: **[Delhi 2023, Set-I, A]**

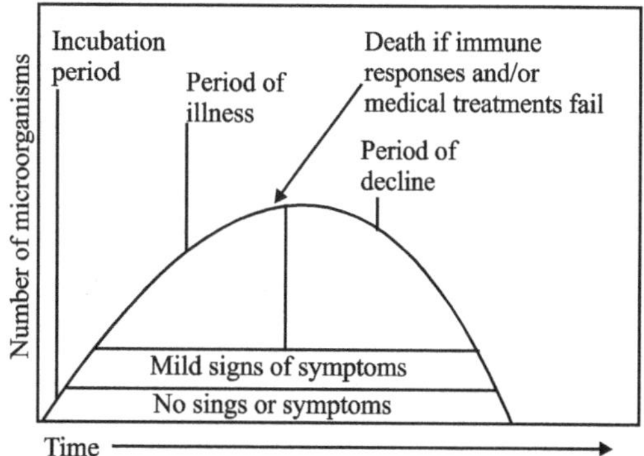

(a) In which period, according to the graph there are maximum chances of a person transmitting a disease/infection and why?

(b) Study the graph and write what is an incubation period. Name a sexually transmitted disease that can be easily transmitted during this period. Name the specific type of lymphocytes that are attacked by the pathogen of this disease.

8. During a field trip, one of your friend in the group suddenly became unwell, she started sneezing and had trouble in breathing. Name and explain the term associated with such sudden responses. What would the doctor recommend for relief?

[CBSE Sample Paper 2022-23, U]

9. (a) Explain the Life cycle of Plasmodium starting from its entry in the body of female Anopheles till the completion of its life cycle in humans.

[CBSE Sample Paper 2022-23, U]

(b) Explain the cause of periodic recurrence of chill and high fever during malarial attack in humans.

[CBSE Sample Paper 2022-23, U]

10. (a) Identify the nos. (i) to (iv) in the following table:

[Delhi 2019, K]

	Name of disease	Causative organism	Symptoms
w	Penumonia	*Streptococcus*	(i)
x	Typhoid	(ii)	High fever, weakness, headache, stomach pain
y	(iii)	Rhinoviruses	Nasal congestion and discharge, sore throat, cough, headache
z	Ascariasis	*Ascaris*	(iv)

(b) Which one of the above mentioned diseases are transmitted through mechanical carriers?

[Delhi 2019, K]

11. Name a human disease, its causal organism, symptoms (any three) and vector, spread by intake of water and food contaminated by human faecal matter. **[Delhi 2017, K]**

12. Name the causative organism of the disease amoebiasis. List three symptoms of the disease. **[Delhi 2016, K]**

13. List the symptoms of *Ascariasis*. How does a healthy person acquire this infection? **[All India 2014, U]**

14. A student on a school trip started sneezing and wheezing soon after reaching the hill station for no explained reasons. But, on return to the plains, the symptoms

disappeared. What is such a response called? How does the body produce it ? **[Delhi 2013, Ap]**

Long Answer Questions (5 Marks)

15. Explain the role of Primary and Secondary Lymphoid organs with the help of suitable examples.

[CBSE Sample Paper 2023-24, U]

Case Based Questions

16. The diagram shows the life cycle of a pathogenic protozoan. **[All India 2023, Set-I, A]**

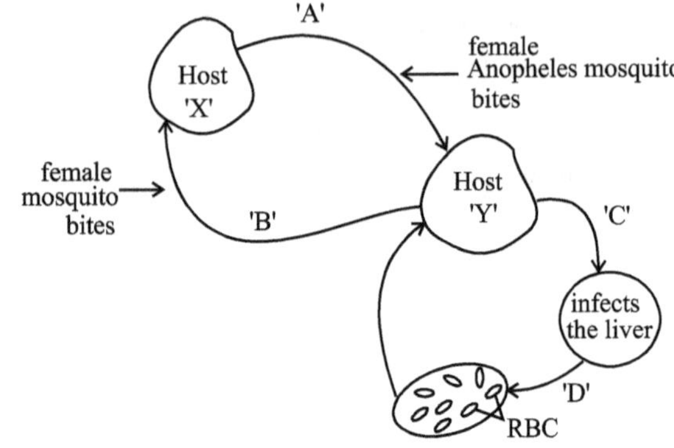

(i) Name the parasitic stage that is being transferred from host 'X' to host 'Y'.

(ii) Write the changes the parasite undergoes in the liver.

(iii) Write the changes the parasite undergoes when it enters the RBC.

(iv) (a) Trace the changes the parasite undergoes when the host 'X' takes its blood meal from infected host 'Y'.

OR

(iv) (b) At which stage during the life cycle of the pathogen does the host 'Y' experience the symptoms of the disease? Name the disease and the toxic substance responsible for these symptoms. **[All India 2023, Set-I, A]**

17. Community Service department of your school plans a visit to a slum area near the school with an objective to educate the slum dwellers with respect to health and hygiene.

[All India 2014, Ap]

(a) Why is there a need to organize such visits?

(b) Write the steps you will highlight, as a member of this department, in your interaction with them to enable them to lead a healthy life.

Topic-2: *Immunity*

Multiple Choice Questions (1 Mark)

1. Select the options which is/are incorrect statement(s) with respect to T-lymphocytes in the human body.

   [All India 2023, Set-I, K]

   (i) They are a type of white blood cells.

   (ii) They are produced in bone marrow.

   (iii) They remain active at all times in the body.

   (iv) They mature in the bone marrow.

   (a) (i) and (iv) only   (b) (iii) only

   (c) (iv) only   (d) (iii) and (iv) only

2. The decrease in the T-lymphocytes count in human blood will result in :   **[Delhi 2023, Set-I, K]**

   (a) Decrease in antigens   (b) Decrease in antibodies

   (c) Increase in antibodies (d) Increase in antigens

3. *Apis mellifera* are killer bees possessing toxic bee venom. Identify the treatment and the type of immunity developed from the given table to treat a person against the venom of this bee.   **[CBSE Sample Paper 2022-23, U]**

	Remedy	Immunity
(a)	Inactivated proteins	Active
(b)	Proteins of the venom	Passive
(c)	Preformed antibodies	Passive
(d)	Dead micro-organisms	Active

4. Interferons are most effective in making non-infected cells resistant against the spread of which of the following diseases in humans? **[CBSE Sample Paper 2022-23, K]**

   (a) ascariasis   (b) ringworm

   (c) amoebiasis   (d) AIDS

5. The main barrier that prevents the entry of micro-organisms into our body is   **[All India 2020, K]**

   (a) Antibodies   (b) Macrophages

   (c) Monocytes   (d) Skin

Very Short Answer Questions (1 Mark)

6. The graph given below indicates the administration of the first (L) and second dose (M) of a vaccine. The corresponding response of the body is indicated by X and

Y. Interpret the graph and explain the reason for such a response shown by the body.

[CBSE Sample Paper 2023-24, A]

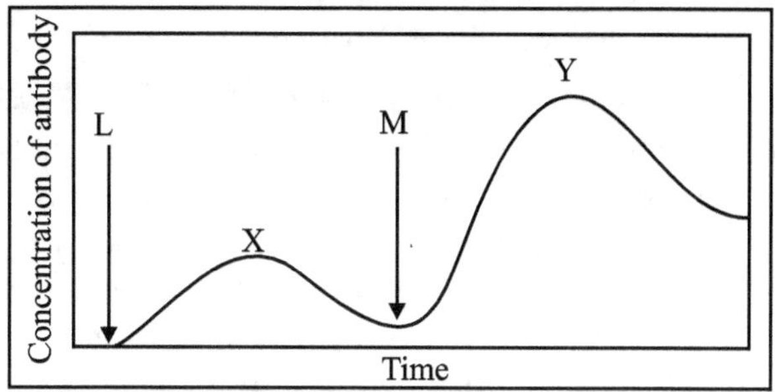

7. Mention the two types of acquired immunity response present in our body. Give one major role of each.

   [All India 2022, Term-II, K]

8. Humans have innate immunity for protection against pathogens that may enter the gut along with food. What are the two barriers that protect the body from such pathogens?

   [CBSE Sample Paper 2021-22, Ap]

9. How do cytokine barriers provide innate immunity in humans?   **[All India 2018, K]**

10. Suggest a method to ensure an anamnestic response in humans.   **[All India 2017, U]**

11. Why is secondary immune response more intense than the primary immune response in humans?

    [All India 2014, U]

12. Name any two types of cells which act as 'Cellular barriers' to provide Innate Immunity in humans. **[Delhi 2014, U]**

13. When does a human body elicit an anamnestic response?

    [All India 2013, U]

5   **Short Answer Questions (2 or 3 Marks)**

14. (a) Draw a schematic labelled diagram of an antibody.

    [Delhi 2023, Set-II, U]

    (b) In which period, the number of immune cells forming antibodies will be the highest in a person suffering from pneumonia? **[Delhi 2023, Set-II, U]**

15. Highlight the structural importance of an antibody molecule with a diagram. Name the four types of antibodies found to give a humoral immune response, mentioning the functions of two of them you have studied.

OR

(a) Explain the Life cycle of Plasmodium starting from its entry in the body of female Anopheles till the completion of its life cycle in humans.

[CBSE Sample Paper 2023-24, K]

(b) Explain the cause of periodic recurrence of chill and high fever during malarial attack in humans.

[CBSE Sample Paper 2023-24, K]

16. Recognition of an antigenic protein of a pathogen or exposure to a pathogen occurs during many types of immune responses, including active immunity and induced active immunity. Specify the types of responses elicited when human beings get encountered by a pathogen.

[CBSE Sample Paper 2021-22, Ap]

17. Differentiate between the roles of B-lymphocytes and T-lymphocytes in generating immune responses

[All India 2019, K]

OR

Principle of vaccination is based on the property of "memory" of the immune system.　**[All India 2019, K]**
Taking one suitable example, justify the statement.

18. Give reasons for the following:　　　**[Delhi 2019, U]**

(a) Antibody mediated immunity is called humoral immunity.

(b) How is a child protected from a disease for which he/she is vaccinated?

(c) Name the type of cells the AIDS virus enters after getting into the human body.

19. (a) What precaution(s) would you recommend to a patient requiring repeated blood transfusion?

[All India 2017, U]

(b) If the advise is not followed by the patient, there is an apprehension that the patient might contract a disease that would destroy the immune system of his/ her body.

Explain with the help of schematic diagram only how the immune system would get affected and destroyed.

20. Mention one application for each of the following :

(a) Passive immunization　　　　**[Delhi 2017, K]**

(b) Antihistamine

(c) Colostrum

(d) Cytokinin-barrier

21. (a) It is generally observed that the children who had suffered from chicken-pox in their childhood may not contract the same disease in their adulthood. Explain giving reasons, the basis of such an immunity in an individual. Name this kind of immunity.

[All India 2016, U]

(b) What are interferons? Mention their role.

[All India 2016, U]

22. A heavily bleeding and bruised road accident victim was brought to a nursing home. The doctor immediately gave him an injection to protect him against a deadly disease.

[All India 2015, Ap]

(a) Write what did the doctor inject into the patient's body.

(b) How do you think this injection would protect the patient against the disease?

(c) Name the disease against which this injection was given and the kind of immunity it provides.

23. Write the events that take place when a vaccine for any disease is introduced into the human body.

[Delhi 2013, U]

OR

Why is a person with cuts and bruises following an accident administered tetanus antitoxin? Give reasons.

[Delhi 2013, U]

6　　　*Long Answer Questions (5 Marks)*

24. Following a road accident four injured persons were brought to a nearby clinic. The doctor immediately injected them with tetanus antitoxin.　**[Delhi 2020, K]**

(a) What is tetanus antitoxin?

(b) Why were the injured immediately injected with this antitoxin?

(c) Name the kind of immunity this injection provided.

Topic-3:　　*AIDS*

4　　　*Very Short Answer Questions (1 Mark)*

1. Name and mention the events that occur in the cells when HIV gets into blood after gaining entry into the human body.　　　**[All India 2020, U]**

2. Why sharing of injection needles between two individuals is not recommended?　　　**[Delhi 2013, U]**

3. Retroviruses have no DNA. However, the DNA of the infected host cell does possess viral DNA. How is it possible?　　　**[All India 2015, U]**

 **Long Answer Questions (5 Marks)**

4. With the help of a flow chart illustrate how an infected animal cell can survive while viruses are being replicated or released.   **[CBSE Sample Paper 2023-24, Ap]**

5. Study the diagram showing the entry of HIV into the human body and the processes that are followed:

[Delhi 2020, U]

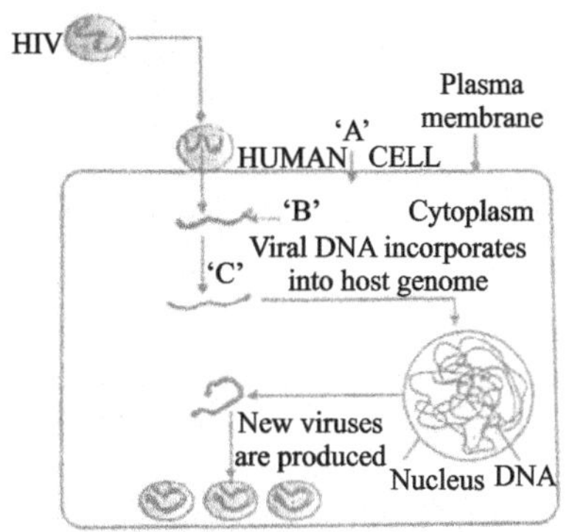

(a) Name the human cell 'A' HIV enters into.

(b) Mention the genetic material 'B' HIV releases into the cell.

(c) Identify enzyme 'C'.

6. A person in your colony has recently been diagnosed with AIDS. People/residents in the colony want him to leave the colony for the fear of spread of AIDS.

[All India 2013, A]

(a) Write your view on the situation, giving reasons.

(b) List the possible preventive measures that you would suggest to the residents of your locality in a meeting organised by you so that they understand the situation.

(c) Write the symptoms and the causative agent of AIDS.

 *Topic-4:* **Cancer**

 **Very Short Answer Questions (1 Mark)**

1. Why a malignant tumour considered to be more damaging than a benign tumour? Explain. **[Delhi 2023, Set-I, K]**

2. Immunotherapy these days is one of the most efficient way of treatment of cancer. The therapy involved activates the immune system and destroys the tumour.

[Delhi 2023, Set-III, K]

(i) Write an example of one such biological response modifier used in immunotherapy.

(ii) Why do patients need such substances if immune system is already working in body?

(iii) State what is 'Contact inhibition'.

3. Indiscrimate diagnostic practices using X-rays etc., should be avoided. Give one reason.   **[Delhi 2015, K]**

 **Short Answer Questions (2 or 3 Marks)**

4. Name any two techniques used to detect the cancer of internal organs and write about any one of them.

[Delhi 2023 (Set-II), K]

5. (a) Write down a short note on contact inhibition in cancer cell?   **[All India 2022, K]**

(b) Write a short note on a-interferons?

[All India 2022, K]

6. How do normal cells get transformed into cancerous neoplastic cells? Elaborate giving three examples of inducing agent. OR A person is suffering from a high-grade fever. Which symptoms will help to identify if he/she is suffering from Typhoid, Pneumonia or Malaria?

[CBSE Sample Paper 2021-22, A]

7. What are the different ways of treat cancer?

[All India 2019, K]

 **Long Answer Questions (5 Marks)**

8. (a) Cancer is one of the most dreaded diseases of humans. Explain 'Contact inhibition' and 'Metastasis' with respect to the disease.   **[Delhi 2014, U]**

(b) Name the group of genes which have been identified in normal cells that could lead to cancer and how they do so ?   **[Delhi 2014, U]**

(c) Name any two techniques which are useful to detect cancers of internal organs.   **[Delhi 2014, U]**

(d) Why are cancer patients often given a-interferon as part of the treatment ?   **[Delhi 2014, U]**

9. What are the different causes of cancer? **[Delhi 2013, U]**

Topic-5:   *Drug and Alcohol Abuse*

1   *Multiple Choice Questions (1 Mark)*

1. A patient was advised to have a kidney transplant. To suppress the immune reaction, the doctor would administer him: **[CBSE Sample Paper 2021-22, U]**

   (a) statins produced from *Monascus purpureus*

   (b) statins produced from *Streptococcus thermophilus*

   (c) cyclosporin A produced from *Trichoderma polysporum*

   (d) cyclosporin A produced from *Clostridium butylicum*

4   *Very Short Answer Questions (1 Mark)*

2. Differentiate between opioids and cannabinoids on the basis of their   **[Delhi 2020, K]**

   (a) specific receptor site in human body.

   (b) mode of action in human body.

3. Identify the compound chemical structure is shown below. State any three of its physical properties.

   [CBSE Sample Paper 2021-22, U]

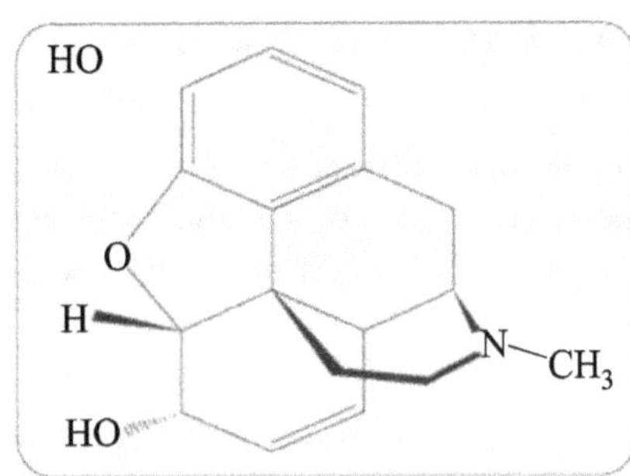

5   *Short Answer Questions (2 or 3 Marks)*

4.   **[All India 2023, Set-I, K]**

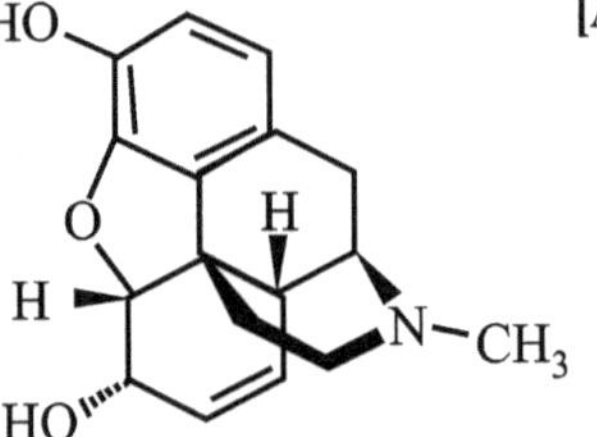

   (a) Name the category of drugs represented by the chemical structure given above.

(b) If the methyl group is substituted by acetyl group we get a bitter crystalline compound. Name the compound.

(c) Name the natural source of these compounds.

(d) State the harmful effects of this class of drugs on the human body.

5. (a) Write the scientific names of the source plants from where opioids and canabinoids are extracted.

   [Delhi 2019, K]

   (b) Write their receptor sites in the human body. How do these drugs affect the human beings?

   [Delhi 2019, K]

6. (a) Name the source plant of heroin drug. How is it obtained from plant?   **[All India 2018, K]**

   (b) Write the effects of heroin on the human body?

   [All India 2018, K]

7. (a) Why is there a fear amongst the guardians that their adolescent wards may get trapped in drug/alcohol abuse?   **[Delhi 2017, K]**

   (b) Explain 'addiction' and 'dependence' in respect of drug/alcohol abuse in youth.   **[Delhi 2017, K]**

8. Prior to a sports event blood & urine samples of sportspersons are collected for drug tests.   **[Delhi 2016, U]**

   (a) Why is there a need to conduct such tests ?

   (b) Name the drugs the authorities usually look for.

   (c) Write the generic names of two plants from which these drugs are obtained.

9. A team of students are preparing to participate in the interschool sports meet. During a practice session you find some vials with labels of certain cannabionoids.

   [Delhi 2015, U]

   (a) Will you report to the authorities ? Why ?

   (b) Name a plant from which such chemicals are obtained.

   (c) Write the effect of these chemicals on human body.

7   *Case Based Questions*

10. The data below shows the concentration of nicotine smoked by a smoker taking 10 puffs/ minute.

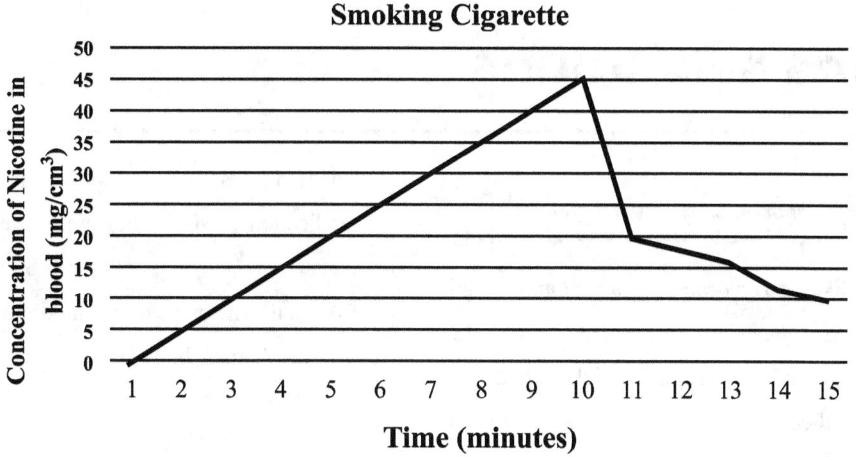

[CBSE Sample Paper 2022-23, **A**]

(a)   With reference to the above graph explain the concentration of nicotine in blood at 10 minutes.

(b)   How will this affect the concentration of carbon monoxide and haembound oxygen at 10 minutes?

(c)   How does cigarette smoking result in high blood pressure and increase in heart rate?

OR

(c)   How does cigarette smoking result in lung cancer and emphysema?   [CBSE Sample Paper 2022-23, **A**]

Hints & Solutions

Topic-1: *Common Diseases in Humans*

1. **(d)** Bacteria like *Streptococcus pneumoniae* and *Haemophilus influenzae* are responsible for the disease pneumonia in humans which infects the alveoli (air filled sacs) of the lungs. **(1 Mark)**

2. **(c)** Interferon is a protein secreted by cells in response to infection by a virus, but it does not directly inhibit the virus's multiplication. The function of interferon is to protect the uninfected cells from infection by virus. **(1 Mark)**

3. **(b)** Mary Mallon, also called Typhoid Mary, was identified as a carrier of the typhoid bacterium and was the source of multiple outbreaks of typhoid fever in New York City and Long Island during 1900-1907. After eating food or drinking water contaminated with the Salmonella typhi bacteria, the bacteria moves down into the digestive system, where it will multiply quickly. **(1 Mark)**

4. During the initial stage of infection, memory cells are generated in the body. The memory cells create information about the pathogen that causes measles in the human body for the first time and produce antibodies for them. During the second stage of measles infection, the memory cells are activated that are formed during first encounter. These memory cells produce an antibody against the antigen that cause measles and kills the virus that causes measles. **(1 Mark)**

Note

Acquired immunity is pathogen specific and is characterised by memory. This means that our body when it encounters a pathogen for the first time produces a response called primary response which is of low intensity.

5. The two diseases whose spread can be controlled by the eradication of *Aedes* mosquitoes are chikungunya and dengue. **(1 Mark)**

6. **(a)** In the life cycle of Plasmodium, Plasmodium enters the human body as sporozoites (infectious form) through the bite of infected female Anopheles mosquito. The parasites initially multiply within the liver cells and then attack the red blood cells (RBCs) resulting in their rupture. The rupture of RBCs is associated with release of a toxic substance, haemozoin, which is responsible for the chill and high fever recurring every three to four days. When a female Anopheles mosquito bites an infected person, these parasites enter the mosquito's body and undergo further development. The parasites multiply within them to form sporozoites that are stored in their salivary glands. When these mosquitoes bite a human, the sporozoites are introduced into his/ her body, thereby initiating the events mentioned above. Hence, malarial parasite requires two hosts – human and mosquitoes – to complete its life cycle. **(3 Marks)**

Note

Different species of plasmodium (P vivax, P malaria annd P falciparum) are responsible for causing malaria.

OR

(b) Health can be defined as a state of complete physical, mental and social well-being. When people are healthy, they are more efficient at work. This increases productivity and brings economic prosperity. Health also increases longevity of people and reduces infant and maternal mortality.

(1½ Marks)

There are various way to achieve a good health:

(i) Balanced diet, personal hygiene and regular exercise are very important to maintain good health.

(ii) Yoga has been practised since time immemorial to achieve physical and mental health.

(iii) Awareness about diseases and their effect on different bodily function are also necessary for achieving good health.

(iv) Vaccinations (immunisation) against infectious diseases are necessary for achieving good health.

(v) Proper disposal of wastes is important,

(vi) Control of vectors and maintenance of hygiene in food and water resources are necessary for achieving good health. **(1½ Marks)**

7. **(a)** In the period of illness, there are maximum chances of a person transmitting a disease because during this period the number of micro- organisms is highest.

(1 Mark)

(b) Incubation period (also known as the **latent period** or **latency period**) is the time elapsed between exposure to a pathogenic organism, a chemical, or radiation, and when symptoms and signs are first apparent.

AIDS (Acquired immune deficiency syndrome) can be easily transmitted during incubation period.

T lymphocytes (helper T cells are attacked by the pathogen of HIV.

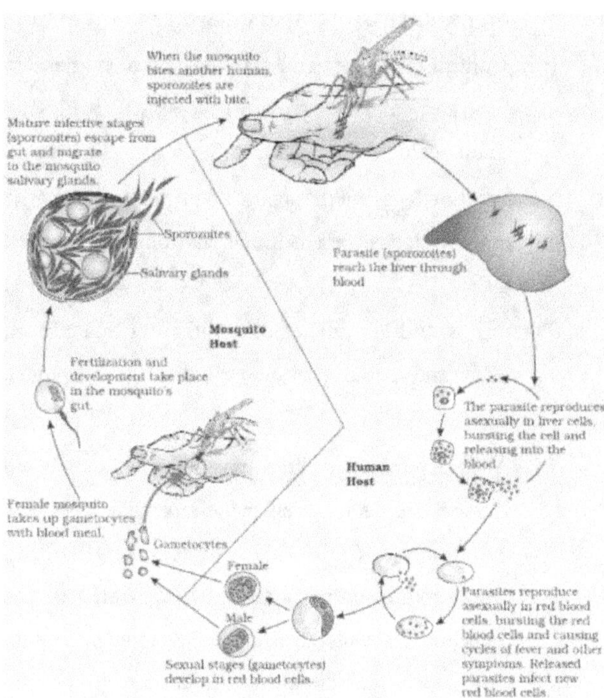

(2 Marks)

OR

(b) Health can be defined as a state of complete physical, mental and social well-being. When people are healthy, they are more efficient at work. This increases productivity and brings economic prosperity. Health also increases longevity of people and reduces infant and maternal mortality.

(1 Mark)

There are various way to achieve a good health:

(i) Balanced diet, personal hygiene and regular exercise are very important to maintain good health.

(ii) Yoga has been practised since time immemorial to achieve physical and mental health.

(iii) Awareness about diseases and their effect on different bodily function are also necessary for achieving good health.

(iv) Vaccinations (immunisation) against infectious diseases are necessary for achieving good health.

(v) Proper disposal of wastes is important,

(vi) Control of vectors and maintenance of hygiene in food and water resources are necessary for achieving good health. **(2 Marks)**

8. Allergy, the exaggerated response of the immune response to certain antigens present in the environment is called allergy. **(1 Mark)**

   Doctors would administer drugs like antihistamines, adrenaline and steroids (any one) to reduce the symptoms. **(2 Marks)**

9. (a) When a female Anopheles mosquito bites an infected person, the parasites enter the mosquito's body as **gametocytes** (½ Mark). It leads to **fertilization and development in the gut** (½ Mark) of the mosquito and undergoes further development to form **sporozoites** that are **stored in salivary glands** (½ Mark) until their transfer to human body.

      In the human body – the **sporozoites reach the liver and reproduce asexually** (½ Mark), bursting the cells and releasing them into the **RBCs as gametocytes** (½ Mark). *(Labeled diagram explaining the mentioned stages can also be considered)* **(1 Mark)**

   (b) The **rupture of RBCs releases a toxic substance called haemozoin,** (½ mark) which is responsible for the chill and high fever. **(1 Mark)**

10. (a) (i) Fever, chills, cough, cold and headache. In severe cases, the lips and fingernails may turn grey to bluish in color.

       (ii) *Salmonella typhi*

       (iii) Common cold

       (iv) Internal bleeding, muscular pain, fever, anaemia and blockage of intestinal passage. **(2 Marks)**

    (b) None of the above mentioned diseases are transmitted through mechanical carriers. **(1 Mark)**

11. The infectious disease that is caused because of the intake of contaminated food and water by human faecal matter is Amoebic dysentery or Amoebiasis.

    This disease is caused by a protozoa *Entamoeba histolytica*.

Its symptoms involve constipation, abdominal pain and cramps, stools with excess mucous and blood clots. Houseflies act as carrier for the transmission of parasites from faeces of infected person to food and water.

(3 Marks)

12. Amoebiasis or amoebic dysentery is caused by *Entamoeba histolytica*. **(2 Marks)**

    Symptoms of Amoebiasis:

    - Appearance of blood in the stool.
    - Pain in the abdomen.
    - Fever
    - Diarrhoea

13. The symptoms of Ascariasis are as follows:

    - Constipation
    - Abdominal pain and cramps
    - Stools with excess mucous and blood clots

    Houseflies act as mechanical carriers and serves to transmit the parasite from faeces of infected person to food and food products. Drinking water and food contaminated by the faecal matter are the main source of infection. **(3 Marks)**

14. The student is suffering from allergy and the substances to which such as immune response is produced are called allergens. Allergy is because of the release of chemicals such as histamine and serotonin from the mast cells.

(2 Marks)

The antibodies produced to allergic response are of IgE type.

15. - Lymphoid organs: These are the organs where origin and/or maturation and proliferation of lymphocytes occur.

    - The primary lymphoid organs are bone marrow and thymus where immature lymphocytes differentiate into antigen–sensitive lymphocytes.

    - After maturation the lymphocytes migrate to secondary lymphoid organs like spleen, lymph nodes, tonsils, Peyer's patches of small intestine and appendix.

    - The secondary lymphoid organs provide the sites for interaction of lymphocytes with the antigen, which then proliferate to become effector cells.

- The bone marrow is the main lymphoid organ where all blood cells including lymphocytes are produced.

- The thymus is a lobed organ located near the heart and beneath the breastbone.

- Both bone–marrow and thymus provide micro–environments for the development and maturation of T–lymphocytes.

- The spleen is a large bean – shaped organ. It mainly contains lymphocytes and phagocytes.

- It acts as a filter of the blood by trapping blood–borne micro – organisms. Spleen also has a large reservoir of erythrocytes.

- The lymph nodes are small solid structures located at different points along the lymphatic system. Lymph nodes serve to trap the micro-organisms or other antigens, which happen to get into the lymph and tissue fluid. Antigens trapped in the lymph nodes are responsible for the activation of lymphocytes present there and cause the immune response.

There is lymphoid tissue also located within the lining of the major tracts (respiratory, digestive and urogenital tracts) called mucosa - associated lymphoid tissue (MALT). It constitutes about 50 per cent of the lymphoid tissue in human body.

(0.5 × 10 =5 Marks)

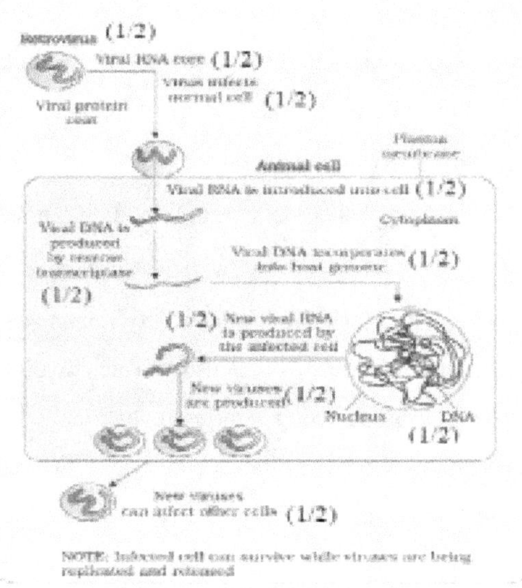

Figure Replication of retrovirus

16. (i) Sporozoite is the parasitic stage that is being transferred from host X (mosquito) to host Y (human).

    (1 Mark)

    (ii) The parasite reproduce asexually in the liver cells of the human host. It leads to bursting of cells and the parasite spreads into the bloodstream. **(1 Mark)**

    (iii) Parasite when enters in to the red blood cells reproduces asexually causing bursting of the red blood cells. Further causing the cycle of fever and other symptoms. Released parasites from ruptured red blood cells infect new red blood cells. **(1 Mark)**

    (iv) (a) Host X is mosquito which will feed on host Y to obtain its blood meal and the host Y is already been infected by the parasite which is at the sexual stage (gametocytes) develop in red blood cells of the host Y. The host X will take up gametocytes with blood meal. **(1 Mark)**

    OR

    (iv) (b) When the parasite enters into the red blood cells of the host it reproduces asexually, when the red blood cells get burst this causes cycles of fever and other symptoms. The disease is malaria and the rupture of RBCs is associated with release of a toxic substance, haemozoin, which is responsible for the chill and high fever recurring every three to four days. **(1 Mark)**

17. (a) There is need to Organize Community Service Department to visit a slum area is to create awareness about disease and their effects on the body and health and hygiene. **(1 Mark)**

    (b) The steps we will highlight, as a member of this department in our interaction with them to enable them to lead a healthy life will be:

    - Explain them the importance of healthy life and healthy people more efficient at work.

    - Health also increases productivity, economy, longevity and also reduces infants as well as maternal mortality.

- To make them aware of the various diseases and their effect.

- Teach people about the proper disposal of waste, control of vectors like mosquitoes, importance of hygienic food and drinking, balanced diet.

- Maintenance of hygienic environment, proper disosal of waste, and control of vector.   **(1 Mark)**

Topic-2:   *Immunity*

1. **(d)** Fully matured T lymphocytes circulate in all tissues and organs of the lymphatic system including the tonsils, spleen and lymph nodes. They can also circulate in the bloodstream. These cells do not remain active all time during life span but get activated during pathogenic invasion in the body. These cells are produced in the bone marrow but get matured in the thymus.   **(1 Mark)**

2. **(b)** The B-lymphocytes produce an army of proteins in response to pathogens into our blood to fight with them. These proteins are called antibodies. The T-cells themselves do not secrete antibodies but help B cells to produce them. Hence, decreases in number of T- lymphocytes automatically reduce the count of antibodies.   **(1 Mark)**

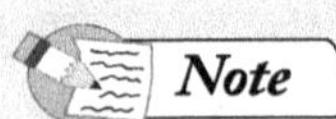

Note

If you have low number of lymphocytes, you are at higher risk of infections.

3. **(c)** Preformed Antibodies, Passive   **(1 Mark)**

4. **(d)** AIDS   **(1 Mark)**

5. **(d)** The main barrier that prevents the entry of microorganisms into our body is skin. Skin on human body serves as the main physical barrier that prevents the entry of the microorganisms.   **(1 Mark)**

6. On administration of the first dose of the vaccine (L), the body shows a response of low intensity (X) as the immune system comes in contact with the antigenic protein of the weakened/inactivated pathogen for the first time. This is called primary immune response.

On subsequent encounter with the same antigenic protein in the second dose (M), the body elicits a highly intensified secondary response (Y). Because of the memory of the first contact with the antigen, the secondary immune response is faster and stronger, leading to more effective pathogen elimination in comparison to the primary immune response.   **(1 Mark)**

7. The two type of acquired immune response present in human body are-

(a) Humoral immune response

(b) Cell- mediated immunity   **(1 Mark)**

Major roles are:

(i) Humoral immune response protects against extracellular virus and bacteria.   **(½ Mark)**

(ii) Cell- mediated immunity is responsible for the graft rejection.   **(½ Mark)**

8. Microbial pathogens enter the gut of humans along with food:

- Physical barriers: Mucus coating of the epithelium lining the gastrointestinal tract helps in trapping microbes entering our body.   **(1Mark)**

- Physiological barriers: Acid in the stomach, saliva in the mouth prevent microbial growth. **(½ + ½ Mark)**

9. Cytokines play a vital role in the innate immune response by means of direct mechanisms which inhibit viral replication by secreting interferon. Interferons are the proteins secreted by viral-infected cells that provide protection to the non-infected cells from further viral infections.   **(1 Mark)**

10.

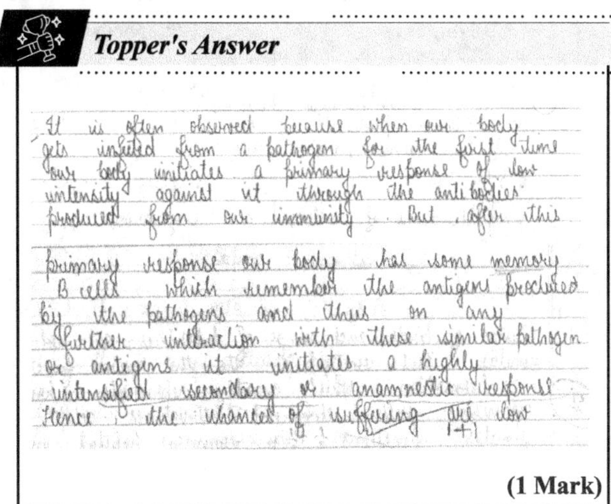

(1 Mark)

Anamestic response is the secondary immune response which is produced when the body encounters the same antigen which is entered previously in the body. As the body recognises the pathogen, immune system starts producing antibodies against the foreign antigens for subsequent encounter and this response is very intense.

(1 Mark)

11. The secondary immune response is more intense than primary immune response because the secondary immune response is based on the memory of the first encounter. The secondary immune response takes place when our body encounters the same antigen for second time. Our body have memory of the first encounter that recognize the pathogen quickly on subsequent exposure and initiates the production of antibodies. **(1 Mark)**

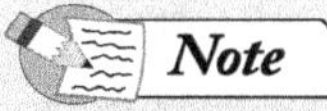

The secondary immune response is pathogen specific and is characterised by memory.

12. Certain types of leukocytes (WBCs) such as Polymorpho-Nuclear Leukocytes (PMNL-neutrophils), monocytes and natural killer cells in the blood as well as macrophages in the tissues that can phagocytise and destroy microbes. These cells act as cellular barriers and provide innate immunity in humans. **(1 Mark)**

Innate immunity is non-specific type of defence which is present at the time of birth.

13. Anamnestic response is the secondary immune response which is produced when the body encounters the same antigen which is entered previously in the body. As the body recognises the pathogen, immune system starts producing antibodies against the foreign antigens for subsequent encounter and this response is very intense. **(1 Mark)**

14. (a)

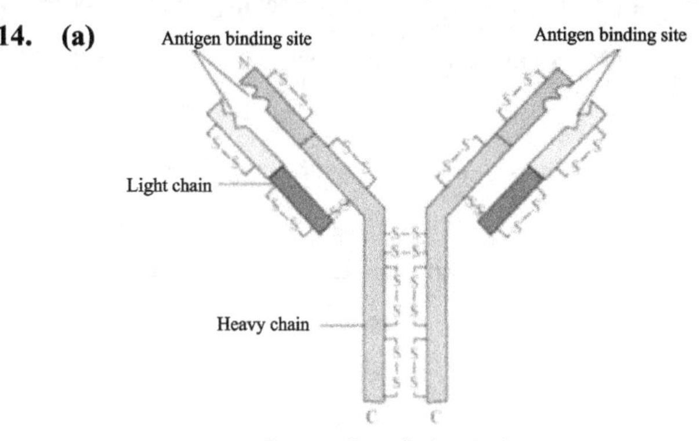

Structure of an antibody molecule

(1 Mark)

(b) In the period of illness, the number of immune cells forming antibodies will be highest in a person suffering from pneumonia. **(1 Mark)**

B-cells (B-lymphocytes) are the immune cells that produce antibodies.

Down syndrome was first described by Langdon Dawy (1866).

15. An antibody molecule consists of four polypeptide chains, two are long called heavy (H) chains while other two are short called light (L) chains. Both are arranged in the shape of Y. Hence, the antibody is represented as $H_2 L_2$.

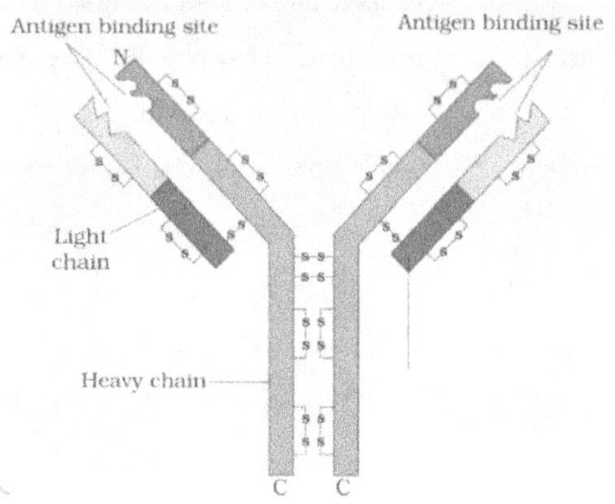

(Diagram with Labels –

Light chain, Heavy Chain   (½ × 2 = 1 **Mark**)

Types of Antibody –

IgA, IgM, IgE,IgG

(1 mark awarded when all 4 types are stated)

IgA – Lactating Mother to protect their infant (½ **Mark**)

Ig E – To protect from allergen   (½ **Mark**)

OR

(a) When a female Anopheles mosquito bites an infected person, the parasites enter the mosquito's body as **gametocytes**. It leads to **fertilization and development in the gut** of the mosquito and undergoes further development to form **sporozoites** that are **stored in salivary glands** until their transfer to human body.   (1½ **Marks**)

In the human body – the **sporozoites reach the liver and reproduce asexually** bursting the cells and releasing them into the **RBCs as gametocytes** (½ Mark). *(Labeled diagram explaining the mentioned stages can also be considered)*

(b) The **rupture of RBCs releases a toxic substance called haemozoin,** which is responsible for the chill and high fever.   (1½ **Marks**)

16. • When our body encounters an antigenic protein or a pathogen for the first time it produces a response which is of low intensity and our body retains memory of the first encounter.   **(1 Mark)**

   • The subsequent encounter with the same pathogen elicits a highly intensified response carried out with the help of two special types of lymphocytes present in our blood, B-lymphocytes, and T-lymphocytes.

                       (1 Mark)

   • The B-lymphocytes produce an army of proteins in response to these pathogens into our blood to fight with them. These proteins are called antibodies. The T-cells themselves do not secrete antibodies but help B-cells produce them.

17.

B-lymphocytes	T-lymphocytes
(i) The B-lymphocytes produces an army of proteins in response to pathogen into the blood and these proteins are called antibodies.	(i) The T-lymphocytes do not secrete any antibodies but help B-cells to produce antibodies.
(ii) The response produced by B-lymphocytes is also called as **humoral immune response.**	(ii) The response produced by T-lymphocytes is also called as **Cell-mediated immune response.**
(iii) B-cells mature in the bone marrow	(iii) T-cells mature in the Thymus.

                       (3 Marks)

Both B-lymphocytes and T-lymphocytes are formed in the bone marrow.

OR

In case of polio vaccination, an antigenic protein preparation of pathogen is introduced into the body which is inactivated or weakened form. The antibodies produced in the body against polio antigens would neutralise the pathogenic agents which responsible for causing polio. The vaccines also generate memory B-and T-cells which recognises the pathogen on subsequent exposure and encounter the pathogen by the production of antibodies.

                       (3 Marks)

18. (a) Antibodies are also called immunoglobulins that are produced by B-lymphocytes in the blood and produces immune response. This type of immune response is called humoral immune response.   **(1 Mark)**

   (b) Vaccination is based on the memory of the immune system. Vaccination involves the preparation of inactivated or weakened pathogens or a preparation of antigenic proteins of pathogen in the host body. The antibodies produced in the body against these antigens neutralise the pathogenic agents during actual infections.   **(1 Mark)**

(c) The AIDS virus after entering into the body get enters into the macrophages. Then the AIDS virus enters into the helper-T cells.   **(1 Mark)**

19. (a) If a patient requires repeated blood transfusion, he must ensure that the donor's blood has been screened for HIV and other pathogens before transfusion.

(1 Mark)

(b) If this advice is not being followed by the patient he might contract AIDS (Acquired Immunodeficiency Syndrome). AIDS is a serious health problem in which the immune system of the patient gets weakened greatly. It is caused by a virus named HIV (Human Immunodeficiency Virus). It is a retrovirus, which attacks the helper T-cells of the body and greatly reduce their number. These helper T-cells are responsible for stimulating the antibody production by B-cells Thus, reduction in their number results in the loss of natural defence of our body. HIV can attack and replicate inside the host cell by using reverse transcription method, which is shown below:

Diagrammatic Representation of replication of reterovirus:-

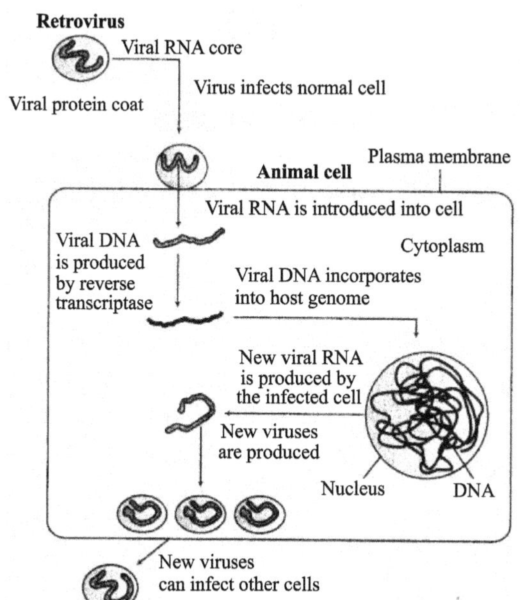

(2 Marks)

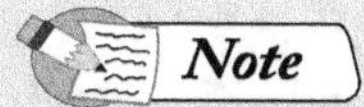

Infected cell can survive while viruses are being replicated and released.

20. (a) Passive immunization: When readymade antibiotics are introduced into the body, then it is called passive immunization. Passive immunization provides quick immune response in the body.   **(½ Mark)**

(b) Anti-histamines: Anti-histamines are the chemicals that are given against allergic reactions. **(½ Mark)**

(c) Colostrum: Colostrum is the yellow fluid produced during the initial days of lactation. It is rich in antibodies IgA. It provides innate immunity to the new baby.   **(½ Mark)**

(d) Cytokinin barrier: It involves interferons. Virus-infected cells secrete proteins called **interferons** that protect non-infected cells from further viral infections.   **(½ Mark)**

21. (a) Children who had suffered from chicken pox in their childhood may not contract the same disease in their adulthood because they have developed antibody against chicken pox virus. The active memory intiates highly intense response during the second encounter. This kind of immunity is called active immunity which provides protection against the same disease as immune cells already produced antibodies against the disease causing antigens.   **(1 Mark)**

(b) Viral infected cells secrete proteins called interferons that protect non-infected cells from further viral infection.   **(1 Mark)**

22. (a) In the patient's body, the doctor has injected antiserum containing preformed antibodies against the causative organism or toxin produced by it.   **(1 Mark)**

(b) The solution injected by the doctor had antibodies; hence, the injection would protect the patient against the disease and provide him humoral immunity.

(1 Mark)

(c) The disease against which this injection was given is tetanus caused by Clostridium tetani, which usually exists in environment as spores and may again access to the body through wound. **(1 Mark)**

The kind of immunity that the injection containing antiserum provides is passive immunity as preformed antibodies are used because fast action is required in this emergency case.

23. The principle of immunisation or vaccination is based on the property of 'memory' of the immune system. In vaccination, a preparation of antigenic proteins of pathogen or inactivated/ weakened pathogens (vaccine) is introduced into the body. The antibodies that are produced in the body against these antigens would neutralise the pathogenic agents during actual infection and vaccines also generate memory B and T-cells that recognise the pathogen quickly on subsequent exposure and encounters the foreign antigen with a massive production of antibodies. **(2 Marks)**

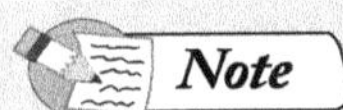

Immunization refers to the process in which a person is made immune or resistant to an infectious disease by the administration of a vaccine.

OR

Person with cuts and bruises following an accident is administered with tetanus antitoxin provides protection from the infection by bacteria *Clostridium tetani*. This bacterium is responsible for causing tetanus infection which can be fatal if left untreated. The bacterium enters into the body through cuts or wounds and is usually found in soil and manure. So, at the time of accidents there is a higher risk of entering bacteria in the skin and hence tetanus antitoxin is administered in order to reduce the chances of infection by providing passive immunity to the bacterial toxin. **(2 Marks)**

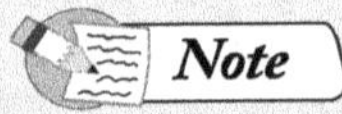

The overall ability of a body to fight against disease - causing mircoorganisms by the immune system is called immunity.

24. **(a)** Antitoxins are the preparation containing antibodies to the toxins. Tetanus antitoxins is preparation that contains antibodies that kill *Clostridium tetnani*. A causal organisms of tetanus. **(1 Mark)**

(b) Tetanus antitoxin is administered to an injured person to neutralize the effect of toxin produced by *Clostridium tetani*. **(1 Mark)**

(c) Tetanus antitoxin provides a short-term passive immunity to injured person. As it contains preformed antibodies against *Clostridium tetani* and produces a quick immune response in the patients. **(3 Marks)**

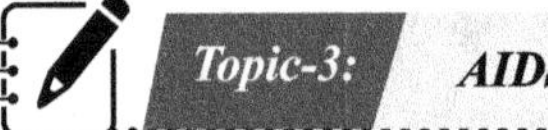

1. Replication of viral RNA genome takes place in the cells when the HIV gets into the blood after gaining entry into the human body. The RNA genome of the HIV virus tends to replicate with the help of an enzyme of reverse transcriptase. The viral DNA gets incorporated into host cell's DNA and directs the infected cells to form virus particles. **(1 Mark)**

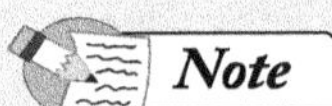

Infected all can survive while viruses are being replicated and released.

2. Sharing of injection needles is not recommended between two individuals because it leads to the transmission of fatal and incurable diseases such as hepatitis B and AIDS that can be transmitted from one person to another on coming in contact with the body fluid of an infected person.

(1 Mark)

3. After attacking the host cell, retrovirus enters into macrophages (as in case of HIV) where RNA genome of the virus replicates to form viral DNA with the help of enzyme reverse transcriptase. This viral DNA gets incorporated into the host cell's DNA and directs the infected cells to produce more viruses. The macrophages continue to produce virus and works as a HIV factory. Hence, the infected host cell possesses viral DNA.

(1 Mark)

4. (i) The human cell 'A' is animal cell in which HIV virus enters. **(1 Mark)**

(ii) Viral RNA is introduced into the cell. **(1 Mark)**

(iii) Viral DNA is produced by reverse transcriptase enzyme and then the viral DNA is incorporates into the host genome. **(1 Mark)**

5. **(a)** Recently AIDS is diagnosed in our area and it is a life-threatening disease. So it is our prime responsibility to create awareness among the people in order to combat the situation. There is no need to isolate the person who is suffering from AIDS from the society. The infected person needs help and sympathy instead of being shunned by society. We must have educated people about AIDS. **(1 Mark)**

(b) In a society meeting, we must have to educate people about the mode of infection of AIDS as it cannot be spread through direct contact with the infected person. It can be spread by following reasons:

- Sexual intercourse with multiple partners
- Transfusion of contaminated blood and blood products
- By sharing of infected needle as in case of intravenous drug abusers
- From infected mother to her foetus through placenta.

Preventive measures involves:

- Use of condom during sexual intercourse with the infected person.
- Proper disposal of needles after use
- Use clean needle
- Pregnant women take medical care immediately
- Avoid sharing of sharp objects or needles **(2 Marks)**

(c) AIDS is Acquired Immunodeficiency Syndrome and is caused by the Human Immuno deficiency Virus (HIV), which is a group of viruses called retrovirus. This virus has an envelope that encloses the RNA genome.

Symptoms: The infected person is suffering from a bouts of fever, diarrhoea and weight loss. Due to decrease in the number of helper T lymphocytes, T person starts suffering from infections caused by *Mycobacterium,* viruses, fungi and even parasites like *Toxoplasma.*

The infected person becomes immune deficient as the patient is unable to protect themselves from such infections. **(2 Marks)**

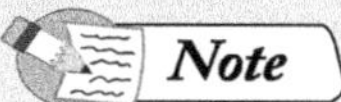

Note

*AIDS can be diagnosed by **Enzyme Linked Immuno-sorbent assay (ELISA)**. It can be treated by using anti-retroviral drugs which is partially effective and such drugs only prolong the life of the patient but cannot prevent death and is inevitable.*

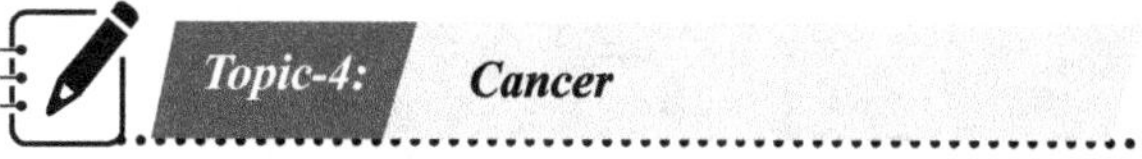

1. Benign tumors normally remain confined to their original location and do not spread to other parts of the body and cause little damage. The malignant tumors, on the other hand are a mass of proliferating cells called neoplastic or tumor cells. These cells grow very rapidly, invading and damaging the surrounding normal tissues. As these cells actively divide and grow they also starve the normal cells by competing for vital nutrients. Cells sloughed from such tumors reach distant sites through blood, and wherever they get lodged in the body, they start a new tumor there. **(1 Mark)**

2. (i) Alpha-interferon is the example of biological response modifier used in immunotherapy.

(ii) Tumor cells have been shown to avoid detection and destruction by immune system. Therefore, the patients are given alpha interferon that activates their immune system and helps in destroying the tumor.

(iii) Contact inhibition is a process of arresting cell growth when cells come in contact with each other. As a result, normal cells stop proliferating but cancerous cells do not show this property. Cancerous cells just continue to divide giving rise to masses of cells called tumors. **(1 Mark)**

3. Indiscrimate diagnostic practices using X-rays should be avoided because excessive use of X-rays leads to cause mutation and cancer. **(1 Mark)**

> **Note**
>
> *X-rays are ionizing radiation that can affect the atoms in living things. Cells on exposure to ionizing radiation lead to cause tissue and DNA damage.*

4. Techniques like radiography, CT (computed tomography) and MRI (magnetic resonance imaging) are used to detect cancer growth in the internal organs. A biopsy is the removal of a small amount of tissue for examination under a microscope. Other tests can suggest that cancer is present, but only a biopsy can make a definite diagnosis for most cancers. **(2 Marks)**

5.

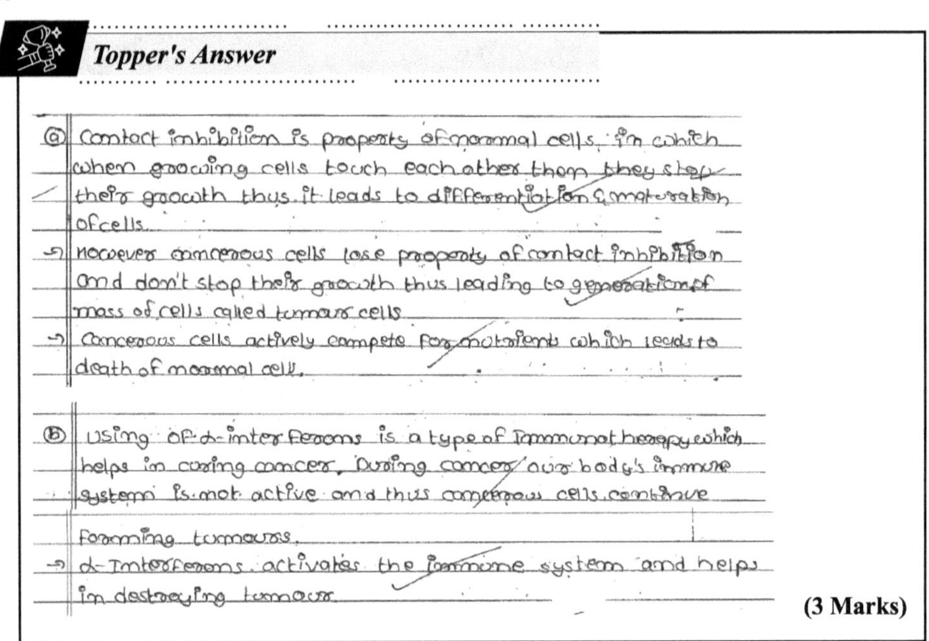

Topper's Answer

(a) Contact inhibition is property of normal cells, in which when growing cells touch each other then they stop their growth thus it leads to differentiation & maturation of cells.

→ However cancerous cells lose property of contact inhibition and don't stop their growth thus leading to generation of mass of cells called tumour cells

→ Cancerous cells actively compete for nutrients which leads to death of normal cell.

(b) Using of α-interferons is a type of Immunotherapy which helps in curing cancer. During cancer our body's immune system is not active and thus cancerous cells continue forming tumours.

→ α-Interferons activates the immune system and helps in destroying tumour.

(3 Marks)

(a) In our body, cell growth and differentiation is highly controlled and regulated. In cancer cells, there is breakdown of these regulatory mechanisms. Normal cells show a property called contact inhibition by virtue of which contact with other cells inhibits their uncontrolled growth. Cancer cells appears to have lost this property. As a result of this, cancerous cells just continue to divide giving rise to masses of cells called tumors. Tumors are of two types: benign and malignant. Benign tumors normally remain confined to their original location and do not spread to other parts of the body and cause little damage. The malignant tumors, on the other hand are a mass of proliferating cells called neoplastic or tumor cells. These cells grow very rapidly, invading and damaging the surrounding normal tissues. As these cells actively divide and grow they also starve the normal cells by competing for vital nutrients. Cells sloughed from such tumors reach distant sites through blood, and wherever they get lodged in the body, they start a new tumor there. This property called metastasis is the most feared property of malignant tumors. **(2 Marks)**

(b) Tumor cells have been shown to avoid detection and destruction by immune system. Therefore, the patients are given substances called biological response modifiers such as a-interferon which activates their immune system and helps in destroying the tumor. **(1 Mark)**

6. Transformation of normal cells into cancerous neoplastic cells may be induced by following physical, chemical or biological agents causing DNA damage:

- Ionising radiations like X-rays and gamma rays

- Non-ionizing radiations like UV.

- Chemical carcinogens present in tobacco smoke

- Cellular oncogenes (c-onc) or proto-oncogenes, when activated under certain conditions cause cancer. Viruses with oncogenes can transform normal cells to cancerous cells.

(3 Marks)

7.

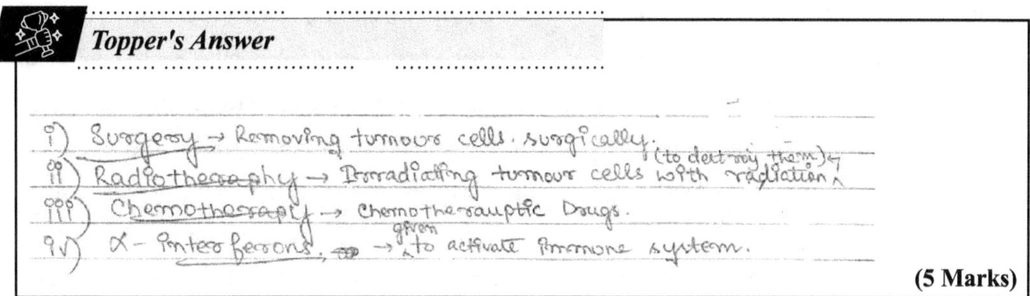

Topper's Answer

(5 Marks)

Surgery: An operation where doctors cut out tissue with cancer cells. **(5 Marks)**

Chemotherapy: Special medicines that shrink or kill cancer cells that we cannot see.

Radiation therapy: Using high-energy rays (similar to X-rays) to kill cancer cells.

Hormone therapy: Blocks cancer cells from getting the hormones they need to grow.

Immunotherapy: A treatment that works with your body's immune system to help it fight cancer cells or to control side effects from other cancer treatments.

Stem cell transplant (bone marrow transplant): Replace bone marrow cells lost due to very high doses of chemotherapy of radiation therapy. Most commonly used to treat blood cancers and cancers that start in the lymph nodes.

8. (a) Normal cells show a property called contact inhibition by virtue of which contact with other cells that inhibits their uncontrolled growth. Cancer cells lack the property of contact inhibition because of thus the cancerous cells divides continuously and give rise to masses of cells called tumors.

There are two types of tumors such as benign and malignant. Benign tumors normally remains at their original location and do not spread to the other parts of the body results in little damage. Whereas the malignant tumors are a mass of proliferating cells called neoplastic or tumor cells. Such cells grow rapidly, invading and also damaging the surrounding normal tissue. All the tumor cells divide actively and grow. These cells also starve the normal cells by competing for vital nutrients. The cells sloughed from such tumors reach distant sites through blood and they get lodged in the body. Then they start a new tumor at new location and this property is called **metastasis** which is the most feared property of malignant tumors. **(1 Mark)**

(b) **Cause of cancer:** The transformation of normal cells into cancerous neoplastic cells is induced by physical, chemical or biological agents. These agents are called carcinogens. Ionising radiations such as X-rays and gamma rays while non-ionizing radiation involves UV cause DNA damage results in neoplastic transformation. **(1 Mark)**

(c) The chemical carcinogens present in tobacco smoke causes lung cancer. Cancer causing viruses called oncogenic viruses that have genes called viral oncogene. Certain genes called cellular oncogene or proto oncogene that have been identified in normal cells that are activated under several conditions that leads to cause oncogenic transformation of the cells. Techniques such as techniques as radiotherapy, CT (Computer Tomography) and MRI (Magnetic Resonance Imaging) are useful for the detection of cancers in the internal organ. **(2 Marks)**

(d) Cancer patients are treated with substances called biological response modifiers called **alpha-interferon**. It activates their immune system and help in destroying the tumor. **(1 Mark)**

9. **Causes of cancer:**

(i) Transformation of normal cells into cancerous neoplastic cells may be induced by physical,

chemical or biological agents. These agents are called **carcinogens**.

(ii) Ionising radiations like X-rays and gamma rays and non-ionizing radiations like UV cause DNA damage leading to neoplastic transformation.

(iii) The chemical carcinogens present in tobacco smoke have been identified as a major cause of lung cancer. Cancer causing viruses called **oncogenic viruses** have genes called **viral oncogenes**.

(iv) Furthermore, several genes called **cellular oncogenes** (c-onc) or **proto oncogenes** have been identified in normal cells which, when activated under certain conditions, could lead to oncogenic transformation of the cells.

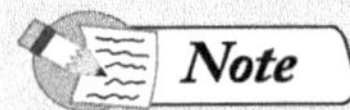

Topic-5:   *Drug and Alcohol Abuse*

1. (c) Cyclosporin A produced from *Trichoderma polysporum*

(1 Mark)

2. **Difference between opioids and cannabinoids:**   **(1 Mark)**

	Categories	Opioids	Cannabinoids
(a)	**Specific receptor site in human body**	**Opioid** receptors present in the central nervous system and gastrointestinal tract of human beings.	**Cannabinoid** receptors present in the brain. **(½ Mark)**
(b)	**Mode of action in human body**	**Opioids** such as heroin act a depressant and slow down body functions.	**Cannabinoids** such as marijuana, hashish, charas and ganja effects on cardiovascular system of the body.

(½ + ½ = 1 Mark)

> **Note**
>
> *Opioids are the drugs that are obtained from the latex of poppy plant called Papaver somniferum. Whereas cannabinoids are the group of chemicals that are naturally obtained from the inflorescences of the plant Cannabis sativa.*

3. It is Morphine. **(½ Mark)**

Physically it appears as a white, odourless, crystalline compound. **(1½ Mark)**

> **Note**
>
> *Morphine are used as analgesics.*

4. (a) The given drug is morphine that belongs to the category of opioids. Opioids are the drugs, which bind to specific opioid receptors present in our central nervous system and gastrointestinal tract.

(½ Mark)

(b) Heroin, commonly called smack is chemically diacetylmorphine which is a white, odourless, bitter crystalline compound. This is obtained by acetylation of morphine, which is extracted from the latex of poppy plant Papaver somniferum. Generally taken by snorting and injection, heroin is a depressant and slows down body functions. **(1 Mark)**

(c) *Papaver somniferum* is the natural source of these compounds. **(½ Mark)**

(d) The harmful effects of opioids include drowsiness, constipation, euphoria, nausea, vomiting and slowed breathing. A person using opioids over time can develop tolerance, physical dependence and opioid used disorder, with the risk of overdose and death. **(1 Mark)**

5. **(a)** Opioids are the drugs that are obtained from the latex of poppy plant called *Papaver somniferum*. Whereas cannabinoids are the group of chemicals that are naturally obtained from the inflorescences of the plant *Cannabis sativa*. **(1 Mark)**

(b) Opioids are the drugs that get bids with the specific opioid receptors present in the central nervous system and gastrointestinal tract of human beings. Opioids such as heroin acts a depressant and slows down body functions.

Cannabinoids are a group of chemicals that interact with cannabinoid receptors present in the brain. Cannabinoids such as marijuana, hashish, charas and ganja effects on cardiovascular system of the body. **(2 Marks)**

6. **(a)** *Papaver somniferum* is the source plant for heroin drug. This is obtained by the acetylation of morphine, which is extracted from the latex of poppy plant.

(b) Heroin is a depressant and used to slow down body functions. **(2 Mark)**

Note

Heroin is a opioids. Opioids are the drugs, which bind to specific opioids receptors that are present in central nervous system and gastrointestinal trait.

7. **(a)** The adolescent's wards may get trapped in drug/alcohol abuse involves following reasons:

- Peer pressure
- Curiosity and need to try for adventure, excitement and experiment.
- To escape from stress, frustration and depression.
- To overcome hardships of life.
- Unstable or unsupportive family structure.

(1½ Marks)

(b) **Addiction:** Addiction is defined as the psychological attachment to certain effects such as Euphoria or temporary feeling of well-being.

Dependence: Dependence is defined as the tendency of the body to show withdrawal syndrome or appearance of symptoms because of regular doses of drug or alcohol abuse is abruptly discontinued. **(1½ Marks)**

8. **(a)** There is a need to conduct blood and urine test for sports persons because some sports persons take narcotics analgesics, anabolic steroids, diuretics and several hormones in order to increase their muscle strength and performance. These tests help to determine whether a sports person has taken any drugs and it also ensures a fair play. **(1 Mark)**

(b) The sports authorities are usually looking for narcotic drugs such as analgesics, diuretics and hormones such as gonadotropins and steroids, opiates such as oxy contin and cannabinoids. **(1 Mark)**

(c) The generic names of two plants are given below:

- Smack or heroin is obtained from the Papaver somniferum. **(½ Mark)**
- Ganja and marijuana is obtained from the Cannabis sativa. **(½ Mark)**

9. **(a)** Yes, I would like to report the matter to the higher sports authorities because cannabinoids are classified under drugs and its abuse is considered as an illegal practice. **(1 Mark)**

(b) Natural cannabinoids are obtained from the inflorescences of the plant *Cannabis sativa.* **(1 Mark)**

(c) Cannabinoids are the group of chemicals that interact with the cannabinoids receptors present in the brain. It affects the cardiovascular system of the body. **(1 Mark)**

10. (a) Concentration of nicotine is maximum at 10 minutes/ conc. of nicotine increases steadily in the blood to reach $45mg/cm^3$ **(1 Mark)**

(b) The Concentration of CO will increase resulting in reduced concentration of haemboundoxygen. **(1 Mark)**

(c) Nicotine results in stimulating the adrenal gland which results in release of adrenaline / nor - adrenaline in the blood resulting in increase of blood pressure and heart rate. **(2 Marks)**

OR

(c) Chemical carcinogens present in tobacco smoke are the major cause of lung cancer. **(1 Mark)**

The cigarette smoke irritates the air passages of the lungs causing them to produce mucus which causes cough resulting in enlarging air spaces/ reduce surface area/lose their elasticity (any point can be mentioned) thus difficulty in breathing causing emphysema. **(1 Mark)**

8 Chapter — Microbes in Human Welfare

 **Microbes in Household Products**

1. Multiple Choice Questions (1 Mark)

1. Identify the fungus that ripens the famous 'Roquefort' cheese: **[All India 2023, Set-I, K]**
   (a) *Saccharomyees cerevisiae*
   (b) *Propionibacterium sharmanii*
   (c) *Monascus purpureus*
   (d) *Penicillium notatum*

2. The microbes commonly used in kitchens are
   (a) Lactobacillus and Yeast **[All India 2020, K]**
   (b) Penicillium and Yeast
   (c) Microspora and E. coli
   (d) Rhizopus and Lactobacillus

3. Large-holes in 'Swiss-Cheese' are due to **[Delhi 2020, K]**
   (a) *Propionibacterium sharmanii*
   (b) *Saccharomyces cerevisae*
   (c) *Penicillium chrysogenum*
   (d) *Acetobacter aceti*

5. Short Answer Questions (2 or 3 Marks)

4. Name the group of bacteria involved in setting milk into curd. Explain the process they carry in doing so. Write another beneficial role of such bacteria. **[All India 2019, U]**

5. Mention a product of human welfare obtained with the help of each one of the following microbes :
   (a) LAB **[Delhi 2015, K]**
   (b) *Saccharomyces cerevisiae*
   (c) *Propionibacterium sharmanii*
   (d) *Aspergillus niger*

6. Name the bacterium response for the large holes seen in "Swiss Cheese". What are these holes due to?
   [All India 2013, U]

 **Microbes in Industrial Products**

3. Matching Based Questions (1 Mark)

1. Given below are the list of the commercially important products and their source organisms. Select the option that gives the correct matches. **[Delhi 2023, Set-I, K]**

List A		List B	
S. No.	Bioactive Products	S. No.	Microbes (Source Organism)
(A)	Cyclosporin A	(i)	*Streptococcus*
(B)	Statins	(ii)	*Tricoderma polysporum*
(C)	Streptokinase	(iii)	*Penicillium notatum*
(D)	Penicillin	(iv)	*Monascus purpureus*

Options :
(a) (A)-(i), (B)-(ii), (C)-(iii), (D)-(iv)
(b) (A)-(iii), (B)-(iv), (C)-(ii), (D)-(i)
(c) (A)-(iv), (B)-(iii), (C)-(ii), (D)-(i)
(d) (A)-(ii), (B)-(iv), (C)-(i), (D)-(iii)

2. (a) Match the microbes listed under Column-A with the products mentioned under Column-B.
   [All India 2019, U]

Column – A	Column – B
(H) *Penicillium notatum*	(i) Statin
(I) *Trichoderma polysporum*	(ii) ethanol
(J) *Monascus purpurea*	(iii) antibiotic

(K) *Saccharomyces cerevisiae*   (iv) Cyclosporin-A

(b) Why does 'Swiss Cheese' develop large holes ?

 **4**   *Very Short Answer Questions (1 Mark)*

3. Name the source organism (scientific name) that produces statins. Mention its use in medical field and how does it act.   **[All India 2022, Term-II, U]**

4. Describe the contributions of Alexander Fleming, Ernest Chain and Howard Florey in the field of microbiology.

     [Delhi 2020, U]

 **5**   *Short Answer Questions (2 or 3 Marks)*

5. (a) A patient had suffered myocardial infarction and clots were found in his blood vessels. Name a 'clot buster' that can be used to dissolve the clots and the micro-organism from which it is obtained.

     [Delhi 2019, K]

(b) A woman had just undergone a kidney transplant. A bioactive molecular drug is administered to oppose kidney rejection by the body. What is the bioactive molecule? Name the microbe from which this is extracted.   **[Delhi 2019, K]**

(c) What do doctors prescribe to lower the blood cholesterol level in patients with high blood cholesterol? Name the source organism from which this drug can be obtained.   **[Delhi 2019, K]**

6. (a) Why are the fruit juices bought from market clearer as compared to those made at home?   **[Delhi 2013, K]**

(b) Name the bioactive molecules produced by *Trichoderma oolysoorurn* and *Monaseus purpureus*.

     [Delhi 2013, K]

 **Topic-3:**   *Microbes in Sewage Treatment*

 **4**   *Very Short Answer Questions (1 Mark)*

1. State the impact of constant mechanical agitation and pumping of air in the aeration tank on the sewage during the biological treatment.   **[All India 2022, Term-II, U]**

2. Water samples were collected at points A, B and C in a segment of a river near a sugar factory and tested for BOD level. The BOD levels of samples A, B and C were 400 mg/L, 480 mg/L and 8 mg/L respectively. What is this indicative of? Explain why the BOD level gets reduced considerably at the collection point C?

     [CBSE Sample Paper 2021-22, U]

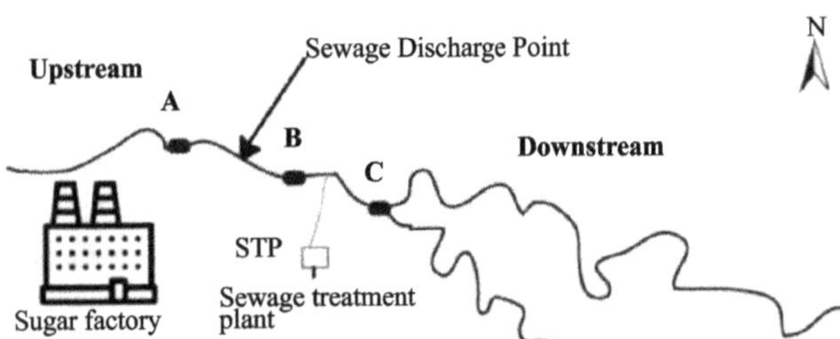

3. "Micro-organisms play an important role for the biological treatment of sewage." Justify.

     [All India 2020, K]

4. What are 'flocs', formed during secondary treatment of sewage ?   **[All India 2019, U]**

5   *Short Answer Questions (2 or 3 Marks)*

5. How the flocs help in reducing the box of sewage water?

     [All India 2022, Term-II, U]

6. What is the similarity between Rhizobium & Anabena.

     [All India 2022, Term-II, U]

7. Explain the effect on the characteristics of a river when urban sewage is discharged into it.   **[All India 2018, K]**

8. Describe how do 'flocs' and 'activated sludge' help in Sewage Treatment.   **[All India 2017, K]**

9. Secondary treatment of the sewage is also called Biological treatment. Justify this statement and explain the process.   **[Delhi 2017, U]**

10. Explain the different steps involved during primary treatment phase of sewage.   **[All India 2015, K]**

11. "Determination of Biological Oxygen Demand (BOD) can help in suggesting the quality of a water body." Explain.   **[Delhi 2015, U]**

Topic-4:	*Microbes in Production of Biogas*

4 | *Very Short Answer Questions (1 Mark)*

1. What are 'flocs', formed during secondary treatment of sewage ? **[All India 2019, K]**

5 | *Short Answer Questions (2 or 3 Marks)*

2. **(a)** Name the two institutes which developed the technology of biogas production in India.
[All India 2023, Set-I, K]

   (b) Explain the main principle used in this technology.
[All India 2023, Set-I, K]

3. **(a)** Cattle excreta is important source for producing a domestic fuel. Name the fuel and write its main components. **[All India 2022, Term-II, U]**

   (b) Write the biological process that is responsible for the production of this fuel.
[All India 2022, Term-II, U]

4. What are methanogens? How do they help to generate biogas? **[All India 2015]**

Topic-5:	*Microbes as Bicontrol Agent*

4 | *Very Short Answer Questions (1 Mark)*

1. A patient admitted in ICU was diagnosed to have suffered from myocardial infarction. The condition of coronary artery is depicted in the image below. Name two bioactive agents and their mode of action that can improve this condition. **[CBSE Sample Paper 2021-22, U]**

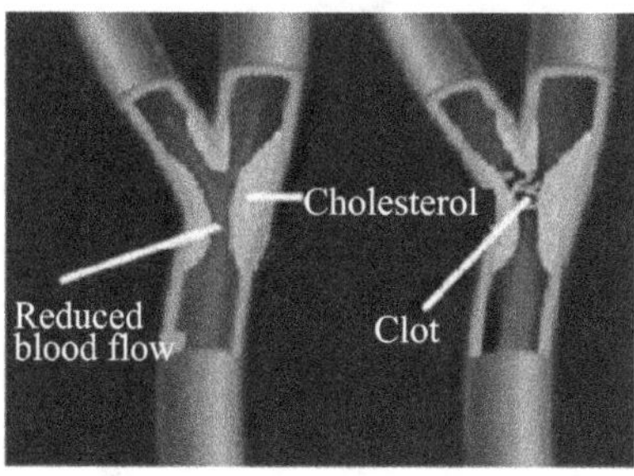

OR

Substantiate by giving two reasons as to why a holistic understanding of the flora and fauna the cropland is required before introducing an appropriate biocontrol method.

2. Name the genus of bacolovirus that acts as a biological control agent in spite of being a pathogen. Justify by giving three reasons that make it an excellent for the job.
[All India 2020, K]

4 | *Very Short Answer Questions (1 Mark)*

3. Give an example of a genus of virus used as narrow spectrum insecticidal biocontrol agent.

[Delhi 2023, Set-I, K]

5 | *Short Answer Questions (2 or 3 Marks)*

4. **(a)** Give an example of viral biocontrol agent.
[All India 2022, Term-II, U]

   (b) Why are they considered to be desirable when an ecologically sensitive area is being treated?
[All India 2022, Term-II, U]

5. **(a)** Organic farmers prefer biological control of diseases and pests to the use of chemicals for the same purpose. Justify. **[All India 2018, K]**

   (b) Give an example of a bacterium, a fungus and an insect that are used as biocontrol agents.

6. Name a genus of baculovirus. Why are they considered good biocontrol agents? **[All India 2016, U]**

7. Given below is a list of six micro-organisms. State their usefulness to humans. **[Delhi 2016, U]**

   (a) Nucleopolyhedrovirus

   (b) Saccharomyces cerevisiae

   (c) Monascus purpureus

   (d) Trichoderma polysporum

   (e) *Penicillium notatum*

   (f) *Propionibacterium sharmanii*

Topic-6:   *Microbes as Biofertilizer*

5   *Short Answer Questions (2 or 3 Marks)*

1. (i)   Give an example of a genus of fungi that forms mycorrhizial association with plants.

    (ii) How does the plant derive benefits from this association?   **[Delhi 2023, Set-II, U]**

2. Certain specific bacterial spores are mixed in water and sprayed over Brassica crop to control butterfly caterpillars.

    Name this bacterium and its mode of action on the butterfly caterpillars.   **[Delhi 2023, Set-III, U]**

3. Explain giving reason the action plan followed by organic farmers that support their key belief "biodiversity furthers health of crop lands."

    [All India 2022, Term-II, U]

4. Enumerate the main sources of bio-fertilisers giving one example of each.   **[All India 2022, Term-II, U]**

5. How are the members of genus Glomus useful to organic farmers?   **[Delhi 2019, U]**

6. How does the application of the fungal genus, Glomus, to the agricultural farm increase the farm output?

    [All India 2017, U]

7. Choose any three microbes, from the following which are suited for organic farming which is in great demand these days for various reasons. Mention one application of each one chosen. Mycorrhiza; Monascus; Anabaena; Rhizobium; Methanobacterium; Trichoderma.

    [Delhi 2015, U]

8. Explain the significant role of the genus *Nucleopolyhedrovirus* in an ecological sensitive area.

    [All India 2014]

9. Name the type of association that the genus *Glomus* exhibits with higher plants.   **[All India 2014]**

Hints & Solutions

| **Topic-1:** | *Microbes in Household Products* |

1. **(b)** *Propionobacterium sharmanii* is responsible for repening of chosse. **(1 Mark)**

2. **(a)** **(1 Mark)**

3. **(a)** The large holes in the 'Swiss-cheese' are due to the production of a large amount of carbon dioxide by bacterium *Propionibacteriumsharmanii.* **(1 Mark)**

4. Lactic acid bacteria (LAB) are involved in setting milk into the curd. **(½ Mark)**

   Process of curd formation from milk: Milk is converted into curd by the process of fermentation. Milk consists of globular proteins called casein. The curd forms because of the chemical reaction between the lactic acid bacteria and casein. During fermentation, the bacteria use enzymes to produce energy (ATP) from lactose. Under suitable condition, these bacteria multiply and produce acids which coagulate and partially digest the milk proteins and change the milk into curd. Lactobacilli bacteria present in curd multiply in milk and convert the lactose sugar into lactic acid. **(1 Marks)**

   Beneficial role played by lactic acid bacteria are:

   (i) they are used in food fermentation.

   (ii) also found in the human stomach where these bacteria prevent the growth of certain disease-causing microbes.

   (iii) improve lactose digestion and increases the content of vitamin B_{12} in curd.

   (iv) play a role in preventing and treating diarrhoea and act on the immune system, helping the body to resist and fight infection. **(½ Mark)**

5. **(a)** **LAB (Lactic acid bacteria):** LAB are commonly grow in milk and helps in the conversion of milk into curd. It produces acid that helps in coagulation and partial digestion of milk proteins. LAB also plays essential role in checking disease causing microbes. **(½ Mark)**

   (b) *Saccharomyces cerevisiae*: It is also called baker's yeast. It is used for making bread and also used in beverage industry. **(½ Mark)**

   (c) *Propionibacterium sharmanii:* It is used for the production of large holes in 'Swiss cheese'. Large holes are produced in the cheese because of the production of large amount of carbon dioxide by bacteria. **(½ Mark)**

   (d) *Aspergillus niger:* It is a fungus used for the production of citric acid. **(½ Mark)**

6. The production of large holes in 'Swiss cheese' is because of the production of a large amount of carbon dioxide by a bacterium named *Propionibacterium sharmanii.*

   (2 Marks)

| **Topic-2:** | *Microbes in Industrial Products* |

1. **(d)** **Statins** produced by the yeast *Monascus purpureus* have been commercialised as blood-cholesterol lowering agents.

   Cyclosporin A, that is used as an immunosuppressive agent in organ-transplant patients, is produced by the fungus *Trichoderma polysporum.*

   Penicillin was the first antibiotic to be discovered extracted from *Penicillium notatum.*

   Streptokinase is used as a clot buster is obtained from bacteruim *streptococcus.* **(1 Mark)**

2. **(a)**

Column A	Column B	Correct Options
(H) *Penicillium notatum*	(i) Statin	**(H) – (iii)**
(I) *Trichoderma polysporum*	(ii) ethanol	**(I) – (iv)**
(J) *Monascus purpurae*	(iii) antibiotic	**(J) – (i)**
(K) *Saccharomyces cerevisae*	(iv) cyclosporin-A	**(K) – (ii)**

(b) The development of large holes in 'Swiss cheese' is because of the production of large amount of carbon dioxide by the bacterium *Propionibacterium-sharmanii.* **(1 Mark)**

3. Statins produced by the yeast *Monascus purpureus.*

(1 Mark)

Statins have been commercialised as **blood cholesterol lowering agent**. It acts by competitively inhibiting the enzyme responsible for synthesis of cholesterol.

4. Alexander Fleming while working on *Staphylococci* bacteria observed that a mould growing in one of his unwashed culture plates around which *Staphylococci* could not grow. During this, he found that it was due to a chemical produced by the mould and he named it as Penicillin after the *Penicillium notatum.* Ernest Chain and Howards Florey give its full potential to prove it as an effective antibiotic. This antibiotic was used for treatment of American soldiers that wounded in World War II. Fleming, Chain and Florey were awarded the Nobel Prize in 1945 for this discovery. **(1 Mark)**

5. **(a)** Streptokinase is used as clot buster for patients suffering from myocardial infraction. It is produced from bacterium *Streptococcus*. **(1 Mark)**

(b) Cyclosporin A is a bioactive molecule that is used as an immunosuppressive agent in organ-transplant patients. It is produced by a fungus *Trichoderma polysporum*. **(1 Mark)**

(c) Statins is a blood-cholesterol lowering agents produced by yeast *Monascus purpureus*. It competitively inhibits the enzyme that is responsible for the synthesis of cholesterol. **(1 Mark)**

6. **(a)** The bottled juices that we have brought from the market are clearer as compared to those made at home because the bottled juices are clarified by the use of pectinases and proteases enzymes. **(1½ Marks)**

(b) Trichoderma polysporum is fungus that produces an bioactive molecule called cyclosporin A that is used as an immunosuppressive agents in organ-transplant patients.

Monascus purpureus is an yeast that produces statin which is used as a blood-cholesterol lowering agent.

(1½ Marks)

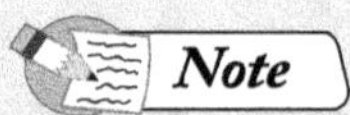
Note

Statin acts by competitively inhibiting the enzyme responsible for synthesis of cholesterol.

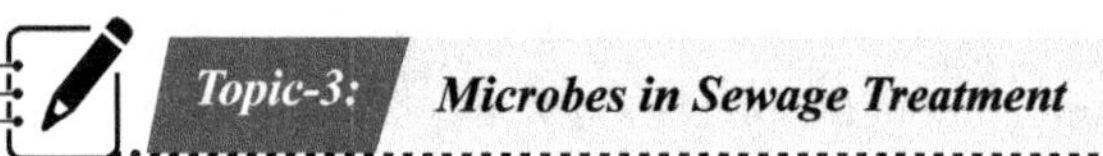
Topic-3: *Microbes in Sewage Treatment*

1. The primary effluent is passed into large aeration tanks, where it is constantly agitated mechanically and air is pumped into it. This allows vigorous growth of useful aerobic microbes into flocs (masses of bacteria associated with fungal filaments to form mesh like structures). While growing, these microbes consume the major part of the organic matter in the effluent. This significantly reduces the BOD (biochemical oxygen demand) of the effluent.

(1 Mark)

2. At collection points A and B, the BOD level is high due to high organic pollution caused by sugar factory and sewage discharge.

At the collection point C, the water was released after secondary treatment/ biological treatment (where vigorous growth of useful aerobic microbes into flocs consume the major part of the organic matter present in the river water or effluent due to sugar factory and sewage discharge).

(1 Mark)

3. Secondary treatment of sewage is also called biological treatment because it involves biological organisms such as aerobic and anaerobic microbes and fungi for digestion of organic waste.

In this, the primary effluent is passed into the large aeration tanks and is constantly agitated mechanically. In this, air is pumped and this allows the vigorous growth of useful aerobic microorganisms into flocs. These microbes consume the maximum part of the organic matter in the effluent. This significantly reduces the biochemical oxygen demand (BOD) of the effluent. The sewage water is treated till the BOD is reduced. **(1 Mark)**

4. The secondary treatment plant allows the vigorous growth of useful microbes into **flocs. Flocs** are the masses of bacteria associated with fungal filaments to form mesh like structures. They are formed when the primary effluent is passed into large aeration tanks where it is constantly agitated mechanically and then air is pumped into it. **(1 Mark)**

5.

Topper's Answer

Flocs are the mesh like structures formed by bacterias and fungal filaments during secondary treatment of sewage water.

Biochemical oxygen demand is amount of oxygen required by bacteria to oxidise organic waste in one litre of sewage. Thus these flocs helps in reducing BOD of sewage water and make it less polluted so that it can be sent back to rivers.

(3 Marks)

In Secondary treatment or Biological treatment The primary effluent is passed into large aeration tanks where it is constantly agitated mechanically and air is pumped into it. This allows vigorous growth of useful aerobic microbes into **flocs** (masses of bacteria associated with fungal filaments to form mesh like structures). While growing, these microbes consume the major part of the organic matter in the effluent. This significantly reduces the **BOD (biochemical oxygen demand)** of the effluent. BOD refers to the amount of the oxygen that would be consumed if all the organic matter in one liter of water were oxidised by bacteria. The sewage water is treated till the BOD is reduced. The BOD test measures the rate of uptake of oxygen by micro-organisms in a sample of water and thus, indirectly, BOD is a measure of the organic matter present in the water. The greater the BOD of waste water, more is its polluting potential. **(3 Marks)**

6.

Topper's Answer

Both the organisms act as biofertilisers

i) Rhizobium
It is a type of bacteria which forms symbiotic association with roots of mainly leguminous plants and fixes atmospheric nitrogen into nitrites and nitrates which can be absorbed by plants and in turn take shelter & food from plants
Thus it reduces reliance on chemical fertilisers

ii) Anabaena
It is a type of cyanobacteria which fixes atmospheric nitrogen into absorbable forms.
Thus both of them improves soil fertility by increasing nitrogen content in soil.

(1½ + 1½ Marks)

(i) **Rhizobium:**

The main sources of biofertilisers are bacteria, fungi and cyanobacteria. You have studied about the nodules on the roots of leguminous plants formed by the symbiotic association of Rhizobium. These bacteria fix atmospheric nitrogen into organic forms, which is used by the plant as nutrient. Other bacteria can fix atmospheric nitrogen while free-living in the soil (examples Azospirillum and Azotobacter), thus enriching the nitrogen content of the soil. **(1½ Marks)**

(ii) **Anabena:**

Cyanobacteria are autotrophic microbes widely distributed in aquatic and terrestrial environments many of which can fix atmospheric nitrogen, e.g. Anabaena, Nostoc, Oscillatoria, etc. In paddy fields, cyanobacteria serve as an important biofertiliser. Blue green algae also add organic matter to the soil and increase its fertility. **(1½ Marks)**

7. Accelerated eutrophication is caused by the nutrient enrichment of lake due to passage of sewage, agricultural & industrial wastes into them. These wastes are rich in nitrates & phosphates which over-stimulate the growth of algae (algal bloom) & other plants, causing unsightly scum and unpleasant odours, and robbing the water of dissolved oxygen vital to other aquatic life. This along with decomposition of dead aquatic plants & animals deplete the water's dissolved oxygen content & a lake can literally choke to death in escalated method. **(3 Marks)**

8. During sewage treatment the bacteria naturally present in sewage helps in the process. After primary treatment the effluent is passed into large aeration tanks where vigorous growth of useful aerobic microbes form flocs. Flocs are masses of bacteria associated with fungal filaments to form mesh like structures. These microbes consume major part of the organic matter in the effluent reducing biochemical oxygen demand of the effluent. After this effluent is passed into a settling tank where these flocs are allowed to sediment and called activated sludge. This is passed to anaerobic sludge digesters where other kinds of anaerobic bacteria digest the bacteria and fungi of sludge. During this digestion the bacteria produces a mixture of gases like methane, hydrogen sulphide, carbon dioxide forming biogas which is used as a fuel. **(3 Marks)**

9. Secondary treatment of sewage is also called biological treatment because it involves biological organisms such as aerobic and anaerobic microbes and fungi for digestion of organic waste.

In this, the primary effluent is passed into the large aeration tanks and is constantly agitated mechanically. In this air is pumped and this allows the vigorous growth of useful aerobic microorganisms into **flocs.** These microbes consume the maximum part of the organic matter in the effluent. This significantly reduces the biochemical oxygen demand (BOD) of the effluent. The sewage water is treated till the BOD is reduced. **(3 Marks)**

Note

Flocs are the masses of bacteria associated with fungal filaments to form a mesh like structures. BOD refers to the amount of oxygen consumed if all the organic matter in one litre of water were oxidised by bacteria.

10. The steps involved in the primary treatment of sewage involves:

- This involves the physical removal of large and small particles from the sewage through filtration and sedimentation.

- Floating debris are removed by sequential filteration.

- Then the girt (soil and small pebbles) are removed by sedimentation.

- All solids that settle form the primary sludge, and the supernatant forms the effluents.

- The effluent from the primary settling tank is taken for secondary treatment. **(2 Marks)**

11. BOD (Biological oxygen demand) refers to the amount of oxygen consumed if all the organic matter in one litre of water were oxidised by bacteria.

BOD of the water body helps in the determination of quality of water body. Presence of more organic waste increases the BOD that consumes a large amount of oxygen from water. Greater the BOD of waste water indicates that water is more polluting by microorganisms.

(3 Marks)

 **Topic-4:** **Microbes in Production of Biogas**

1. The secondary treatment plant allows the vigorous growth of useful microbes into **flocs**. **Flocs** are the masses of bacteria associated with fungal filaments to form mesh like structures. They are formed when the primary effluent is passed into large aeration tanks where it is constantly agitated mechanically and then air is pumped into it. **(1 Mark)**

2. (a) The technology of biogas production was developed in India mainly due to the efforts of Indian Agricultural Research Institute (IARI) and Khadi and Village Industries Commission (KVIC). **(1 Mark)**

(b) Principle of Biogas: Biogas is produced by decomposition of organic matter. Biogas is mainly composed of methane.

- A mixture of farm waste is fed into the biogas plant. This waste is mixed to make a slurry.

- Slurry is then fed into the digester. Digester is an air-tight chamber and oxygen is not present in it.

- Anaerobic bacteria in digester carry out decomposition process of slurry. This results in production of biogas.

(1 Mark)

- Biogas is sent out through an outlet so that it can be suitably used.

- Decomposed matter is taken out and it can be used as manure. **(1 Mark)**

3. (a) The excreta of cattle, commonly called gobar, is rich in bacteria. Dung can be used for generation of biogas, commonly called **gobar gas.** Biogas contains methane gas. **(1 Mark)**

(b) Some bacteria, which grow anaerobically, fermented the cattle excreta in the sludge. During this digestion, bacteria produce a mixture of gases such as methane, hydrogen sulphide and carbon dioxide. These gases form biogas and can be used as a source of energy as it is inflammable. **(1 Mark)**

 **Note**

Biochemical oxygen demand (BOD):
BOD is defined as the amount of oxygen consumed by bacteria and other micro-organisms while they decompose organic matter under aerobic conditions at a specified temperature.

4. Methanogens are anaerobic bacteria growing on cellulosic material and produce large amount of methane alongwith CO_2 and H_2 gas.

These bacteria are commonly found in the anaerobic sludge during sewage treatment. Examples are: *methana bacterium, Methanococcus.*

Methanogens are the bacteria found in cattle dung (gobar) and in anaerobic sludge during sewage treatment. They grow anaerobically on cellulosic material and produce a large amount of methane (main constituent of biogas) alongwith CO_2 and H_2. Thus, methanogens are used in biogas production. **(3 Marks)**

 **Topic-5:** **Microbes as Bicontrol Agent**

1. Streptokinase (produced by the bacterium Streptococcus) is used as a 'clot buster' for removing clots from the blood vessels of patients who have undergone myocardial infarction. **(1 Mark)**

Statins (produced by the yeast *Monascus purpureus*) act as blood-cholesterol lowering agents. **(1 Mark)**

OR

Eradication of pests will disrupt predator-prey relationships, where beneficial predatory and parasitic insects which depend upon flora and fauna as food or hosts, may not be able to survive. **(1 Mark)**

Holistic approach ensures that various life forms that inhabit the field, their life cycles, patterns of feeding and the habitats that they prefer are extensively studied and considered. **(1 Mark)**

2. Baculoviruses are the pathogens which attack insects and other arthropods and are used as a biological control agents. Baculoviruses belongs to the genus *Nucleopolyhedrovirus.* These viruses are used as an excellent source for species-specific, narrow specturum insecticidal applications. They are not harmful for plants, mammals, birds, fishes and on target insects. **(2 Marks)**

3. *Nucleopolyhedrovirus* are excellent candidates for species-specific, narrow spectrum insecticidal applications.

   (1 Mark)

4. (a) **Baculoviruses** is the one of the best example of viral biocontrol agent. **(½ Mark)**

   (b) Baculoviruses showed no negative impacts on plants, mammals, birds, fish or non-target insects. This is especially desirable when beneficial insects are being conserved to aid in the overall integrated pest management (IPM) programme, or when an ecologically sensitive area is being treated. **(1½ Marks)**

5. (a) Biological pest control has important advantages compared to chemical pest control, such as being safer for humans and the environment. Chemical methods often kills both useful and harmful life forms indiscriminately. Eradication of the creatures that are often described as pests in not only possible, but also undesirable, for without them the beneficial predatory and parasitic insects which depend upon them as food or hosts would not be able to survive. **(1½ Marks)**

   (b) Bacterium, a fungus and an insect that are used as biocontrol agents are:

   Insects = Ladybird and Dragonflies.

   Bacteria = *Bacillus thuringiensis.*

   Fungus = *Trichoderma* **(1½ Marks)**

6. Baculoviruses are the pathogen that attack insects and other arthropods. The baculoviruses are used as a biological control agent. They belong the genus *Nucleopolyhedrovirus.* These viruses are excellent candidates for species-specific, narrow spectrum insecticidal applications. **(2 Marks)**

7. (i) *Nucleopolyhedovirus : Nucleopolyhedovirus* is a biological control agent that is used as a species-specific insecticide. **(½ Mark)**

   (ii) *Saccharomyces cerevisiae : Saccharomyces cerevisiae* is also called baker's yeast. It is used in baking and beverage industry. It is used for making breads, south Indian cuisine, cakes and in beverages it is used for making alcohol. **(½ Mark)**

   (iii) *Monscus perpureus :* It is yeast that is used for the production of a blood-cholesterol lowering agents called as **statins.** **(½ Mark)**

   (iv) *Trichoderma polysporum:* It is fungus used for the formation of bioactive molecule called **cyclosporine A.** It is used as an immuno suppressive agent in organ-transplant patients. **(½ Mark)**

   (v) *Penicillium notatum:* It is a bacteria used for the production of antibiotics. **(½ Mark)**

   (vi) *Propionibacterium sharmanii:* It is a bacterium used for the production of "Swiss cheese". The appearance of large holes in the 'Swiss cheese" is because of the production of carbon dioxide by bacteria. **(½ Mark)**

 **Topic-6:**   *Microbes as Biofertilizer*

1. (i) Glomus is an example of a genus of fungi that forms mycorrhizal association with plants. **(1 Mark)**

   (ii) Many members of the genus Glomus form mycorrhizal association with plant. **(1 Mark)**

   The fungal symbiont in these associations absorbs phosphorus from soil and passes it to the plant. Plants having such associations show other benefits also, such as resistance to root-borne pathogens, tolerance to salinity and drought, and an overall increase in plant growth and development.

2. An example of microbial biocontrol agent is bacteria Bacillus thuringiensis (Bt). It can be introduced in order to control butterfly caterpillars.

These are available in sachets as dried spores that are mixed with water and sprayed onto vulnerable plants such as Brassica and fruit trees, where these are eaten by the insect larvae. In the gut of larvae, the toxin is released and the larvae get killed. The bacterial disease will kill the caterpillars, but leaves other insect unaffected. **(3 Marks)**

3. Yes, the organic farmer indeed believes that biodiversity furthers health.

- An **organic farmer** depends on composting and using absolutely natural ingredients in conducting his cultivation.

- There is no use of pesticides or chemicals and crop cultivation is done in an all-natural environment.

- Farmer uses biodiversity to counter the problems of cultivation and by doing so he believes that this helps in overall health improvement.

- As no chemical is used and only **natural produce is utilized** so this indeed improves the health of all. **(3 Marks)**

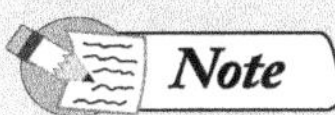
Note

Organic farming can be defined as "an integrated farming system that strives for sustainability, the enhancement of soil fertility and biological diversity. It increased species richness by about 30%.

4. **Biofertilisers** are organisms that enrich the nutrient quality of the soil.

The main sources of biofertilisers are **bacteria, fungi** and **cyanobacteria.**

(i) The **bacteria** fix atmospheric nitrogen into organic forms, which are used by the plant as a nutrient. Other bacteria can fix atmospheric nitrogen while free-living in the soil (example, *Azospirillum* and *Azotobacter*), thus enriching the nitrogen content of the soil. **(1 Mark)**

(ii) The **fungal** symbiont in these associations absorbs phosphorus from soil and passes it to the plant. Plants having such associations show other benefits also, such as resistance to root-borne pathogens, tolerance to salinity and drought, and an overall increase in plant growth and development. **(1 Mark)**

(iii) In paddy fields, **cyanobacteria** serve as an important biofertiliser. Blue-green algae also add organic matter to the soil and increase its fertility. **(1 Mark)**

Note

Biofertiliser can be defined as biological products containing living micro-organisms that, when applied to seed, plant surfaces, or soil, promote growth by several mechanisms such as increasing, the supply of nutrients, increasing root biomass or root area & increasing nutrient uptake capacity of the plant.

5. *Glomus* forms mycorrhiza. It is symbiotic association between the fungi and root nodules of leguminous plants. They absorbs phosphorus from the soil and transport it to the plants. **(1 Mark)**

6. *Glomus* belongs to the genus fungi that are found in symbiotic relationship with the roots of the seed plants (mycorrhiza). Phosphorus is absorbed by the fungi from the soil and passed into the plants and in return derives sugar from the plant cell for survival. Thus the application of the fungal genus, *Glomus*, to the agricultural farm increases the farm output due to increased phosphorus availability to the crops. **(2 Marks)**

7. (a) *Mycorrhiza:* It is an fungi that plays an essential role in the symbiotic association with plants and involves in nitrogen fixation in plants. It is also involved in the absorption of phosphorus from soil and passes it to the plants. **(½ Mark)**

(b) *Monascus purpureus:* It is yeast that is used for the commercial production statins used as a blood-cholesterol lowering agents. **(½ Mark)**

(c) *Anabaena:* It is a cyanobacteria that is involved in nitrogen fixation. They are autotrophic and free-living. They are also used as a good source of biofertiliser.

(½ Mark)

(d) *Rhizobium:* It forms symbiotic association with the root nodules of the leguminous plant. They fix atmospheric nitrogen into organic and absorbable forms for plants that can be used as a source of nutrient. **(½ Mark)**

(e) *Methanobacterium:* It is an bacteria used for the biological generation of methane by anaerobic processes. **(½ Mark)**

(f) *Trichoderma polysporum:* It is a fungus used for the production of bioactive molecule called cyclosporine A that is used as an immunosuppressive agent in organ-transplant patients. **(½ Mark)**

8. The genus *Nucleopolyhedrovirus* are baculoviruses that are used as a biological control agents. These viruses are excellent source for species-specific, narrow spectrum insecticidal applications. There will be negative impact on plants, mammals, birds, and fish or even on non-target insects. Such viruses are used for integrated pest management programme (IPM). **(2 Marks)**

9. Fungi are able to form symbiotic association with the root nodules of plants and are called mycorrhiza. So many members of the genus *Glomus* form mycorrhiza. The fungal symbiont in this association absorbs phosphorus from soil and passes it to the plant. Plants having such associations show other benefits such as these are resistance to root-borne pathogens, tolerance against salinity and drought. It also promotes the overall growth and development of plant. **(2 Marks)**

Chapter 9: Biotechnology : Principles and Processes

[5] *Short Answer Questions (2 or 3 Marks)*

1. What are plasmids? How are they different from cloning vectors? Give one example each for a viral and a bacterial cloning vector. **[All India 2022, Term-II, K]**

[1] *Multiple Choice Questions (1 Mark)*

1. Given below is the restriction site of a restriction endonuclease Pst-I and the cleavage sites on a DNA molecule. **[Delhi 2023, Set-I, Ap]**

   5' C - T - G - C - A $\downarrow$ G 3'

   3' G $\uparrow$ A - C - G - T - C 5'

   Choose the option that gives the correct resultant fragments by the action of the enzyme Pst-I.

   (a) 5' C - T - G   C - A - G 3'
        3' G - A - C - G - T   C 5'

   (b) 5' C - T   G - C - A - G 3'
        3' G - A - G - C   T - C 5'

   (c) 5' C - T - G - C   A - G 3'
        3' G - A - C - G   T - C 5'

   (d) 5' C - T - G - C - A   G 3'
        3' G   A - C - G - T - C 5'

2. Identify the activity of endonuclease and exonuclease in the given image. **[CBSE Sample Paper 2023-2024, A]**

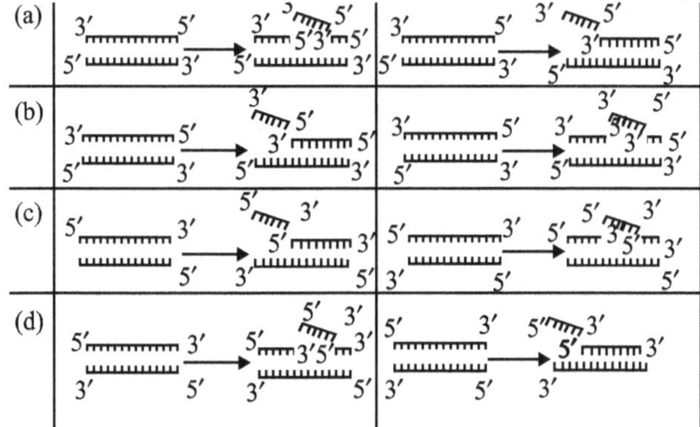

[5] *Short Answer Questions (2 or 3 Marks)*

3. (a) 'Insertional inactivation' is a method to detect recombinant DNA. Explain the method. **[All India 2023, Set-I, U]**

   (b) Explain how recombinant DNA technology is used to detect a disease even before any clinical symptom appears. **[All India 2023, Set-I, U]**

4. (a) State the principle involved in separation of DNA fragments using gel electrophoresis. **[Delhi 2023, Set-II, K]**

   (b) How are DNA fragments visualised once they are separated by gel electrophoresis? **[Delhi 2023, Set-II, K]**

5. The image below shows the result of plating bacteria in chromogenic medium after incorporating the gene of interest in plasmid. Some plates had blue colonies; some plates had white colonies. A single bacterium extracted from Plate I, II, III is shown below: **[CBSE Sample Paper 2023-2024, A]**

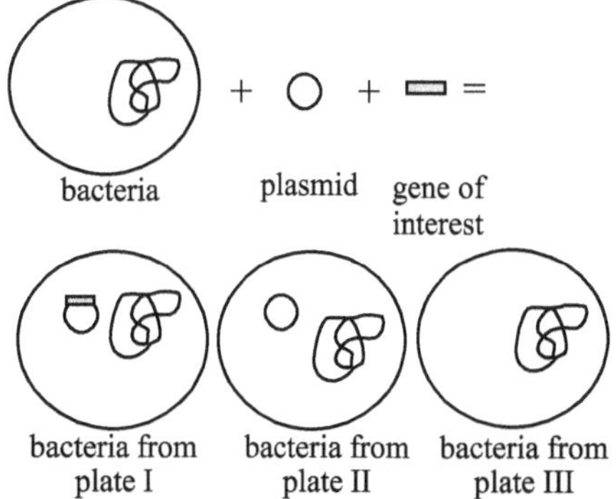

On the basis of your observations

(a) Identify the plate(s) which is/are white. Give a reason.

(b) Identify the plate(s) which is/are blue. Give a reason.

6. (i) State the role of a selectable marker in r-DNA technology. **[All India 2022, Term-II, Ap]**

(ii) Name one such selectable marker which is considered to be useul for *E.coli*. **[All India 2022, Term-II, Ap]**

(iii) Give one reason why is it considered to be a useful marker. **[All India 2022, Term-II, Ap]**

7. In an E. coli cloning vector pBR 322, state the role of the following genes: **[All India 2020, U]**

(a) ori gene

(b) Antibiotic resistance gene

(c) rop gene

8. All cloning vectors do have a 'selectable marker'. Describe its role in recombinant DNA-technology. **[Delhi 2020, K]**

9. Name two natural cloning vectors usid in recombinant DNA technology. Write the chracteristics of biological section. **[Delhi 2020, K]**

10. Write by taking a suitable example, the convention followed for naming the restriction enzymes. **[Delhi 2019, U]**

11. Study the figure of vector pBR322 given below: **[Delhi 2019, U]**

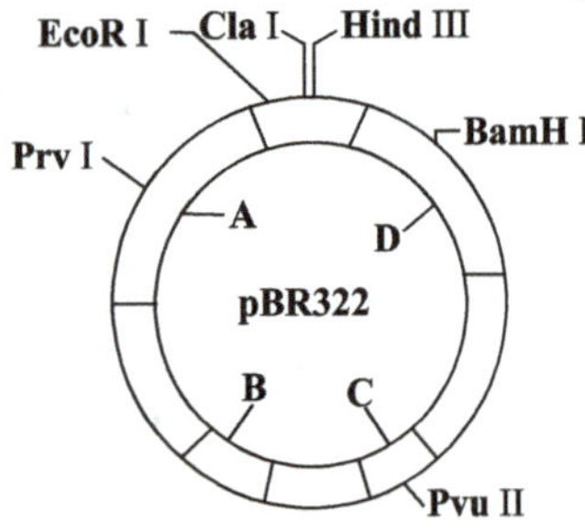

Identify A, B, C and D and explain their roles in cloning a vector.]

12. Explain the roles of the following with the help of an example each in recombinant DNA technology.

(a) Restriction Enzymes **[All India 2018, K]**

(b) Plasmids

13. Explain the role(s) of the following in Biotechnology.

(a) Restriction endonuclease **[All India 2017, U]**

(b) Gel - electrophoresis

(c) Selectable markers in pBR322

14. (a) Explain the significance of 'palindromic nucleotide sequence' in the formation of recombinant DNA. **[Delhi 2017, U]**

(b) Write the use of restriction endonuclease in the above process. **[Delhi 2017, U]**

15. (a) Name the selectable markers in the cloning vector pBR322? Mention the role they play. **[All India 2016, U]**

(b) Why is the coding sequence of an enzyme β galactosidase a preferred selectable marker in comparison to the one named above? **[All India 2016, U]**

16. Explain with the help of a suitable example the naming of a restriction endonuclease. **[Delhi 2014, U]**

17. How are 'sticky ends' formed on a DNA strand ? Why are they so called ? **[Delhi 2014, U]**

18. (a) Mention the difference in the mode of action of exonuclease and endonuclease. **[Delhi 2013, U]**

(b) How does restriction endonuclease function ? **[Delhi 2013, U]**

6   *Long Answer Questions (5 Marks)*

19. Answer the following questions with respect to recombinant DNA technology: **[All India 2023, Set-I, U]**

(i) Why is plasmid considered to be an important tool in rDNA technology? From where can plasmids be isolated? (Any two sources)

(ii) Explain the role of 'ori' and selectable marker in a cloning vector.

(iii) "r-DNA technology cannot proceed without restriction endonuclease." Justify.

20. Draw a digram representing the formation of recombinant DNA. **[All India 2022, Term-II, K]**

21. Write down the process of separation & isolation of DNA fragments. **[Delhi 2013, K]**

7   *Case Based Questions*

22. The structure below shows pUC18 which is similar to pBR322 in its function. However, they differ in some of their restriction sites and number of ori. The ori number for pBR322 is approximately 20.

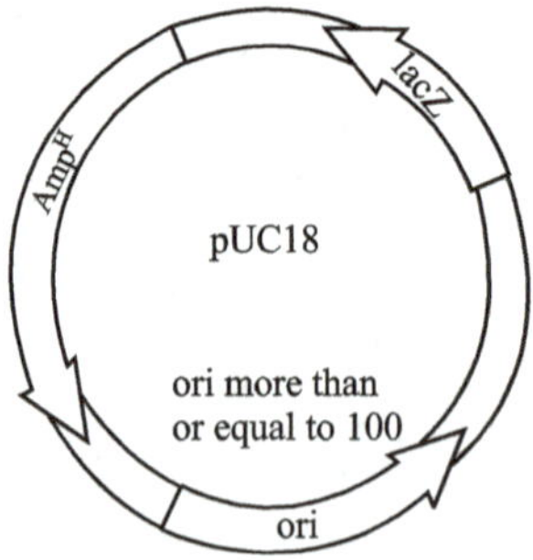

(a) How are puc18 and pBR322 used in biotechnology studies? **[CBSE Sample Paper 2023-24, A]**

OR

What will be the impact if ori in the above structure gets damaged?

(b) The lac z gene has many recognition sites. Study the segment of DNA given below and answer the questions.

5' ... ATC GTA AAG CTT CAT ... 3'

3' ... TAG CAT TTC GAA GTA ... 5'

(i) Applying your knowledge of palindrome sequences identify and mark the possible region where the restriction enzyme X will act.

(ii) Restriction enzyme Y was used to extract gene of interest from a plant. This gene needs to be inserted in the given DNA segment which has been treated with restriction enzyme X. Will there be a successful recombination? Explain with a reason.

(c) Which one of the two (pUC18 and pBR322) would you prefer for biotechnological studies? Justify.

[CBSE Sample Paper 2023-24, A]

23. Some restriction enzymes break a phosphodiester bond on both th7e DNA strands, such that only one end of each molecule is cut and these ends have regions of single stranded DNA. BamH1is one such restriction enzyme which binds at the recognition sequence, 5'-GGATCC-3'and cleaves these sequences just after the 5'- guanine on each strand.

[CBSE Sample Paper 2021-22, A]

(a) What is the objective of this action?

(b) Explain how the gene of interest is introduced into a vector.

(c) You are given the DNA shown below.

5' ATTTTGAGGATCCGTAATGTCCT 3'

3' TAAAACTCCTAGGCATTACAGGA 5'

If this DNA was cut with BamHI, how many DNA fragments would you expect? Write the sequence of these double-stranded DNA fragments with their respective polarity.

(d) A gene M was introduced into E.coli cloning vector PBR322 at BamH1 site. What will be its impact on the recombinant plamids? Give a possible way by which you could differentiate non recombinant to recombinant plasmids.

Topic-3: *Process of Recombinant DNA Technology*

1   *Multiple Choice Questions (1 Mark)*

1. The given schematic illustration shows three steps 'P', 'Q' and 'R' of the polymerase chain reaction.

[All India 2023, Set-I, A]

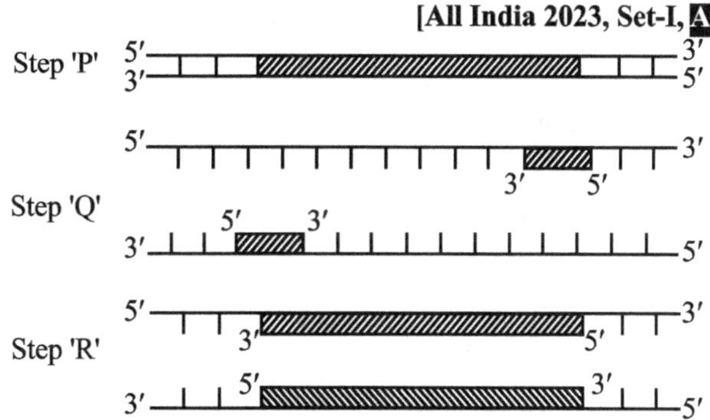

Which of the following statements are correct with reference to the illustration given above?

(i) Step 'P' is showing denaturation at low temperature.

(ii) Step 'Q' is a denaturation of DNA strand at high temperature, followed by annealing.

(iii) Step 'R' is the extension of DNA in presence of thermostable DNA polymerase.

(iv) Step 'Q' is extension with two sets of primers.

(a) (i) and (iii) only

(b) (ii) and (iii) only

(c) (ii) only

(d) (i) only

2   *Assertion Reason/Two Statement Type Questions (1 Mark)*

2. **Assertion (A) :** Synthetic oligonucleotide polymers are used during Annealing in a PCR. **[Delhi 2023, Set-I, K]**

Reason (R) : The primers bind to the double stranded DNA at their complementary regions.

(a) Both (A) and (R) are true and (R) is the correct explanation of (A).

(b) Both (A) and (R) are true, but (R) is not the correct explanation of (A).

(c) (A) is true, but (R) is false.

(d) (A) is false, but (R) is true.

4　　　*Very Short Answer Questions (1 Mark)*

3. (a) Write the scientific name of the source organism of the themostable DNA polymerase used in PCR.
   [Delhi 2023, Set-I, U]

   (b) State the advantage of using Thermostable DNA polymerase. **[Delhi 2023, Set-I, U]**

4. Name the enzymes that are used for the isolation of DNA from bacterial and fungal cells for recombinant DNA technology. **[All India 2014, U]**

5. Mention the type of host cells suitable for the gene guns to introduce an alien DNA. **[Delhi 2014, U]**

6. Why is the enzyme cellulase needed for isolating genetic material from plant cells and not from the animal cells?
   [Delhi 2013, U]

5　　　*Short Answer Questions (2 or 3 Marks)*

7. In a pathological lab, a series of steps were undertaken for finding the gene of interest. Describe the steps, or make a flow chart showing the process of amplification of this gene of interest.
   [CBSE Sample Paper 2021-22, U]

8. Explain the three steps carried out in the formation of recombinant DNA using the enzyme EcoRI.
   [All India 2020, K]

9. How is a continuous culture system maintained in bioreactors and why ? **[All India 2019, K]**

10. Describe the formation of recombinant DNA by the action of EcoRI. **[All India 2019, U]**

   OR

   Describe the process of amplification of "gene of interest" using PCR technique. **[All India 2019, U]**

11. Restriction endonucleases have played a very significant role in rDNA technology. Explain the roles of EcoRI and DNA ligase in formation of recombinant DNA.
    [Delhi 2019, U]

12. (a) How has the development of bioreactor in biotechnology? **[All India 2018, U]**

    (b) Name the most commonly used bioreactor and describe its working. **[All India 2018, U]**

13. Write the steps you would suggest to the undertaken to obtain a foreign-gene-product. **[All India 2017, K]**

14. Describe the roles of heat, primers and the bacterium *Thermus aquaticus* in the process of PCR.
    [Delhi 2017, K]

15. Suggest and describe a technique to obtain multiple copies of a gene of interest *in vitro*. **[Delhi 2016, U]**

16. Rearrange the following in the current sequences to accomplish an important biotechnological reaction:
    [All India 2015, Ap]

    (a) In vitro synthesis of region of DNA of interest

    (b) Chemically synthesised oligonucleotides

    (c) Enzyme DNA-polymerase

    (d) Complementary region of DNA

    (e) Genomic DNA template

    (f) Nucleotides provided

    (g) Primers

    (h) Thermostable DNA-polymerase (from *Thermus aquaticus*)

    (i) Denaturation of ds-DNA

17. Draw a labelled sketch of sparged-stirred-tank bioreactor. Write its application. **[Delhi 2015, U]**

18. How does a restriction nuclease function? Explain.
    [All India 2014, U]

19. Name and describe the technique that helps in separating the DNA fragments formed by the use of restriction endonuclease. **[All India 2014]**

20. Name the source of the DNA polymerase used in PCR technique. Mention why it is used. **[All India 2013, K]**

21. Write any four ways used to introduce a desired DNA segment into a bacterial cell in recombinant technology experiments. **[All India 2013, K]**

22. Recombinant DNA-technology is of great importance in the field of medicine. With the help of a flow chart, show how this technology has been used in preparing genetically engineered human insulin. **[Delhi 2015, U]**

23. Name two commonly used bioreactors. State the importance of using a bioreactor. **[Delhi 2013, K]**

24. Expand the following and mention one application of each:

    (i) PCR　(ii) ELISA **[Delhi 2013, U]**

 **Long Answer Questions (5 Marks)**

25. Bioreactors are the containment vehicles of any biotechnology-based production process. For large scale production and for economic reasons the final success of biotechnological process depends on the efficiency of the bioreactor. **[Delhi 2023, Ap]**

Answer the following questions w.r.t. the given paragraph:

(i) List the operational guidelines that must be adhered to so as to achieve optimisation of the bioreactor system. Enlist any four.

(ii) Mention the phase of the growth we refer to in the statement "Optimisation of growth and metabolic activity of the cells".

(iii) Is the biological product formed in the bioreactor suitable for the intended use immediate? Give reason in support of your answer.

OR

(i) 'EcoRI' has played very significant role in r-DNA technology. **[Delhi 2023, Set-I, U]**

(I) Explain the convention for naming *Eco*RI.

(II) Write the recognition site and the cleavage sites of this restriction endonuclease.

(ii) What are the protruding and hanging stretches of DNA produced by these restriction enzymes called?

Describe their role in formation of r-DNA.

26. Oil spill is a major environmental issue. It has been found that different strains of *Pseudomonas* bacteria have genes to break down the four major groups of hydrocarbons in oil. Trials are underway to use different biotechnological tools to incorporate these genes and create a genetically engineered strain of *Pseudomonas* - a '*super-bug*', to break down the four major groups of hydrocarbons in oil. Such bacteria might be sprayed onto surfaces polluted with oil to clean thin films of oil.

[CBSE Sample Paper 2022-2023, U]

(a) List two advantages of using bacteria for such biotechnological studies?

(b) For amplification of the gene of interest PCR was carried out. The PCR was run with the help of polymerase which was functional only at a very low temperature. How will this impact the efficiency of the PCR? Justify.

(c) If such bacteria are sprayed on water bodies with oil spills, how will this have a positive or negative effect on the environment? Discuss.

27. (a) Explain the different steps carried out in Polymerase Chain Reaction, and the specific roles of the enzymes used. **[All India 2020, U]**

(b) Mention application of PCR in the field of

(i) Biotechnology

(ii) Diagnostics

28. Mention the steps carried put in the formation of recombinant DNA using EcoRI.

[Delhi 2020, K]

Hints & Solutions

Topic-1: ***Principles of Biotechnology***

1. Plasmids are autonomously replicating circular extra – chromosomal DNA, present only in prokaryotic organisms.

    (1 Mark)

    Plasmids can able to replicate within bacterial cells independent of the control of chromosomal DNA. While cloning vector is a small piece of DNA, taken from any organism into which a foreign DNA fragment can be inserted for cloning purposes.   **(1 Mark)**

    The example of viral cloning vector is Bacteriophage.

    (½ Mark)

    The example of bacterial cloning vector is *E.coli*. **(½ Mark)**

Topic-2: ***Tools of Recombinant DNA Technology***

1. **(d)** Restriction endonucleases make cuts at specific positions within the DNA. Restriction enzymes cut the strand of DNA a little away from the centre of the palindrome sites, but between the same two bases on the opposite strands. Therefore resultant fragment will be

    5' C – T – G – C- A   G 3'

    3' G   A – C – G – T – C 5'

    (1 Mark)'

2. **(d)**   **(1 Mark)'**

3. **(a)** Insertional inactivation technique of recombinant DNA technology used to select bacteria that carry recombinant plasmids; a fragment of foreign DNA is inserted into a restriction site within a gene for antibiotic resistance, thus causing that gene to become nonfunctional. It is often used to identify recombinant vectors in gene cloning and in turn to distinguish a recombinant vector from a non-recombinant vector. For example, insertion of a piece of foreign DNA into a cloning site which is located on an antibiotic-resistant gene on the vector can lead to loss of the antibiotic resistance phenotype by insertional inactivation. The recombinant vector will, therefore, specify antibiotic sensitivity, whilst the non-recombinant vector will specify antibiotic resistance.   **(1½ Marks)**

    (b) PCR, ELISA and autoradiography are some of the recombinant DNA technologies that can be used for the detection of disease even before any clinical symptom appears.

    PCR is now routinely used to detect HIV in suspected AIDS patients. It is being used to detect mutations in genes in suspected cancer patients too. It is a powerful technique to identify many other genetic disorders.   **(1½ Marks)**

    A single stranded DNA or RNA, tagged with a radioactive molecule (probe) is allowed to hybridise to its complementary DNA in a clone of cells followed by detection using autoradiography. The clone having the mutated gene will hence not appear on the photographic film, because the probe will not have complementarity with the mutated gene. This can be help in detection of mutated gene responsible for causing disease. ELISA is based on the principle of antigen-antibody interaction. Infection by pathogen can be detected by the presence of antigens (proteins, glycoproteins, etc.) or by detecting the antibodies synthesised against the pathogen.

4. (a) DNA fragments are the negatively-charged molecules as a result DNA molecules are forced to move towards an anode under an electric field through an agarose medium. The DNA fragment separates according to their size through sieving effect provided by agarose gel. Hence, the smaller the size of the molecule faster it will move. **(1½ Marks)**

(b) The DNA fragments after being separated by are treated with ethidium bromide followed by UV radiation exposure. This enables us to view the DNA fragments. **(1½ Marks)**

5. (a) Plate I, b–galactosidase enzyme is responsible for blue colour. Gene is inserted in the b–galactosidase site of the plasmid thereby causing insertional inactivation of the enzyme, so no blue colour is made. **(1 Mark)**

(b) Plate II – Gene of interest not inserted in the plasmid

(1 Mark)

6. (i) A selectable marker helps in identifying and eliminating non-transformants and selectively permitting the growth of the transformants. **(1 Mark)**

(ii) Ampicillin is considered useful selectable marker for *E. coli.* **(1 Mark)**

(iii) The selectable markers are the gene substances that are injected into the cell so that they can offer resistance to the action of the antibiotics. **(1 Mark)**

7. (a) **ori gene:** It is origin of replication. A gene sequence that initiates the process of replication. It controls the copy number of linked DNA. **(1 Mark)**

(b) **Antibiotic resistance gene:** Some genes encoding resistance to antibiotics such as ampicillin, chloramphenicol, tetracycline or kanamycin are considered as useful selectable markers for *E.coli.* The normal *E.coli* cells that does not carry resistance against any of these antibiotics. Antibiotic resistance gene helps in the selection of transformants. **(1 Mark)**

(c) **rop gene:** The rop gene present in pBR322 cloning vectors codes for the protein which is involves in the replication of plasmid. **(1 Mark)**

8. The use of selectable marker in Recombinant DNA helps in the identification and elimination of non-transformants. It selectively permitting the growth of the transformants.

Transformation refers to the process through which a piece of DNA is introduced in a host bacterium and the genes encoding resistance to antibiotics such as ampicillin, chloramphenicol, tetracycline or kanamycin are considered as useful selectable marker for *E.coli.* **(2 Marks)**

9.   **(3 Marks)**

Topper's Answer

The two natural cloning vectors are plasmid of E. coli and plasmid of Agrobacterium tumifaciens. Infact retroviruses also provides their plasmids in order to provide genes of desired interest. Moreover pBR322 and pUC8 are also two widely used plasmids responsible for acting as a cloning vector to deliver gene of interest.

These plasmids and bacteriophages can inculate themselves with host DNA and produce their multiple copies according to their copy numbers. Thus, these extra chromosomal self replicating DNA helps a lot in delivering gene of interest and act as cloning vector.

The two characteristics of these vectors should be :-

(a) Presence of Origin of Replication

These cloning vectors should possess ori (origin of replication) as the presence of it is required to initiate any kind of replication without these the process of replication cannot be carried out. Also, one must ensure that the vectors should support origin of replication with high copy numbers to support too many copies.

(b) Selection of Transformants from Selectable marker

These cloning vectors must contain antibiotic resistant genes like tetracyclin and ampicillin etc. to select transformants from non-transformants after the creation of recombinant DNA. These selectable markers are very much needed to identify transformants from non transformants. Hence, it is a very important attribute indeed.

plasmids and bacteriophages have the ability to replicate within bacterial cells independent of the control of chromosomal DNA. Bacteriophages because of their high number per cell, have very high copy numbers of their genome within the bacterial cells. Some plasmids may have only one or two copies per cell whereas others may have 15-100 copies per cell. Their numbers can go even higher. If we are able to link an alien piece of DNA with bacteriophage or plasmid DNA, we can multiply its numbers equal to the copy number of the plasmid or bacteriophage. Vectors used at present, are engineered in such a way that they help easy linking of foreign DNA and selection of recombinants from non-recombinants.

The following are the features that are required to facilitate cloning into a vector.

(i) Origin of replication (ori) : This is a sequence from where replication starts and any piece of DNA when linked to this sequence can be made to replicate within the host cells. This sequence is also responsible for controlling the copy number of the linked DNA. So, if one wants to recover many copies of the target DNA it should be cloned in a vector whose origin support high copy number.

(ii) Selectable marker : In addition to 'ori', the vector requires a selectable marker, which helps in identifying and eliminating nontransformants and selectively permitting the growth of the transformants. Transformation is a procedure through which a piece of DNA is introduced in a host bacterium (you will study the process in subsequent section). Normally, the genes encoding resistance to antibiotics such as ampicillin, chloramphenicol, tetracycline or kanamycin, etc., are considered useful selectable markers for E. coli. The normal E. coli cells do not carry resistance against any of these antibiotics.

(iii) Cloning sites: In order to link the alien DNA, the vector needs to have very few, preferably single, recognition sites for the commonly used restriction enzymes. Presence of more than one recognition sites within the vector will generate several fragments, which will complicate the gene cloning. The ligation of alien DNA is carried out at a restriction site present in one of the two antibiotic resistance genes. For example, you can ligate a foreign DNA at the BamH I site of tetracycline resistance gene in the vector pBR322. The recombinant plasmids will lose tetracycline resistance due to insertion of foreign DNA but can still be selected out from non-recombinant ones by plating the transformants on tetracycline containing medium. The transformants growing on ampicillin containing medium are then transferred on a medium containing tetracycline. The recombinants will grow in ampicillin containing medium but not on that containing tetracycline. But, non- recombinants will grow on the medium containing both the antibiotics. In this case, one antibiotic resistance gene helps in selecting the transformants, whereas the other antibiotic resistance gene gets 'inactivated due to insertion' of alien DNA, and helps in selection of recombinants.   **(3 Marks)**

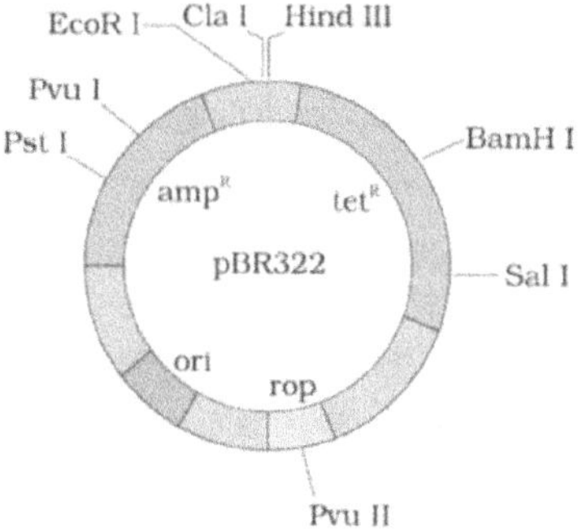

Fig.: E. coli cloning vector pBR322 showing restriction sites (Hind III, EcoR I, BamH I, Sal I, Pvu II, Pst I, Cla I), ori and antibiotic resistance genes (ampR and tetR). rop codes for the proteins involved in the replication of the plasmid.

10. The convention for naming these enzymes is the first letter of the name that comes from the genes and the second two letters come from the species of the prokaryotic cell from which they were isolated for *e.g.,* EcoRI comes from *Escherichia coli* RY13.

In EcoRI, in this the letter 'R' is derived from the name of strain. Roman numbers following the names indicate the order in which the enzymes were isolated from that strain of bacteria. **(3 Marks)**

11. In the given figure, A is ampicillin resistance gene, B is origin of replication, C is repressor of primer, D is tetracycline resistance gene.

   (a) Ampicillin resistance gene (amp^R): It acts as a selectable marker that provides resistance against ampicillin antibiotic.

   (b) ori: It is origin of replication. A sequence that initiates the process of replication. It controls the copy number of linked DNA.

   (c) rop (repressor of primer): This site is responsible for the restricting the plasmid copy number.

   (d) tet^R: It is tetracyclin resistance gene that acts as a selectable marker which provides resistance against tetracyclin antibiotic. **(3 Marks)**

12. (a) Restriction enzymes :

   (i) Restriction enzymes belongs to class of enzymes nucleases which breaks nucleic acids by cleaving their phosphodiester bonds.

   (ii) Since restriction endonucleases cuts DNA at specific recognition site, they are used to cut the donor DNA to isolate the desired gene.

   (iii) The desired gene has sticky ends which can be easily ligated to cloning vector which was cut by same restriction enzymes having complementary sticky ends to form recombinant DNA.

   (iv) An example is EcoRI which is obtained from E.coli bacteria "R" strain which cuts DNA at specific palindromic recognition site. **(1½ Marks)**

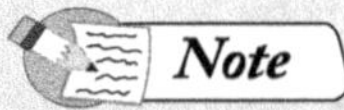

Pallindromes are the group of letters that form the same words when read both forward and backward for e.g. MALAYALAM.

(b) Plasmids :

   (i) Plasmids are autonomous, extra chromosomal circular double stranded DNA of bacteria.

   (ii) They are small and self-replicating, and they are used as cloning vectors in genetic engineering.

   (iii) Some plasmids have antibiotic resistance genes which can be used as marker genes to identify recombinant plasmids from non-recombinant ones.

   (iv) The plasmids are cut and ligated with desired genes and transformed into host cell for amplification to obtain the desired products.

   (v) An example of artificial modified plasmids is pBR322 or pUC. **(1½ Marks)**

13. (a) Restriction endonuclease - These are molecular scissors or biological scissors that recognizes and cuts double stranded DNA at specific points. They are used in biotechnology to form recombinant molecules which are composed of DNA from different sources. To insert a foreign DNA into an intact DNA, it must be cut from its source and the intact DNA also must be cut open. Both these processes are carried by using the same restriction endonucleases. **(1 Mark)**

(b) Gel electrophoresis is a molecular biology technique which is used for the separation of DNA fragments. DNA fragments are produced by cutting with restriction.

DNA fragments are negatively charged molecules they can be separated by forcing them to move towards the anode under an electric field through a medium/matrix. The smaller, the fragment size, the farther it moves.   **(1 Mark)**

> *Note*
>
> *Ethidium bromide is an intercalating agent which is used to visualise the separated DNA fragments followed by exposure to UV ratiation.*

(c) pBR322 has two antibiotic resistance genes, one for ampicillin and other one for tetracycline. Antibiotic resistance serves as selectable marker. If the foreign DNA is ligated at the site of tetracycline resistance gene in pBR322 vector, the recombinant plasmid will lose tetracycline resistance due to insertion of foreign DNA but can still be selected out from non-recombinants by plating the transformants on ampicillin containing medium. The transformants growing on ampicillin containing medium are then transferred on a medium containing tetracycline. The recombinants will grow in ampicillin containing medium but not on the tetracycline-containing medium. However the non-recombinants will grow on both. Thus by using antibiotic resistant genes as selectable markers, we can differentiate between recombinants and non-recombinants.   **(1 Mark)**

14. (a) The palindromic sequences are the groups of letters that form the same word that is when both read forward and backward. For e.g "MALAYALAM". Palindrome where the same word is read in both directions, the palindrome in DNA is a sequence of base pairs that reads the same on the two strands when orientation of reading is kept the same.

For example: The following sequences read the same on the two strands in 5'→3' direction. The same sequence read in the 3'→5' direction.

5'-----GAATTC----3'

3'----CTTAAG----5'   **(1½ Marks)**

(b) On finding the palindrome, the endonuclease binds to the DNA. It cuts the opposite strands of DNA, but between the same bases on both the strands and form 'Sticky-ends'. This 'sticky ends' facilitates the action of enzyme DNA ligase and also helps in the formation of recombinant DNA.   **(1½ Marks)**

15. (a) Selectable markers are used for the identification and elimination of non-transformants that selectively permits the growth of the transformants. The genes encoding resistance to antibiotics such as ampicillin, chloramphenicol, tetracycline and kanamycin are commonly used selectable markers.

                                    (1½ Marks)

> *Note*
>
> *Transformation is a procedure through which a piece of DNA is introduced in a host bacterium.*

(b) The selectable markers are developed to differentiate recombinants from non-recombinants on the basis of their ability to produce colour in the presence of chromogenic substrate.

In this, a recombinant DNA is inserted within the coding sequence of an enzyme, which is referred as **insertional inactivation**. The presence of a chromogenic substrate gives blue coloured colonies if the plasmid in the bacteria does not have insert.

The presence of insert results in **insertional inactivation** of the beta-galactosidase enzyme and the colonies does not produce any colour and are identified as recombinant colonies.   **(1½ Marks)**

16. The convention for naming enzyme restriction endonucleases such as ECoRI contains the first letter of the name that comes from the genes and the second two letters comes from the species of the prokaryotic cell from which they were isolated.

For example: in case of ECoRI comes from *Escherichia coli* RY 13. In this, the letter 'R' is derived from the name of strain. Roman numbers following the names indicate the order in which the enzymes were isolated from that strain of bacteria. **(3 Marks)**

17. The sticky ends are produced by the restriction enzymes. The restriction enzymes cut the strand of the DNA a little away from the centre of the palindromic sites, but between the same two bases on the opposite strands. This leaves single stranded portions at the ends. There are overhanging stretches called sticky ends on each strand.

They are called sticky ends because they form hydrogen bonds with their complementary cuts. This stickiness of the ends facilitates the action of the enzyme DNA ligase.

(2 Marks)

Diagrammatic Representation of action of Restriction Enzymes:

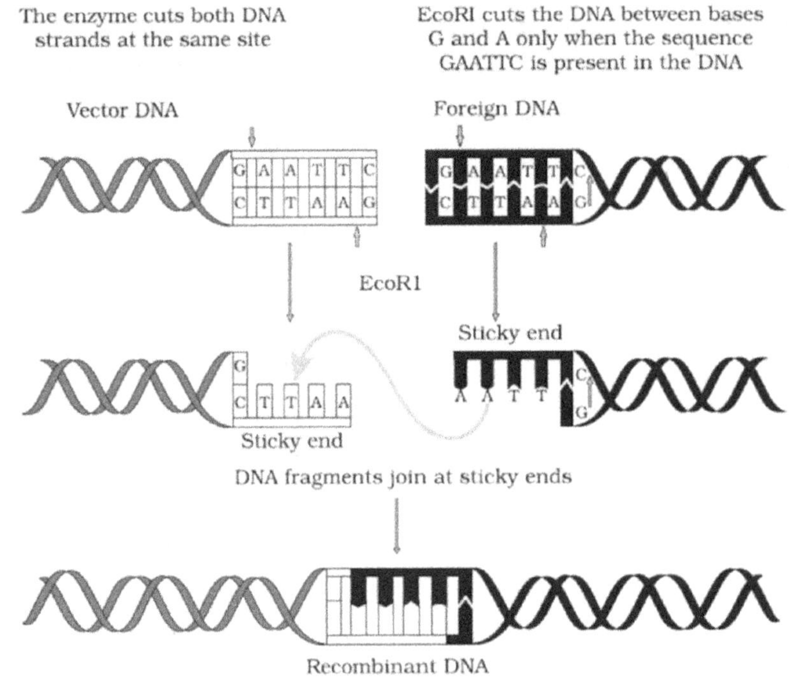

(1 Mark)

18. **(a)** Restriction enzymes are larger class of enzymes called nucleases and they are of two types exonucleases and endonucleases.

Exonucleases remove nucleotides from the ends of the DNA whereas endonucleases make cuts at specific positions within the DNA.

(b) Restriction endonuclease functions by 'inspecting' the length of a DNA Sequence and one it recognise the sequence, it will get bind with the DNA and cut each of the two strands of the double helix at specific points in their sugar-phosphate backbones.

Each restriction endonuclease recognises a specific nucleotide sequences the DNA. Restriction enzymes cut the strand of DNA away from the centre of the palindrome sites but between the same two bases on the opposite strands.

This leaves single stranded portions at the ends and there are overhanging stretches called **sticky ends** on each strand. These are named so because they form hydrogen bonds with their complementary cut. This stickiness of the ends facilitates the action of the enzyme DNA ligase.

Restriction endonucleases are used in genetic engineering for formation of 'recombinant' molecules of DNA, which are composed of DNA from different sources or genomes.   **(2 Marks)**

Diagrammatic representation of steps involved in the formation of recombinant DNA by action of restriction endonuclease:

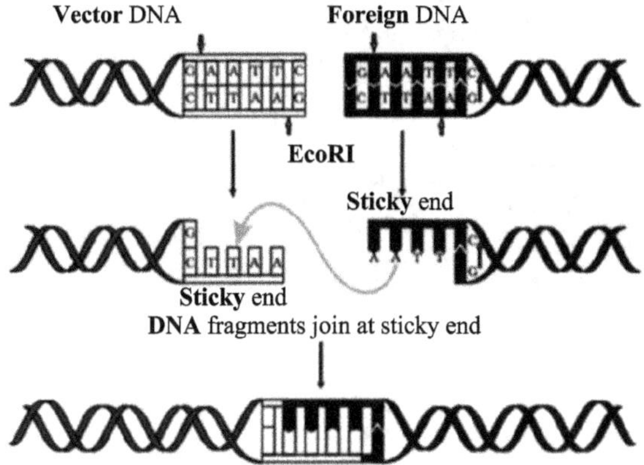

19. (i) Plasmids used in genetic engineering are called vectors. They are used to transfer genes from one organism to another. Plasmid is helps in linking of foreign DNA and selection of recombinants from non-recombinants. Some plasmids may have only one or two copies per cell whereas others may have 15-100 copies per cell. Their numbers can go even higher. The two sources of plasmid are E.coli and Agrobacterium tumifaciens.   **(1 Mark)**

(ii) Origin of replication (ori) : This is a sequence from where replication starts and any piece of DNA when linked to this sequence can be made to replicate within the host cells. This sequence is also responsible for controlling the copy number of the linked DNA. So, if one wants to recover many copies of the target DNA it should be cloned in a vector whose origin support high copy number.   **(2½ Marks)**

Selectable marker : In addition to 'ori', the vector requires a selectable marker, which helps in identifying and eliminating nontransformants and selectively permitting the growth of the transformants. Transformation is a procedure through which a piece of DNA is introduced in a host bacterium (you will study the process in subsequent section). Normally, the genes encoding resistance to antibiotics such as ampicillin, chloramphenicol, tetracycline or kanamycin, etc., are considered useful selectable markers for E. coli. The normal E. coli cells do not carry resistance against any of these antibiotics.

(iii) The r-DNA technology cannot proceed without restriction endonuclease because this enzyme cuts the DNA very precisely and thus eliminates the infecting organisms. It cuts double stranded DNA at specific recognition sites. It was used to restrict the growth of viruses when it was discovered in bacteria.   **(1½ Marks)**

20. **(3 Marks)**

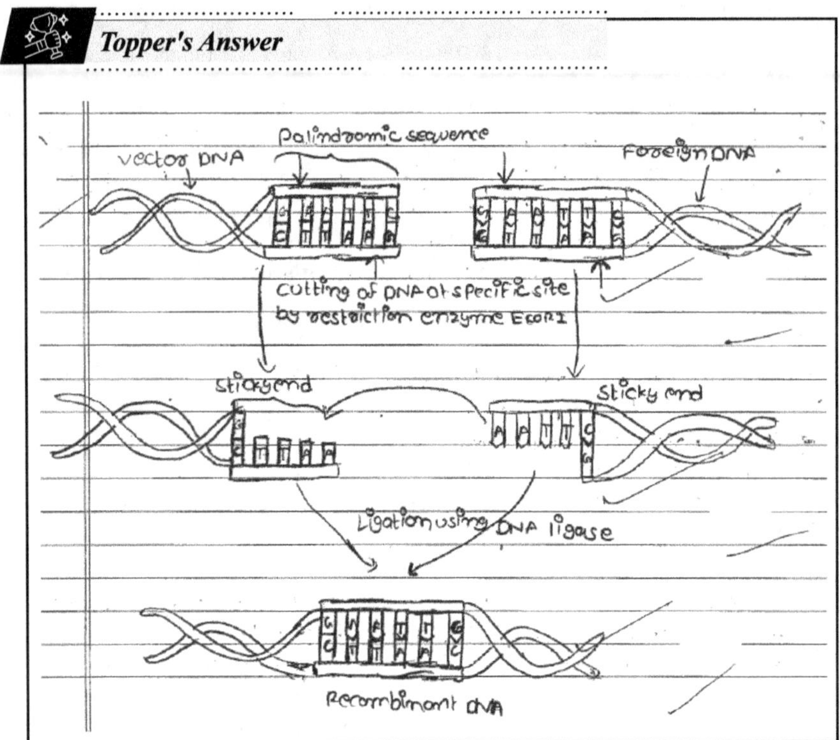

Each restriction endonuclease functions by 'inspecting' the length of a DNA sequence. Once it finds its specific recognition sequence, it will bind to the DNA and cut each of the two strands of the double helix at specific points in their sugar -phosphate backbones. Each restriction endonuclease recognises a specific palindromic nucleotide sequences in the DNA. **(3 Marks)**

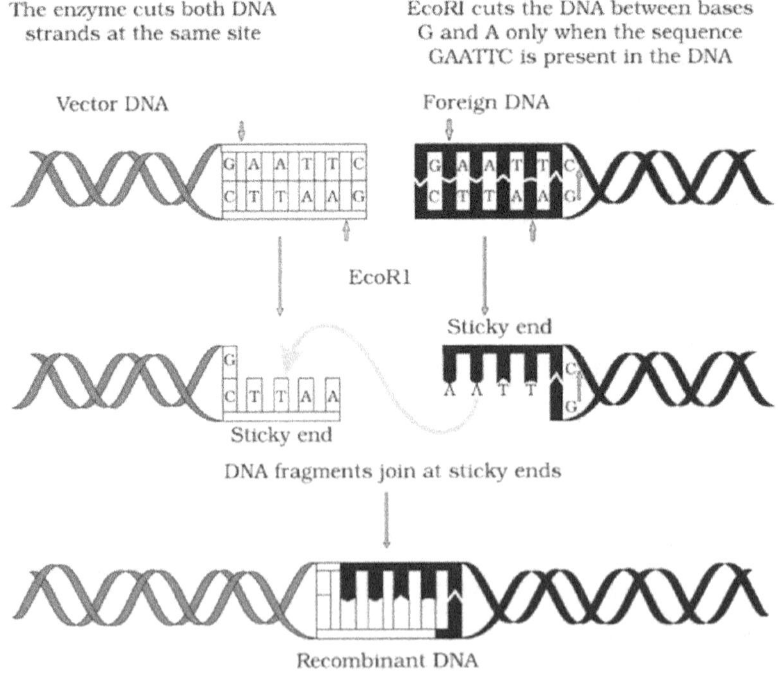

Fig.: Steps in formation of recombinant DNA by action of restriction endonuclease enzyme - EcoRI

21. The cutting of DNA by restriction endonucleases results in the fragments of DNA. These fragments can be separated by a technique known as gel electrophoresis. Since DNA fragments are negatively charged molecules they can be separated by forcing them to move towards the anode under an electric field through a medium/ matrix. Nowadays the most commonly used matrix is agarose which is a natural polymer extracted from sea weeds. The DNA fragments separate (resolve) according to their size through sieving effect provided by the agarose gel. Hence, the smaller the fragment size, the farther it moves. **(5 Marks)**

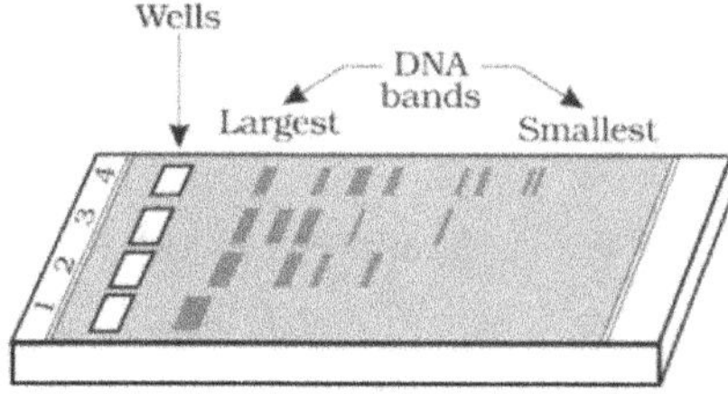

Fig.: A typical agarose gel electrophoresis showing migration of undigested (lane 1) and digested set of DNA fragments (lane 2 to 4

The separated DNA fragments can be visualised only after staining the DNA with a compound known as ethidium bromide followed by exposure to UV radiation (you cannot see pure DNA fragments in the visible light and without staining). You can see bright orange coloured bands of DNA in a ethidium bromide stained gel exposed to UV light (Figure 11.3). The separated bands of DNA are cut out from the agarose gel and extracted from the gel piece. This step is known as elution. The DNA fragments purified in this way are used in constructing recombinant DNA by joining them with cloning vectors.

22. **(a)** Plasmids which can be used to insert the geneof interest from a desired organism into a host/ they act as vectors to transfer gene of interest into the host.

4(1)

OR

Ori– Origin of replication (ori) – No replication will take place resulting in no copies of linked DNA.

(b) (i) 5' ... ATC GTA/AAG CTT /CAT ... 3'

    3' ... TAG CAT/TTC GAA /GTA ... 5'

        (1 mark for both strand)

OR

    5' ... AAG CTT ...3'

    3' ... TTC GAA ...5'   **(1 mark for both strand)**

(ii) No, as the restriction enzymes need to be the same which cut the DNA of the plasmid and the gene of interest from the plant. **(0.5+0.5=1)**

(c) PUC18 as it has a higher copyrate. **(0.5+0.5=1)**

23. **(a)** The two different DNA molecules will have compatible ends to recombine. **(½Mark)**

(b) Restriction enzyme cuts the DNA of the vector and then ligates the gene of interest into the DNA of the vector. **(1 Mark)**

(c) 2 fragments **(½ Mark)**

   5' ATTTTGAG 3'5'GATCCGTAATGTCCT 3'

   3' TAAAACTCCTAG 5'.3'GCATTACAGGA 5'

        (1 Mark)

(d) BamH1 site will affect tetracycline antibiotic resistance gene, hence the recombinant plasmids will lose tetracycline resistance due to inactivation of the resistance gene. **(1 Mark)**

Recombinants can be selected from non recombinants by plating into a medium containing tetracycline, as the recombinants will not grow in the medium because the tetracycline resistance gene is cut.

        (1 Mark)

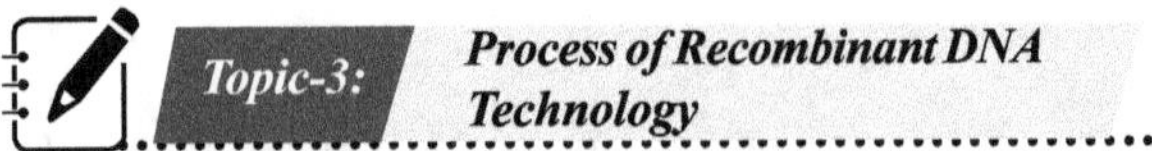

Topic-3: Process of Recombinant DNA Technology

1. (b) In the given polymerase chain reaction, in option (b) there is correct explanation of steps Q and R. Moreover, step P is not showing the denaturation process, it is a single stranded DNA molecule and in step Q only annealing process is occurring but no extension. **(1 Mark)**

2. (b) In polymerase chain reaction, multiple copies of the gene (or DNA) of interest is synthesised *in vitro* using two sets of primers (small chemically synthesised oligonucleotides that are complementary to the regions of DNA) and the enzyme DNA polymerase. The enzyme extends the primers using the nucleotides provided in the reaction and the genomic DNA as template. **(1 Mark)**

3. (a) *Thermus aquaticus* is the source organism of the thermostable DNA polymerase used in PCR.

(1 Mark)

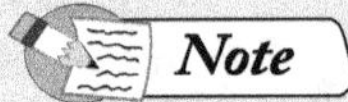

Note

PCR stand for Polymerase chain reaction. In this reaction multiple copies of gene of interest is synthezied in vitro.

(b) Advantages **of using thermostable DNA polymerase is-** It remains active during the high temperature induced denaturation of double stranded DNA. **(1 Mark)**

4. Enzymes that can be used for the isolation of DNA from bacterial cell is lysozyme and for fungal cell is chitinase for recombinant DNA technology. **(1 Mark)**

5. An undifferentiated plant cells are the most suitable host cells for the gene guns or biolistics gun. Plant cells are used because they have rigid cell wall that can be broken easily by bombarding them with high velocity micro-particles of gold or tungsten coated with DNA in a gene gun. **(1 Mark)**

6. Plants cells have cellulose in their cell wall that can be degraded by cellulase enzyme in order to isolate DNA. While in case of animal cell, cell wall is absent and due to this, cellulase enzyme is not required for isolation of DNA **(1 Mark)**

Note

Lysozyme enzyme is used for breaking bacterial cell whereas chitinase enzyme is used for breaking fungal cells.

7. The flow chart shows the three steps involved in the process of PCR showing the following

– Denaturation The DNA strands are treated with a temperature of 940C (Heat) and the strands are separated.

– Annealing The primers anneal to the complementary strands.

– Extension The DNA polymerase facilitates the extension of the strands. **(1 × 3 = 3 Marks)**

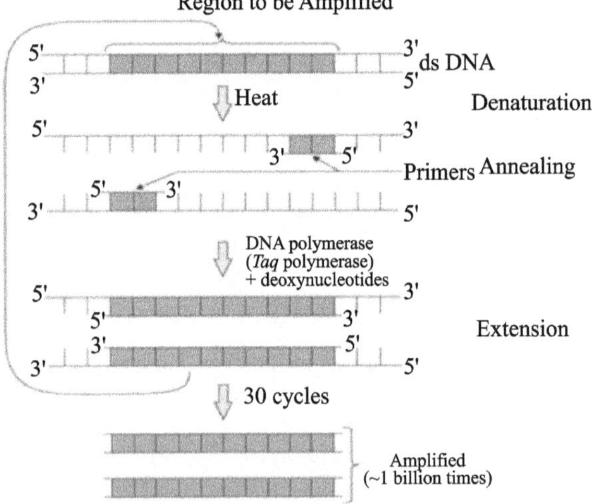

Diagram : Polymerase Chain Reaction

8. The steps involved in the formation of recombinant DNA by the action of restriction endonuclease enzymes EcoRI:

- EcoRI cuts the DNA between the nitrogenous bases G and A only when the sequence GAATTC is present in the DNA.

- The restriction endonuclease enzyme cuts both the DNA strands such as vector DNA and foreign DNA at the same site.

- Then, the DNA fragments are joined at sticky ends and recombinant DNA is produced.   **(2 Marks)**

Diagrammatic representation of steps involved in the formation of recombinant DNA by action of restriction endonuclease enzyme EcoRI.

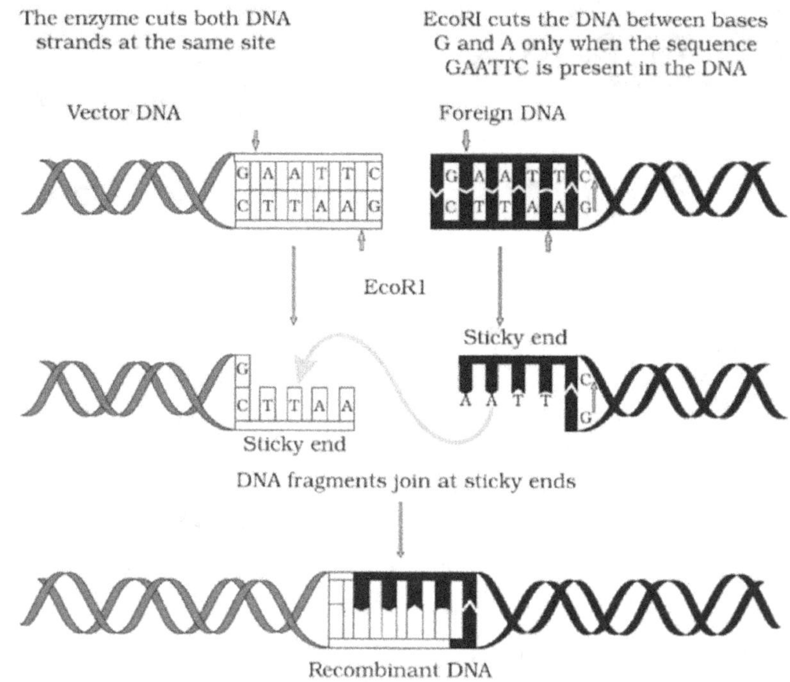

(1 Mark)

9. A continuous culture system is maintained in a bioreactor by continuously and regularly feeding with culture medium steadily and by providing optimum growth conditions such as pH, temperature, vitamins, salts, oxygen. The used medium is drained out from one side of the bioreactor and the fresh medium is added from the other side. Continuous culture system is maintained in bioreactors in order to maintain the cells in their physiologically most active log/ exponentially phase. This type of culturing method produces a large biomass results in higher yield of the desired protein.   **(2 Marks)**

10. The various steps involved in the formation of recombinant DNA by the action of *Eco*RI are as follows:

- Both vector DNA and foreign DNA is cut with EcoRI.

- Both DNAs will possess smaller fragments with overhanging stretches called sticky ends on each strand.

- After digestion, both vector DNA and foreign DNA are mixed and allowed to join together with the help of DNA ligase enzyme. This results in the formation of recombinant DNA molecules.   **(2 Marks)**

Diagrammatic representation of steps involved in the formation of recombinant DNA by action of restriction endonuclease enzyme-EcoRI:

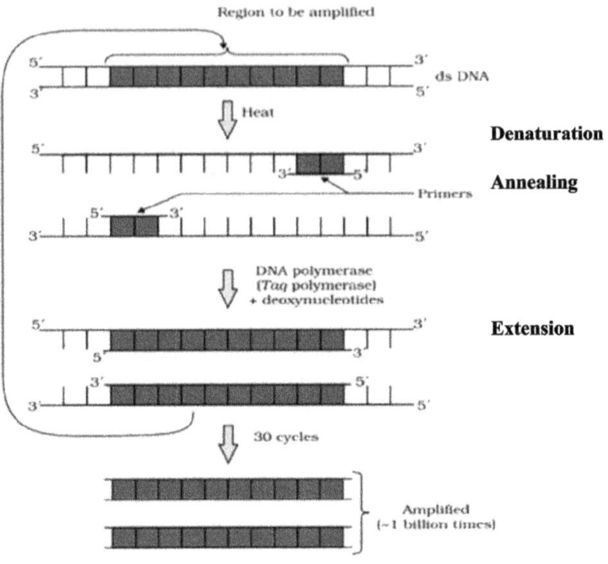

(1 Mark)

OR

With the help of recombinant DNA technology called Polymerase Chain Reaction technique (PCR) multiple copies of the 'gene of interest' are obtained in *Vitro*. A single PCR amplification cycle involves three steps which are as follows:

(a) **Denaturation:** This is the first step of PCR, in which the target DNA is heated at high temperature such as 94-96°C. It facilitates the separation of two strands of DNA. Each separated strand of DNA acts as a template for synthesis of DNA.

(b) **Annealing:** This is the second step of PCR, in which two oligonucleotide primers are used to hybridize each single-stranded template DNA. The sequence of primers is complementary to 3' end of the template DNA strand.

This step of PCR occurs at low temperature 40-60°C than denaturation. The annealing temperature depends upon the length and sequence of the primers.

(c) **Extension:** This is the third and the last step of PCR, in which enzyme *Taq*DNA polymerase synthesizes the DNA between the primers. This step also requires dNTPs and Mg2++. The optimum temperature for an extension is 72°C.

Diagrammatic representation of steps involved in PCR:

(3 Marks)

Enzyme used in PCR is a DNA polymerase such as Taq polymerase. This enzyme is stable at high temperature as it is isolated from thermostable bacteria Thermus aquaticus.

11. In Recombinant DNA technology, EcoRI cuts the DNA between bases G and A only when the sequences GAATTC is present in the DNA. It acts as a molecular scissors that serves as tool for DNA at specific palindromic sites at specific points.

DNA ligase enzyme is also called molecular gum as it is involved in joining the two segments of DNA by creating phosphodiester bond between the two fragments of DNA. **(2 Marks)**

A recombinant DNA molecule is formed from the segments of two or more different DNA molecules.

12. **(a)** Small volume cultures cannot yield appreciable quantities of products. In order to produce in large quantities, bioreactor are developed in which, large volumes (100 - 1000 litres) of culture can be processed. Thus, bioreactors can be thought of as vessels in which raw materials are biologically converted into specific products, individual enzymes, etc., using microbial plant, animal or human cells. **(1½ Marks)**

 *Note*

Bioreactor is defined as a vessel that carries out a biological reaction and is used to culture aerobic cells for conducting cellular or enzymatic immobilization.

(b) The most commonly used bioreactors are of stirring type. A stirred - tank reactors is usually cylindrical or with a curved base to facilitate the mixing of the reactor contents. The stirrer facilitates even mixing and oxygen availability throughout the bioreactor. The bioreactor has an agitator system, an oxygen delivery system and a foam control system, a temperature control system. pH control system and sampling ports so that small volumes of the culture can be withdrawn periodically. **(1½ Marks)**

13. Recombinant DNA technology allows DNA to be produced via artificial means. The procedure has been used to change DNA in living organisms and may have even more practical uses in the future. Recombinant DNA technology works by taking DNA from two different sources and combining that DNA into a single molecule.

To obtain rDNA steps involved are:

(a) The DNA fragment containing the gene sequence to be cloned (also known as ('insert') is isolated.

(b) Insertion of these DNA fragments into a host cell using a 'vector' (carrier DNA molecule).

(c) The rDNA molecules are generated when the vector self replicates in the host cell.

(d) Transfer of the rDNA molecules into an appropriate host cell.

(e) Selection of the host cells carrying the rDNA molecule using a marker.

(f) Replication of the cells carrying rDNA molecules to get a genetically identical cells population or clone.

(3 Marks)

14. **Role of heat in PCR:**

Heat helps in the denaturation process in PCR. In this process, the dsDNA is heated in this process at very high temperature (94-96°C) results in the separation of two strands of DNA into single strands.

Role of primers in PCR:

Primers are the short synthetic single stranded DNA fragments that are complementary to DNA sequences that flank the target region of the DNA.

DNA polymerase enzyme extends the primers by using the nucleotides provided in the reaction and the genomic DNA as template. It helps in the extension of new chain.

Role of Bacterium *Thermus aquaticus:*

The bacteria *Thermus aquaticus is* thermostable bacteria. An enzyme Taq DNA polymerase is isolated from these thermostable bacteria. This enzyme remains active during high temperature during denaturation of double stranded DNA. **(3 Marks)**

15. With the help of recombinant DNA technology called Polymerase Chain Reaction (PCR) technique multiple copies of gene of interest are obtained in *Vitro*. A single PCR amplification cycle involves three steps which are as follows:

(a) **Denaturation:** This is the first step of PCR, in which the target DNA is heated at high temperature such 94-96°C. It facilitates the separation of two strands of DNA. Each separated strand of DNA acts as a template for synthesis of DNA.

(b) **Annealing:** This is the second step of PCR, in which two oligonucleotide primers are used to hybridize each single stranded template DNA. The sequence of primers is complementary to 3' end of the template DNA strand.

This step of PCR occurs at low temperature 40-60°C than denaturation. The annealing temperature depends upon the length and sequence of the primers.

(c) **Extension:** This is third and last step of PCR, in which enzyme *Taq*DNA polymerase synthesizes the DNA between the primers. This step also requires dNTPS and Mg^{2++}. The optimum temperature for extension is 72°C. **(3 Marks)**

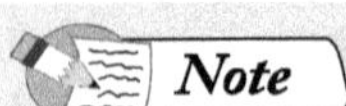

Note

Enzyme used in PCR is a DNA polymerase such as Taq DNA polymerase. This enzyme is stable at high temperature as it is isolated from thermostable bacteria Thermus aquaticus.

16. The given steps refer to the steps involved in the polymerase chain reaction:

    (b) Chemically synthesised oligonucleotides

    (f) Nucleotides provided

    (h) Thermostable DNA-polymerase (from Thermus aquaticus)

    (i) Denaturation of ds DNA

    (g) Primers

    (e) Genomic DNA template

    (c) Enzyme DNA-polymerase

(d) Complementary region of DNA

(a) In *vitro* synthesis of region of DNA of interest

(3 Marks)

17. **Diagrammatic representation of sparged-stirred-tank bioreactors:**

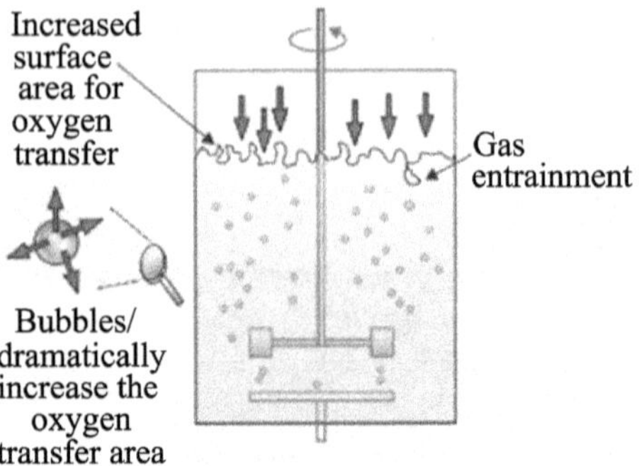

Bioreactors refers to an apparatus in which a biological reaction is carried out.

Application of sparged-stirred-tank bioreactor:

- Sparged-stirred tank bioreactors are used for the production of large amount of proteins.

- It is also used for the large-scale production of alcohol. **(3 Marks)**

18. Restriction enzymes belong to a larger class of enzymes called nucleases. They are of two types such as endonuclease and exanucleases. Restriction endonuclease is the most widely used enzyme in recombinant DNA technology and molecular biology. This enzyme is involved in the process of gene modification. It recognizes specific sequences of nucleotides that is known as recognition site and produces a double strand nick in the desired DNA. The action of restriction endonuclease can be on palindromic sequences. For example, *EcoRI*cuts the DNA at the following palindromic sequence:

    5' GAATTC 3'   3' C T T A A G 5'

Exonucleases remove nucleotides from the ends of the DNA. **(2 Marks)**

Pallindromes are groups of letters that form the same words when read both forward and backward. For example "MALAYALAM"

19. The technique that is used for separating DNA fragments in the lab is called gel electrophoresis. In this technique, restriction endonuclease is used for cutting DNA fragments. **(3 Marks)**

- The DNA fragments are negatively charged molecules so they can be separated by forcing them to move towards the anode under an electric field through a medium or matix.

- The most commonly used matrix is called agarose that is a natural polymer extracted from sea weeds.

- The DNA fragments separate according to their size through sieving effect provided by the agarose gel

- So, the smaller the fragment size, farther, it moves.

- The separated DNA fragments can be visualised only after staining the DNA with a compound known as ethidium bromide followed by exposure to UV radiation.

- A DNA marker with fragments of known lengths is usually run through the gel at the same time as the samples.

- By comparing the bands of the DNA samples with those from the DNA marker one can work out at the approximate length of the DNA fragments in the samples.

(3 Marks)

20. DNA polymerase used in PCR is *Taq* DNA polymerase which is isolated from a bacterium *Thermus aquaticus*. This bacterium is found in hot springs and hydrothermal vents.

The *Taq* polymerase remains active at high temperature during denaturation process of PCR. **(3 Marks)**

PCR stands for Polymerase Chain Reaction is a molecular biology technique used for the formation of large number of copies of samples produced in small quantities. PCR amplification is commonly used by medical and forensic applications.

21. The four ways used for the introduction of a desired DNA segment into bacterial cell in the recombinant DNA technology are as follows: **(½ × 4 = 2 Marks)**

(i) **Chemical method:** In this process, the bacterial cells must be first made 'competent' to take up DNA. It is done by treating the bacterial cell with a specific concentration of a divalent cation such as calcium that increases the efficiency with which DNA enters the bacterium through pores in its cell wall. Recombinant DNA can then be forced into such cells by incubating the cells with recombinant DNA on ice, followed by placing them briefly at 42°C (heat shock). Then, putting them back on ice. So, this enables the bacteria to take up the recombinant DNA.

(ii) **Microinjection:** In this method, recombinant DNA is directly injected into the nucleus of an animal cell.

(iii) **Biolistics or gene gun:** This method is suitable for plants, as cells are bombarded with high velocity micro-particles of gold or tungsten coated with DNA.

(iv) **Disarmed pathogen:** In this method, vector is allowed to infect the cell results in the transfer of the recombinant DNA into the host.

22. **Representation of flow chart for the production of recombinant insulin:**

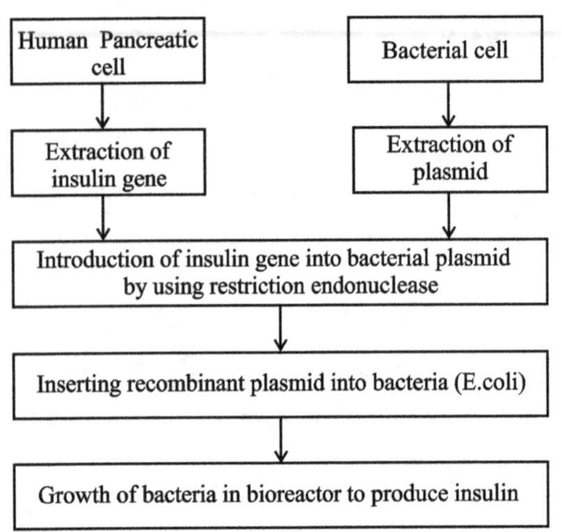

Diagrammatic representation of recombinant insulin:

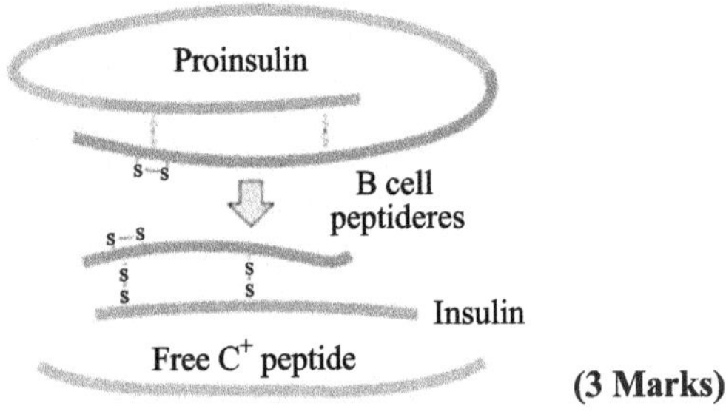

(3 Marks)

23. The two commonly used bioreactors are stirred-tank bioreactor and sparged stirred-tank bioreactor.

A stirred-tank bioreactor is cylindrical or with a curved base in order to facilitate the mixing of reactor contents and stirrer facilitates the mixing and availability of oxygen throughout the bioreactor. Alternatively air can be bubbled through the reactor. Whereas in a sparged stirred-tank bioreactor, a sparge which is a ring made of metal or glass that facilitates the mixing and oxygen availability throughout the bioreactor.

Bioreactors are important as large volume (100-1000 litres) of culture can be processed. Bioreactor provides optimal conditions for growth such as temperature, pH, substrate, salts, vitamins and oxygen for production of desired product. **(2 Marks)**

24. (i) PCR stand for Polymerase Chain Reaction. It is a molecular biology for the synthesis of many copies of a specific DNA in vitro. It is used for the diagnosis of infectious diseases even if the small is present in minute quantities.

PCR requires sets of primers (small chemically synthesised oligonucleotides that are complementary to the regions of DNA) and Enzyme Taq DNA polymerase. **(1½ Marks)**

Note

The enzyme Taq DNA polymerase is a thermostable enzyme as it can tolerate higher temperature (upto 96 °C) as it is extracted from a bacterium Thermus aquaticus.

(ii) ELISA stands for Enzyme Linked Immunosorbent Assay is a molecular biology and immunological technique used for the diagnosis of AIDS. It is used for the measurement of antibodies in the blood and the test can be used for the determination of antibodies in the blood during infection. **(1½ Marks)**

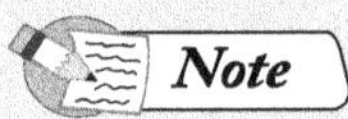

Note

The enzyme used in ELISA is horseradish peroxidise.

25. (i) The four operational guidelines that must be adhered to for achieving optimization of the bioreactor system:

1 **Monitoring and control of key parameters:** In order to achieve optimal growth and productivity of the biological system, it is essential to monitor and control key parameters such as temperature, pH, dissolved oxygen, and nutrient levels. This can be achieved by using sensors and control systems that can adjust these parameters as needed. **(1 Mark)**

2. **Optimization of mixing and aeration:** Proper mixing and aeration are essential for ensuring uniform distribution of nutrients and oxygen to the biological system. The mixing and aeration rate should be optimized based on the specific requirements of the system, as well as the characteristics of the bioreactor being used.

(1 Mark)

3. **Minimizing contamination:** Contamination can have a significant impact on the productivity of the biological system, so it is essential to minimize the risk of contamination by maintaining aseptic conditions throughout the process. This can be achieved by using sterile equipment, air filtration systems, and other appropriate measures. **(1 Mark)**

4. **Maintenance and cleaning of the bioreactor:** Regular maintenance and cleaning of the bioreactor are essential for ensuring optimal performance and longevity of the system. This includes routine inspection of the system, cleaning of all components, and replacement of any worn or damaged parts as needed. **(1 Mark)**

(ii) The cells can also be multiplied in a continuous culture system wherein the used medium is drained out from one side while fresh medium is added from the other to maintain the cells in their physiologically most active log/exponential phase.

(iii) After completion of the biosynthetic stage, the product has to be subjected through a series of processes before it is ready for marketing as a finished product. The processes include separation and purification, which are collectively referred to as downstream processing. The product has to be formulated with suitable preservatives. Such formulation has to undergo thorough clinical trials as in case of drugs. Strict quality control testingfor each product is also required. The downstream processing and quality control testing vary from product to product. **(1½ Marks)**

OR

(I) EcoRI comes from *Escherichia coli* RY 13. In EcoRI, the letter 'R' is derived from the name of strain. Roman numbers following the names indicate the order in which the enzymes were isolated from that strain of bacteria.

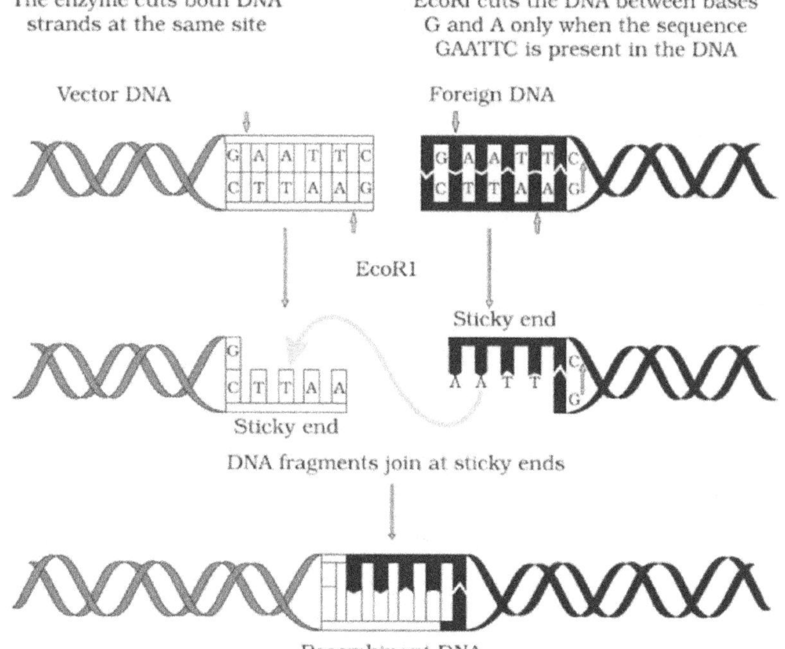

(2 Marks)

Steps in formation of recombinant DNA by action of restricted endonuclease enzyme - *Eco*RI

(II) Restriction endonuclease cut the strand of DNA a little away from the centre of the palindrome sites, but between the same two bases on the opposite strands. This leaves single stranded portions at the ends. There are overhanging stretches called sticky ends on each strand. These are named so because they form hydrogen bonds with their complementary cut counterparts. This stickiness of the ends facilitates the action of the enzyme DNA ligase

(ii) Restriction endonucleases are used in genetic engineering to form recombinant molecules of DNA,which are composed of DNA from different sources/Genomes. When cut by the same restriction enzyme, the resultant DNA fragments have the same kind of 'sticky-ends' and these can be joined together (end-to-end) using DNA ligases.

(3 Marks)

26. (a) You can easily grow a large quantity of the bacteria/ no ethical issues/have plasmids/ can easily transform

    (b) PCR will not amplify the gene. **(1 Mark)**

    If the polymerase enzyme denatures at low temp, it will not be able to withstand **high temperature which is essential for separating/opening/unwinding/ denaturing DNA** strand to open. Thus subsequent step of **extending the primers using the nucleotides provided in the reaction and the genomic DNA as template will not occur.** **(1½ Marks)**

    (c) Positive effect: oil spills can be treated and the environment becomes better/ cleaner/ water becomes

more potable/ safe for aquatic forms/ safe for water birds like sea gulls.

Negative effect: the bacteria can mutate/ can harm other organisms/ can conjugate with other non-virulent forms and make them super bugs with detrimental effect/ unpredictable/ for a longer duration it may reduce the dissolved oxygen and leading to mortality of aquatic organisms . (any one)

(2 Marks)

27. **(a)** With the help of recombinant DNA technology called Polymerase Chain Reaction technique (PCR) multiple copies of gene of interest are obtained in *Vitro*. A single PCR amplification cycle involves three steps which are as follows:

    (i) **Denaturation:** This is the first step of PCR, in which the target DNA is heated at high temperature such 94-96°C. It facilitates the separation of two strands of DNA. Each separated strand of DNA acts as a template for synthesis of DNA.

    (ii) **Annealing:** This is the second step of PCR, in which two oligonucleotide primers are used to hybridize each single stranded template DNA. The sequence of primers is complementary to 3′ end of the template DNA strand.

    This step of PCR occurs at low temperature 40-60°C than denaturation. The annealing temperature depends upon the length and sequence of the primers.

    (iii) **Extension:** This is third and last step of PCR, in which enzyme *Taq* DNA polymerase synthesizes the DNA between the primers. This step also requires dNTPS and Mg2++. The optimum temperature for extension is 72°C. **(3 Marks)**

Diagrammatic representation of PCR cycle:

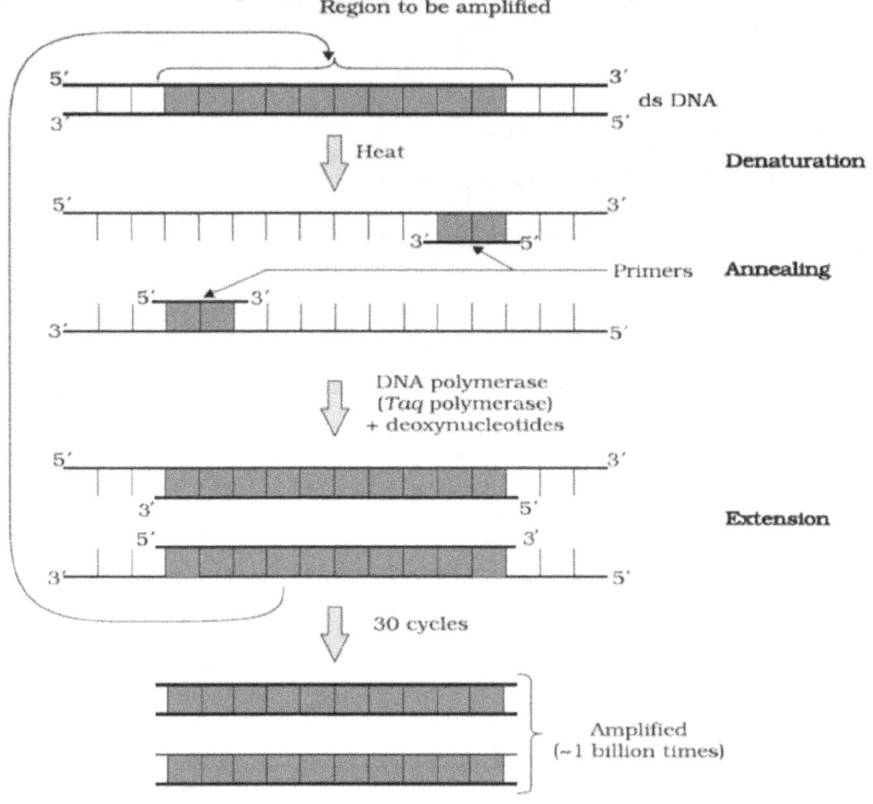

(b) (i) **Application of PCR in the field of biotechnology:** Polymerase Chain Reaction is a widely used method in the field of biotechnology as it helps in amplification billions of copies of desired DNA sequence from small sample of DNA.

(ii) **Application of PCR in the field of diagnostic:** Now days, PCR can be used in molecular diagnostic and biochemical analyses. Even with the help of small sequence of DNA, the genotypes can be determined. PCR helps in diagnosis of genetic disorder. **(2 Marks)**

28. **(5 Marks)**

The three steps carried out in the formation of recombinant DNA using enzyme EcoRI are:

a) **Isolation of Desirable gene containing Foreign DNA**

The DNA containing desirable gene is identified and isolated by using several enzymes. The cell wall is digested by using cellulase enzyme in plants, lysozyme in bacteria etc. Further it is subjected to RNAse and Protease to digest RNA and proteins. Finally pure desired DNA is spooled after addition of chilled ethanol in it.

(b) **Digestion or Cutting of Desired foreign DNA and Vector DNA by the same restriction endonuclease (EcoRI).**

The obtained desired DNA is cut in between specific nitrogeneous bases in recognition sequence and the vector DNA or plasmids are also subjected to be cut by restriction endonuclease also called as "molecular scissors" in order to create sticky ends.

(c) The foreign DNA is joined with vector DNA resulting in formation of rDNA

The foreign DNA with desirable gene is ligated with plasmid (vector DNA). The sticky ends of both DNA are joined together and the recombinant DNA is formed.

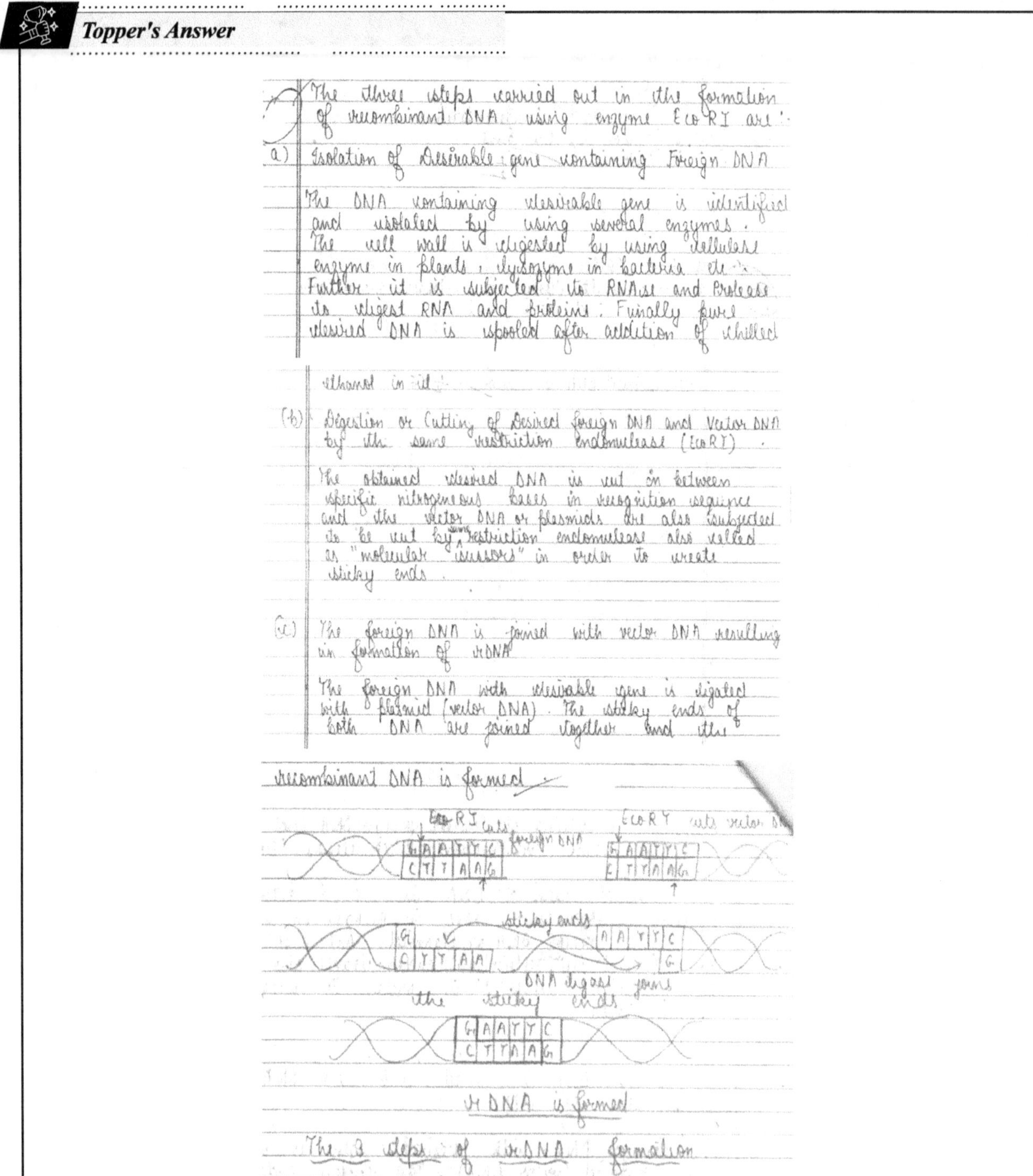

The 3 steps of rDNA formation

Chapter 10 — Biotechnology and its Applications

1 — Multiple Choice Questions (1 Mark)

1. The main objective of production of pest resistance GM crops is to **[CBSE Sample Paper, 2023-2024, U]**
(a) encourage eco–friendly pesticides
(b) reduce pesticide accumulation in food chain
(c) eliminate pests from the field without the use of manual labour
(d) retain maximum nutritional content in the crop that would be otherwise consumed by pest

2. ' 'Cry' protein' coded by gene Cry IAb controls
(a) Cotton bollworm **[All India 2020, K]**
(b) Corn borer
(c) Tobacco budworm
(d) Mosquito

4 — Very Short Answer Questions (1 Mark)

3. Mention the form in which inactive protein toxin is produced by *Bacillus thuringiensis*. How does it get activated in the pest body to kill it? **[Delhi 2019, U]**

4. What are Cry genes ? In which organism are they present? **[Delhi 2017, K]**

5. State the role of transposons in silencing of mRNA in eukaryotic cells. **[All India 2013, U]**

6. Explain how recombinant DNA technology is used to detect a disease even before any clinical symptom appears. **[All India 2023, Set-I, K]**

5 — Short Answer Questions (2 or 3 Marks)

7. (a) Write the scientific name of the nematode that infests the tobacco plants and the part that it infests. **[All India 2023, Set-I, U]**
(b) How is Agrobacterium used to protect tobacco plant from this attack? **[All India 2023, Set-I, U]**

8. On spraying *Bacillus thuringiensis* on an infected cotton crop field the pests are killed by the toxin, however the toxin although produced by the bacteria does not affect it. Explain giving reason. **[Delhi 2023, Set-I, U]**

9. (a) Name (i) a GM cereal crop having enhanced nutritional value, (ii) the nutrient it is rich in.
(b) State any two benefits of Genetically modified crops. **[Delhi 2023, Set-III, K]**

10. A farmer grew 2 varieties of corn crop in field A and B. He grew normal corn crops in field A and GM corn crops in field B. He observed corn borers attacked only in field A. To control it, spores of Bt were sprayed in field A.
(a) Name the gene in the spores responsible for the control of this pest.
(b) What effect will the spores of Bt have on the insect pest?
(c) How has field B developed resistance against this pest? **[CBSE Sample Paper 2023-24, A]**

11. Why GMOs are so called? List the different ways in which GMO plants have benefitted and have become useful to humans. **[Delhi 2020, K]**

12. List any four ways by which GMO's have been useful for enhanced crop output. **[All India 2019, K]**

13. How has the use of *Agrobacterium* as vectors helped in controlling *Meloidegyne incognita* infestation in tobacco plants ? Explain in correct sequence. **[All India 2018, K]**

14. Why do lepidopterans die when they feed on Bt cotton plant? Explain how does it happen. **[All India 2017, U]**

15. What is a GMO ? List any five possible advantages of a GMO to a farmer. **[Delhi 2016, K]**

16. How has RNAi technique helped to prevent the infestation of roots in tobacco plants by a nematode *Meloidegyne incognitia* ? **[Delhi 2016, U]**

17. State how has *Agrobacterium tumifuciens* been made a useful cloning vector to transfer DNA to plant cells. **[Delhi 2014, U]**

18. How did the process of RNA interference help to control the nematode from infecting roots of tobacco plants ? Explain. **[Delhi 2014, U]**

19. Name the pest that destroys the cotton bolls.

    Explain the role of *Bacillus thuringiensis* in protecting the cotton crop against the pest to increase the yield. **[All India 2013, K]**

---

6   *Long Answer Questions (5 Marks)*

---

20. Answer the following questions based on Bt-crops: **[All India 2023, Set-I, U]**

(i) Why do farmers prefer to grow. Bt cotton crop than genetically unmodified cotton crops?

(ii) Name any two insects that are killed by Bt toxin.

(iii) Explain the mechanism by which Bt toxin kills the insects but not the bacterium which possesses the toxin.

21. "RNA interference has been used to produce transgenic tobacco plants to protect them from the infestation by specific nematodes." Explain the novel strategy exploited by the biotechnologists. **[Delhi 2023, Set-I, U]**

22. Insects in the Lepidopteran group lay eggs on maize crops. The larvae on hatching feed on maize leaf and tender cob. In order to arrest the spread of three such Lepidopteran pests, Bt maize crops were introduced in an experimental field.

A study was carried out to see which of the three species of lepidopteran pests was most susceptible to Bt genes and its product. The lepidopteran pests were allowed to feed on the same Bt-maize crops grown on 5 fields (A-E).

The graph below shows the leaf area damaged by these three pests after feeding on maize leaves for five days.

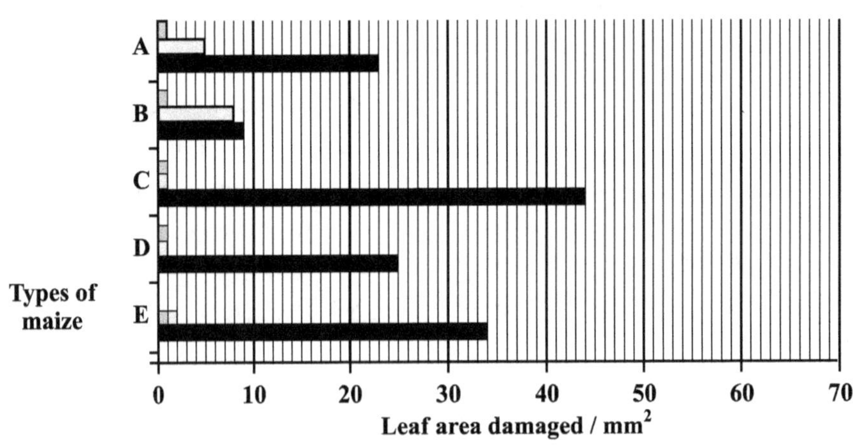

Insect gut pH was recorded as 10, 8 and 6 respectively for Species I, II and III respectively.

[CBSE Sample Paper 2022-23, U]

(a) Evaluate the efficacy of the Bt crop on the feeding habits of the three species of stem borer and suggest which species is least susceptible to Bt toxin.

(b) Which species is most susceptible to Bt-maize, explain why?

(c)   Using the given information, suggest why similar effect was not seen in the three insect species?

23. (a)   Name the insect that attacks cotton crops and causes log of damage to the crop. How has Bt cotton plants overcome this problem and saved the crop? Explain.

[Delhi 2020, U]

(b)   Write the role of gene Cry IAb.   **[Delhi 2020, U]**

24. Write down the steps in development of Bt cotton?

[Delhi 2013, U]

25. Why does cryproteins act as a toxic proteins?

[Delhi 2013, U]

7   *Case Based Questions*

26. To save the crop plant from the attack of various insect pests the biotechnologists have developed many pest resistant plants. One such example is Bt corn plant. In this plant 'cry' genes were introduced which produces cry-proteins in the plant that has toxic effect on the pest (corn borer). Thus saves the corn plant from the attack of the corn borer. An experimental field study was conducted by the scientists to see the efficacy of the Bt corn plant against the attack of corn borers. Three different species of corn borers namely 'A', 'B', 'C' were collected and were independently fed on non Bt corn plants and Bt corn plants separately for the same period. The extent of the damage caused to the leaf area of the plant was observed and noted down. With the help of the observations and data collected the following bar graph was plotted. Study the graph and answer the questions that follow.

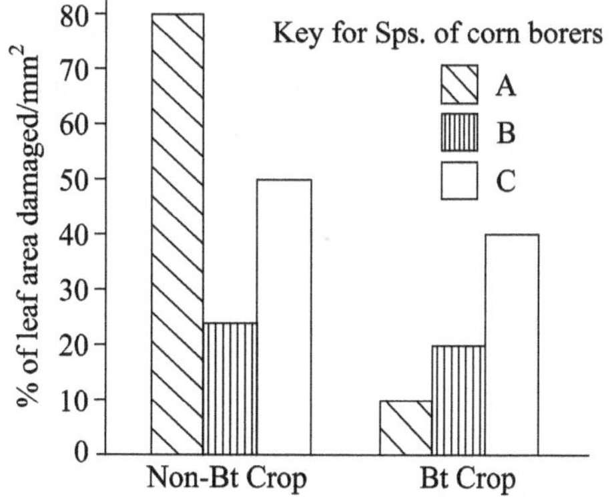

(i)   Identify the species of the corn borer that was most successfully controlled by Bt corn plant. Give appropriate reason for your inference.

(ii)   Identify the species of the corn borers which shows least impact of toxin produced by Bt genes.

(iii)   What would be your advise as a Scientist, to the farmers for growing this particular Bt corn variety in the area which is infested by species-'B' of corn borers?

(iv)   Name one Bt gene that encodes protein in corn plants to control corn borers.   **[All India 2022, A]**

27. GM crops especially Bt crops are known to have higher resistance to pest attacks. To substantiate this an experimental study was conducted in 4 different farmlands growing Bt and non Bt-Cotton crops. The farm lands had the same dimensions, fertility and were under similar climatic conditions. The histogram below shows the usage of pesticides on Bt crops and non-Bt crops in these farm lands.   **[CBSE Sample Paper 2021-22, Term-II, A]**

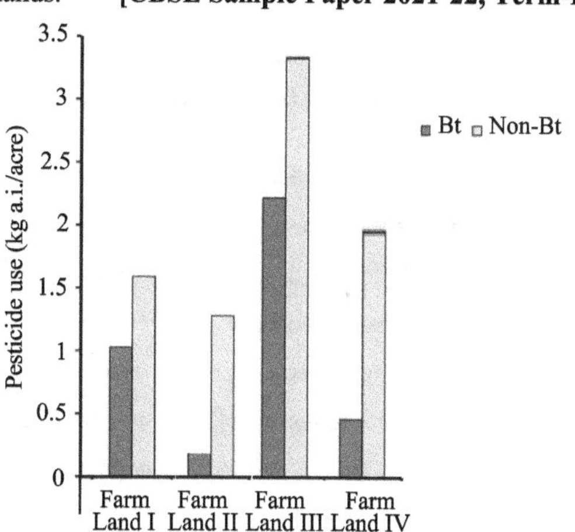

(a)   Which of the above 4 farm lands has successfully applied the concepts of Biotechnology to show better management practices and use of agrochemicals? If you had to cultivate, which crop would you prefer (Bt or Non- Bt) and why?

(b)   Cotton Bollworms were introduced in another experimental study on the above farm lands wherein no pesticide was used. Explain what effect would a Bt and Non Bt crop have on the pest.

| Topic-2: | ***Biotechnological Applications in Medicine*** |

2 *Assertion Reason/Two Statement Type Questions (1 Mark)*

1. **Assertion:** Functional ADA cDNA genes must be inserted in the lymphocytes at the early embryonic stage.

    [CBSE Sample Paper 2022-23, U]

    Reason: Cells in the embryonic stage are mortal, differentiated and easy to manipulate.

4 *Very Short Answer Questions (1 Mark)*

2. Mention the chemical change that proinsulin undergoes, to be able to act as mature insulin. **[All India 2018, U]**

3. Why do children cured by enzyme-replacement therapy for adenosine deaminase deficiency need periodic treatment? **[All India 2015, U]**

4. State the role of C-peptide in human insulin.

    [All India 2014, U]

5 *Short Answer Questions (2 or 3 Marks)*

5. Lipoprotein lipase deficiency (LPLD) is a genetic disorder in which a person has a defective gene for lipase. This leads to high triglycerides, stomach pain, fat deposits under the skin. It may eventually affect the liver, pancreas and may also cause diabetes. The disorder occurs if a child acquires defective genes from both parents (autosomal recessive). ERT (enzyme replacement treatment) is one of the treatments offered to patients with LPLD.

    (a) (i) What procedure is followed in ERT?

         (ii) What could be one possible drawback of ERT?

    (b) How can LPLD be treated using Biotechnology? Elaborate. **[CBSE Sample Paper, 2023-2024, A]**

6. (i) Name three molecular diagnostic techniques for diagnosis of a disease. **[All India 2022, Term-II, U]**

    (ii) List three advantages of molecular diagnostic techniques over conventional method of diagnosis.

    [All India 2022, Term-II, U]

7. Insulin in the human body is secreted by pancreas as prohormone/proinsulin. The schematic polypeptide structure of proinsulin is given below. This proinsulin needs to undergo processing before it becomes functional in the body. Answer the questions that follow:

    [All India 2020, U]

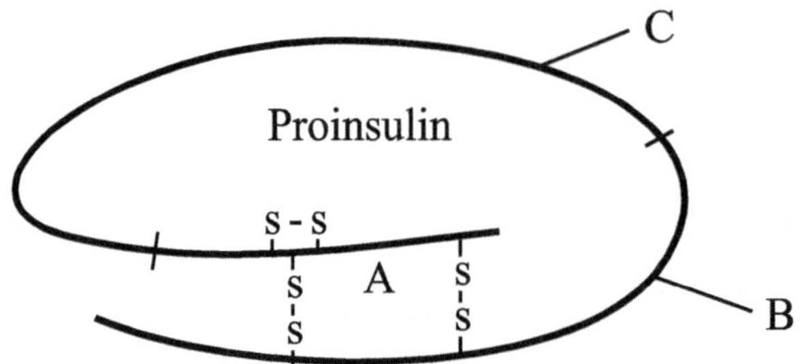

    (a) State the change the proinsulin undergoes at the time of its processing to become functional.

    (b) Name the technique the American company Eli Lilly used for the commercial production of human insulin.

    (c) How are the two polypeptides of a functional insulin chemically held together?

8. Explain the various steps involved in the production of artificial insulin. **[Delhi 2019, U]**

9. Explain enzyme-replacement therapy to treat adenosine deaminase deficiency. Mention two disadvantages of this procedure. **[All India 2016, K]**

10. Recombinant DNA-technology is of great importance in the field of medicine. With the help of a flow chart, show how this technology has been used in preparing genetically engineered human insulins. **[Delhi 2015, Ap]**

11. How did an American Company, Eli Lilly use the knowledge of r-DNA technology to produce human insulin?

    [All India 2015, U]

12. Why is proinsulin so called? How is insulin different from it? **[All India 2013]**

6   *Long Answer Questions (5 Marks)*

13. (a) Name the disease for which ADA deficieny can be cured.   **[All India 2022, Term-II, U]**
    (b) Write down the application of enzyme replacement therapy.   **[All India 2022, Term-II, U]**

Topic-3: *Transgenic Animals*

5   *Short Answer Questions (2 or 3 Marks)*

1. How have transgenic animals proved to be beneficial in:

    (a) Production of biological products

    (b) Chemical safety testing   **[All India 2014, U]**

2. (a) Why are transgenic animals so called ?   **[Delhi 2013, U]**

    (b) Explain the role of transgenic animals in (i) Vaccine safety and (ii) Biological products with the help of an example each.   **[Delhi 2013, U]**

Topic-4: *Ethical Issues*

4   *Very Short Answer Questions (1 Mark)*

1. What is biopiracy?   **[All India 2017, K, All India 2016, K, Delhi 2015, K]**

6   *Long Answer Questions (5 Marks)*

2. What are some ethical issues in genetically modified organisms? Write down the steps taken by Indian Government to stop biopiracy?   **[All India 2013, K]**

Hints & Solutions

| | *Topic-1:* | *Biotechnological Applications in Agriculture* |

1. **(b)** Reduce pesticide accumulation in food chain. **(1 Mark)**

2. **(b)** The *Bt* toxin genes were isolated from *Bacillus thuringiensis.* The toxin which is coded by a gene called cry. The 'Cry' protein encoded by gene *Cry IAb* controls corn borer. **(1 Mark)**

3. **Gel electrophoresis** is a molecular biology technique and is also used for the early diagnosis of symptoms of diseases. In this technique, DNA sequences are separated according to their size. **(1 Mark)**

4. *Cry* genes are present in bacterium *Bacillus thuriengiensis.* It codes for toxin called Bt toxin. The proteins encoded by the genes *cryI*Ac and *cryII*Ab control the cotton bollworms whereas *cryI*Ab controls corn borer. **(1 Mark)**

5. Transposons are also called as mobile genetic elements and the process of mRNA silencing is used for the prevention of mRNA translation. In mRNA silencing, transposons are acts as a complementary RNA in order to stop the process of mRNA translation. **(1 Mark)**

Note

Transposons are repetitive DNA sequences that have capability to move from one genome location to another genome location.

6. PCR, ELISA and autoradiography are some of the recombinant DNA technologies that can be used for the detection of disease even before any clinical symptom appears.

PCR is now routinely used to detect HIV in suspected AIDS patients. It is being used to detect mutations in genes in suspected cancer patients too. It is a powerful technique to identify many other genetic disorders.

(2 Marks)

A single stranded DNA or RNA, tagged with a radioactive molecule (probe) is allowed to hybridise to its complementary DNA in a clone of cells followed by detection using autoradiography. The clone having the mutated gene will hence not appear on the photographic film, because the probe will not have complementarity with the mutated gene. This can be help in detection of mutated gene responsible for causing disease. ELISA is based on the principle of antigen-antibody interaction. Infection by pathogen can be detected by the presence of antigens (proteins, glycoproteins, etc.) or by detecting the antibodies synthesised against the pathogen.

7. **(a)** A nematode *Meloidegyne incognitia* infects the roots of tobacco plants and causes a great reduction in yield. **(1½ Marks)**

   (b) Using Agrobacterium vectors, nematode-specific genes were introduced into the host plant. The introduction of DNA was such that it produced both sense and anti-sense RNA in the host cells. These two RNA's being complementary to each other formed a double stranded (dsRNA) that initiated RNAi and thus, silenced the specific mRNA of the nematode. The consequence was that the parasite could not survive in a transgenic host expressing specific interfering RNA. The transgenic plant therefore got itself protected from the parasite. **(1½ Marks)**

8. Some strains of *Bacillus thuringiensis* produce proteins that kill certain insects such as lepidopterans (tobacco budworm, armyworm), coleopterans (beetles) and dipterans (flies, mosquitoes).

B. thuringiensis forms protein crystals during a particular phase of their growth. These crystals contain a toxic insecticidal protein. The *Bt* toxin protein exist as inactive *protoxins* but once an insect ingest the inactive toxin, it is converted into an active form of toxin due to the alkaline pH of the gut which solubilise the crystals. The activated toxin binds to the surface of midgut epithelial cells and creates pores that cause cell swelling and lysis and eventually cause death of the insect. **(3 Marks)**

9. (a) (i) Golden rice is a GM cereal crop having enhanced nutritional value. **(1½ Marks)**

   (ii) Golden rice is a rich source of Vitamin A.

   (b) (i) They are more tolerant to environmental stresses like drought, salt, heat and cold.

   (ii) The crops are of high nutritional value.

   (1½ Marks)

10. (a) Cry I Ab **(1 Mark)**

    (b) The spores of Bt contain crystalline toxin which is inactive; for this crystalline toxin protein to become active it needs alkaline pH, which is present in insect gut. The gut linking is broken down/mid gut epithelial cells become porous/swollen/cell lysis.

    (1 Mark)

    (c) The Bt–toxin gene is cloned and inserted into the plant genome by recombinant DNA technology. These genetically modified (GM) plants express the Bt–toxin genes and become pest–resistant.

    (1 Mark)

11. **GMOs** are Genetically Modified Organisms that are produced by alteration in genes of plants, bacteria, fungi and animals. GM plants are useful in many ways such as:

    - Genetic modification made crops more tolerant to abiotic stresses such as cold, drought, salt and heat.

    - It also reduces the reliance of chemical pesticides such as pest-resistant crops

    - It helps to reduce post-harvest losses.

    - It also increases the efficiency of mineral usage by plants

    - GM enhanced nutritional value of foods such as vitamin A enriched rice. **(3 Marks)**

12. The four ways by which GMO's have been useful for enhanced crop output are as follows:

    - GMOs made crop more tolerant to abiotic stress such as cold, drought, salt and heat.

    - It reduces dependency on chemical pesticides such as pest-resistant crops.

    - It helped in the reduction post harvest losses.

    - GMOs increases the efficiency of mineral usage by plants and this helps in the prevention of early exhaustion of fertility of soil.

    - GMOs also enhance nutritional value of food such as vitamin 'A' enriched rice. **(2 Marks)**

13. A nematode *Meloidegyne incognita* infects the roots of tobacco plants and causes a great reduction in yield. A novel strategy was adopted to prevent this infestation which was based on the process of RNA inteference (RNAi). Using *Agrobacterium* vectors, nematode-specific genes were introduced into the host plants. The introduction of DNA was such that it produced both sense and anti-sense RNA in the host cells. These two RNA's being complementary to each other formed a double stranded (dsRNA) that initiated RNAi and thus, silenced specific mRNA of the nematode. The consequence was that the parasite could not survive in a transgenic host expressing specific interfering RNA. The transgenic plant therefore got itself protected from the parasite.

    (3 Marks)

14. *Bt* cotton is an insect resistant plant which resist attack of Lepidopterans insects. The plant *Bt* toxin gene cause death of insect larvae by causing cell lysis and swelling of epithelium of midgut. *Bt* toxin is biologically produced by bacterium called *Bacillus thuringiensis (Bt)*. This toxin is insecticidal protein crystal (cry proteins) produced in bacteria (inactive form in bacteria) during a particular phase of growth. Inactive protein (protoxin) is converted into active form of toxin due to alkaline pH of gut of insect which solubilize crystals. The activated

toxin binds to surface of midgut epithelial cell and creates pores that cause cell swelling and lysis and eventually death of the insect.   **(3 Marks)**

15. **GMOs are Genetically modified organisms**. They are defined as a living organisms whose genes are manipulated or altered by using recombinant DNA technology.

     The advantages of GMOs are as follows:

     (i)   GMOs are resistant to diseases, pest and insects. So it reduces the use of harmful pesticides and other chemical fertilisers that harm the crops.

     (ii) GMOs crops are more tolerant to abiotic stress such as cold, drought, heat and salt stress.

     (iii) Such crops have high crop yield and nutritional value.

     (iv) GMOs reduce post-harvest loss of crops.

     (v)   GMOs increase the efficiency of mineral usage by plants and also prevents exhaustion of soil.

                                                            (3 Marks)

Note

Golden rice is genetically modified crop which is obtained by recombinant DNA technology. It contains good quantities of beta-carotene which is a principal source of vitamin A. Due to the presence of beta-carotene, the rice grain appear golden in colour.

16. *Meloidogyne incognitia* is a nematode that causes infections in the root of tobacco plants. This reduces the yield of tobacco plants. In order to protect the tobacco plants from infection, a process called **RNA interference** occurs in all eukaryotic organisms as a method of cellular defense. The process of RNA interference involves **mRNA silencing** because of complementary dsRNA molecule that get binds to and prevents the translation of mRNA.

     The complementary RNA is obtained due to the infection by viruses that contain a RNA genome or mobile genetic elements (transposons). It replicate via a RNA intermediate.

By using *Agrobacterium* vectors, nematode-specific gene were used to introduced into the host plant. After the introduction of DNA into the host, it produces both sense and anti-sense RNA in the host cells.

The two RNA's are complementary to each other formed a double strand (dsRNA) that initiates the process of RNAi and silenced the specific mRNA of the nematode. After that, the nematode is not able to survive in a transgenic host expressing specific interfering RNA.

In this way, the transgenic plant got itself to be protected from the parasite.   **(3 Marks)**

17. *Agrobacterium tumifaciens,*is a pathogen of several dicot plants is able to deliver a piece of DNA known as 'T-DNA' to transform normal plant cells into tumor.

     •   To direct these tumor cells to produce the chemical required by the pathogen.

     •   Retroviruses in animals have ability to transform normal cells into cancerous cells.

     •   The tumor inducing (Ti) plasmid of Agrobacterium tumifaciens has modified into a cloning vector and is no more pathogenic to the plants and is used to deliver genes of interest into a variety of plants.

     •   The Ti plasmid contains genes that codes for the synthesis of auxin and cytokinin hormone and its introduction in a plant helps to produce its own nutrient machinery.   **(3 Marks)**

18. *Meloidogyne incognitia* is a nematode that causes infections in the root of tobacco plants. This reduces the yield of tobacco plants. In order to protect the tobacco plants from infection, a process called **RNA interference** occurs in all eukaryotic organisms as a method of cellular defense. The process of RNA interference involves **mRNA silencing** because of complementary dsRNA molecule that get binds to and prevents the translation of mRNA.

     The complementary RNA is obtained due to the infection by viruses that contain an RNA genome or mobile genetic elements (transposons). It replicate via an RNA intermediate.

By using *Agrobacterium* vectors, nematode-specific gene were used to introduced into the host plant. After the introduction of DNA into the host, it produces both sense and anti-sense RNA in the host cells.

The two RNA's are complementary to each other formed a double strand (dsRNA) that initiates the process of RNAi and silenced the specific mRNA of the nematode. After that, the nematode is not able to survive in a transgenic host expressing specific interfering RNA.

In this way, the transgenic plant got itself to be protected from the parasite. **(3 Marks)**

19. Cotton bollworms destroy the cotton bolls. The strains of *Bacillus thuringiensis* produce proteins that kill several insects such as lepidopterans, coleopterans and dipterans. *Bacillus thuringiensis* forms protein crystals contain a toxic called insecticidal protein. This toxin protein exists in an inactive form protoxins but once an insect ingest the inactive toxin, then it is converted into an active form of toxin due to the alkaline pH of the gut which solubilise the crystals.

The activated toxin binds to the surface of the midgut epithelial cells and creates pores that cause cell swelling and lysis results in death of the insect. The toxin is coded by a gene name **cry**. So, the protein encoded by the genes cryIAB controls corn borer. **(3 Marks)**

20. (i) Specific Bt toxin genes were isolated from Bacillus thuringiensis and incorporated into the several crop plants such as cotton. The choice of genes depends upon the crop and the targeted pest, as most Bt toxins are insect-group specific. The toxin is coded by a gene cryIAc named cry. There are a number of them, for example, the proteins encoded by the genes cryIAc and cryIIAb control the cotton bollworms, that of cryIAb controls the growth of corn borer infecting the healthy cotton plants. The genetically

unmodified cotton crops will remain unprotected with the corn borer and this will negatively affect the cotton crops.

(2½ Marks)

(ii) Cotton bollworm and corn borer are the two insects that are killed by Bt toxin. **(1 Mark)**

(iii) Bt toxin is produced by bacteria Bacillus thuriengiensis. During sporulation, these bacteria forms intracellular crystalline proteins. Bt toxin does not kill the bacterium that produces it, but kills the insect that ingests it because the endotoxin that accumulates in the bacterium is an inactive precursor. It gets activated only in the alkaline gut of insect. When insect ingests it, then protoxin is cleaved by proteases (alkaline conditions in gut), resulting is shorter versions of the protein that display the toxic activity, by binding to the inside of the insects mid gut and damages the surface epithelium by creating pores that cause swelling and lysis. So, that insect is unable to feed and consequently starves to death.

(1½ Marks)

21. RNA interference can be defined as the method used to develop nematode resistance in tobacco plants. This process leads to post- transcriptional gene silencing. The steps involved in this process are; at first, the disease- causing genes are identified and isolated from the nematode Meloidogyne incognita. Then this gene would be incorporated into the genome of tobacco plants with the help of a vector. It is then introduced into the tobacco plant in such a way that both sense and antisense mRNA is produced. These RNAs being complementary to each other get paired to form double-stranded RNA. This double-stranded RNA induces RNAi in the tobacco plants which neutralize the mRNA of the nematode. Thus, the nematode is unable to live in such a transgenic host. Therefore, the tobacco plant became resistant to pests. **(5 Marks)**

22. **(a)** Species III is least susceptible **(1 Mark)**

(b) Bt toxin **protoxins are converted into an active form in the gut** which solubilises the toxin crystals.

The **activated toxin binds to the surface of midgut epithelial cells** and **create pores** that **cause cell swelling and lysis** and eventually cause death of the insect **(2 Marks)**

(c) Insect **species I and II have alkaline gut pH** which **solubilises the insecticidal protein crystals of protoxin and makes it active**. Species **III has an acidic** and the **protoxin continues to remain in an inactive form** doing no harm to insect species III

(2 Marks)

23. **(a)** Cotton bollworms are the insect that attacks and destroy the cotton crops. Some strains of *Bacillus thuringiensis* produces proteins that kill insects that the cotton crops. They forms protein crystals during a particular phase of their growth. These crystals contain a toxic called insecticidal protein.

This protein exists in an inactive form but once it is ingested by the insect, this protein is converted into an active form of toxin because of alkaline pH of the gut. It tends to solubilise the crystals. Then the activated toxin binds to the surface of midgut epithelial cells and creates pores that cause cell swelling as well as lysis and eventually results in the death of the insect. **(4 Marks)**

(b) The gene *cryIAb* controls the growth of cotton corn borer. **(1 Mark)**

24. **Bt Cotton :** Some strains of Bacillus thuringiensis produce proteins that kill certain insects such as lepidopterans (tobacco budworm, armyworm), coleopterans (beetles) and dipterans (flies, mosquitoes). B. thuringiensis forms protein crystals during a particular phase of their growth. These crystals contain a toxic insecticidal protein. Actually, the Bt toxin protein exist as inactive protoxins but once an insect ingest the inactive toxin, it is converted into an active form of toxin due to the alkaline pH of the gut which solubilise the crystals. The activated toxin binds to the surface of midgut epithelial cells and create pores that cause cell swelling and lysis and eventually cause death of the insect. **(5 Marks)**

25.

Topper's Answer

Cry prooteins are the toxic prooteins coded by cry genes present in Bacteria <u>Bacillus thuringiensis</u>.

⮕ Thus it acts as a bio pesticide

⮕ For eg.. BE cotton is pest resistant crop

• when an insect comes and attacks Bt cotton it ingest the cells having cry genes which have produced Cry prooteins in inactive foorm.

• when insect ingest the cry prooteins, due to alkaline pH of gut of insect cry prooteins activate and stick to midgut of insects and starts foormation of poores.

• This leads to for swelling of gut and ultimately death of insect thus it act as biopesticide.

(3 + 2 Marks)

Specific Bt toxin genes were isolated from Bacillus thuringiensis and incorporated into the several crop plants such as cotton. The choice of genes depends upon the crop and the targeted pest, as most Bt toxins are insect-group specific. The toxin is coded by a gene cryIAc named cry. There are a number of them, for example, the proteins encoded by the genes cryIAc and cryIIAb control the cotton bollworms, that of cryIAb controls corn borer.

(5 Marks)

26. (i) The species 'A' of the corn borer was most successfully controlled by the Bt corn plant. It is because cry gene is expressed in plants to provide resistance to insects. And show less damage in comparison to species B and C. **(1 Mark)**

(ii) Species B shows very less impact of the Bt gene because the damage rate is almost equal in plant species of non-Bt crop and Bt crop. **(1 Mark)**

(iii) The scientist we must give advice to farmer are –

• When different species of plants are cultivated on the same field, there is a definite distance between crops of the same species. So, it is efficient in attracting pests away from their target host plant.

• To manage pests, the crop rotation farming method also increases the fertility of the soil.

• Organic pesticides allow the farmers to turn agricultural outputs into natural pesticides and do not affect their health or damage the crops. like farmers can use *Bacillus thuringiensis* (bacteria) on their crops to reduce the effect of insects on the plant. **(2 Marks)**

(iv) The cry gene protein is the Bt gene that encodes protein in corn plants. **(1 Mark)**

27. (a) From the above 4 farm lands, "Farm land II" has successfully applied the concept of Biotechnology to show better management practices this is because it exhibit low concentration of pesticide. If I had to cultivate, I would prefer Bt-crop because they are least resistant to the pesticides. **(2 Mark)**

(b) In Bt cotton a cry gene has been introduce from bacterium Bacillus thuringiensis (Bt) which causes synthesis of a toxic protein. This protein becomes active in the alkaline gut of bollworm feeding on cotton, punching holes in the lining causing death of the insect. **(2 Marks)**

However; a Non Bt crop will have no effect on the cotton bollworm/ the yield of cotton will decrease / non Bt will succumb to pest attack. **(1 Mark)**

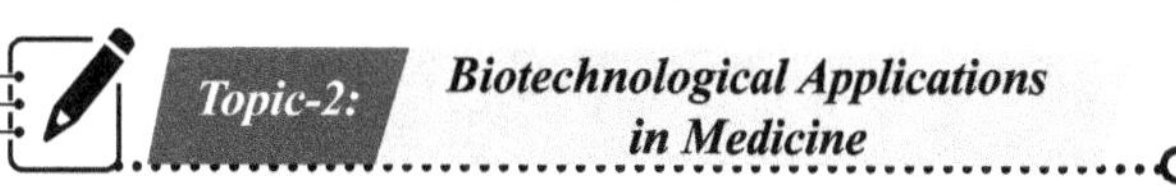

1. (c) A is true but R is false **(1 Mark)**

2. Mature functional protein is produced by the processing or pro-hormone insulin which contains an extra peptide called C-peptide or connecting peptide. This C-peptide is removed during the maturation of proinsulin, and A & B chains are linked by disulphide linkage. **(1 Mark)**

An American company Elilily in 1983 prepared two DNA sequences corresponds to A and B, chains of human insulin and introduced them in plasmids of E.coli to produce insullin chains.

3. The introduction of genetically engineered lymphocytes into an ADA deficiency patient is not a permanent cure because, the genetically engineered lymphocytes die after somedays. Hence, the patient requires periodic infusion of genetically engineered lymphocytes, so the cure is not permanent. **(1 Mark)**

4. The C-peptide in human insulin is a short stretch of amino acids that is present in proinsulin and during the process of maturation of insulin this C-peptide is removed. So, it is involved in the synthesis of mature insulin. **(1 Mark)**

An American company Eli lily in 1983 prepared two DNA sequence corresponding to A and B chains of human insulin and introduced them in plasmids of E.coil to produce insulin chains. Chain A & chain B were separately produced & joined together by disulphide bond.

5. (a) (i) Functional enzyme lipase is given to the patient by injection. **(0.5)**

   (ii) This procedure is not completely curative. **(0.5)**

(b) • The disease can be treated by using Gene therapy. **(0.5)**

   • Gene therapy is a collection of methods that allows correction of a gene defect that has been diagnosed in a child/embryo. **(0.5)**

   • Here genes are inserted into a person's cells and tissues to treat a disease. Correction of a genetic defect involves delivery of a normal gene into the individual or embryo to take over the function of and compensate for the non–functional gene. **(1)**

6. (i) Recombinant DNA technology, Polymerase Chain Reaction (PCR) and Enzyme Linked Immuno sorbent Assay (ELISA) are some of the techniques that serve the purpose of early diagnosis. **(1 Mark)**

   (ii) Advantages of molecular diagnostic techniques are:

   • It is being used to detect mutations in genes in suspected cancer patients too.

   • It is a powerful technique to identify many other genetic disorders.

   • Infection by a pathogen can be detected by the presence of antigens (proteins, glycoproteins, etc) or by detecting the antibodies synthesised against the pathogen. **(2 Marks)**

7.

Topper's Answer

(a) Proinsulin undergoes maturation by dropping C-peptide free from it and the mature insulin only contains A and B polypeptide joined together by disulphide linkage.

(b) The company used recombinant DNA technology in order to produce two different polypeptides A and B and then obtained it from E. coli. The company further joined the two polypeptides with disulphide linkage.

(c) The two polypeptides are joined together by disulphide bridges or linkages.

(3 Marks)

8.　The various steps involved in the production of artificial insulin are as follows:

- The artificial insulin consists of two short polypeptide chains such as chain A and chain B.

- These two short polypeptide chains are linked together by disulphide bond.

- In mammals such as humans, insulin is synthesised as a prohormone that contains an extra stretch called the **C peptide**.

- This **C peptide** is not present in mature insulin and is removed during maturation into insulin.

- The two DNA sequences corresponding to A and B polypeptide chains of human insulin were prepared and these were introduced into *E.coli* in order to produce A and B chains separately, and these chains were extracted and then combined by creating disulphide bonds.

Diagrammatic representation of artificial insulin:

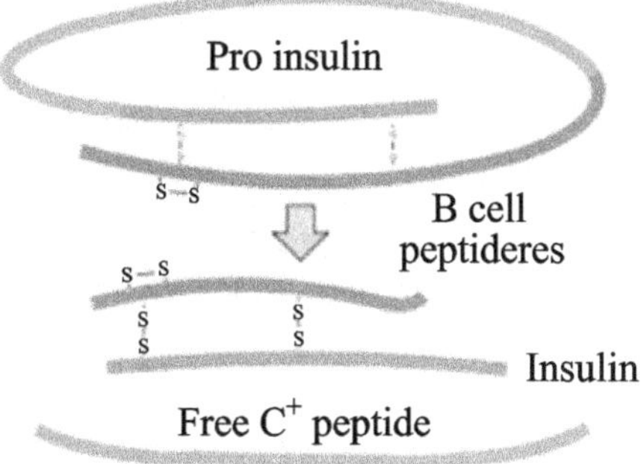

(3 Marks)

9.　ADA (Adenosine deaminase deficiency) can be treated by enzyme replacement therapy in which functional ADA is given to the patient by injection. In this process:

- Lymphocytes from the blood of the patients are grown in a culture outside the body.

- A functional ADA cDNA (using a retroviral vector) is then introduced into these lymphocytes which are subsequently returned to the patient.

Disadvantages associated with enzyme-replacement therapy are:

- This method is not completely curative

- The cells are immortal as the patients require periodic infusion of such genetically engineered lymphocytes.　　**(3 Marks)**

10.　**Representation of flow chart for the production of recombinant insulin:**

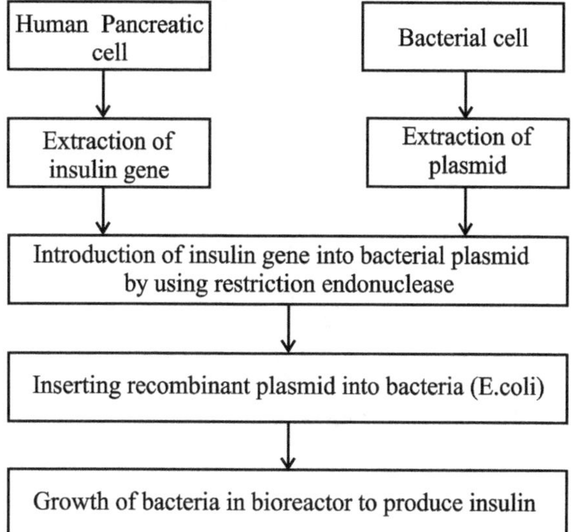

Diagrammatic representation of recombinant insulin:

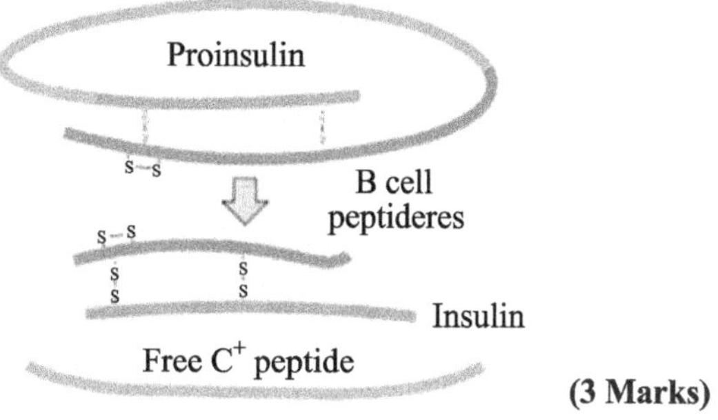

(3 Marks)

11.　Insulin hormone is released as a pro-hormone, which consists of three peptide chains; A, B and C. This pro-hormone insulin is converted to mature insulin by removal of C peptide. The American company, Eli Lilly, used the knowledge of rDNA technology as follows:

(i)　DNA sequences corresponding to the two polypeptide, A and B of insulin are synthesised *invitro*.

                                                                      Biology

(ii) They are introduced into plasmid DNA of *E.coli*.

(iii) This bacterium is cloned under suitable conditions.

(iv) The transgenes expressed in the form of polypeptides-A and B, secreted into the medium.

(v) They are extracted and combined by creating disulphide bridge to form human insulin. **(3 Marks)**

12. In humans, insulin is synthesised as a prohormone that contains an extra stretch called the **C peptide** and it is not present in the mature insulin. As a mature insulin contains two short polypeptide chains such as Chain A and Chain B that are linked together by a disulphide bond. The prohormone is non-functional whereas mature insulin is functional. **(2 Marks)**

13.

Topper's Answer

> i) The disease for which gene therapy was used for first time is for Adenosine Deaminase deficiency (ADA deficiency) or SCID (severe combined Immuno Deficiency).
>
> ii) Enzyme replacement therapy is used to cure the disease
> 1. Lymphocytes from blood of patients are extracted and cultured in laboratory.
> 2. ADA c-DNA (complimentary DNA) containing gene for ADA is inserted to lymphocytes using retroviral agents.
> 3. lymphocytes are injected back to patient. thus lymphocytes
> → This therapy is not a permanent cure because lymphocyte of human are not immortal thus they die after sometime & patient co requires periodic injections of lymphocyte
>
> iii) The permanent cure for disease is to extract DNA coding for Adenosine deaminase enzyme from bone marrow and inserting it in embryo stage of the child.

Gene therapy is an attempt to do this. Gene therapy is a collection of methods that allows correction of a gene defect that has been diagnosed in a child/embryo. Here genes are inserted into a person's cells and tissues to treat a disease. Correction of a genetic defect involves delivery of a normal gene into the individual or embryo to take over the function of and compensate for the non-functional gene. The first clinical gene therapy was given in 1990 to a 4-year old girl with adenosine deaminase (ADA) deficiency. This enzyme is crucial for the immune system to function. The disorder is caused due to the deletion of the gene for adenosine deaminase. In some children ADA deficiency can be cured by bone marrow transplantation; in others it can be treated by enzyme replacement therapy, in which functional ADA is given to the patient by injection. But the problem with both of these approaches that they are not completely curative. As a first step towards gene therapy, lymphocytes from the blood of the patient are grown in a culture outside the body. A functional ADA cDNA (using a retroviral vector) is then introduced into these lymphocytes, which are subsequently returned to the patient. However, as these cells are not immortal, the patient requires periodic infusion of such genetically engineered lymphocytes. However, if the gene isolate from marrow cells producing ADA is introduced into cells at early embryonic stages, it could be a permanent cure. **(5 Marks)**

| Topic-3: | *Transgenic Animals* |

1. (a) The first transgenic cow called Rosie was made in 1997 that produces human-protein-enriched milk. The milk of that cow contains human alpha-lactalbumin and was nutritionally a more balanced diet for human babies than normal natural- cow.

(1 Mark)

(b) Transgenic animals carry genes that make them more sensitive to toxic substances and the results obtained in less time. **(1 Mark)**

2. (a) Animals that have had their DNA manipulated to possess and express a foreign of interest are known as transgenic animals. Transgenic animals such as rats, rabbits, pigs, sheep, cows and fish have been produced. **(1 Mark)**

(b) (i) Vaccine safety: Transgenic mice are being developed for use in testing the safety of vaccines before they are used on humans. Transgenic mice are being used for testing the safety of the polio vaccine. **(1 Mark)**

(ii) Biological products: Medicines required for treatment of certain human diseases that contains biological products but are expensive to make. **(1 Mark)**

So, transgenic animals that produce useful biological

products can be created by the introduction of the portion of DNA (or genes) that codes for a particular product such as human protein called alpha-1-antitrypsin) which is used for the treatment of emphysema.

Similarly, transgenic animals are used for the treatment of phenylketonuria (PKU) and cystic fibrosis. In 1997, the first transgenic cow, Rosie, produced human protein-enriched milk (2.4 grams per litre). The milk contained the human alpha-lactalbumin and was nutritionally a more balanced product for human babies than natural cow-milk.

| Topic-4: | *Ethical Issues* |

1. Biopiracy is the term used to refer to the use of bio-resources by multinational companies and organisations without proper authorisation from the countries and people concerned without compensatory payment. For example, basmati is a type of fragrant rice variety grown in India. But some US based companies crossed this Indian basmati rice with their local variety and produced Texmati - a new American fragrant rice variety and used it commercially. **(1 Mark)**

2. The manipulation of living organisms by the human race cannot go on any further, without regulation. Some ethical standards are required to evaluate the morality of all human activities that might help or harm living organisms.

Going beyond the morality of such issues, the biological significance of such things is also important. Genetic modification of organisms can have unpredicatable results when such organisms are introduced into the ecosystem.

Therefore, the Indian Government has set up organisations such as **GEAC** (Genetic Engineering Approval Committee), which will make decisions regarding the validity of GM research and the safety of introducing GM-organisms for public services.

The modification/usage of living organisms for public

services (as food and medicine sources, for example) has also created problems with patents granted for the same.

There is growing public anger that certain companies are being granted patents for products and technologies that make use of the genetic materials, plants and other biological resources that have long been identified, developed and used by farmers and indigenous people of a specific region/country.

Rice is an important food grain, the presence of which goes back thousands of years in Asia's agricultural history. There are an estimated 200,000 varieties of rice in India alone. The diversity of rice in India is one of the richest in the world. Basmati rice is distinct for its unique aroma and flavour and 27 documented varieties of Basmati are grown in India. There is reference to Basmati in ancient texts, folklore and poetry, as it has been grown for centuries. In 1997, an American company got patent rights on Basmati rice through the US Patent and Trademark Office. This allowed the company to sell a 'new' variety of Basmati, in the US and abroad. This 'new' variety of Basmati had actually been derived from Indian farmer's varieties. Indian Basmati was crossed with semi-dwarf varieties and claimed as an invention or a novelty. The patent extends to functional equivalents, implying that other people selling Basmati rice could be restricted by the patent. Several attempts have also been made to patent uses, products and processes based on Indian traditional herbal medicines, e.g., turmeric neem. If we are not vigilant and we do not immediately counter these patent applications, other countries/individuals may encash on our rich legacy and we may not be able to do anything about it.

Biopiracy is the term used to refer to the use of bio-resources by multinational companies and other organisations without proper authorisation from the countries and people concerned without compensatory payment.

Most of the industrialised nations are rich financially but poor in biodiversity and traditional knowledge. In contrast the developing and the underdeveloped world is rich in biodiversity and traditional knowledge related to bio-resources. Traditional knowledge related to bio-resources can be exploited to develop modern applications and can also be used to save time, effort and expenditure during their commercialisation.

There has been growing realisation of the injustice, inadequate compensation and benefit sharing between developed and developing countries. Therefore, some nations are developing laws to prevent such unauthorised exploitation of their bio-resources and traditional knowledge.

The Indian Parliament has recently cleared the second amendment of the Indian Patents Bill, that takes such issues into consideration, including patent terms emergency provisions and research and development initiative.   **(5 Marks)**

Topic-1: Population Attributes

1   Multiple Choice Questions (1 Mark)

1. Important attributes belonging to a population but not to an individual are : **[Delhi 2023, Set-I, U]**
   (i) Birth rate and death rate
   (ii) Male and female
   (iii) Birth and death
   (iv) Sex-ratio
   Select the correct option from the given options :
   (a) (i) only   (b) (ii) only
   (c) (ii) and (iii)   (d) (i) and (iv)

5   Short Answer Questions (2 or 3 Marks)

2. Identify the type of each pyramid.

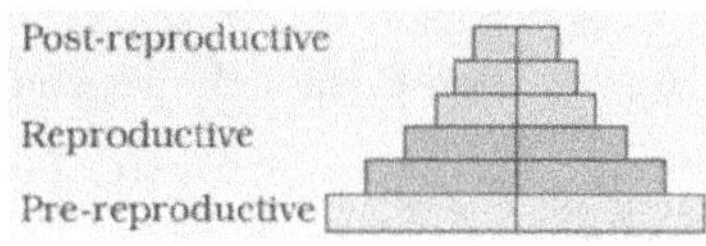

[All India 2022 Term-II, K]

3. Study the age pyramid 'A', 'B' and 'C' of the human population given below and answer the questions that follow: **[All India 2020, U]**

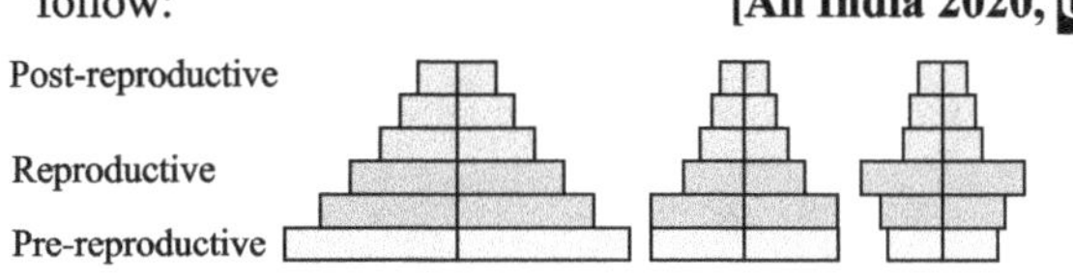

   (a) Identify pyramid 'B' and 'C'.
   (b) Write the basis on which the above pyramids are plotted.

4. List the proceses that are responsible fro increasing and decreasing the population density? **[All India 2019, U]**

5. (a) How will you measure population density of fish in a lake? **[Delhi 2019, U]**

   (b) In a pond there are 100 frogs. 20 more were born in a year. Calculate the birth rate of this population.

[Delhi 2019, U]

OR

Draw a "stable" human age pyramid. Comment on the population growth rate that is depicted by it.

[Delhi 2019, U]

6. Study the graph given below and answer the questions that follow : **[Delhi 2014, U]**

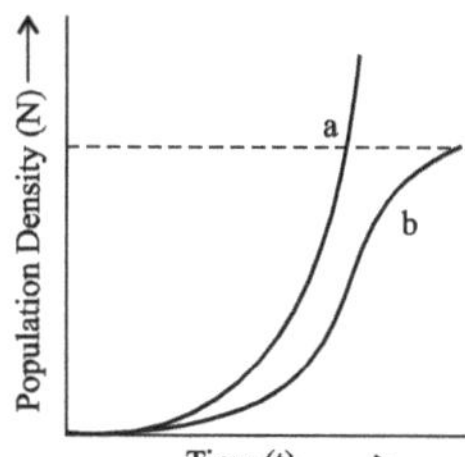

   (i) Write the status of food and space in the curves (a) and (b).

   (ii) In the absence of predators, which one of the two curves would appropriately depict the prey population?

   (iii) Time has been shown on X-axis and there is a parallel dotted line above it. Give the significance of this dotted line.

6 *Long Answer Questions (5 Marks)*

7. "The population of a metro city experiences fluctuations in its population density over a period of time."

[Delhi 2020, U]

(a) When does the population in a metro city tend to increase?

(b) When does the population in metro city tend to decline?

(c) If 'N' is the population density at the time 't', write the population density at the time 't + 1'.

8. (a) What is "population" according to you as a biology student ? [All India 2019, U]

(b) "The size of a population for any species is not a static parameter." Justify the statement with specific reference to fluctuations in the population density of a region in a given period of time. [All India 2019, U]

9. (a) What is an age-pyramid? [All India 2017, U]

(b) Name three representative kinds of age-pyramids for human population and list the characteristics for each one of them. [All India 2017, U]

10. (a) List the different attributes that a population has and not an individual organism. [All India 2015, U]

(b) What is population density? Explain any three different ways the population density can be measured, with the help of an example each.

[All India 2015, U]

  **Topic-2:** *Population Growth*

1 *Multiple Choice Questions (1 Mark)*

1. Swathi was growing a bacterial colony in a culture flask under ideal laboratory conditions where the resources are replenished. Which of the following equations will represent the growth in this case?

(*Where population size is N, birth rate is b, death rate is d, unit time period is t, and carrying capacity is K*).

[CBSE Sample Paper 2022-23, A]

(a) dN/dt = KN (b) dN/dt = r N

(c) dN/dt = r N(K-N/K) (d) dN/dt = r N(K+N/K)

4 *Very Short Answer Questions (1 Mark)*

2. Study the graph given below, showing the population growth curves 'A' and 'B' respectively. Answer the following questions: [All India 2022, Term-II, A]

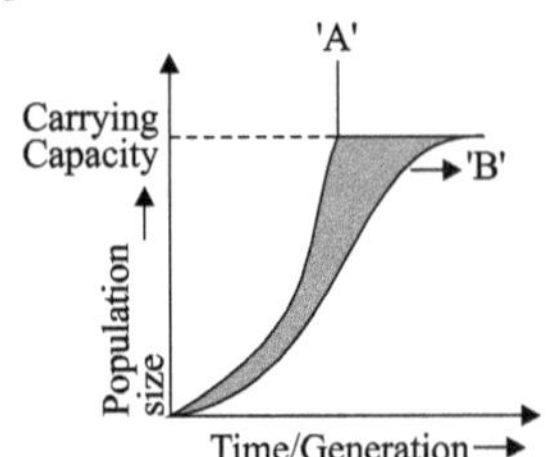

(a) What is 'Carrying Capacity' in respect of Curve 'B' indicative of?

(b) Mention the action of possible natural forces that could have lead to curve 'B'.

3. An ecologist study an area with population A, thriving on unlimited resources and showing exponential growth, introduced population B and C to the same area. What will be the effect on the growth pattern of the population A, B and C when living together in the same habitat?

[All India 2021-22, Term-II, A]

5 *Short Answer Questions (2 or 3 Marks)*

4. (a) What does the equation dN/dt = rN express in terms of population growth? [All India 2022, Ap]

(b) Write the significance of 'r' in a population survey.

[All India 2022, Ap]

5. Study the population growth curve given below and answer the questions that follow: [All India 2020, U]

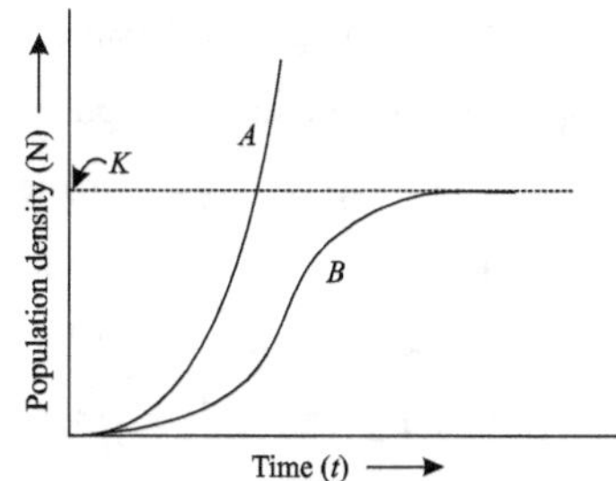

(a) Identify 'A' and 'B' shown in the graph.

(b) When and why do such curves occur in a population?

6   *Long Answer Questions (5 Marks)*

6. Compare, giving reasons, the J-shaped and S-shaped models of population growth of a species.

[Delhi 2017, **U**]

7. (a) Name the two growth models that represent population growth and draw the respective growth curves they represent.   [All India 2016, **U**]

(b) State the basis for the difference in the shape of these curves.   [All India 2016, **U**]

(c) Which one of the curves represent the human population growth at present? Do you think such a curve is sustainable? Give reason in support of your answer.   [All India 2016, **U**]

Topic-3:   *Population Interaction*

1   *Multiple Choice Questions (1 Mark)*

1. A Tight one-to-one relationship between many species of fig tree and certain wasps is an example of -

[Delhi 2023, Set-I, **U**]

(a) Commensalism   (b) Parasitism

(c) Amensalism   (d) Mutualism

2. Intersection between clown fish living among the stinging tentacles of sea anemone is an example of-

[Delhi 2023 (Set-II), **U**]

(a) Amensalism   (b) Parsitism

(c) Mutualism   (d) Commensalism

3. Sea Anemone gets attached to the surface of the hermit crab. The kind of population interaction exhibited in this case is   [CBSE Sample Paper 2022-23, **K**]

(a) amensalism   (b) commensalism

(c) mutualism   (d) parasitism

4   *Short Answer Questions (2 or 3 Marks)*

4. "Cattle and goats do not browse the *Calotropis* plant." Justify the statement giving reasons.

[Delhi 2023 (Set-I), **Ap**]

5. Mention how have plants developed mechanical and chemical defence against herbivores to protect themselves with the help of one example of each.   [Delhi 2020, **K**]

6. Mention the term used to describe a population interaction between an orchid growing on a forest tree.

[All India 2019, **K**]

7. Explain mutualism with the help of any two examples. How is it different from commensalism ?

[Delhi 2013 (Set-I), **U**]

6   *Long Answer Questions (5 Marks)*

8. Explain the following population interactions with the help of one example each: [All India 2023, Set-I, **K**]

(a) Brood Parasitism

(b) Co-evolution of mutualists

9. Differentiate between commensalism and mutualism.

[All India 2020, **K**]

10. Name and explain the type of interaction that exists in mycorrhizae and between cattle egret and cattle.

[All India 2016, **U**]

11. What is mutualism? Mention any two examples where the organisms involved are commercially exploited in agriculture.   **[All India 2015, U]**

12. Describe the mutual relationship between Fig. tree and wasp and comment on the phenomenon that operates in their relationship.   **[All India 2014, U]**

7   *Case Based Questions*

13. Observe the graph given below.

The graph represents inter–specific interaction between two species of Paramecia competing for the same resource in a culture medium. Paramecium caudatum and Paramecium aurelia were grown in separate cultures as well as in mixed cultures. It was found that each species grew in numbers according to the logistic equation.

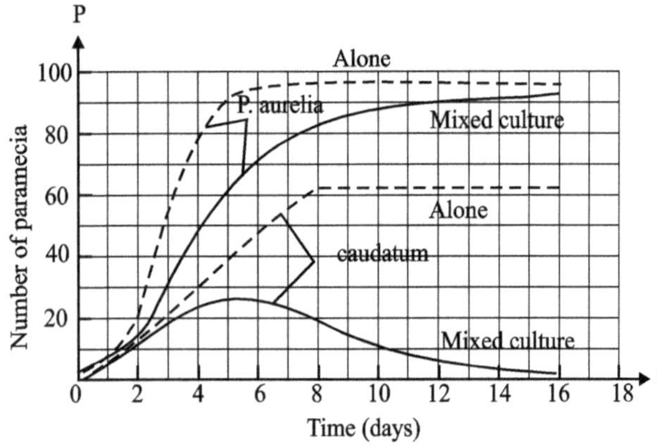

[CBSE Sample Paper 2023-24, A]

(a) Which species is competitively superior? Support it with the data provided in the graph.

(b) State the underlying principle for the above result and name the scientist associated with this principle.

(c) Explain the mechanism in which two or more species competing with each other can co – exist.

OR

Graphs A and B shown below depict interaction of two species. Which graph indicates Mutualism? Give reason.

[CBSE Sample Paper 2023-24, A]

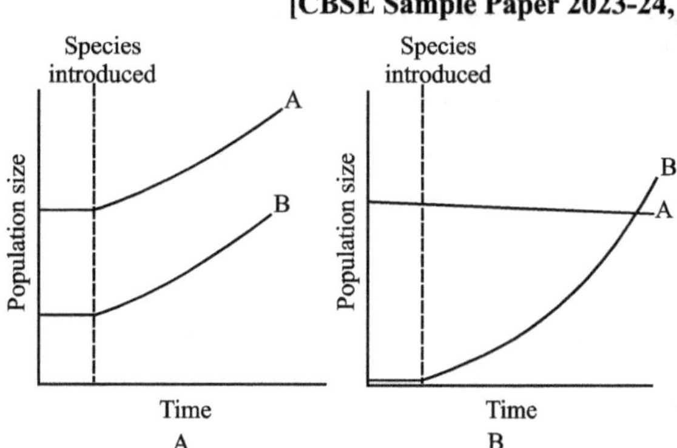

Hints & Solutions

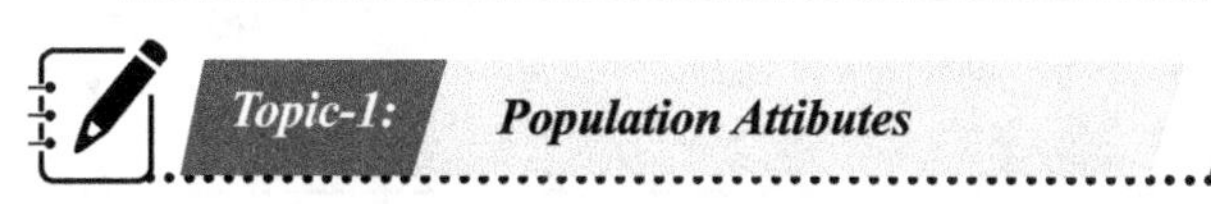

1. **(d)** A population has certain attributes whereas, an individual organism does not. An individual may have births and deaths, but a population has *birth rates* and *death rates*. In a population these rates refer to *per capita* births and deaths. Another attribute characteristic of a population is *sex ratio*. An individual is either a male or a female but a population has a sex ratio. **(1 Mark)**

2.

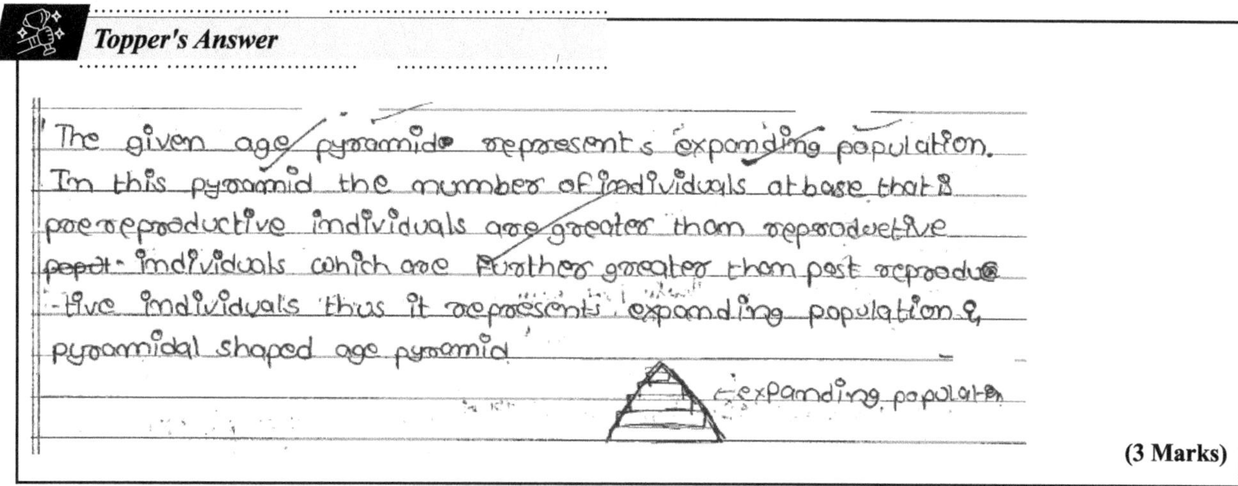

(3 Marks)

A population at any given time is composed of individuals of different ages. If the age distribution (per cent individuals of a given age or age group) is plotted for the population, the resulting structure is called an age pyramid. For human population, the age pyramids generally show age distribution of males and females in a diagram. The shape of the pyramids reflects the growth status of the population - (a) whether it is growing, (b) stable or (c) declining.

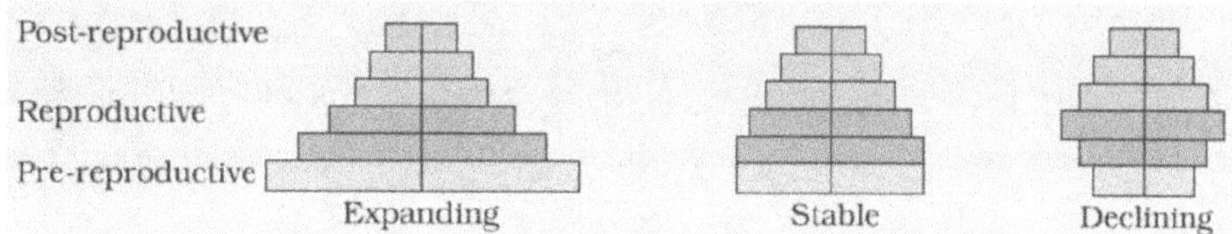

Fig.: Representation of age pyramids for human population

The size of the population tells us a lot about its status in the habitat. Whatever ecological processes we wish to investigate in a population, be it the outcome of competition with another species, the impact of a predator or the effect of a pesticide application, we always evaluate them in terms of any change in the population size. The size, in nature, could be as low as <10 (Siberian cranes at Bharatpur wetlands in any year) or go into millions (Chlamydomonas in a pond). Population size, technically called population density (designated as N), need not necessarily be measured in numbers only. Although total number is generally the most appropriate measure of population density, it is in some cases either meaningless or difficult to determine. In an area, if there are 200 carrot grass (Parthenium hysterophorus) plants but only a single huge banyan tree with a large canopy, stating that the population density of banyan is low relative to that of carrot grass amounts to underestimating the enormous role of the Banyan in that community. In such cases, the per cent cover or biomass is a more meaningful measure of the population size. Total number is again not an easily adoptable measure if the population is huge and counting is impossible or very time-consuming.   **(3 Marks)**

3.

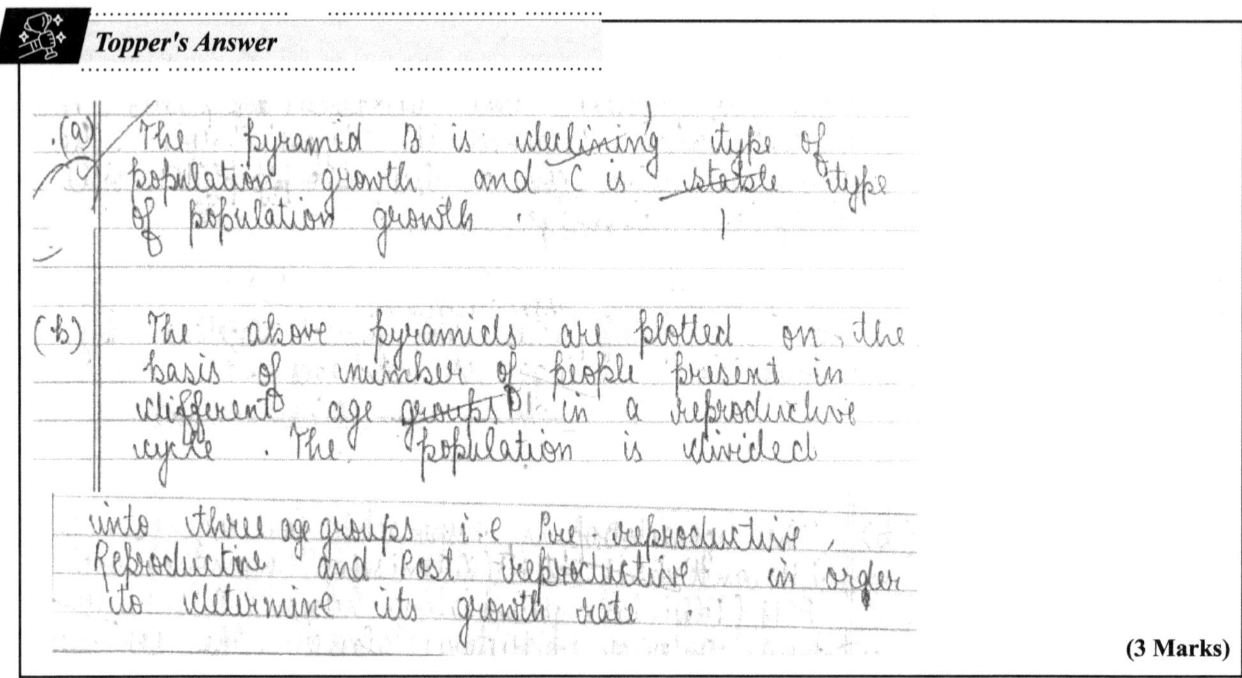

(3 Marks)

(a) The pyramid **B** is stable while pyramid **C** is declining.

(1 Mark)

(b) Age pyramid is defined as a way for representing the age-sex structure of a population. There are three types of age distribution pyramids such as expanding, stable and declining. A population is composed of individuals of different age groups.

In a stable or Bell-shaped age pyramid the number of pre-reproductive and reproductive individuals is almost equal. If the post-reproductive individuals are comparatively fewer then the population size remains stable as it is neither growing nor diminishing.

The declining or urn-shaped age pyramid indicates the number of reproductive individuals is higher than that of number of pre-reproductive individuals. The declining age pyramid indicates declining growth.   **(2 Marks)**

 **Note**

The structure of age pyramids for human population emphasis on providing food to population, development of proper health care facilities and so on.

4.

a) 1 → Natality (B)
2 → Immigration (I)
3 → Mortality (D)
4 → Emigration (E)

$$N_{t+1} = N_t + \{(B+I) - (D+E)\}$$

b) Determining the total no. of individuals in a population is best method but sometimes it is cumbersome.

i) measuring per cent cover or biomass. ✓
e.g. in an area with 200 Parthenium plants & a single banyan tree, the latter produces more biomass

ii) determining relative densities
e.g. no. of fishes present per trap. in a river.

iii) Indirect method (without actually calculating (OR) counting them)

E.g. tiger census is based on pug marks & faecal pellets

(3 Marks)

Whatever might be the ultimate reasons, the density of a population in a given habitat during a given period, fluctuates due to changes in four basic processes, two of which (natality and immigration) contribute to an increase in population density and two (mortality and emigration) to a decrease.

(i)   Natality refers to the number of births during a given period in the population that are added to the initial density.

(ii) Mortality is the number of deaths in the population during a given period.

(iii) Immigration is the number of individuals of the same species that have come into the habitat from elsewhere during the time period under consideration.

(iv) Eigration is the number of individuals of the population who left the habitat and gone elsewhere during the time period under consideration.

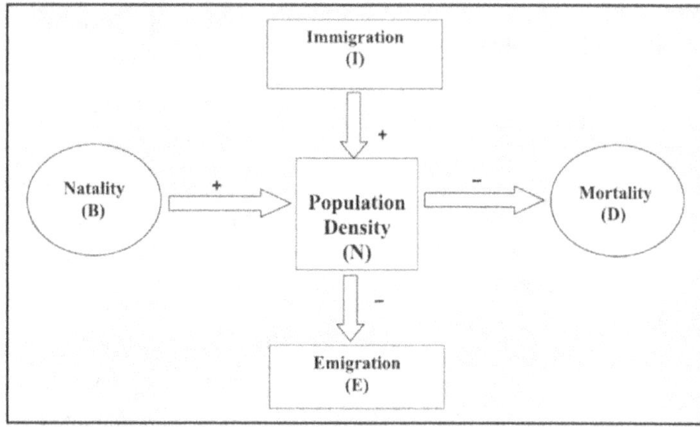

So, if N is the population density at time t, then its density at time t +1 is

$$N_{t+1} = N_t + [(B + I) - (D + E)]$$

You can see from the above equation (Fig. 13.5) that population density will increase if the number of births plus the number of immigrants (B + I) is more than the number of deaths plus the number of emigrants (D + E). Under normal conditions, births and deaths are the most important factors influencing population density, the other two factors assuming importance only under special conditions. For instance, if a new habitat is just being colonised, immigration may contribute more significantly to population growth than birth rates. **(3 Marks)**

5. **(a)** The population density of a fishes in a lake is determined by the fish caught per trap. Population density refers to the measure to determine the number of individuals of a species in a particular unit area. The relative densities are used to determine the population size in a specific area. **(1 Mark)**

(b) To calculate the birth rate of population

$$= \frac{\text{Number of births}}{\text{Total population}} \times 100$$

The birth rate of a frog population $= \frac{20}{120} \times 100$

$$= 16.66 \text{ per year} \qquad \textbf{(1 Mark)}$$

OR

In a stable or Bell-shaped age pyramid the number of pre-reproductive and reproductive individuals is almost equal. If the post-reproductive individuals are comparatively fewer than the population size remains stable as it is neither growing nor diminishing.

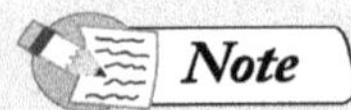

Note

Age pyramid is defined as a way for representing the age-sex structure of population.

Diagrammatic Representation of Stable Age pyramid:

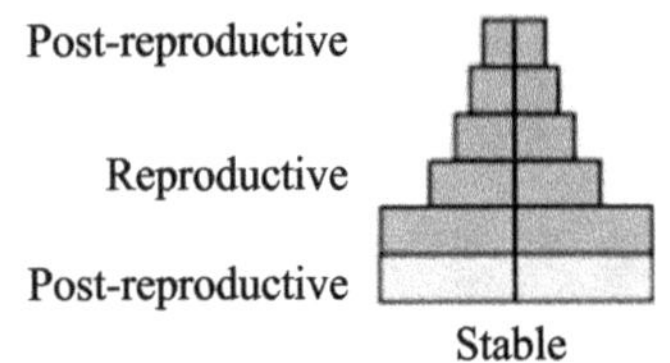

(2 Marks)

6. **(i)** The curve (a) represents exponential growth of the population when the responses are not limiting the growth. Whereas curve (b) represents logistic growth of the population when responses are limiting the growth. **(1 Mark)**

(ii) In the absence of predator, the curve (a) is increasing as the responses are not limiting the growth. So in the absence of predator, prey population continuously increases. **(1 Mark)**

(iii) The parallel dotted line represents K (carrying capacity). **Carrying capacity** is defined as in nature; a given habitat has enough resources to support a maximum possible number beyond which no further growth is possible. **(1 Mark)**

7. **(a)** The size of a population changing with time and it depends on various factors such as availability of food, predation pressure, weather conditions. So the size of population in a metro city tends to increase when all the conditions are favourable. The size of population in a particular habitat fluctuates because of four basic processes such as natality, mortality, immigration and emigration. Out of which **Natality** (refers to the number of births during a given period of time in a population) and **Immigration** (refers to the number of individuals of the same species that have come into the habitat from somewhere else in a specific time period) tends to increase the population size in a given locality. **(2 Marks)**

(b) **Mortality** (refers to the number of deaths in the population during a given period) and **Emigration** (refers to the number of individuals of a population who left the habitat and gone somewhere else during the time period) tends to decreases the population. **(2 Marks)**

(c) If N is the population density at time t, then its density at time t + 1 is:

$$N_{t+1} = N_t + ((B + I) - (D + E))$$

Where B = Natality

I = Immigration

E = Emigration

D = Mortality **(1 Mark)**

8. **(a)** Population is the number of people or animals of the same group or species, living in a particular geographical area, and have the capability of interbreeding. **(2½ Marks)**

(b) The size of a population for any species is not a static parameter because it keeps changing with time, depending on various factors including food availability, predation, pressure and adverse weather. The density of a population in a given area during a period fluctuates due to changes in four basic processes two of which are natality and immigrationcontribute to an increase in population density and two are mortality and emigration to a decrease. **(½ Marks)**

(i) **Natality:** Number of births during a given period in the population that are added to the initial density.

(ii) **Mortality:** Number of deaths in the population during a given period. **(½ Marks)**

(iii) **Immigration:** Number of individuals of the same species that have come into the habitat from elsewhere during given time period. **(½ Marks)**

(iv) **Emigration:** Number of individuals of the population who had left the habitat and gone elsewhere during given time period. **(½ Mark)**

9. (a) An age pyramid is a graphical representation of the distribution of various age groups within a population of a region forming the shape of a pyramid when the population (percent individual of a given age or age group) is growing. **(2 Marks)**

(b) For human population, the age pyramid shows age distribution of males and females in a combined diagram. These age groups are pre-reproductive, reproductive and post-reproductive. The shape of the pyramids reflects the growth status of the population, Three types of pyramids namely, pyramid with broad base, bell shaped and an urnlike structure indicate rapidly growing population, stable population and a declining population respectively.
(2 Marks)

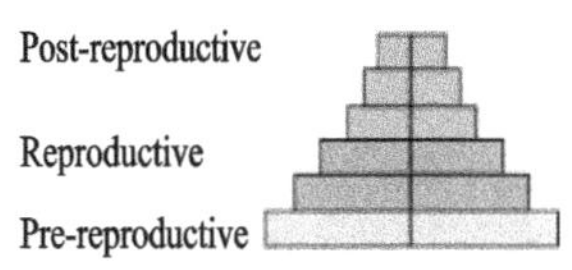

10. (a) A population certain characteristics that an individual organisms does not have are as follows:

(i) Natality refers to the number of birth during a given period in the population that are added to the initial density.

(ii) Mortality refers to the number of deaths in the population during a given period.

(iii) Percentage revers to the sex-ratio of male and female. **(2½ Marks)**

(b) Population density means number of individuals present per unit area. Population density can be measured by determining the population size. The different methods to study population size are as follows:

(1) **Quadrat method:** It is a method that involves the use of square of particular dimensions to measure the number of organisms.

Example: The number of *Parthenium* plants in a given area can be measured using the quadrat method.

(2) **Direct observation:** It involves the counting of organisms in the given area.

Example: In order to determine the number of bacteria growing in a petridish, their colonies are counted.

(3) **Indirect method:** In this method, there is no need to count the organisms individually.

Example: The number of fishes caught per trap gives the measure of their total density in a given water body. **(2½ Marks)**

Topic-2: *Population Growth*

1. (b) dN/dt = r N **(1 Mark)**

2. (a) In logistic growth, a population's per capita growth rate gets smaller and smaller as population size approaches a maximum imposed by limited resources in the environment, known as the carrying capacity (K).
$$dN/dt = rN(K – N/K)$$ **(1 Mark)**

(b)
- Resources for growth for most animal populations are finite and become limiting sooner or later, the logistic growth model is considered a more realistic one.
- The 'fittest' individual will survive and reproduce.
- In nature, a given habitat has enough resources to support a maximum possible number, beyond which no further growth is possible. **(1 Mark)**

3. This interaction will lead to competition between the individuals of population A,B and C for resources. Eventually the 'fittest' individuals will survive and reproduce. **(1Mark)**

The resources for growth will become finite and limiting, and population growth will become realistic. **(1 Mark)**

4. (a) The equation dN/dt = rN express for Exponential growth. **(1 Mark)**

   (b) The r in this equation is called the 'intrinsic rate of natural increase' and is a very important parameter chosen for assessing the impacts of any biotic or abiotic factor on population growth. **(1 Mark)**

5. (a) **A** in the given graph is $\dfrac{dN}{dt} = rN$ that indicates exponential growth and **B** in the given graph is

   $dN = rN\ \dfrac{(K-N)}{K}$ that indicates logistic growth.

   (1½ Marks)

   (b) The exponential growth occurs when the resources such as food and space are available unlimited. While the logistic growth occurs when the resources are limited and there is competition between the individuals in a given habitat. So, only the 'fittest' individual will survive and reproduce. **(3 Marks)**

6. The difference between J shaped-growth curve and S shaped-growth curve are as follows:

J shaped-growth curve	S shaped-growth curve
(i) In this type of growth curve, the resources are unlimited.	In this type of growth curve, the resources are limited.
(ii) In J shaped-growth curve, growth is exponential.	In S shaped-growth curve, growth is logistic.
(iii) Because of the availability of unlimited resources, all individuals will survive and reproduce.	This type of curve favours the survival and reproduction of the fittest one.
(iv) Growth equation for J shaped-shaped curve is dN/dt = R_n	Growth equation for S shaped-curve is dN/dT = rN

(5 Marks)

7. (a) The two growth curves are exponential growth curves and logistic growth curves.

   Diagrammatic representation of Growth curves:

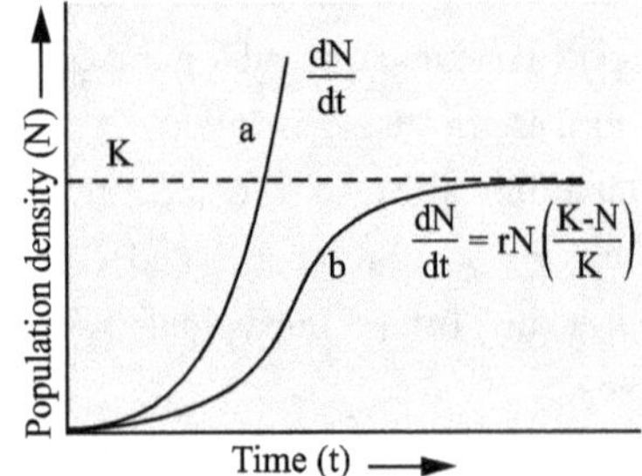

A represents exponential growth curve whereas b represents logistic growth curve. **(2 Marks)**

   (b) The exponential growth curve is formed when the availability of resources in the habitat are unlimited. A J-shaped curve is formed in exponential growth curve.

The exponential growth equation is $N_t = N_0 e^{rt}$
   where

   N_t = Population density after time t

   N_0 = Population density at time zero

   r = intrinsic rate of natural increase

   e = the base of natural logarithms

Logistic growth occurs when the available resources are limited results in competition between individuals for limited resources. So, the fittest individual will survive and reproduce.

A S-shaped or sigmoid growth curve is formed. The logistic growth equation is

$$\dfrac{dN}{dt} = rN\left[\dfrac{K-N}{K}\right]$$

where,

   N = Population density at time t

   r = Intrinsic rate of natural increase

   K = Carrying capacity **(2 Marks)**

   (c) The human population at present is represented by the logistic growth. No, the growth is not sustainable because with the growing population and the depleting natural resources, it would be difficult in the future to fulfil the demands of growing population. **(1 Mark)**

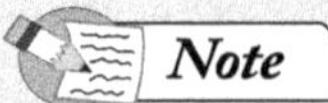

Note

Carrying capacity (K) is defined as in a given habitat that has enough resources to support a maximum possible number, beyond which no further growth is possible.

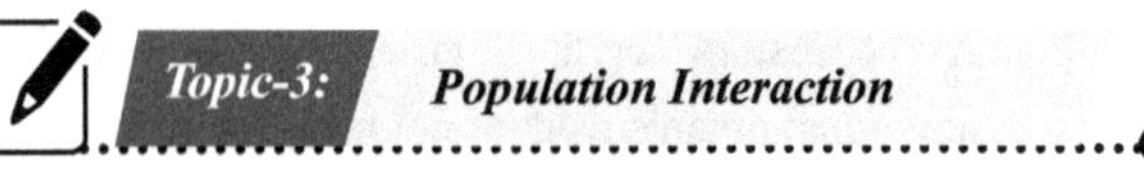

Topic-3: *Population Interaction*

1. (d) The interaction confers benefits on both the interacting species. Such type of interaction is called **Mutualism**. One of the most common examples of mutualism is, the female wasp uses the fruit not only as an oviposition (egg-laying) site but uses the

developing seeds within the fruit for nourishing its larvae. The wasp pollinates the fig inflorescence while searching for suitable egg-laying sites. In return for the favour of pollination the fig offers the wasp some of its developing seeds, as food for the developing wasp larvae. **(1 Mark)**

2. **(d)** Clownfish and sea anemone interact via a symbiotic association called commensalism. In this type of interaction, one species is benefited while the other is neither harmed nor benefited. Sea anemone possesses stinging tentacles that provide protection to clownfish from predators. The anemone does not receive any benefit from the clown fish. **(1 Mark)**

3. **(b)** commensalism **(1 Mark)**

4. The plant *Calotropis* produces highly poisonous cardiac glycosides and that is why we never see any cattle browsing on this plant. **(1 Mark)**

A wide variety of chemical substances that we can extract from plants on a commercial scale (nicotine, caffeine, quinine, strychnine, opium, etc.,) are produced by them actually as defences against grazers and browsers.

(1 Mark)

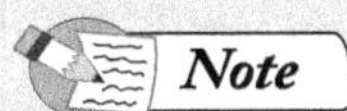
Note

Menstrual cycle starts with a menstrual phase, when menstrual flow occurs and it last for 3-5 days

5. Unlike animals, plants cannot move away from their predators. So they developed a variety of mechanical and chemical defences against herbivores. Herbivores are predator. Some plants such as *Acacia* and *Cactus* develop specific structures like thorns for defence. Many plants produce and store chemicals that make herbivore sick when they are eaten as they inhibit feeding and digestion. This chemical also disrupts its reproduction or even kills it. **(1 Mark)**

For example: A weed called *Calotropis* growing in abandoned fields produces a highly poisonous cardiac glycosides that causes cardiac arrest in herbivores. **(1 Mark)**

6. The term used to describe a population interaction between an orchids growing on a forest tree is called commensalism. Commensalism is a biological interaction between two organisms in which one organism gets benefits from others while the other organism is neither benefited nor harmed.

An orchid growing on the branch of a forest tree is an epiphyte (plants that are growing on other plants). In this biological interaction, the orchid gets support, more sunlight for photosynthesis and nutrients from the mango tree. Whereas mango tree remains unaffected. **(1 Mark)**

7. Mutualism is a type of population interaction that confers benefits on both the interacting species. For example: lichens represent an intimate mutualistic relationship between a fungus and photosynthesising algae or cyanobacteria. **(1 Mark)**

The Mycorrihzae are associations between fungi and the roots of higher plants. The fungi help the plant in the absorption of essential nutrients from the soil while the plant in turn provides the fungi with energy-yielding carbohydrates.

Commensalism is a type of population interaction in which one species benefits and other is neither harmed nor benefitted. **(1 Mark)**

For example: an orchid growing as an epiphyte on a mango branch and barnacles growing on the back of a whale benefit while neither the mango tree not the whale derives any apparent benefit. **(1 Mark)**

8. (a) Brood parasitism: in birds is a fascinating example of parasitism in which the parasitic bird lays its eggs in the nest of its host and lets the host incubate them. During the course of evolution, the eggs of the parasitic bird have evolved to resemble the host's egg in size and colour to reduce the chances of the host bird detecting the foreign eggs and ejecting them from the nest. **(2½ Marks)**

(b) Co-evolution of mutualists: The most spectacular and evolutionarily fascinating examples of mutualism are found in plant-animal relationships. Plants need the help of animals for pollinating their flowers and dispersing their seeds. Animals obviously have to be paid 'fees' for the services that plants expect from them. Plants offer rewards or fees in the form of pollen and nectar for pollinators and juicy and nutritious fruits for seed dispersers. But the mutually beneficial system should also be safeguarded against 'cheaters', for example, animals that try to steal nectar without aiding in pollination. Plant-animal interactions often involve co-evolution of the mutualists, that is, the evolutions of the flower and its pollinator species are tightly linked with one another. In many species of fig trees, there is a tight one-to-one relationship with the pollinator species of wasp. It means that a given fig species can be pollinated only by its 'partner' wasp species and no other species. The female wasp uses the fruit not only as an oviposition (egg-laying) site but uses the developing seeds within the fruit for nourishing its larvae. The wasp pollinates the fig inflorescence while searching for suitable egg-laying sites. In return for the favour of pollination the fig offers the wasp some of its developing seeds, as food for the developing wasp larvae. **(2½ Marks)**

9.

Topper's Answer

Commensalism type of interaction takes place where one species is benefitted and the other species remain neutral and does n't derieve any loss or benefit. In commensalism the two interacting species closely stays together and interact with each other. There are many examples of commensalism and one such can be witnessed in between cattle egrets and grazing cattles. The cattle egrets carefully follows the grazing cattle and when these cattle stir and flush up vegetation cattle egrets eat the insects in those vegetation which may not be visible to it on its own but is easily found out in staying close to cattle. Here, the cattle does n't derieves anything and stays neutral whereas cattle egrets are benefitted.

In Mutualism whereas the two interacting species both derieve benefits from each other and are mutually profited. But, the two interacting species does n't stays as closer to each other as in commensalism.

One of its examples can be witnessed in the association between fungi and roots of higher plants resulting in the formation of mycorrhizza. Here, both are benefitted as fungi helps plant roots its derieve more nutrients from the soil and fungi inturn is provided with high emerging yielding carbohydrates.

(5 Marks)

Commensalism: This is the interaction in which one species benefits and the other is neither harmed nor benefited. An orchid growing as an epiphyte on a mango branch, and barnacles growing on the back of a whale benefit while neither the mango tree nor the whale derives any apparent benefit. The cattle egret and grazing cattle in close association, a sight you are most likely to catch if you live in farmed rural areas, is a classic example of commensalism. The egrets always forage close to where the cattle are grazing because the cattle, as they move, stir up and flush out insects from the vegetation that otherwise might be difficult for the egrets to find and catch. Another example of commensalism is the interaction between sea anemone that has stinging tentacles and the clown fish that lives among them. The fish gets protection from predators which stay away from the stinging tentacles. The anemone does not appear to derive any benefit by hosting the clown fish.

Mutualism: This interaction confers benefits on both the interacting species. Lichens represent an intimate mutualistic relationship between a fungus and photosynthesising algae or cyanobacteria. Similarly, the mycorrhizae are associations between fungi and the roots of higher plants. The fungi help the plant in the absorption of essential nutrients from the soil while the plant in turn provides the fungi with energy-yielding carbohydrates. **(5 Marks)**

10. *Mycorrhizae* are association between fungi and the root nodules of higher plants. This type of population interaction is called **mutualism.** In this, the fungi help the plant in the absorption of essential nutrients from the soil whereas the plant in turn provides the fungi with energy-yielding carbohydrates. **(2½ Marks)**

The interaction between cattle egret and grazing cattle is **commensalism.** In this type of population interaction, the egrets always forage close to where the cattle are grazing because the cattle, as they move stir up and flush out from the vegetation insects which is difficult for the egrets to find and catch. **(2½ Marks)**

Note

Commensalism *is a type of population interaction in which one species benefits and the other is neither harmed nor benefited.* ***Mutualism*** *is a type of population interaction in which both the interacting species are benefited from each other.*

11. Mutualism is a type of population interaction between the organisms of two species in which both organisms are benefited from each other. **(1 Mark)**

Examples of the organisms involved that are commercially exploited in agriculture are as follows:

(i) **Commercial exploitation of *Rhizobium* in agriculture:** Continuous growth of crops leads to the nutrient deficiency in soil. Farmers, then grow leguminous crops containing *Rhizobium* in its roots to replenish the lost nutrients (especially nitrogen) in the soil. **(1½ Marks)**

(ii) **Commercial exploitation of Mycorrhiza in agriculture:** Mycorrhiza is an association of the soil fungus with the roots of higher plants. Farmers use Mycorrhiza commercially in agriculture as it improves the soil quality and reduces soil erosion by improving plant rooting capacity. The fungal hyphae spread into the root tissues and help the plants to optimally use the soil's water and minerals. Thus, to increase the yield of plants and to replenish the soil nutrients. Mycorrhiza is commercially exploited in agriculture. **(1 Marks**

12. The relationship between the fig tree and wasp shows mutualism, the wasp lays its egg and also pollinates the fig's. On the other hand, the fig not only provides shelter (fruit) for oviposition to wasp but also allows its larva to feed on seeds. **(5 Marks)**

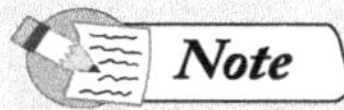

Note

Mutualism is a type of population interaction that confers benefits on both the interacting species.

13. **(a)** P. aurelia species is competitively superior P. aurelia grows in numbers more quickly than P. caudatum and shows more individuals in the same volume of culture/ 100 Paramecia aurelia in 6 days whereas 60 P. caudatum in 8 days. **(1)**

(b) Competitive Exclusion Principle' which states that two closely related species competing for the same resources cannot co–exist indefinitely and the competitively inferior one will be eliminated.G.F. Gause, **(1)**

(c) One such mechanism is 'resource partitioning'. If two species compete for the same resource, they could avoid competition by choosing different times for feeding or different foraging patterns, to avoid competition and co–exist due to behavioural differences in their foraging activities. **(1)**

OR

Graph A – As both species grow simultaneously.

(1)

Chapter 12 — Ecosystem

Topic-1: *Ecosystem: Structure and Function*

1   *Multiple Choice Questions (1 Mark)*

1. Which of the following food chains is the major conduit for energy flow in terrestrial and aquatic ecosystems respectively?   **[CBSE Sample Paper 2022-23, U]**

	Terrestrial Ecosystem	Aquatic Ecosystem
(a)	Grazing	Grazing
(b)	Detritus	Grazing
(c)	Detritus	No growth
(d)	Grazing	Detritus

4   *Very Short Answer Questions (1 Mark)*

2. On August 22 in the year 2022, 3358 fires were detected in the rainforests. Write one short-term and one long-term effect of this event on the biotic and abiotic components of the environment.   **[All India 2023, Set-I, K]**

3. How is 'stratification' represented in a forest ecosystem?   **[Delhi 2014, U]**

4. Why are green algae not likely to be found in the deepest strata of the ocean?   **[All India 2013, U]**

5   *Short Answer Questions (2 or 3 Marks)*

5. "In a food-chain, a trophic level represents a functional level, not a species." Explain.   **[Delhi 2016, U]**

6   *Long Answer Questions (5 Marks)*

6. (a) Taking an example of a small pond, explain how the four components of an ecosystem function as a unit.   **[All India 2016, Ap]**

    (b) Name the type of food chain that exists in pond.   **[All India 2016, Ap]**

Topic-2: *Productivity*

1   *Multiple Choice Questions (1 Mark)*

1. The primary productivity in an ecosystem is expressed as :   **[Delhi 2023, Set-I, U]**

    (a) gm–2 yr-1

    (b) gm-2 yr

    (c) K cal m-2 yr-1

    (d) K cal m-2

4   *Very Short Answer Questions (1 Mark)*

2. Write the equation that helps in deriving the net primary productivity of an ecosystem.   **[Delhi 2013, Ap]**

5   *Short Answer Questions (2 or 3 Marks)*

3. Explaing the equation : $NPP = GPP - R$.   **[All India 2019, U]**

4. Describe the inter-relationship between productivity, gross primary productivity and net productivity.   **[Delhi 2017, K]**

5. Many fresh water animals can not survive in marine environment. Explain.   **[Delhi 2015, U]**

    OR

    How are productivity, gross productivity, net primary productivity and secondary productivity interrelated ?   **[Delhi 2015, U]**

6. (i) What is primary productivity? Why does it vary in different types of eco-systems?   **[Delhi 2014, U]**

    (ii) State the relation between gross and net primary productivity.   **[Delhi 2014, U]**

Topic-3: *Decomposition*

Multiple Choice Questions (1 Mark)

1. Observe the contents 1, 2, 3 and 4 of soil samples A, B and C shown in the graph. If the temperature and soil moisture of all soil samples are identical, which soil sample (s) will show faster decomposition?

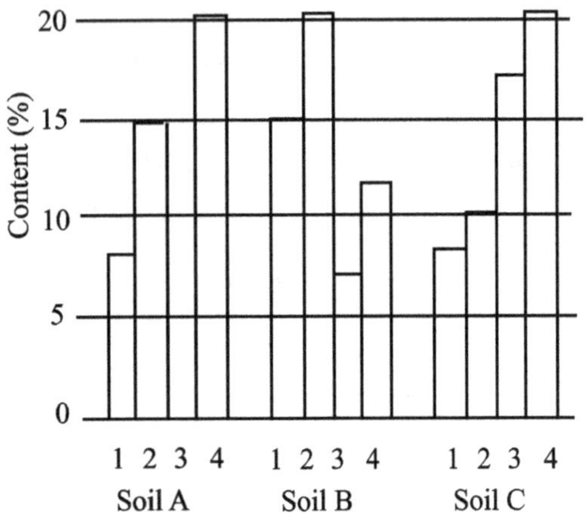

(a) Soil Sample A   [CBSE Sample Paper 2023-24, **A**]

(b) Soil Sample B

(c) Soil Samples A and B both

(d) Soil Sample C

Assertion Reason/Two Statement Type Questions (1 Mark)

2. **Assertion (A) :** Decomposition process is slower if detritus is rich in lignin and chitin.[**Delhi 2023, Set-I, K**]

   Reason (R) : Decomposition is largely an oxygen requiring process.

   (a) Both (A) and (R) are true and (R) is the correct explanation of (A).

   (b) Both (A) and (R) are true, but (R) is not the correct explanation of (A).

   (c) (A) is true, but (R) is false.

   (d) (A) is false, but (R) is true.

Very Short Answer Questions (1 Mark)

3. Name and explain the processes earthworm and bacteria carry on detritus.   [**Delhi 2020, K**]

Topic-4: *Energy Flow*

Very Short Answer Questions (1 Mark)

1. Given below is a food web that involves nine organisms.

   [**All India 2023, Set-I, K**]

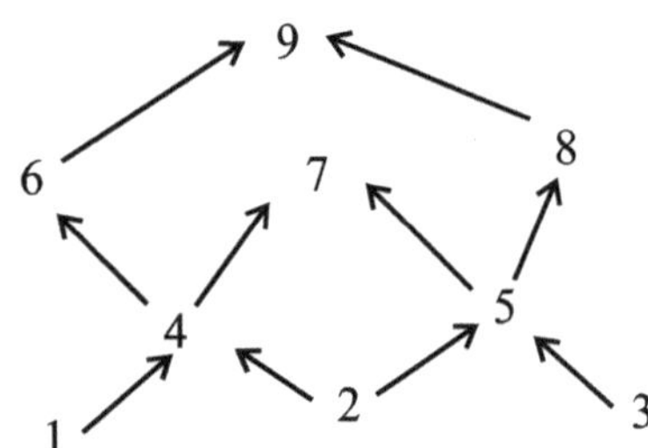

   (a) Identify two producers and two carnivores shown in the food web.

   (b) Is it possible to make an ecological pyramid depicting this food web? Give reason in support of your answer.

2. State what does 'standing crop' of a trophic level represent.   [**All India 2013, Set-I, U**]

Short Answer Questions (2 or 3 Marks)

3. Apart from being part of the food chain, predators play other important roles. Mention any two such roles supported by examples.   [**Delhi 2014, U**]

4. "It is possible that a species may occupy more than one trophic level in the same ecosystem at the same time." Explain with the help of one example.

   [**All India 2013, U**]

Long Answer Questions (5 Marks)

5. (a) What is a trophic level in an ecosystem? What is 'standing crop' with reference to it?

   [**All India 2018, U**]

   (b) Explain the role of the 'first trophic level' in an ecosystem.   [**All India 2018, U**]

   (c) How is the detritus food chain connected with the grazing food chain in a natural ecosystem?

   [**All India 2018, U**]

Topic-5: *Ecological Pyramid*

2 *Assertion Reason/Two Statement Type Questions*
(1 Mark)

1. Given below is the Age Pyramid of population in one of the states in India as per 2011 census. It depicts the male population on the left hand side, female population on the right hand side, newborns towards the base and gradually increasing age groups as we move from base to the top, with the oldest population at the top. Study this pyramid and comment upon the appropriateness of the Assertion and the Reason.

[CBSE Sample Paper 2022-23, A]

Assertion: It is a stable population.

Reason: The pre-reproductive and reproductive individuals are almost in equal numbers and the post-reproductive individuals are relatively fewer.

(a) Both (A) and (R) are true and (R) is the correct explanation of (A).

(b) Both (A) and (R) are true, but (R) is not the correct explanation of (A).

(c) (A) is true, but (R) is false.

(d) (A) is false, but (R) is true.

4 *Very Short Answer Questions (1 Mark)*

2. Biomass of a standing crop of phytoplankton is 4 kg/m^2 which supports a large standing crop of zooplankton having a biomass 11 kg/m^2. This is consumed by small fishes having biomass 25 kg/m^2 which are then consumed by large fishes with the biomass 37 kg/m^2.

Draw an ecological pyramid indicating the biomass at each stage and also name the trophic levels. Mention whether it is an upright or inverted pyramid.

[CBSE Sample Paper 2023-24, Ap]

OR

Use the information provided in the table given below to answer the following questions:

Tropic level	Net Production ($KJm^{-2}y^{-1}$)	Respiration ($KJm^{-2}y^{-1}$)
Top Carnivore	50	35
Carnivores	420	378
Herbivores	4490	4041
Producers	45000	40,367

(a) Calculate the gross primary productivity.

(b) Analyze the trend in the Net Production from Producers to Top Carnivore. Give a reason for your observation. **[CBSE Sample Paper 2023-24, Ap]**

5 *Short Answer Questions (2 or 3 Marks)*

3. Construct an age pyramid which reflect an expanding growth status of human population.

[All India 2014, Ap]

4. Construct an age pyramid which reflects a stable growth status of human population. **[Delhi 2014, Ap]**

5. Differentiate between two different types of pyramids of biomass with the help of one example of each.

[All India 2013, U]

6. Why the pyramid of energy is always upright ? Explain.

[Delhi 2013, K]

7. (a) Given below is a pyramid of biomass in an ecosystem where each bar represents the standing crop available in the trophic level. With the help of an example explain the conditions where this kind of pyramid is possible in nature?

[CBSE Sample Paper 2022-23, A]

Trophic Level 2 [   ]
Trophic Level 1 [   ]

(b) Will the pyramid of energy be also of the same shape in this situation? Give reason for your response.

[CBSE Sample Paper 2022-23, U]

OR

(a) Draw a pyramid of numbers where a large number of insects are feeding on the leaves of a tree. What is the shape of this pyramid?

(b) Will the pyramid of energy be also of the same shape in this situation? Give reason for your response.

[CBSE Sample Paper 2022-23, U]

---

6 *Long Answer Questions (5 Marks)*

---

8. (a) What is an ecological pyramid ? Compare the pyramids of energy, biomass and numbers.

[Delhi 2017, K]

(b) Write any two limitations of ecological pyramids.

[Delhi 2017, K]

9. (a) Represent diagrammatically three kinds of age-pyramids for human populations. **[Delhi 2016, Ap]**

(b) How does an age pyramid for human population at given point of time helps the policy-makers in planning for future. **[Delhi 2016, Ap]**

10. "It is often said that the pyramid of energy is always upright. On the other hand, the pyramid of biomass can be both upright and inverted." Explain with the help of examples and sketches. **[All India 2015, Ap]**

11. "Analysis of age-pyramids for human population can provide important inputs for longterm planning strategies." Explain. **[Delhi 2015, U]**

Hints & Solutions

Topic-1: *Ecosystem, Structure and Function*

1. **(c)** Detritus; Grazing food chain respectively.

2. One short term impact of forest fire:

   On biotic component of the environment is mortality of large number of species causing biodiversity loss.

   On abiotic component of the environment is the deterioration of the quality of air and water.

   One long term impact of forest fire:

   On biotic component of the environment is co-extinction of species.

   On abiotic component of the environment will not support the survival of future species. **(1 Mark)**

3. Stratification refers to the vertical distribution of different species occupying different levels. It involves trees occupy top vertical strata or layer of a forest, shrubs the second and herbs and grasses occupy the bottom layers.

   (1 Mark)

4. The green algae acts as producer and they synthesise their own food by the process of photosynthesis. In the deepest strata such as in the benthic zone sunlight is not available. The green algae are not likely found in the deepest strata of the ocean because of the non-availability of sunlight for the process of photosynthesis. **(1 Mark)**

5. In a trophic level, the position of species is determined by their function as well as mode of nutrition in a specific food chain. The species may occupy more than one trophic level within the same ecosystem. **(1 Mark)**

   If the mode of nutrition of species changes results in the change in trophic level of species. One species can become primary level of consumer in one food chain and also become secondary level of consumer in another food chain.

   (1 Mark)

6. **(a)** The four function functions of an ecosystem are as follows:

   • **Productivity:** The productivity is defined as the rate of biomass production. Productivity is represented by the autotrophic phytoplanktons, algae, floating abd submerged plants. **(1 Mark)**

   • **Decomposition:** Decomposers such as fungi, bacteria, flagellates. The decomposers break down complex organic matter into inorganic substances such as carbon dioxide, water and nutrients. **(1 Mark)**

   • **Energy flow:** There is a unidirectional flow of energy from the sun to producers and then to consumers.

     (1 Mark)

   • **Nutrient cycling:** The movement of nutrient elements through the various components of an ecosystem. The pond ecosystem involves the process of conversion of inorganic substances into organic material with the help of solar energy. **(1 Mark)**

   (b) In the pond ecosystem, the Grazing Food chain is the major food chain for the energy flow:

   Producer → Primary consumer → Secondary consumer → Tertiary consumer

   (Phytoplankton)   (Zooplanktn)   (small fishes)   (Large fishes)

   (1 Mark)

Topic-2: *Productivity*

1. **(a)** The rate of biomass production is called productivity. It is expressed in terms of $gm^{-2}yr^{-1}$ or $(kcalm^{-2}) yr^{-1}$.

   (1 Mark)

Note

Productivity of an ecosystem can be divided into gross primary productivity and net primary productivity.

2. Net primary productivity is defined as the Gross primary productivity (GPP) minus respiration losses (R).

   $NPP = GPP - R$

   Where Gross primary productivity of an ecosystem is defined as the rate of production of organic matter during photosynthesis.

   (1 Mark)

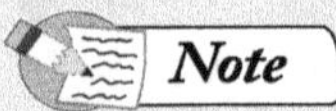
Note

Productivity refers to the rate of biomass production whereas primary productivity refers to the amount of biomass or organic matter produced per unit area over a time period by plants during photosynthesis.

3.

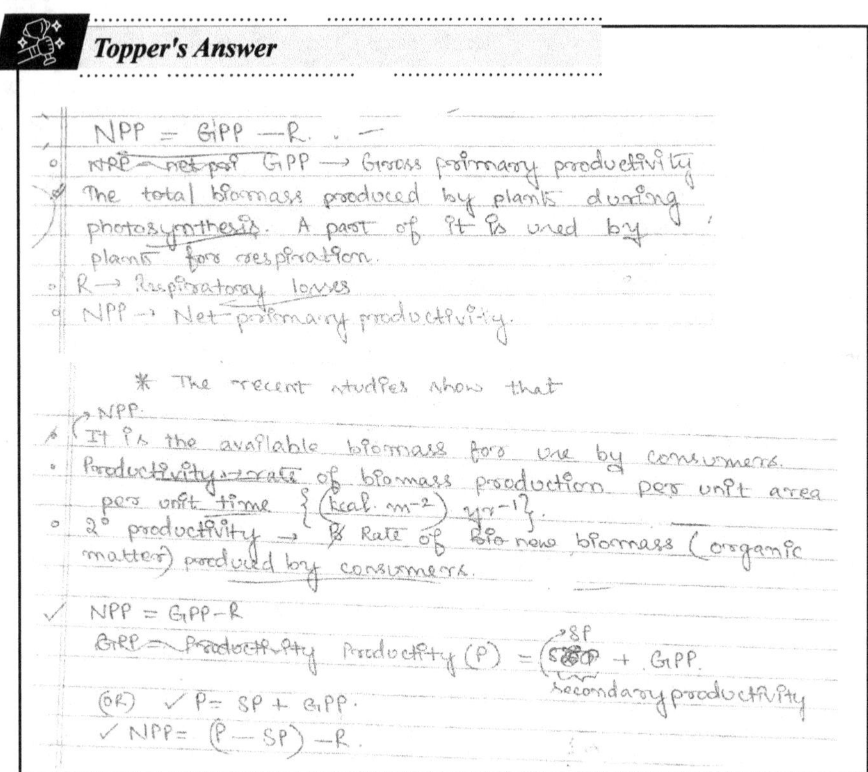

A constant input of solar energy is the basic requirement for any ecosystem to function and sustain. Primary production is defined as the amount of biomass or organic matter produced per unit area over a time period by plants during photosynthesis. It is expressed in terms of weight (gm–2) or energy (kcal m–2). The rate of biomass production is called productivity. It is expressed in terms of gm–2 yr–1 or (kcal m–2) yr–1 to compare the productivity of different ecosystems. It can be divided into gross primary productivity (GPP) and net primary productivity (NPP). Gross primary productivity of an ecosystem is the rate of production of organic matter during photosynthesis. A considerable amount of GPP is utilised by plants in respiration. Gross primary productivity minus respiration losses (R), is the net primary productivity (NPP).

$$GPP - R = NPP$$

Net primary productivity is the available biomass for the consumption to heterotrophs (herbiviores and decomposers). Secondary productivity is defined as the rate of formation of new organic matter by consumers.

Primary productivity depends on the plant species inhabiting a particular area. It also depends on a variety of environmental factors, availability of nutrients and photosynthetic capacity of plants. Therefore, it varies in different types of ecosystems. The annual net primary productivity of the whole biosphere is approximately 170 billion tons (dry weight) of organic matter. Of this, despite occupying about 70 per cent of the surface, the productivity of the oceans are only 55 billion tons. Rest of course, is on land.

3. **Productivity:** Productivity is defined as the rate of biomass production. **(1 Mark)**

   Gross primary productivity: Gross primary productivity is defined as the rate of organic matter production during photosynthesis. **(1 Mark)**

   Net primary productivity: Net primary productivity involves the gross-productivity minus respiratory losses (R).

   So, NPP = GPP-R

   As per their definitions, all the terms are interrelated to each other. **(1 Mark)**

4. Many fresh water fishes cannot survive in the marine environment because their bodies are not adapted to the marine environment. As freshwater fishes lose body water because the surrounding water has higher salt concentration (hypertonic solution) and this makes the survival of fresh water fishes difficult in marine water. **(2 Marks)**

   OR

   Productivity: Productivity is defined as the rate of biomass production.

   Gross primary productivity: Gross primary productivity is defined as the rate of organic matter production during photosynthesis. **(1 Mark)**

   Net primary productivity: Net primary productivity involves the gross-productivity minus respiratory losses (R).

   So, NPP = GPP-R **(1 Mark)**

   Secondary productivity: Secondary productivity is defined as the rate of formation of new organic matter by consumers.

   As per their definitions, all the terms are interrelated to each other. **(2 Marks)**

5. (i) Primary productivity is defined as the amount of biomass or organic matter produced per unit area over a time period by plants during photosynthesis. The primary productivity depends on different plant species present in a given ecosystem and each of their photosynthetic efficiency. The environmental factors, availability of various nutrients vary in different ecosystems results in variations in primary productivity. **(1 Mark)**

   (ii) Gross primary productivity of an ecosystem is the rate of production of organic matter during photosynthesis. A considerable amount of Gross primary productivity is utilized by the plants in respiration. Net primary productivity or NPP is the Gross primary productivity minus the respiratory losses (R).

   NPP = GPP-R **(1 Mark)**

Note

*The rate of biomass production is called **Productivity** and it is expressed in terms of $g^{-2}\ yr^{-1}$ or $(kcal\ m^{-2})\ yr^{-1}$.*

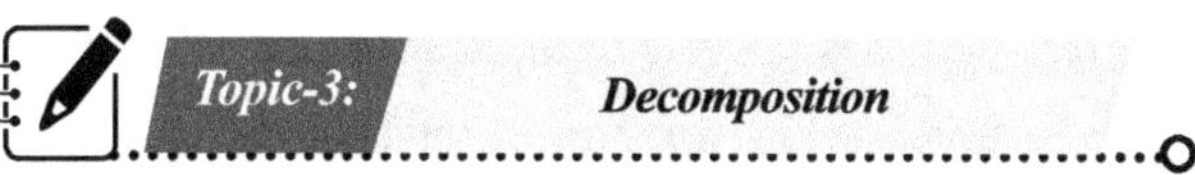

Topic-3: *Decomposition*

1. (d) Soil Sample C **(1 Mark)**

2. (b) Decomposition is largely an oxygen-requiring process. The rate of decomposition is controlled by chemical composition of detritus and climatic factors. In a particular climatic condition, decomposition rate is slower if detritus is rich in lignin and chitin, and quicker, if detritus is rich in nitrogen and water-soluble substances like sugars.

   (1 Mark)

3. Decomposition is a process in which the Earthworm and bacteria carry on detritus. Detritus is composed of dead remains of plants such as leave, bark, flowers and dead remains of animals involves fecal matter. All these material serves as a raw material for decomposition.

   Detritivores such as earthworm breakdown detritus into smaller particles and this process is called fragmentation. Then, by the process of leaching, the water soluble inorganic nutrients go down into the soil horizon and get precipitated as unavailable salts. Bacterial and fungal enzymes degrade detritus into simpler inorganic substances by the process called as catabolism. During the process of decomposition, humifiation and mineralisation also occurs. **(1 Mark)**

 *Note*

Humification *involves the process of accumulation of dark coloured amorphous substance that is highly resistant to microbial action. Whereas humus is further degraded by some microbes and release of inorganic nutrients occurs and this process is called **mineralisation**.*

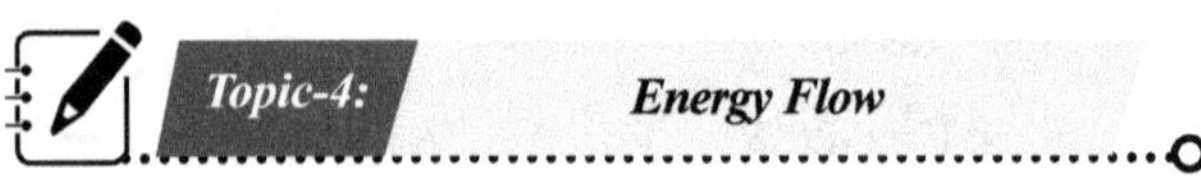

Topic-4:   **Energy Flow**

1. (a) According to the given food web, the producers are 1 and 2 whereas the two carnivores are 6 and 7.

    (1 Mark)

    (b) Yes, it is possible to make an ecological pyramid using the food web provided as it includes organisms at the producer, primary consumer, secondary consumer and tertiary consumer trophic levels. So, there will be transfer of energy from lower to higher trophic level leading to the formation of an upright ecological pyramid. **(1 Mark)**

2. Standing crop at a trophic level is referred to the amount of biomass or mass of living material at a successive trophic level at a given time. **(1 Mark)**

3. Important roles played by predators apart from being a part of the food chain:

    • Predators check the prey-population.

    • They prevent the over-population of prey and

    • Predators also help in maintaining the biodiversity in an ecosystem. **(2 Mark)**

4. Yes, it is possible that a species may occupy more than one trophic level in the same ecosystem at the same time.

    (1 Mark)

    For example, man is an omnivore as he can consume plants so they are called as a primary consumer and when man consumes animals such as goat and chicken which consume plants and become secondary consumer. In this way, a species occupying more than one trophic level in the same ecosystem at the same time. **(1 Mark)**

5. (a) **Tropic level :** Organisms occupy a place in the natural surroundings or in a community according to their feeding relationship with other organisms. Based on the source of their nutrition or food, organisms occupy a specific place in the food chain and this is known as trophic level. Each trophic level has a certain mass of living material at a particular time and this is called as **(1 Mark)**

    Standing crop: It is measured as the mass of living organisms (biomass) or the number in a unit area.

    (1 Mark)

    (b) **First trophic level** is formed by producers. This is the basic unit. These organisms can live without feeding on any another level. The only thing that these organisms need to survive is sunlight and water which they can turn into energy themselves. All other trophic levels depend on this level for energy. **(1 Mark)**

    (c) GFC is Grazing Food Chain : It is depicted as below : Producers Primary consumers Secondary consumers DFC is Detritus Food Chain : It begins with dead organic matter. It is made up of decomposers which are heterotrophic organisms like fungi, bacteria etc. GFC is the major conduct for energy flow. DFC may be connected with GFC at some levels : Some of the organisms of DFC are prey to the GFC animals. **(1 Mark)**

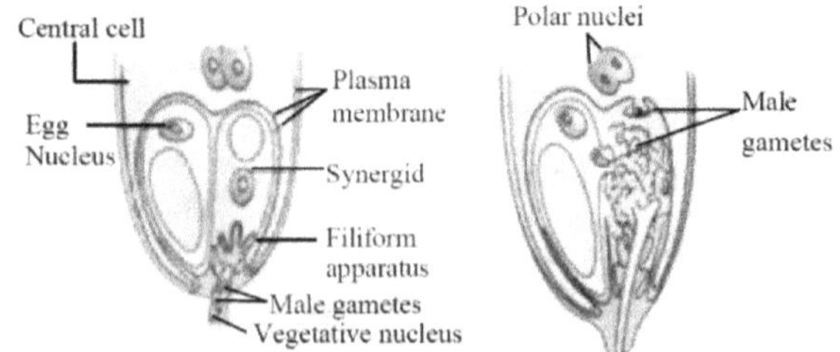

These natural inter connection of food chains forms food web. **(1 Mark)**

 *Note*

Food chain refers to the a linear network of links in a food web which represents the flow of energy from one trophic level to another.

Topic-5: *Ecological Pyramid*

1. **(a)** Both A and R are true and R is the correct explanation of A. **(1 Mark)**

2.

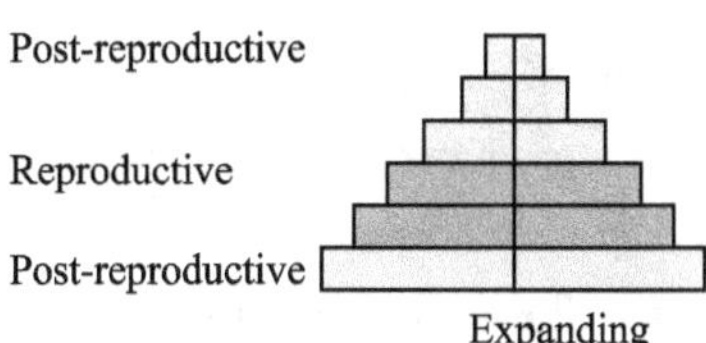

Tertiary consumer	Large Fishes	37 kg/m²
Secondary consumer	Small Fishes	25 kg/m²
Primary consumer	Zooplankton	11 kg/m²
Primary producer	Phytoplankton	4 kg/m²

Inverted Pyramid of Biomass

(1 Mark)

OR

(a) Gross Primary Productivity is 45000 + 40367 = 85367 KJm^{-2}y^{-1} **(1)**

(b) Net production is gradually reducing as we move from producers to consumers due to heat loss/respiration/10% law. **(1)**

3. **Diagrammatic Representation of Expanding age pyramid:**

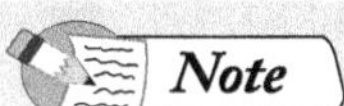

Expanding age pyramid indicates that the population is growing. **(2 Marks)**

4. **Diagrammatic Representation of Stable Age pyramid:**

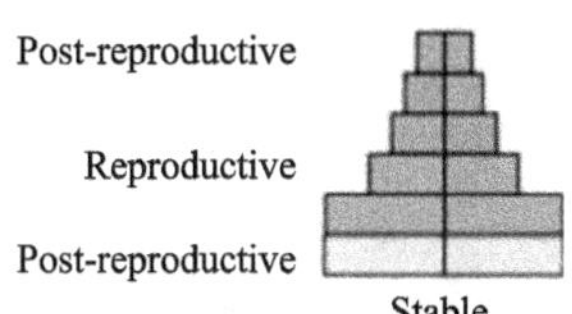

Stable age pyramid indicates equal proportion of population in each age group. **(2 Marks)**

5. The two types of pyramid of biomass are as follows:

(i) 

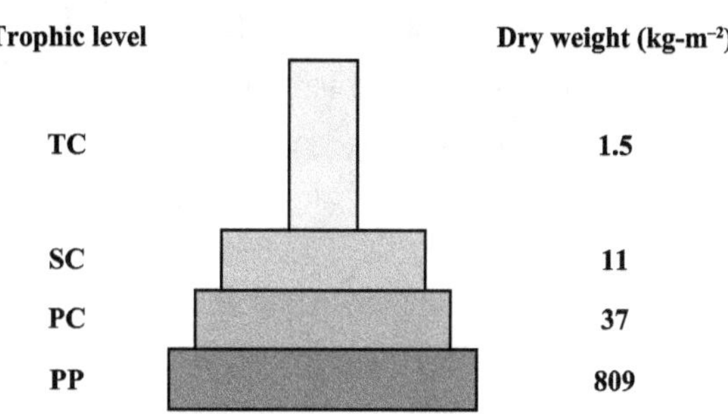

Trophic level		Dry weight (kg-m^{-2})
TC		1.5
SC		11
PC		37
PP		809

Pyramid of biomass is upright and it occurs in grasslands where the biomass of the producers is much higher than that of primary consumer. This indicates that there is sharp decrease in biomass at higher trophic level.

(1½ Marks)

(ii)

Pyramid of biomass is inverted and it occurs in aquatic ecosystems and the biomass of producers is much lower than that of primary consumers. This inverted pyramid indicates that a small standing crop of phytoplankton supports large standing crop of zooplankton. **(1½ Marks)**

6. The pyramid of energy is always upright because the energy flow in a food chain is always unidirectional and also with every increasing trophic level, some amount of energy is lost into the environment and never goes back to the sun. **(1 Mark)**

Diagrammatic Representation of Pyramid of energy:

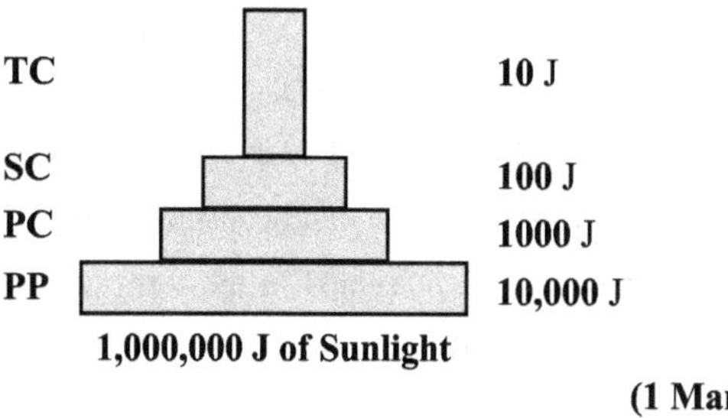

(1 Mark)

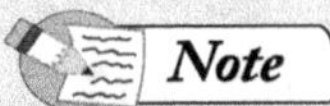

The pyramid of energy represents that primary producers converts only 1% of the energy in the sunlight available to them into NPP.

7. (a) Inverted pyramids of biomass are seen in aquatic conditions where a small standing crop of phytoplankton supports a large standing crop of zooplankton/fish/In terrestrial ecosystem where a large number of insects are feeding on the leaves of a tree. **(1 Mark)**

(b) No, the Pyramid of energy is always upright, and can never be inverted because when energy flows from one trophic level to the next trophic level some amount of energy is always lost as heat at each step.

(1 Mark)

OR

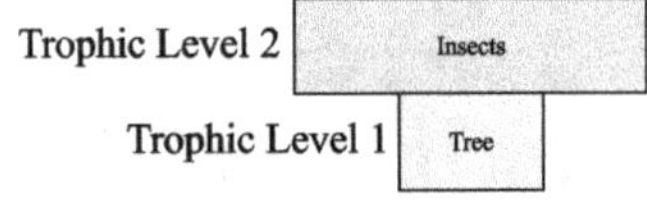

(a) Inverted pyramid because a large number of insects feed on one tree. **(1 Mark)**

(b) No, the Pyramid of energy is always upright, and can never be inverted because when energy flows from one trophic level to the next trophic level some amount of energy is always lost as heat at each step.

(1 Mark)

8. (a) Ecological pyramid is defined as the relationship between producers and consumers in an ecosystem that can be graphically represented in the form of a pyramid.

Different types of ecological pyramids are as follows:

(i) **Pyramid of number:** It is defined as the relationship between producers and consumers in an ecosystem that can be presented in the form of a pyramid in terms of number.

Diagrammatic Representation of Pyramid of number:

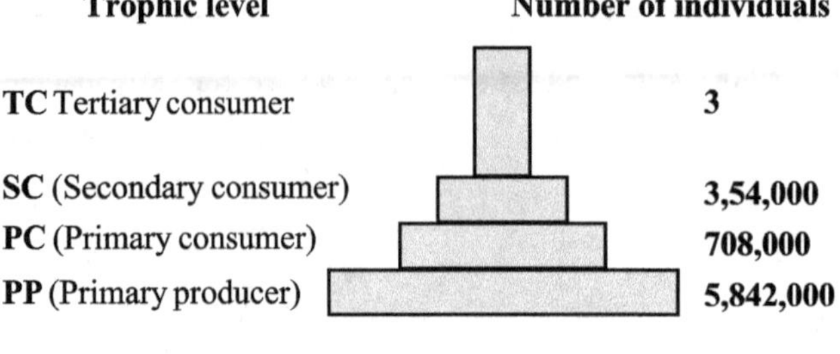

Trophic level	Number of individuals
TC Tertiary consumer	3
SC (Secondary consumer)	3,54,000
PC (Primary consumer)	708,000
PP (Primary producer)	5,842,000

(1 Mark)

(ii) **Pyramid of biomass:** It is defined as the relationship between producers and consumers in an ecosystem that can be represented in the form of a pyramid in terms of biomass. It can be upright or inverted.

Diagrammatic Representation of Pyramid of Biomass:

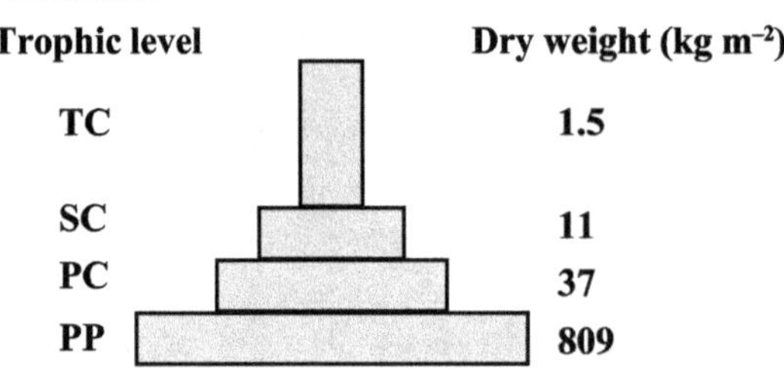

Trophic level	Dry weight (kg m^{-2})
TC	1.5
SC	11
PC	37
PP	809

(1 Mark)

(iii) **Pyramid of energy:** It is defined as the relationship between producer and consumers in an ecosystem that can be represented in the form of pyramid in terms of flow of energy. It is always upright as the energy is lost as heat at each step.

Diagrammatic Representation of Pyramid of energy:

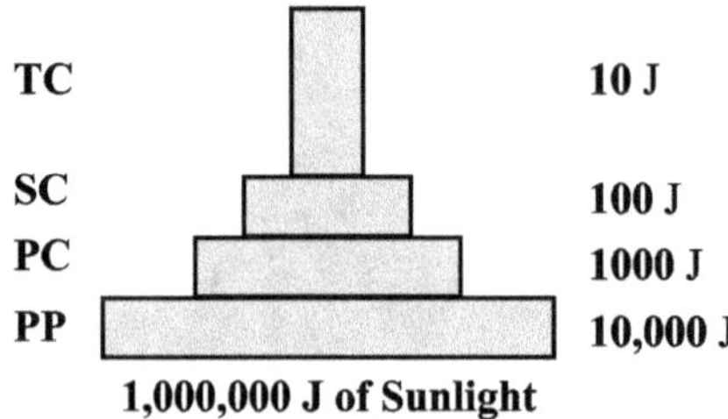

TC	10 J
SC	100 J
PC	1000 J
PP	10,000 J

1,000,000 J of Sunlight

(1 Mark)

(b) The limitations of ecological pyramids are as follows:

- It levels takes into account the same species belonging to two or more trophic levels. **(1 Mark)**

- Ecological pyramids assume a simple food chain that never existed in nature. **(1 Mark)**

9. (a) Age pyramid is defined as a way for representing the age-sex structure of a population. There are three types of age distribution pyramids such as expanding, stable and declining. A population is composed of individuals of different age groups.

(1½ Marks)

Diagrammatic representation of age pyramids for human population:

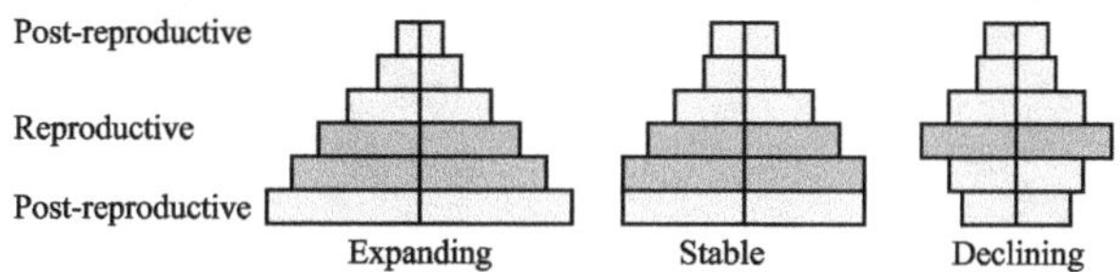

(1 Mark)

(b) The structure of age pyramid helps in the determination of growth status of the population. It involves three types of structure that represents that whether the population is expanding, stable or declining. The structure of age pyramids for human population emphasis on providing food to population, development of proper health care facilities and so on. **(1½ Marks)**

For example: If the human population is growing then, the policy makers will make the policies to increase the food resources for **(1 Mark)**

10. TC (Tertiary consumer)

SC (Secondary consumer)

PC (Primary consumer)

PP (PrimaryProducer)

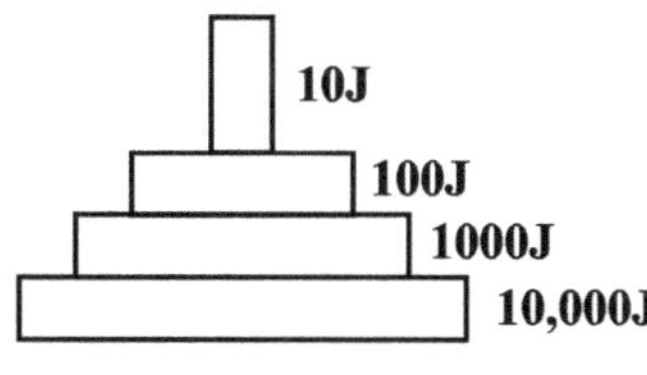

1,000,000 J of Sunlight

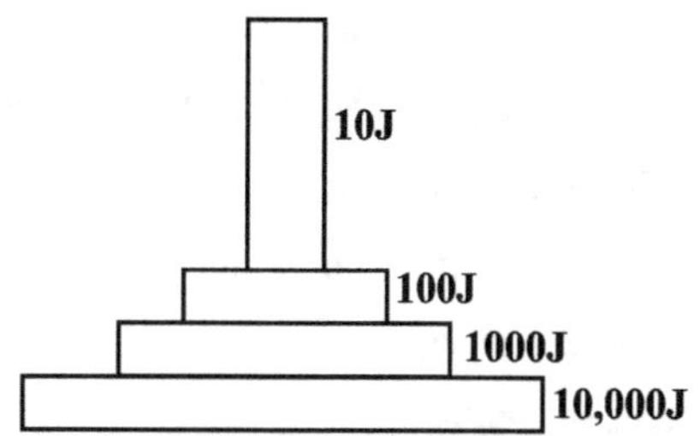

(2 Marks)

Pyramid of energy is always upright because when energy flows from a particular trophic level to the next trophic level, some energy is always lost as heat as well as for performing various activities at each step. Maximum energy is present at the producers level and minimum at level of top carnivores (top consumers). Thus, pyramid of energy is always upright. **(1 Mark)**

(a) The pyramid of biomass in a sea ecosystem is inverted. Because, the sum total of the weight of phytoplankton (producer) is far less than a few fishes feeding at higher trophic levels.

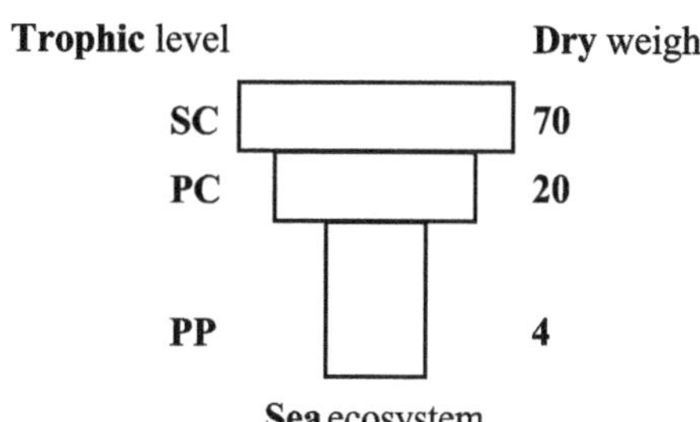

(1 Mark)

(b) Pyramid of biomass in a forest ecosystem is upright because producers are more in biomass than primary consumers. Primary consumers are more than secondary consumers and secondary consumers are more than tertiary consumers (top). **(1 Mark)**

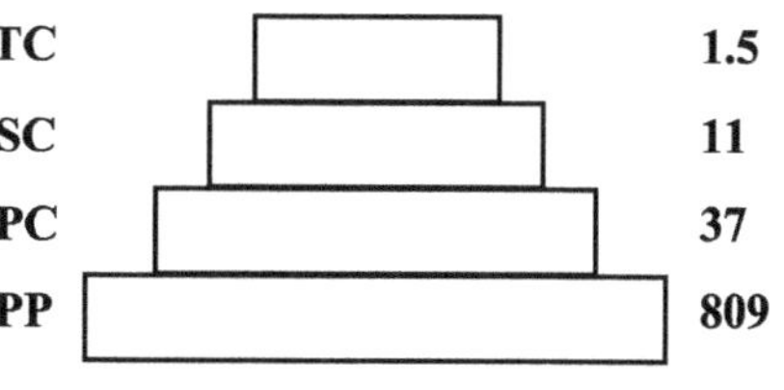

11. Age pyramid is defined as a way for representing the age-sex structure of a population. There are three types of age distribution pyramids such as expanding, stable and declining. A population is composed of individuals of different age groups. **(1 Mark)**

The analysis of age pyramid helps in the determination of growth status of the population. It involves three types of structure that represents that whether the population is expanding, stable or declining. The structure of age pyramids for human population emphasis on providing food to population, development of proper health care facilities and so on. **(2 Marks)**

Diagrammatic representation of age pyramids for human population:

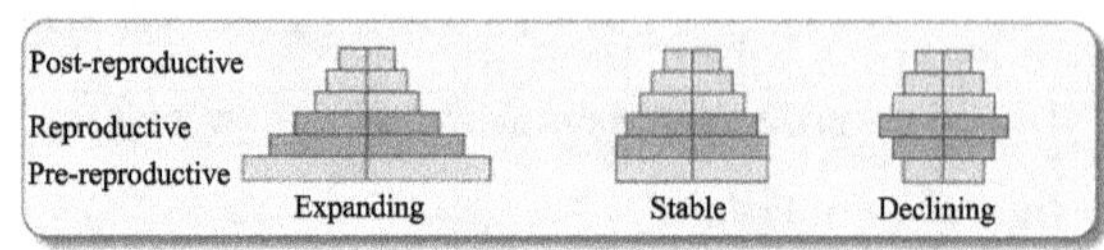

(2 Marks)

Chapter 13: Biodiversity and Conservation

Topic-1: *Types of Biodiversity*

1   *Multiple Choice Questions (1 Mark)*

1. The IUCN Red Data List (2004) in the last 500 years documents the extinction of nearly 784 species including: **[Delhi 2023, Set-I, U]**
   - (a) 330 invertebrates
   - (b) 338 invertebrates
   - (c) 359 invertebrates
   - (d) 362 invertebrates

2   *Assertion Reason/Two Statement Type Questions (1 Mark)*

2. **Assertion (A):** Biologists are sure about how many prokaryotic species are living now. **[All India 2023, Set-I, A]**
   Reason (R): The conventional taxonomic methods are not suitable for identifying microbial species.
   - (a) Both Assertion (A) and Reason (R) are true and Reason (R) is the correct explanation of the Assertion (A).
   - (b) Both Assertion (A) and Reason (R) are true, but Reason (R) is not the correct explanation of the Assertion (A).
   - (c) Assertion (A) is true, but Reason (R) is false.
   - (d) Assertion (A) is false, but Reason (R) is true.

5   *Short Answer Questions (2 or 3 Marks)*

3. "Biodiversity plays a major role in many ecosystem services that nature provides." **[Delhi 2023, Set-I, K]**
   - (a) Describe any two broadly utilatarian arguments to justify the given statement.
   - (b) State one ethical reason of conserving biodiversity.

4. (a) "India has greater ecosystem diversity than Norway." Do you agree with the statement ? Give reasons in support of your answer. **[All India 2018, U]**
   (b) Write the difference between genetic biodiversity and species biodiversity that exists at all the levels of biological organisation. **[All India 2018, U]**

5. Mention the kind of biodiversity of more than a thousand varieties of mangoes in India represent. How is it possible? **[Delhi 2016, U]**

6. Identify 'a' and 'b' in the figure given below representing proportionate number of major vertebrate taxa. **[Delhi 2014, U]**

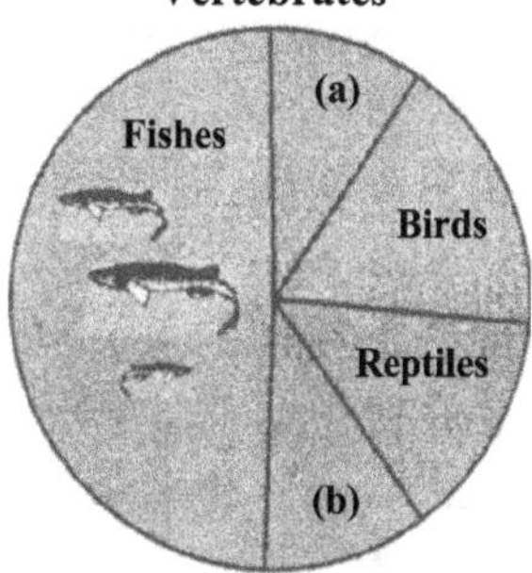

7. Name the type of biodiversity represented by the following: **[All India 2013, U]**
   - (i) 1000 varieties of mangoes of India.
   - (ii) Variations in terms of potency and concentration of reserpine in *Rauwolfia vomitoria* growing in different regions of Himalayas.

8. Where would you expect more species biodiversity – in tropics or in polar regions? Give reasons in support of your answer. **[All India 2013, U]**

9. Name the type of biodiversity represented by the following: **[Delhi 2013, U]**
   - (a) 50,000 different strains of rice in India
   - (b) Estuaries and alpine meadows in India.

Topic-2: *Pattern of Biodiversity*

5   *Short Answer Questions (2 or 3 Marks)*

1. "Stability of community depends upon its species richness." How did David Tilman show this experimentally? **[All India 2022, Term-II, K]**

2. (a) There was loss of biodiversity in an ecosystem due to a new construction project in that area. What would be its impact on the ecosystem? State any three. **[CBSE Sample Paper 2022-23, U]**
   (b) List any three major causes of loss of biodiversity? **[CBSE Sample Paper 2022-23, U]**

 **Topic-3:** *Loss of Biodiversity*

1 *Multiple Choice Questions (1 Mark)*

1. Human settlement often leads to habitat loss which leads to fragmentation, forming smaller patches of habitats. Select the statements that describe how a small patch differs from a large patch of the same habitat.

[All India 2023, Set-I, U]

(i) Invasive species will never be seen here.
(ii) Population of large animals decreases.
(iii) Biodiversity decreases.
(iv) Competition from surrounding habitats increases.

(a) (ii), (iii) and (iv) only (b) (ii) and (iv) only
(c) (i) and (iii) only   (d) (i), (ii) and (iii) only

2. Which one of the following groups faces maximum threat of extinction?   **[CBSE Sample Paper 2021-22, K]**

(a) Gymnosperms   (b) Birds
(c) Amphibian   (d) Mammals

4 *Very Short Answer Questions (1 Mark)*

3. State Gause's Competitive Exclusion Principle.

[All India 2014, K]

5 *Short Answer Questions (2 or 3 Marks)*

4. The histogram given below representing the data for annual shark harvest in the great barrier reef / coral reed located on the east coast of Queensland, Australia, Study the histogram and answer the questions that follow.

[All India 2022, Term-II, A]

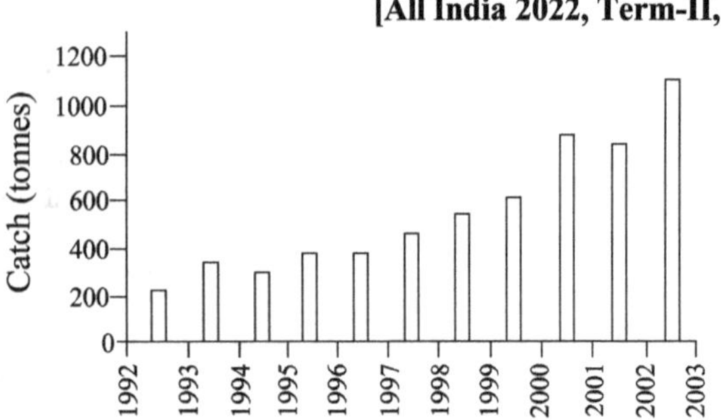

(a) Write your interpretation of the data given.
(b) Write the impact on the biodiversity of the area that you can interpret on the basis of given data.

 **Topic-4:** *Biodiversity Conservation*

1 *Multiple Choice Questions (1 Mark)*

1. Which one among the following regions is not a hotspot of biodiversity?   **[All India 2023, Set-I, U]**

(a) The Indo-Burma Region
(b) Jaintia Hills in Meghalaya

5. Bio-diversification of life started to occur almost 3 billion years ago. Since then new species have been evolving and then disappearing en masse from earth.

[All India 2022, Term-II, U]

(a) How many episodes of mass extinctions of species have already taken place and which one is in progress in the current era?
(b) How is current episode in progress different from the previous episodes and why? Explain.

6. (a) 'The Evil Quartet' describes the rates of species extinction due to human activities. Explain how the population of organisms is affected by fragmentation the habitats.   **[CBSE Sample Paper 2021-22, U]**

(b) Introduction of alien species has led to environmental damage and decline of indigenous species. Give any one example of how it has affected the indigenous species?   **[CBSE Sample Paper 2021-22, U]**

(c) Could the extinction of Steller's sea cow and passenger pigeon be saved by man? Give reasons to support your answer.

[CBSE Sample Paper 2021-22, U]

7. Substantiate with the help of one example that in an ecosystem mutualists (i) tend to co-evolve and (ii) are also one of the major causes of biodiversity loss.

[All India 2019, U]

8. Name and describe any three causes of bio-diversity losses.   **[All India 2017, U]**

9. Since the origin of life on earth, there were five episodes of mass extinction of species.   **[All India 2014, U]**

(i) How is the 'Sixth Extinction', presently in progress, different from the previous episodes ?
(ii) Who is mainly responsible for the 'Sixth Extinction'?
(iii) List any four points that can help to overcome this disaster.

6 *Long Answer Questions (5 Marks)*

10. (a) List any two ways the biodiversity loss affects any region.   **[Delhi 2019, U]**

(b) Explain any two causes the biodiversity loss affects any region.   **[Delhi 2019, U]**

(c) The Western Ghats and Sri Lanka
(d) The Himalayas

2. Which of the following is an example of ex situ conservation?   **[CBSE Sample Paper 2023-24, K]**

(a) Sacred Groves   (b) National Park
(c) Biosphere Reserve (d) Seed Bank

5   *Short Answer Questions (2 or 3 Marks)*

3. "Biodiversity plays a major role in many ecosystem services that nature provides." **[Delhi 2023, Set-I, K]**
(a) Describe any two broadly utilatarian arguments to justify the given statement.
(b) State one ethical reason of conserving biodiversity.

4. (a) The image shown below is of a sacred grove found in India. Explain how has human involvement helped in the preservation of these biodiversity rich regions. **[CBSE Sample Paper 2021-22, A]**

(a) Value of Z (regression coefficient) is considered for measuring the species richness of an area. If the value of Z is 0.7 for area A ,and 0.15 for area B, which area has higher species richness and a steeper slope? **[CBSE Sample Paper 2021-22, A]**

5. Differentiate between "Pioneer-species"; "Climax-community" and "Seres". **[Delhi 2020, K]**

OR

Explain any three ways other than zoological parks, botanical gardens and wildlife safaries, by which threatened species of plants and animals are being conserved 'ex situ'. **[Delhi 2020, K]**

6. List six advantages of "ex-situ" approach to conservation of biodiversity. **[All India 2019, U]**

7. What is cryopreservation? Mention how it is used in conservation of biodiversity. **[Delhi 2019, K]**

8. "In-situ' Conversation can help endangered/threatened species. Justify the statement. **[All India 2017, U]**

9. List four benefits to human life by eliminating the use of CFCs. **[Delhi 2017, K]**

OR

Suggest two practices giving one example of each, that help protect rare or threatened species. **[Delhi 2017, K]**

10. Why are sacred grooves highly protected?
[All India 2016, K]

11. List any four techniques where the principle of ex-situ conservation of biodiversity has been employed.
[All India 2015, U]

12. Many plant and animal species are on the verge of their extinction because of loss of forest land by indiscriminate use by the humans. As a biology student what method would you suggest along with its advantages that can protect such threatened species from getting extinct ?
[Delhi 2015, U]

6   *Long Answer Questions (5 Marks)*

13. (a) Why should we conserve biodiversity ? How can we do it ? **[Delhi 2016, U]**
(b) Explain the importance of biodiversity hot-spots and sacred groves. **[Delhi 2016, U]**

Hints & Solutions

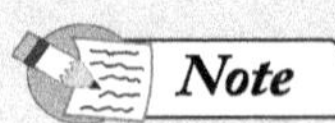
Topic-1:   *Types of Biodiversity*

1. **(c)** The IUCN Red List (2004) documents the extinction of 784 species (including 338 vertebrates, **359 invertebrates** and 87 plants) in the last 500 years.
    (1 Mark)

2. **(d)** Biologists are not sure about how many prokaryotic species there might be. This is because of the fact that conventional taxonomic methods are not sufficient for identifying microbial species and many prokaryotic species are not culturable under laboratory conditions. **(1 Mark)**

3. **(a)** The broadly utilitarian argument says that biodiversity plays a major role in many ecosystem services that nature provides. **(1 mark)**

    The two broadly utilitarian arguments are:

    (i) The fast dwindling Amazon forest is estimated to produce, through photosynthesis, 20 per cent of the total oxygen in the earth's atmosphere.

    (ii) Pollination (without which plants cannot give us fruits or seeds) is another service, ecosystems provide through pollinators layer – bees, bumblebees, birds and bats. **(2 marks)**

    (b) The ethical argument for conserving biodiversity relates to what we owe to millions of plant, animal and microbe species with whom we share this planet. Philosophically or spiritually, we need to realise that every species has an intrinsic value, even if it may not be of current or any economic value to us.

4. **(a)** Yes, India has greater ecosystem diversity than Norway as India has deserts, rain forests, mangroves, coral reefs, wetlands, estuaries, and alpine meadows.
    (1 Mark)

Ecosystem diversity refers to the variations in ecosystems within a geographical location and its overall impact on existance of human population in an environment.

    (b) Genetic diversity:

    (i) It is the total number of genetic characteristics in the genetic makeup of a species.

    (ii) A single species might show high diversity at the genetic level (E.g. Man : Chinese, Indian, American, African etc.). India has more than 50,000 genetically different strains of rice, and 1,000 varieties of mango.

    (iii) It allows species to adapt to changing environments. This diversity aims to ensure that some species survive drastic changes and thus carry on desirable genes.
    (1 Mark)

    Species diversity:

    (i) It is the ratio of one species population over total number of organisms across all species in the given biome. 'Zero' would be infinite diversity, and 'one' represents only one species present.

    (ii) It is a measure of the diversity within an ecological community that incorporates both species richness (the number of species in a community) and the evenness of species.

    (iii) For example, the Western Ghats have greater amphibian species diversity than the Eastern Ghats. There are more than 2, 00,000 species in India of which several are confined to India (endemic). **(1 Mark)**

The genetic variation shown by the medicinal plant Rouwolfia vomitoria growing in different Himalayan ranges have potency and concentration of the active chemical (reserpine) that the plant produces.

5. In India, there are around 1000 different varieties of mangoes produced due to genetic diversity. Genetic diversity is produced due to difference in soil found in different regions. It also occur due to different agricultural practices as well as use of various horticulture techniques that are used in India. **(2 Marks)**

6. In the given figure, **a** represents amphibians and **b** represents mammals. **(1 + 1 = 2 Mark)**

7. (i) Genetic diversity refer to the total number of genetic characteristics in the genetic makeup of a species. 1000 varieties of mangoes in India is an example of genetic diversity. The vast genetic diversity in India is observed as it lies within tropical latitudes that provide a constant and predictable environment as well as availability of more solar energy results in higher productivity. **(1 Mark)**

    (ii) The genetic variation represented by the medicinal plant *Rouwolfia vomitoria* which is growing in different Himalayan ranges is because of the potency and concentration of the active chemical (reserpine) produced by this plant. It is an example of genetic diversity. **(1 Mark)**

8. Tropics has more species diversity than polar regions because of the availability of sufficient sunlight that promotes higher productivity. Less seasonal variations are observed in tropic regions than Polar Regions and tropics remains undisturbed form many years so they have a long evolutionary time for diversification of species. **(2 Marks)**

Lysozyme enzyme is used for breaking bacterial cell whereas chitinase enzyme is used for breaking fungal cells.

9. **(a)** The availability of 50,000 genetically different strains of rice is an example of genetic diversity. Genetic diversity is produced due to difference in soil found in different regions. It is also occurs due to different agricultural practices as well as use of various horticulture techniques that are used in India.
    (1½ Marks)

Genetic diversity is defined as the type of diversity in which the number and types of genes as well as chromosomes that are found in different species. It leads to variation in the genes and their alleles in the same species. It leads to speciation as well as evolution of new species.

(b) The availability of estuaries and alpine meadows in India is an example of ecological diversity. India has a greater ecosystem diversity than a Scandinavian country like Norway. **(1½ Marks)**

Topic-2: *Pattern of Biodiversity*

1. A stable community should not show too much variation in productivity from year to year; it must be either resistant or resilient to occasional disturbances, and it must also be resistant to invasions by alien species. Tilman found that plots with more species showed less year to-year variation in total biomass. He also showed that in his experiments, increased diversity contributed to higher productivity. The rich biodiversity is not only essential for ecosystem health but imperative for the very survival of the human race on this planet. **(2 Marks)**

2. Impacts of loss of biodiversity on the ecosystem:
   (a) (i) Decline in plant production
       (ii) Lowered resistance to environmental perturbations such as drought
       (iii) Increased variability in certain ecosystems – processes such as plant productivity, water use, pest and disease cycles. **(½ × 3 = 1½ Marks)**
   (b) (i) Habitat loss and fragmentation
       (ii) Over-exploitation
       (iii) Alien invasive species
       (iv) Co-extinctions. **(Any three - ½ × 3 = 1½)**

Topic-3: *Loss of Biodiversity*

1. Due to habitat loss and fragmentation, following changes are expected to happen as a result of transformation from large population to small population:
   1. Population of large animals decreases: This occurs because the large animals require larger territory to survive which is not possible at small patch. The population of large animals like herbivores or predators is likely to reduce.
   2. Biodiversity decreases: Due to habitat loss and fragmentation of large patch into small patch the number of species is likely to reduce.
   3. Competition from surrounding habitats increases: As the small patch developed after habitat loss and fragmentation there will be limited number of resources available so the population of small patch is likely to compete with members of the other neighboring patches for resources like food, water and shelter.
   Invasive species will never be seen here is an incorrect option because small patch of population will be more prone to the attack of invasive species. The invasive species will be able to outcompete the population of small patch for resources. **(1 Mark)**

2. (c) Among the options given, amphibians face maximum threat of extinction. According to the IUCN regional red listing guidelines, 12% all the birds species, 23%

all mammals species, 31% all gymnosperms species and 32% all amphibian species in world face the threat of extinctions and have a highest percentage of endangered species, and the threats including habitat loss, fragmentation and degradation, pollution, climate change, and invasive alien species. **(1 Mark)**

3. Gause's *Competitive Exclusion Principle'* states that two closely related species competing for the same resources cannot co-exist indefinitely and the competitively inferior one will be eventually eliminated. **(1 Mark)**

4. (a) The annual catching data of shark is gradually increases and reached upto 1200 tonnes in a year of 2003. **(1 Mark)**
   (b) Healthy shark populations may aid the recovery of coral reefs. But if shark populations in a coral reef system are severely reduced due to commercial fishing, herbivorous fish that graze on algae may also decline. Fewer herbivorous fish keep algae growth in check, which in turn, harms coral reefs. **(1 Mark)**

5. (a) During the long period (> 3 billion years) since the origin and diversification of life on earth, there were five episodes of mass extinction of species.
   Presently, 12 per cent of all bird species, 23 per cent of all mammal species, 32 per cent of all amphibian species and 31per cent of all gymnosperm species in the world face the threat of extinction. **(1½ Marks)**
   (b) The difference is in the rates between the current episode and the previous episode; the current species extinction rates are estimated to be 100 to 1,000 times faster than in the pre-human times and our activities are responsible for the faster rates. Ecologists warn that if the present trends continue, nearly half of all the species on earth might be wiped out within the next 100 years. **(1½ Marks)**

6. (a)

Topper's Answer

Alien species invasion is definitely a great threat to biodiversity as described as one of "EVIL SOBRIQUET" i.e "EVIL QUARTLET"

These alien species when introduced in a new habitat compete with the existing species for the limited resources and tends to eliminate the already existing species in the absence of their predator species in the new natural habitat. They multiply at a faster rate and tends to grow at a phenomenal rate in the absence of their predator.

One of the most sought example in this is of Eichhornia crassipies and Lanthana. Eichhornia also known as "Terror of Bengal" was introduced in India is aquatic bodies for their beautiful shape of leaves but due to the absence of its natural predator it propagated at a phenomenal rate in water bodies, thus draining the amount of dissolved oxygen from it and killing other aquatic plants and animals.

The three other causes for such a loss of biodiversity are:

(a) Habitat loss and Fragmentation
(b) Overexploitation by humans
(c) Co-extinction

(2 + 2 = 4 Mark)

(a) When alien species are introduced unintentionally or deliberately for whatever purpose, some of them turn invasive, and cause decline or extinction of indigenous species. The Nile perch introduced into Lake Victoria in east Africa led eventually to the extinction of an ecologically unique assemblage of more than 200 species of cichlid fish in the lake. You must be familiar with the environmental damage caused and threat posed to our native species by invasive weed species like carrot grass (Parthenium), Lantana and water hyacinth (Eicchornia). The recent illegal introduction of the African catfish Clarias gariepinus for aquaculture purposes is posing a threat to the indigenous catfishes in our rivers.

(b) Humans have always depended on nature for food and shelter, but when 'need' turns to 'greed', it leads to over-exploitation of natural resources.

(c) Yes; Humans have overexploited natural resources for their 'greed' rather than 'need' leading to extinction of these animals. Sustainable harvesting could have prevented extinction of these species. **(1 Mark)**

7. (i) In nature, mutualists often co-evolve such as in Mediterranean orchid *Ophrys*. *Ophrys* employs sexual deceit to get pollinated by a species of bee. One petal of flower resemble to female bee. If female bee changes its colour pattern ever slightly the success of pollination will be reduced unless orchid flower co-evolves to maintain resemblance with female bee. **(1 Mark)**

(ii) Co-extinction is one of the 'Evil Quartet' in which organisms with obligatory relationship like plant pollinator mutualism will result in extinction of one partner if other is eliminated in nature. **(1 Mark)**

8. Three causes of biodiversity losses are:

1. **Habitat destruction-** It is considered as the primary cause of biodiversity loss. It leads to the extinction or decrease in the number of animals living in that particular habitat. Urbanisation, industrialization, clearing forest for agriculture, filling wetlands, caused extinction of endemic species. **(1 Mark)**

2. **Alien species invasion-** Non-native species introduced for economic and other uses, invaded and drive away the local species. Exotic/alien species have proved harmful to both aquatic and terrestrial ecosystem. **(1 Mark)**

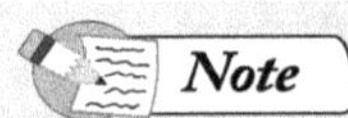 **Note**

The Nile Perch introduced into lakevictoria in east Africa led eventually to the extinction of an ecologically unique assemblage of more than 200 species of cichild fish in the lake. Illegal introduction of the African catfish Clarias gariephinus for aquaculture purposes in posing a threat to the indigenous catfishes in our rivers.

3. **Over exploitation of natural resources-** Over-exploitation of resources has been one of the major contributor to this. Due to increasing human population, resource demands have increased which has resulted into exploitation of already present resources and development of various forms of energy resources.Development of these energy sources modifies natural habitat and accelerates loss of biodiversity. **(1 Mark)**

9. (i) The sixth extinction is different from previous extinctions in several ways:
The sixth extinction occurs rapidly such as the reduction in a number of species per unit area per unit time. It is accelerated by human activities such as deforestation, industrialization and so on. **(1 Mark)**

(ii) Human activities that lead to global warming and disruption of environmental as well as ecological balance are responsible for the sixth extinction. **(1 Mark)**

(iii) The disaster can be overcome by following ways:
- Afforestation **(1 Mark)**
- Reduction in over-exploitation of natural resources
- Conservation of species and their natural habitats in order to minimize the losses.
- Create awareness among people regarding global warming and their consequences.

10. (a) Loss of biodiversity in a region may lead to cause following effects such as:
- Decline in plant production,
- Lowered resistance to environmental perturbations such as drought and,
- Increased variability in certain ecosystem processes such as plant productivity, water use and pest and disease cycles. **(2 Marks)**

(b) The causes of biodiversity losses are as follows:

(i) Habitat loss and fragmentation: This is the most important cause of extinction of plants and animals species. Habitat loss comes from tropical rain forests. The Amazon rain forest as it is also called the 'lungs of the planet' harbour millions of species is being cut and cleared for cultivating soya beans or for conversion to grasslands for raising beef cattle. Population also leads to cause degradation of many habitats and threatens the survival of many species. Large habitats are broken into small fragments due to various human activities, mammals and birds require large territories and certain animals with migratory habits are badly affected results in population declines. **(2 Marks)**

(ii) Over-exploitation: Humans are always depended on nature for food and shelter but their need turns into 'greed' and it leads to over-exploitation of natural resources. Many species become extinct in the last decades such as Steller's sea cow, passenger pigeon because of overexploitation by humans. **(1 Mark)**

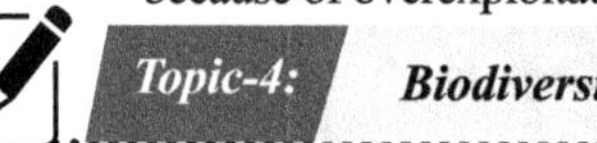 **Topic-4:**   *Biodiversity Conservation*

1. (b) The sacred grooves are the trees which are considered as culturally, socially, medicinally or religiously important. Jaintia Hills in Meghalaya is an example of sacred grove. Three of the hotspots – Western Ghats and Sri Lanka, Indo-Burma and Himalaya – cover our country's exceptionally high biodiversity regions. **(1 Mark)**

2. (d) Seed Bank **(1 Mark)**

3. (a) The broadly utilitarian argument says that biodiversity plays a major role in many ecosystem services that nature provides.
The two broadly utilitarian arguments are:
(i) The fast dwindling Amazon forest is estimated to

produce, through photosynthesis, 20 per cent of the total oxygen in the earth's atmosphere.

(ii) Pollination (without which plants cannot give us fruits or seeds) is another service, ecosystems provide through pollinators layer – bees, bumblebees, birds and bats. **(2 Marks)**

(b) The ethical argument for conserving biodiversity relates to what we owe to millions of plant, animal and microbe species with whom` we share this planet. Philosophically or spiritually, we need to realise that every species has an intrinsic value, even   if it may not be of current or any economic value to us. **(1 Mark)**

4. (a) Indian history of religious and cultural traditions emphasizes on the protection of nature. In many cultures, tracts of forest are set aside, all the trees and wildlife within are venerated and given total protection. Sacred groves in many states are the last refuges for a large number of rare and threatened pl ants. **(2 Marks)**

(b) Area A will have more species richness and a steeper slope. **(1 Mark)**

5. Difference between pioneer species, ecological succession and sere are as follows:

Pioneer species	Ecological succession	Sere
(i) The species that invade a bare area are called pioneer species.	**(i)** The gradual and predictable change in the species composition of a given area is called ecological succession.	**(i)** The entire sequences of communities that successively change in a given area are called sere.

(1 + 1 + 1 = 3 Marks)

OR

Except from zoological parks, wildlife sanctuaries and botanical gardens, ex-situ conservation also involves a method for preservation of endangered or extinct species such as by

Cryopreservation: Gametes (sperms, eggs, tissues and embryo) of several endangered plants and animal species can be preserved by methods involves cryopreservation (–196°C). It can be fertilized in vitro followed by propagation through tissue culture methods.

Seeds of different genetic strains of commercially important plants are also kept for longer period in seed banks. **(1 + 1 + 1 = 3 Marks)**

6. *Ex-situ* ('off site') conservation is a set of conservation techniques involving the transfer of a target species away from its native habitat to a place of safety, such as a zoological garden, botanical garden or seed bank. *Ex-situ* techniques include: seed storage, captive breeding, slow-growth storage, DNA storage.

Advantages of ex-situ conservation

(i) Organisms are completely protected from predation and poaching.

(ii) To preserve gametes of threatened species in viable condition through cryopreservation.

(iii) To grow plants with recalcitrant seeds in orchards where all possible varieties are maintained.

(iv) To conserve seeds of commercially important plants in seed banks. Genetic diversity of the population can be measured

(v) To save endangered or threatened plant that needs urgent measure to save it from extinction in botanical gardens.

(vi) To propagate threatened plants via tissue culture. **(½ × 6 = 3 Marks)**

Note

Ex-situ conservation is a conservation technique that involves the conservation of selected rare or endangered plants and animal species in places outside their natural environment or homes. It involves offsite collection and gene banks.

7. **Cryopreservation:** It is a method used for the preservation of cells and tissue structures in an extremely cold temperature such as at -196°C in a liquid nitrogen. It inhibits metabolism in cells. **(1 Mark)**

Cryopreservation of biodiversity in a following ways: The gametes of endangered plants and animals are kept viable by preserving them at a very low temperature (–196°C) in a liquid nitrogen. **(1 Mark)**

8. In situ Conservation

- It is the conservation and protection of biodiversity in natural habitat. Population is conserved in surroundings, where they have developed their distinctive features.

  Example: National parks, biosphere reserves, wildlife sanctuaries, etc. **(½ Mark)**

- It also includes the introducion of plants and animal species back into agriculural, horticultural and animal husbandry practices so that they are cultivated/reproduced and reused by the farmers. **(½ Mark)**

- It also maintains genetic diversity of crop plants/ flowers by saving seeds for next planting season. **(½ Mark)**

- Biodiversity is permanently protected. **(½ Mark)**

- Facilitates scientific research of the site. **(½ Mark)**

- It may be possible to improve the ecological integrity of the area and restore it if it has been damaged by poaching etc. **(½ Mark)**

9. CFCs (Chlorofluorocarbons) are responsible for affecting the human life. As the chlorinated molecules from CFCs releases leads to cause pollution and ozone layer depletion. Reduction in the use of CFCs helps in following ways:

- It helps in the prevention of ozone layer depletion. **(½ Mark)**

- It also helps in reduction of greenhouse effect. **(½ Mark)**

- It also reduced El Nino effect or odd climatic changes. **(½ Mark)**

- Reduction in CFCs will also help in the prevention of snow blindness and inflammation of cornea. **(½ Mark)** **(½ × 4 = 2 Mark)**

Note

CFCs are widely released into the atmosphere from refrigerators and is discharged in the lower part of atmosphere. Then it move upwards and reach atmosphere. Chlorine atoms are releasing into the atmosphere by the action of UV rays. It results in the ozone depletion.

OR

Practices that help to prevent rare or threatened species are as follows:

(i) **Ex-situ conservation:** In this, the rare or threatened plants and animal species are taken out from their natural habitat and place them in special area where they can be protected and given special care. **(1 Mark)**

(ii) **Cryopreservation:** Gametes (sperms, eggs, tissues and embryo) of several endangered plants and animal species can be preserved by methods involves cryopreservation (-196°C). It can be fertilized in Invitro followed by propagation through tissue culture methods. **(1 Mark)**

(iii) **In-situ conservation:** This approach involves conservation and protection of entire ecosystem, in order to protect its biodiversity at the levels. As if we save forest then we save the tiger. **(1 Mark)**

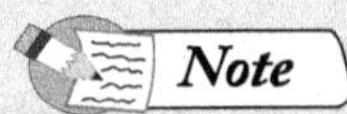 *Note*

Ecologically unique and biodiversity-rich regions in India are legally protected as biosphere reserves, national parks and sanctuaries.

10. The scared grooves are largely protected because they have large number of rare and threatened plants species. They are also protected because of the cultural and religious values of the communities. The scared grooves are found in Khasi and Jaintia Hills in Meghalaya, Aravalli Hills of Rajasthan, Western Ghat regions of Karnataka and Maharashtra and the Sarguja, Chanda and Bastar areas of Madhya Pradesh. **(2 Marks)**

11. Four techniques where the principle of ex-situ conservation of biodiversity has been employed are as follows:

- Botanical gardens, zoological parks and wildlife safari are the conventional methods of ex-situ conservation. **(½ Mark)**
- Gametes of threatened species can be preserved in viable and fertile condition for long periods at a low temperature (–196°C) using cryopreservation techniques. **(½ Mark)**
- Eggs can be fertilised Invitro, and plants can be propagated using tissue culture methods (micropropagation). **(½ Mark)**
- Seeds of many different genetic strains of commercially important plants are kept viable for long periods in seed banks. **(½ Mark)**

(½ × 4 = 2 Marks)

 *Note*

Ex-situ conservation is a conservation approach in which threatened plants and animals are taken out from their natural habitat and placed in special setting where this can be protected and given special care.

12. As a biology student, following method would be suggested in order to protect the threatened species from getting extinct are:

- Ex-situ conservation: In this, the threatened species of plants and animals are taken out of their habitats. Such species of both plants and animals are kept in special habitat such as zoological parks, botanical gardens and wildlife parks to provide natural environment for their survival. **(1 Mark)**
- Gametes of several endangered plants and animal species can be preserved by methods involves cryopreservation. It can be fertilized in vitro followed by propagation through tissue culture methods. **(1 Mark)**
- Seeds are preserved in seed banks and this method is called **off-site conservation method.** **(1 Mark)**

13. (a) There is need to conserve biodiversity because of the following reasons:

- Commercially important products such as food, timber and other essential industrial products are obtained from nature. **(½ Mark)**
- Oxygen production and pollination is totally dependent on nature. **(½ Mark)**
- There is need to conserve the endangered species and protect the biodiversity for our future generations. **(½ Mark)**

Biodiversity can be conserved in two ways:

(i) **In situ conservation:** It involves the conservation of plants and animals species in their natural habitat. For this, biodiversity hotspots are being identified and protected. It involves wildlife sanctuaries, national parks and biosphere reserves. **(½ Mark)**

(ii) **Ex-situ conservation:** The threatened and endangered species are taken out of their natural habitats and kept in special setting like zoological gardens and wildlife parks. **(½ Mark)**

(iii) **Cryopreservation:** The gametes of endangered plants and animals are kept viable by preserving them at a very low temperature (-196°C) in a liquid nitrogen. **(½ Mark)**

(b) Importance of biodiversity hotspots:
Biodiversity hotspots are regions that contain high level of species richness and higher degree of endemism. Such areas are very important because the total number of biodiversity hotspots in the world is 34 and hotspots can reduce the mass extinction by approximately 30%. It involves biodiversity regions such as Western Ghats and Sri-Lanka, Indo-Burma and Himalaya covers high biodiversity regions. **(1 Mark)**
Importance of scared grooves:
Scared grooves are the forest regions that involve all trees and wildlife species. It provide protection all plants and wildlife species.
In India, the scared grooves involve:

- Western Ghats regions of Karnataka and Maharashtra
- Khasi and Jaintia Hills in Meghalaya
- Aravalli Hills in Rajasthan
- Sarguja, Chanda and Baster areas of Madhya Pradesh. **(1 Mark)**